# From Miracle to Mainstream: creating the world's first dialysis organization

# From Miracle to Mainstream: creating the world's first dialysis organization

## EARLY YEARS OF NORTHWEST KIDNEY CENTERS

*Dr. Christopher R. Blagg*

Since 1962 Northwest Kidney Centers has consistently served as a model and national voice for nonprofit kidney care. Putting the patient at the center makes every decision more clear. This history illuminates the hard times in the early years—disbelief in dialysis as a viable therapy, lack of funding and availability of care, the challenge of securing adequate insurance payments—all of which continue in some form today. Yet our organization survives and thrives, driven by our nonprofit mission and vision to be the provider of choice—to patients and our community. The past is prelude to our future.

**Joyce F. Jackson, president and CEO, Northwest Kidney Centers**

# Table of Contents

The History of Northwest Kidney Centers

As historian A. J. P. Taylor said, "Writing history is like W. C. Fields juggling: it looks easy until you try to do it yourself."

# Introduction

———

WHEN CLYDE SHIELDS WAS DYING from chronic kidney failure in University Hospital in Seattle in early March 1960 he and his doctor, Dr. Belding H. Scribner, made medical history. Clyde's life was saved when he was treated using an artificial kidney. The artificial kidney had been used for a number of years to treat patients with acute kidney failure as a result of severe trauma, major surgery and complications of pregnancy. If these patients survived, their kidneys began to work again after two or three weeks and they recovered. However, treatment with the artificial kidney meant that plastic catheters had to be surgically inserted into an artery and vein for each treatment, and so patients with chronic kidney failure whose kidneys had failed permanently could not be treated because (after a few weeks or months) all the accessible blood vessels were used up. Scribner solved this problem by using Teflon™ tubing inserted into the radial artery and a vein in Clyde's left forearm for connection to the machine. Between treatments the two Teflon tubes were connected by a horseshoe-shaped piece of Teflon tube through which blood flowed from artery to vein. When the next dialysis was needed, the connecting tube was removed and the artery and vein connected to the artificial kidney again. This approach had been tried before using glass tubing and early plastics but the connection clotted unless the patient was heparinized and then bleeding often was a problem. With development of Teflon tubing, with its non-stick properties, the connection did not clot for several weeks or months. A previously fatal disease could now be treated by what was called the "shunt."

Scribner had no idea at that time that the world market for dialysis for chronic kidney failure would be more than $60 billion 50 years later and that the number of dialysis patients worldwide would reach 2 million by 2010. Two years later, in 1962, when the Seattle Artificial Kidney Center opened as the world's first out-of-hospital dialysis unit, few would have thought that 50 years later there would be more than 5,500 such units in the United States alone.

The Seattle Community Artificial Kidney Center, later renamed the Seattle Artificial Kidney Center, Northwest Kidney Center and, most recently, Northwest Kidney Centers, from its earliest pioneering days until now has always been recognized as providing one of the best dialysis programs in the world. Together with the Division of Nephrology in the Department of Medicine at the University of Washington in Seattle, it played a major role in the development of dialysis for chronic kidney failure locally, nationally, and elsewhere.

This volume, intended for both professional readers and interested readers from the general public, will include not only the technical and political developments related to kidney dialysis, but also a description of some of the many individuals who were responsible for these developments over the last 50 years.

## CHAPTER 1

# The Origins of Dialysis and the Artificial Kidney: 1860 to 1938

———

THOMAS GRAHAM, FRS, A SCOTTISH physical chemist, is usually regarded as the "father of modern dialysis." He was educated in Scotland and studied chemistry much against the wishes of his father. First a young professor at Anderson University in Glasgow, he then moved to become a professor at University College, London, and in 1855 was made Master of the Mint, a position he held until his death in 1869. He studied the separation of gases by diffusion and developed Graham's law. In the Bakerian Lecture given to the Royal Society of London in 1851 entitled "On Osmotic Force," he described diffusion in fluids when two solutions are layered upon one another and what occurs when the two solutions are separated by a semipermeable membrane. He described an apparatus using a small bell jar with the mouth covered by an animal membrane and filled with the solution to be tested and topped by a capillary tube. The whole was immersed in a glass cylinder of water and he measured the osmotic pressure produced by a variety of solutions and solutes. He noted that "Chemical osmose appears to be particularly well adapted to take part in the animal economy. It is seen that osmose is particularly excited by dilute saline such as animal juices really are." He went on to show that using the right sort of membrane (what he called a "semi-permeable" membrane) in the apparatus he had developed, he could separate sugar and salts (what he called "crystalloids") from a solution that also contained gum arabic, starch, albumin and gelatin (what he called "colloids"). He called this process "dialysis" from the Greek "διάλυσις" or "dialusis," meaning dissolution, and from "dia" meaning through and "ly-sis" meaning loosening or splitting. Previously the word dialysis had meant a dissolution of the strength or weakness of limbs, coming from the Greek word and meaning "to part or sunder." In another experiment he filled an ox bladder with urine and immersed this in a container of water overnight, using the bladder as a semipermeable membrane. He then evaporated off the water, leaving a white residue that he showed was composed primarily of urea. Interestingly, a few years earlier, Richard Bright of Guy's Hospital in London had shown that urea accumulated in the blood of patients with kidney disease.

Dialysis was soon being used in chemistry and physics laboratories for processes like separation and purification of substances. In Germany toward the end of the 19th century, tubes made of the membrane lining the inner wall of a common reed were used by Philippson and others to dialyze blood in vitro and were thought to have advantages over animal membranes or paper-derived materials. They allowed much more rapid but not less complete separation of crystalloids and colloids. But because the tubes were small, 15 cm long and had a volume of eight to ten ml, they were not useful for separation of large volumes of chemical compounds.

It was not until November 10, 1912 that dialysis was first used to separate a substance from blood. Drs. John Jacob Abel, Leonard Rowntree and Bernard Turner at Johns Hopkins in Baltimore developed a device consisting of 32 hollow tubes 40 cm long and 8 mm in diameter made from collodion, a membrane derived from cellulose, and attached to branched glass inlets and outlets, all enclosed in a glass cylinder which contained the dialyzing fluid or dialysate. The device, which they called a "vividiffusion" apparatus, was used to extract salicylate from the blood of anesthetized dogs and rabbits. Blood was circulated by arterial pressure from a carotid artery in the animal's neck and returned to a large vein, clotting of the blood was prevented by using hirudin, an anticoagulant extracted from the crushed heads of leeches, and the dialysate was recirculated. They examined how to minimize the volume of blood in the system with maximum surface area for diffusion and found that, "This can be obtained either by using very small tubes, or by flattening a larger tube until the opposite surfaces nearly touch." In effect they were producing the prototypes of hollow fiber dialyzers and flat plate dialyzers.

Abel first described their preliminary results at the May 1913 meeting of Association of American Physicians in Washington, DC, and in August 1913 the Hopkins group took their device to Europe and demonstrated the removal of salicylate from the blood of rabbits at the meeting of the International Congress of Medicine in London and the International Congress of Physiology in Groningen, Holland. This aroused interest in both the medical and lay press around the world, and on August 11, 1913, a correspondent for The Times of London noted that, "Professor Abel has constructed what is practically an artificial kidney...that may ultimately be adopted in the treatment of disease." The headline in the New York Times of January 18, 1914 was "MACHINE PURIFIES THE BLOOD AND RESTORES IT TO THE BODY" and before long it was suggested that while it might be used to remove poisons from the blood, this device might also be used to remove urea from the blood of patients with kidney failure. It was long known that when the kidneys failed, urea and other poisons normally excreted in urine accumulated in the body, a condition called uremia – literally urea in the blood – and eventually caused death. However, the technical problems that had to be solved before this technique would be useful in humans were considerable, including the need for better membranes and for a better agent to prevent clotting of the blood in the system, as import of leeches as a source of hirudin from Europe became limited during World War I.

By April 1914 the Johns Hopkins group had done 4 dialyses on rabbits and 37 on dogs and all the rabbits and at least 20 of the dogs died after the procedure, hardly in keeping with their comment that the procedure was not prejudicial to life.

Recently, Dr. Charles George, one of Scribner's ex-fellows, published an article about Abel based on a review of his published articles and examination of his laboratory workbooks in the archives of Johns Hopkins Hospital. He pointed out that Abel's primary interest was always in the possibility of removing metabolically active substances including hormones from the blood by dialysis because of his interest in hormones and the alimentary tract. In the group's experiments with both rabbits and dogs they were able to identify amino acids, diastase, bases, sugar, and phosphate in carotid blood and amino acids from the portal blood of normal animals. They were also able to identify sodium salicylate, potassium iodide, and phenolphthalein from the carotid blood of normal animals treated with these compounds but they only appeared to have measured urea in the dialysate from one animal.

As a result of the publicity in Europe and the United States and the suggestion that this treatment might be successful with nephritis, Abel was pressured by his colleagues to treat patients dying with kidney disease. For this he turned to a new procedure, plasmapheresis, described in a German publication, to remove substances from the blood of experimental animals. This involved taking blood from the animal, anticoagulating it with hirudin, separating the plasma by centrifugation, diluting the remaining blood with saline and re-infusing it into the animal. In two months in 1914 they showed that five normal dogs treated by repeated plasmapheresis survived, and that four dogs whose kidneys had been removed and were treated by repeated plasmapheresis showed an initial improvement but died after about 3 ½ days. In December 1914 Abel then tried plasmapheresis on a 32-year-old woman with chronic nephritis and uremia. A surgeon removed 400 ml of blood and Abel took this from the operating room to the laboratory and centrifuged it before bringing it back for reinfusion into the patient. Initially he was excited but a febrile reaction soon occurred, probably due to infection. George could find no record of what had happened to the patient after this. Interestingly, plasmapheresis was also used in experimental animals in the latter 1930s by Drs. Charles Best and William Thalhimer but did not come into general use until 1959 since when it has been used as a treatment for various autoimmune disorders.

The next significant step forward came in Hamburg, Germany, where in 1923 Dr. Heinrich Necheles published his MD dissertation, "On Dialyzing of Flowing Blood in the Living," using a device he had made to dialyze dogs made uremic by removing their kidneys. In this device blood passed between two layers of "gold-beater's skin" made from the peritoneal membrane lining the abdominal cavity of calves and supported by a grid. Several of these devices were connected in a line so the blood went through each in turn and, like Abel and his coworkers, he used hirudin to prevent clotting. Necheles was able to show that the device removed urea from the animals' blood. In 1924 Necheles moved to the Peking Medical College where in 1926 he continued his studies using both hirudin and heparin for anticoagulation, and he was probably the first to use heparin for hemodialysis. He moved to Chicago in 1931, working in gastrointestinal physiology research until his retirement but retaining his interest in dialysis for kidney failure.

Dr. Georg Haas had been experimenting with various membranes for dialysis of animal blood since about 1911 in the biochemistry and physiology laboratories in Strasburg, in Alsace, where he worked on experimental vascular surgery. In the course of this work he removed metabolites from the blood of experimental animals using in-vivo dialysis across semipermeable membranes.

With the advent of World War I, Haas moved to Giessen in Germany where he became interested in renal disease and saw many cases of glomerulonephritis following an epidemic of trench nephritis that often progressed to uremia and death. He noted that the patients were not improved by bloodletting, forced sweating and dietary protein restriction and remembered his earlier experiments with dialysis in animals. But because of the war, he was unaware of the work of Abel, Rowntree and Turner. In 1919 he returned to civilian practice and tried making dialyzers using animal, vegetable and paper membranes but found the best were dialyzers using the collodion membranes that had been developed by Dr. Fritz Pregl. As a result he developed a device very like that of Abel, Rowntree and Turner, but that used fewer and much longer 120 cm U-shaped tubes of collodion immersed in a dialysate bath of Ringer's physiologic solution contained in a glass cylinder. The collodion tubes had to be prepared fresh for each session. He then used a group of up to eight of these glass containers with paired collodion tubes that were connected in series. His dialyzers had a surface area of between 1,512 and

2,160 cm$^2$ and contained a blood volume of 110-120 ml. To exclude leaks and confirm the integrity of the membrane he used pressure testing. He recognized that for continuous dialysis a blood pump would be necessary to overcome the resistance of the opposing blood flow from the radial artery to the dialyzer and back to the cubital vein and so he used a Beck roller pump, initially cranking this by hand and later using an electric motor. This was the first blood pump ever used in extracorporeal blood circuits.

The chief problem was with anticoagulation, and Haas looked at various possible commercial preparations of hirudin in animal experiments but these were very expensive and had side effects including fever and serious or fatal hemorrhage and so he stopped his experiments. He then developed his own chemical techniques to purify hirudin from extracts of leeches but even this was relatively toxic and restricted the duration of the first dialyses to 15-30 minutes.

In October 1924 Haas performed the first human hemodialysis, for just 15 minutes, in a boy dying from kidney failure and showed that the apparatus and procedure were safe and reliable. The procedure was uneventful and he calculated that 150 ml of blood had been treated. He commented afterwards: "In this way, it could be demonstrated for the first time that blood purification ("Blutwaschung") by dialysis in humans is possible without exposing the patient to injury." This effort was supported by funds from the Rockefeller Foundation.

In February 1925 Haas performed his second dialysis in another young patient with end-stage renal disease, this time for 30 minutes, and during 1926 he did a further four dialyses in patients but the treatments lasted only 30 to 60 minutes because of the problems with anticoagulation. In January 1928, after heparin became available as an anticoagulant, he dialyzed a male patient by withdrawing 400 ml of blood, anticoagulating it, and circulating it through the dialyzer for 30 minutes before returning it to the patient, repeating the procedure nine times. Various non-protein nitrogen compounds were removed, the blood urea level fell by about 60% and indican, creatinine and phenol were transferred into the dialysate. The clinical effect of the treatment was marked and lasted for six days, the patient felt better, vomiting and headache ceased, and appetite returned. The next patient was dialyzed on March 29 and again on May 4, 1928. Haas noted that the patient's blood pressure decreased, heart rhythm improved and urine output decreased. He showed that blood volume had decreased during the treatment and that 100 ml of water was removed from the 400-500 ml of blood during the time of its recirculation. This was due to ultrafiltration resulting from the positive pressure in the blood compartment and not by osmosis, as the dialysate was isotonic Ringer's solution. Consequently, he recommended hemodialysis for patients dying from overhydration and nephrotic edema.

In a lecture to the Giessen Medical Society in January 1928 he noted: "There have indeed only been three cleansing organs on a grand scale up to now – and I know that one swallow doesn't make a summer – but despite the limited number of observations, I have already gotten the distinct impression that it is worth the effort to continue along the path taken." However, he then gave up working on dialysis in 1928 because the German medical establishment said the treatment was of little use, that the patients he had treated got only a little benefit from dialysis, and the equipment was difficult to prepare and use because of the fragile collodion tubing. Dr. Franz Volhard, the leading German kidney specialist of the time, had commented at a meeting of the German Society of Internal Medicine that "dialysis is unnecessary and dangerous."

After the end of the Second World War and becoming aware the work of Willem Kolff, Haas commented that he was exhilarated that his ideas had proved correct but was sad that he had not had the means to carry on his own work. In 1965 he visited the newly established dialysis unit in Giessen that was housed in the same building that he had done the first hemodialysis in a patient 41 years earlier.

Most nephrologists today are not aware of Haas's pioneering work in Giessen, Germany, where the first human hemodialysis was done some 17 years before Kolff's first dialysis in Kampen, Holland.

In 1916 Jay Maclean, a medical student at Johns Hopkins working in the laboratory of hematologist and physiologist Dr. William Howell, first described an anticoagulant found in an extract of liver that came to be called heparin in 1918. Within five years a crude version of heparin became available for experimental use and by the 1930s a purified version was in use generally.

Besides the availability of heparin that made anticoagulation much easier and more predictable, the other development related to hemodialysis in the 1930s was the use of a new membrane – regenerated cellulose acetate. This, under the trade name of cellophane, had been widely used as a packing material from about 1910 and in sheet form began to be used in laboratories for dialysis in the 1920s. Cellophane was known to be much sturdier and more easily sterilized than collodion, and the Visking Corporation in Chicago used tubing made from this cheap product to make casings for hot dogs and sausages. It was tough, withstood pressure well, was reliably free of microscopic holes and was ideal for hemodialysis.

Dr. William Thalhimer, a pathologist interested in blood banking working in New York and with Best in Toronto in 1937 and 1938, had used heparin for what he called "exchange transfusion" to cross-circulate dogs whose kidneys had been surgically removed with normal dogs and showed that blood urea levels fell in the nephrectomised dogs and rose in the normal dogs. In 1937 he went on to develop an artificial kidney resembling that of Abel, Rowntree and Turner using purified heparin and commercially available cellophane tubing. With this device, he dialyzed uremic dogs for several hours at a time and showed it was possible to remove significant amounts of urea by this means. As a result, he thought hemodialysis might be used in humans, although he commented that further investigation was still being undertaken in Best's laboratory in Toronto.

The next stage in the early history of dialysis begins with Dr. Willem Kolff in Holland in 1938.

## Selected references

Gottschalk CW. Thomas Graham 1805-1869. *Nephology* 1998;4:211-216.

Eknoyan G. The wonderful apparatus of John Jacob Abel called the "Artificial Kidney." *Semin Dial* 2009;22:287-296.

George CRP. John Jacob Abel reinterpreted: prophet or fraud? *Nephrology* 1998;4:217-222.

George CRP. Hirudin, heparin and Heinrich Necheles. *Nephrology* 1998;4:225-228.

Wizemann V, Benedum J. Nephrology Dialysis and Transplantation 70th Anniversary of Hemodialysis – The pioneering contribution of Georg Haas (1886-1971). *Nephrol Dial Transplant* 1994;9:1829-1831.

Cameron JS. *A History of the Treatment of Renal Failure by Dialysis*. Oxford University Press, 2002.

## CHAPTER 2

# Kolff, Alwall, Murray and Others: Artificial Kidneys: 1938-1950

———

WILLEM ('PIM') KOLFF (1911-2009) WAS a Dutchman who graduated from medical school at the University of Leiden in 1935 and went to work as an unpaid resident in the Department of Medicine at the University of Groningen under Professor Polak Daniels. It was here in 1938 that he saw a patient, Jan Bruning, die from kidney failure and wondered about the possibility of purifying blood by removing the urea that results from protein breakdown. As a result of this experience, he talked with the professor of biochemistry, Dr. Robert Brinkman, who told him about the use of cellophane in the laboratory to dialyze blood. Kolff and Brinkman experimented in the laboratory removing urea from blood using saline as the dialysate and worked out the details of what would be required to dialyze a patient. By early 1940, Kolff had built an upright artificial kidney consisting of a stainless steel drum wrapped with cellophane tubing and sitting in a bath of dialysate, but their studies ended before they could use it on a patient when, on May 10, 1940, the Germans invaded Holland.

On that day Kolff and his wife, Janke, were in The Hague attending the funeral of his grandfather. All blood for transfusion in the Netherlands came from the Central Laboratory for Blood Transfusion Service run by the Red Cross in Amsterdam. The Hague rapidly became isolated because a nearby attack by German paratroops closed the road to Amsterdam and so Kolff immediately offered to set up a local blood transfusion program at the City Hospital. Within four days he had set up this service and had a reserve of 80 bottles of blood. The Dutch capitulated on May 14 and Kolff and Janke returned to Groningen only to find to their distress that Professor Daniels, who was Jewish and who had been Kolff's chief and encouraged his thoughts about an artificial kidney, had committed suicide together with his wife. A Dutch Nazi had been appointed in his place, but because of illness was not able to take up the position for several months. During this time Kolff qualified as a specialist in internal medicine and then left Groningen for Kampen, a small town in central Holland, where he was the first full-time physician appointed to the staff of the Engelenberg Foundation City Hospital. It was here that Kolff contacted Hendrik Berk, an engineer and head of the Kampen Enamel Factory to discuss how to build an artificial kidney. The factory had been taken over by the Wehrmacht for the manu-facture of pots and pans exclusively for the German army and so Berk and one of his engineers, E. C. van Dijk, met with Kolff at 5 a.m.in the factory before the German overseer came to work at 8 a.m. The engineers recom-mended the position of the drum be changed from vertical to horizontal so that gravity would cause blood to sink to the bottom of each loop of cel-lophane, obviating the need for a blood pump to propel the blood through the 30 to 40 meters of cellophane wound around the drum. The drum sat horizontally in a big enamel tank containing the dialysate. Heparin was used as anticoagulant. To get the blood to and from the tubing on the drum they used a coupling based on a Model-T Ford automobile water pump and the drum was rotated by hand or by a second-hand sewing machine motor. Their original artificial kidney used a drum made from corrugated alu-minum and the whole device sat on an aluminum frame made from parts of a German aircraft that had been shot down. This was the first effective artificial kidney for use in humans. Because the enamel factory was taken over by the Germans, Berk ensured that nothing was entered on the books and the first artificial kidney was made for free.

During the winter of 1942-43, Kolff dialyzed his first patient. He was an elderly Jewish man, Gustav Boele, whose family had been transported to Poland but who had been admitted to the hospital because he was too ill to travel. The Germans then apparently forgot about him. He had cancer of the prostate that had grown to obstruct his ureters and caused kidney failure. He went into a coma and was obviously dying so Kolff decided to dialyze him. Because he was concerned about connecting the very sick patient directly to the artificial kidney he withdrew about half a liter of blood at a time from the patient, mixed it with heparin, and passed it through the device. After several such treatments the blood line to the machine leaked and blood fell into the bath causing foaming that overflowed the tank. At the same time the sewing machine motor stopped working and Janke Kolff, who was watching, turned the handle that rotated the drum. The patient did not improve so Kolff discontinued the treatment and the patient died.

The next patient, Janny Schrijver, a 29-year old housemaid dying from chronic kidney failure due to nephritis, was admitted to the hospital on March 16, 1943. She sank into a coma the next afternoon and, after a visit by a minister, she was moved to Kolff's room where the artificial kidney had been prepared. Kolff withdrew about 100 ml of blood from an artery, heparinized it and then passed it through the machine. This was repeated ten times until a liter of blood had been treated. As she did not improve she was dialyzed for six hours the following evening, and while her blood urea level was unchanged and she remained comatose she did not deteriorate further. Consequently on April 4 Kolff connected her directly to the artificial kidney for the first time and, as a result, her blood urea level declined. She was dialyzed again four times over the next two days, the last treatment passing 20 liters of blood through the machine and her blood urea level declined and she woke from her coma. However, after two days, her urea level had risen and she was dialyzed again. On April 27, at her 12th dialysis, it was found that the artery had been so damaged by the repeated use that she could not be dialyzed. She died a week later.

The drum of the second artificial kidney was made of centimeter-thick wooden slats by a local wainwright as aluminum was no longer available and the undercarriage also was made of wood. Fifteen more patients were treated over the next year and all died except for one who might well have recovered without dialysis. The program stopped after two dialyses on July 27 and 31, 1944, because of worsening conditions following the

Allied invasion of Europe, and four more artificial kidneys that had been made for other Dutch hospitals were put into storage until after the war. Consequently, it was not until 14 months later in September 1945 that Kolff dialyzed his 17th patient and he believed she was the first of his patients he felt certain had survived as a result of dialysis. She was a 67-year-old woman, Sofia Schafstadt, who had been a Nazi collaborator and had been imprisoned after the end of war. In early September she developed a gall bladder infection, jaundice, and kidney failure following treatment with sulfonamides for the infection and became desperately ill. On September 11, 1945, she was dialyzed for eleven and a half hours and she remained in a coma until the following afternoon. Kolff said that her first words when she came around were "Now I'm going to divorce my husband." Her recovery was slow at first and Kolff was planning a second dialysis when her kidney function started to return.

Interestingly, like Scribner 15 years later, Kolff did no animal experiments before starting to treat patients; today, neither would be allowed to do this. Kolff's lack of success over the first two years would not be tolerated today either, but he was the only internist in a small provincial hospital and, as he said later, "No one ever tried to stop me."

Over the same time period between 1942 and 1945, Dr. Nils Alwall in Sweden was experimenting with dialysis in rabbits, and Gordon Murray in Canada was dialyzing dogs.

Kolff's first report in English was published in a Scandinavian medical journal in 1944, and in 1946 his University of Groningen thesis was published and later became a classic monograph. The summary of the 17th case in the thesis ends as follows: "The woman described above made such a serious clinical impression before the dialysis that her death was expected. I am sure she would have died had she not been treated with the artificial kidney. If others agree with my opinion it seems to be proved that by dialysis it is possible to save the life of some patients suffering from acute uremia; a great stimulation to continue our research."

Alwall (1906-1986) was a physician interested in kidney disease who worked in Lund, Sweden. By 1942 he had developed a flat plate dialyzer using sheets of cellophane but soon changed the design to use two concentric static vertical metal coils between which cellophane tubing was wound and which were then contained in a closed steel container filled with dialysate. This did away with the need for rotating couplings and for the first time allowed controlled removal of excess fluid from the blood by ultrafiltration. Alwall worked at the University of Lund, and it was not until September 1946, after four years of animal experiments, that he was permitted to treat his first patient with his artificial kidney. The Alwall kidney was used in a number of centers, primarily in Europe, over the next twenty years.

Gordon Murray (1894-1976), a Toronto vascular surgeon, did the first successful hemodialysis in North America in December 1946. He too had been interested in the idea of an artificial kidney since the early 1940s and had been carrying out extensive investigations using dogs. He designed a coil dialyzer using tubing wound around a vertical drum of wire mesh, and between 1946 and 1949 he treated 11 patients, five of whom survived. He then stopped his program because of opposition from the medical establishment and also because he was a very busy surgeon with a large practice and lacked time to supervise dialysis sessions. Even so, with others, he developed a flat plate dialyzer in the 1950s.

These three pioneers laid the groundwork for the development of programs to treat acute reversible kidney failure with an artificial kidney and these increased in number in the United States, England and elsewhere in Europe during the 1950s. Even so, it was not possible to treat patients with permanent chronic kidney failure for more than a few weeks or months because each dialysis required a surgeon to cut-down on an artery and a vein in the arm or leg to insert the arterial and venous cannulas, and patients soon ran out of available vessels. Consequently, with development of kidney biopsy to take tissue from the kidney to establish the cause of kidney failure, it became the practice to biopsy patients who did not begin to recover renal function after two or three week of dialysis. If the biopsy showed chronic kidney failure rather than acute kidney failure, treatment was discontinued and the patient died.

## SELECTED REFERENCES

Jacob van Noordwijk. *Dialyzing for Life: The Development of the Artificial Kidney.* Kluwer Academic Publishers: Dordrecht, The Netherlands; 2001.

Paul Heiney. *The Nuts and Bolts of Life: Willem Kolff and the Invention of the Kidney Machine.* Sutton Publishing Ltd; 2002.

Klinkmann H. Historical review of renal failure therapy – a homage to Nils Alwall. *Cntr Nephrol* 1990;78:1-23.

Shelley McKellar. *Surgical Limits: The Life of Gordon Murray.* University of Toronto Press: Toronto; 2003.

CHAPTER 3

# Acute Renal Failure: 1945-1960

---

ACUTE RENAL FAILURE, OR AS it is now called acute kidney injury (AKI), is generally due to severe shock and low blood pressure damaging the tubules in the kidneys so that urine production ceases or is greatly reduced. Water, salts and the toxins produced from protein metabolism that normally are excreted by the kidneys are retained in the body. The condition is usually reversible, the kidneys recovering within days or weeks, provided the patient can be maintained alive by dialysis until this occurs. Without dialysis, many of these patients would die, usually because of accumulation of potassium in the body.

It was the Second World War that led to a better understanding of acute renal failure. During the blitz in Britain in 1941, Dr. Eric Bywaters and colleagues (1910-2003) showed that crush injuries in individuals buried during the bombing resulted in damaged muscle tissues that released a protein called myoglobin that was toxic to the kidneys and also potassium from within the damaged cells. At that time treatment consisted only of heat to the kidneys aimed at restoring urine output, intravenous saline to increase blood volume and blood pressure, and by the use of diuretics such as caffeine. It was suggested that deep encapsulation of the kidneys should be tried as this had been shown in this very small number of patients to reduce the in-route renal pressure. At the same time, it was becoming obvious that major trauma, with or without crush injuries, led to kidney failure and death among soldiers injured on the battlefield.

After the end of World War II, Kolff donated rotating-drum artificial kidneys to the Hammersmith Hospital in London, England, to a hospital in Cracow, Poland, to the Royal Victoria Hospital in Montreal, Canada, and one he gave to his friend and fellow Dutchman, Professor Isadore Snapper, at Mount Sinai Hospital in New York. This was first used in May 1967 and was reported in Popular Science Monthly under the headline "Machine Cleans Blood While You Wait." However, it was not until January 1948 that this machine was used for the first really successful hemodialysis in the United States by Drs. Al Fishman, Irving Kroop, Evans Leiter and Abraham Hyman. Irving Kroop, now 98, told me recently that dialysis was done in an operating room in the evening and spectators would come to view the procedure from the viewing gallery after going to the theater. Even so, by 1950 dialysis machines were available in only a very few places. Peritoneal dialysis also came in to use as a treatment for acute kidney failure in a few hospitals in the United States and Europe.

Probably the first use of hemodialysis in a patient in the United States was in the spring of 1944 in Philadelphia, when Drs. Jonathon Rhoads and Henry Saltonstall set up 60 feet of sausage casing wound around a test tube rack in a bath of Ringer's solution. The patient was heparinized and blood flowed through the system from an artery to a vein without a pump. The patient, a young woman with postpartum acute kidney and liver failure, died on the following evening, probably because of bleeding and liver failure and despite transfusion.

The first successful hemodialysis in Canada using a rotating-drum artificial kidney was done by Dr. Russell Palmer at the Shaughnessy Hospital in Vancouver in September 1947. Palmer had been in the Canadian army during World War II and had met Kolff in Kampen shortly after the end of the war. Kolff gave him the plans for the Kolff rotating-drum artificial kidney and Palmer constructed one in Vancouver.

Dialysis was tried first in Britain at the Hammersmith Hospital in London in October 1946 by Bywaters and Dr. Mark Joekes using the machine donated by Kolff but the results were disappointing. Ten of their twelve patients died, probably because they either were treated too late or had chronic irreversible kidney failure. No more successful was pathologist Michael Darmady in 1947 in Portsmouth using a replica of the Kolff rotating drum built for him in a local garage. Only two of the nineteen patients that he treated survived. As a result, dialysis in the United Kingdom was abandoned until 1956 because it appeared time consuming, onerous, dangerous and without obvious benefit for patient survival.

During the five years after the war, Kolff in Holland and Alwall in Sweden continued their programs, and a few generally short-lived dialysis programs were established in hospitals in Canada, Britain, France, Germany and Brazil. Even so, there was a general lack of enthusiasm for the procedure in both Europe and the United States, and most physicians were either unconvinced or contemptuous of the value of hemodialysis and saw better prospects with new dietary management. The emphasis was on so-called "conservative" treatment for acute renal failure by limiting fluids and providing a high-calorie intake, usually with glucose. Dr. Graham Bull at Hammersmith Hospital in London had abandoned dialysis and developed a high-calorie, electrolyte-controlled, low-volume diet for the treatment of acute renal failure that was successful in some patients with milder uncomplicated disease. At the same time Dr. Geed Borst in Amsterdam had developed an even more obnoxious diet and did not believe dialysis could save lives, boasting that in fact the dialyzer Kolff had donated to him was rusting, unused in an attic. Peritoneal dialysis also came to use as a treatment for acute kidney failure in a few hospitals in the United States and Europe.

Dr. George Thorn from the Peter Bent Brigham Hospital in Boston had become interested in renal failure during the early 1940s and visited the Mount Sinai Hospital program in order to meet Kolff who was also visiting and to invite him to visit Boston. In 1948 he ordered one of his residents, Dr. John Merrill, to set up a renal failure program using an artificial kidney that had just been donated to Brigham by Kolff. The first dialysis was on June 11, 1948. Merrill went on to become the leading authority on acute renal failure and its treatment in the United States. He was the first to set up an effective dialysis program and within a few years he and his team had treated more than 100 patients with acute renal failure. Thorn also directed surgeon Carl Walter to modify the Kolff artificial kidney and, as a result, Edward Olson was brought in to redesign and build the device using stainless steel and plastics. The result was the Kolff-Brigham artificial kidney that became the most used dialysis equipment in the United States in the 1950s. By 1959 there were more than 110 hospitals in the United States performing hemodialysis.

Dr. Paul Doolan, a physician in the U.S. Navy, was interested in peritoneal dialysis and was trained to do hemodialysis by Merrill's group in Boston. He moved to Georgetown University in Washington, DC, where one of the first Kolff-Brigham artificial kidneys was installed in 1950. In the fall of 1950, he sent Majors Marion McDowell and Paul Teschan for training to Merrill's program in Boston and they returned and established the Walter Reed Hospital dialysis unit in early 1951, also with a Kolff-Brigham artificial kidney.

A major boost to the use of hemodialysis for acute renal failure came with the start of the Korean War in June 1950 and the concern of the U.S. Army Medical Service that experience in World War II had been that the mortality in wounded soldiers who developed acute kidney failure was 90 percent compared with a 10 percent mortality in those who did not. Colonel William Stone, chief of Army Medical Research and Development, set up renal units at Walter Reed and Brooke General Hospitals using Kolff-Brigham dialyzers and staffed by McDowell and Teschan. At the same time, at the request of the Surgeon General and Stone, an Army research and development survey team was sent to Korea and found that survival of soldiers with posttraumatic acute kidney failure had not changed since World War II. Subsequently, an army task force was sent to Korea to investigate the causes of death in battle casualties. One member of the task force was Dr. George Schreiner who had been trained by Doolan and later became the first head of the nephrology division at Georgetown Medical School. On its return, the task force, having noted that casualties with kidney failure often died from the accumulation of high levels of potassium in their blood, recommended that a local artificial kidney unit with supporting laboratory be established in Korea. Consequently, in April 1951, the Walter Reed unit, under the direction of Captains Holley Smith and Robert Post, was moved to the 11th Evacuation Hospital near Pusan, 30 minutes by helicopter from the forward MASH units. Teschan became director of the unit in June 1952. During the course of 1952, 51 patients were treated at the unit for post-traumatic renal failure with fluid restriction, maintenance of caloric intake, use of cation exchange resins, and treatment of anemia and electrolyte disturbances. Thirty-one of the patients were dialyzed a total of 72 times. As a result, the overall mortality rate in these 51 patients was 53 percent. The limiting factors in survival were the extent of the underlying wounds and the development of infection and impaired wound healing. The unit soon was able to show that dialysis improved survival in battle casualties with acute renal failure, as at that time 85 to 95 percent of battle casualties with acute renal failure without access to dialysis died, as compared with 5 to 10 percent of all battle casualties. However, Teschan's most important finding was that aggressive treatment – starting dialysis early and treating patients more frequently – what came to be called prophylactic dialysis, improved survival even more, a finding that became important later with regard to patients with chronic renal failure. In fact, Teschan and his colleagues showed that dialysis more than doubled the rate of survival of battle casualties with acute renal failure from 15 to 62 percent.

Following the end of the war, experience at Walter Reed and Brooke General Hospitals was that too many patients with acute kidney failure continued to die with infections, wasting and wound dehiscence. As a result, Doolan and the Surgeon General arranged a three-day conference in October 1957 at the U.S. Army Surgical Research Unit at Brooke Army Medical Center in Fort Sam Houston, Texas. The Study Group on Acute Renal Failure included everyone who had published experience with dialysis for acute renal failure up to then – Drs. Bill Bluemle, Hadley Conn, Paul Doolan, Garland Herndon, John Kiley, Willem Kolff, Arthur Mason, John Merrill, Milton Rubini and George Schreiner from the U.S., Graham Bull from Belfast and Gabriel Richet from Paris. They had experience with 1,040 patients with an overall mortality of 49 percent, and in patients with acute renal failure following trauma the mortality was 66 percent. The consensus was that the conventional practice of waiting for the development of uremic symptoms or serious chemical abnormalities before dialysis should be abandoned, leading to the concept of prophylactic more frequent hemodialysis.

By the end of 1959, hemodialysis and peritoneal dialysis were being provided as the treatment for patients with acute renal failure in an increasing number of major medical centers. Technology was improving, new dialyzers were being developed and new plastics were becoming available for tubing and catheters. At that time the principal causes of acute renal failure were accidental or surgical trauma, and gynecological causes, including both septic and failed abortion, and severe postpartum bleeding. However, because of the need for a surgical incision on an artery and vein, patients could only be treated for a few weeks or months before accessible vessels in the limbs were exhausted.

In England, the first dialysis unit since the late 1940s was established in the Leeds General Infirmary by the Departments of Urologic Surgery and Medicine in September 1956 using the Kolff-Brigham dialysis machine. The unit was directed by Dr. Frank Parsons, a surgeon, and by Dr. Brian McCracken of the Department of Medicine, and I succeeded Brian in January 1958. A similar unit opened at Hammersmith Hospital in London in January 1957. Leeds served the northern half of the British Isles, patients often being transferred by overnight train and often referred late, needing emergency dialysis as soon as they arrived. Most referrals from outside Leeds and Yorkshire had pregnancy-related AKI and this was also seen in France and in the United States. In Boston at this time, for example, at least half the female patients with acute renal failure had developed it as a pregnancy-related complication and half of these were related to abortion. Today, obstetric acute kidney failure is rare in developed countries with legalized abortion, but was a major problem in the 1950s and 1960s because of relatively unsophisticated management of obstetric complications, problems with mismatched blood transfusions and the relatively common illegal practice of abortion induced by chemical or surgical means. Outcomes in these otherwise fit young women were dramatic.

Dr. John Turney has pointed out that had the early dialysis units been presented with many elderly patients with complex medical and surgical problems and comorbidities such as are seen today, outcomes could have been so much worse that dialysis probably would not have been acceptable. However, some young obstetric cases had irrecoverable bilateral cortical necrosis, and in the late 1950s the moral problems of discontinuing their dialysis stimulated some of the early efforts to attempt cadaveric kidney transplantation.

This all changed in 1960.

## CHAPTER 4

# Chronic Kidney Disease, Kidney Failure and Uremia

———

CHRONIC KIDNEY DISEASE OR CKD is a relatively common disease that affects some 26 million adults in the United States, and many others are at risk. For this reason, individuals should have their urine checked for protein and their blood pressure measured regularly so that the disease can be detected at an early stage. The commonest cause of death in CKD patients is heart disease. CKD causes hypertension and hypertension causes CKD. Individuals at higher risk include those with diabetes, those with high blood pressure, those with a family history of kidney disease, African Americans, Hispanics, Pacific Islanders, Native Americans and the elderly.

The kidneys function to produce urine that removes waste products and fluids from the body and maintains normal levels of water, salt, potassium and other substances. They are also important because they make and release hormones that help regulate blood pressure, stimulate the bone marrow to make red blood cells and help maintain the strength of bones. In addition, they can remove many drugs and other toxins if they are present in the body.

The commonest cause of CKD is diabetes. Diabetic kidney disease accounts for more than half the cases of permanent chronic kidney failure requiring dialysis or kidney transplantation in the United States today. (Permanent kidney failure is also called end-stage renal disease or ESRD). Diabetes is a generalized disease resulting from a lack of the hormone insulin that is produced in the pancreas and regulates sugar levels in blood. Over the years the resulting high levels of blood sugar cause widespread damage to blood vessels throughout the body, causing high blood pressure, heart disease, kidney disease, impaired circulation, blindness and damage to nerves (peripheral neuropathy). The second most common cause of CKD is hypertension, accounting for 20 to 25 percent of ESRD in patients in the U.S. and is particularly common in the African American population, explaining their much higher incidence of kidney failure.

The third commonest cause of CKD is glomerulonephritis. This primary disease of the kidneys results from several types of inflammation that destroy the filtering units in the kidneys. Other causes of CKD include the following: polycystic kidney disease (PKD), an inherited disease that results in development of large cysts in the kidneys that press on the filtering units and may grow to a very large size and usually cause kidney failure in middle age; other congenital problems that affect urine flow; various immune diseases, particularly systemic lupus erythematosus (SLE); obstruction to urine flow due to an enlarged prostate in men; kidney stones; various tumors; and repeated urinary infections.

Unfortunately, the earlier stages of CKD usually do not cause any symptoms. That is why it is wise for patients to have regular checks of blood pressure and of urine for the presence of protein. In the late stages, patients become tired and, lacking energy as a result of anemia, their appetite diminishes. They also may develop swelling around the ankles or around the eyes, especially in the morning, their skin becomes dry and itches, and ultimately they develop nausea and vomiting and may go into a coma and die.

When kidneys fail the products of protein breakdown that normally are excreted through the kidneys accumulate in the body. It has been known for more than 200 years that urea is one of the substances that accumulate with kidney failure and so the condition came to be called uremia. In fact, this is the effect of the accumulation of many different substances that causes the symptoms experienced by patients. In addition, some other problems patients experience include accumulation of water and salt in the body, causing hypertension; accumulation of potassium (hyperkalemia) that may cause muscle weakness and, if very high, can cause heart problems and sudden death; severe anemia because of a lack of the hormone erythropoietin

(EPO) that is made in the kidneys and stimulates bone marrow to produce red blood cells, so the early patients required regular blood transfusions; damage to the peripheral nerves (neuropathy); accumulation of uric acid that can cause gout; and accumulation of phosphate that can cause calcium deposits in the body and that affects bone metabolism.

## CHAPTER 5

# Belding Scribner: Between 1921 and 1960

---

BELDING HIBBARD SCRIBNER WAS BORN in Chicago on January 18, 1921. He was named Belding after his mother, the former Mary Elizabeth Belding. In 1860 her grandfather, Scrib's great grandfather, and his three brothers began buying silk and selling it from house to house from their home in Belding, a small Michigan town about 25 miles north of Grand Rapids that was named Belding because it was the Western homestead of the family that had left the East in 1858. By 1866 they had become Belding Brothers and Company and began manufacturing their own silk thread in a mill in Rockville, Connecticut and expanded their marketing to several major cities in the United States and Canada. Scrib's great grandfather ran their Chicago office. In October 1871 he saved their Chicago operation during the Great Chicago Fire by putting everything in his wagon and hauling the silk north of the Chicago River. By 1872 they had established a second mill in Massachusetts and were selling various goods and embroidery silks of every description. By 1890, further expansion was needed and they established four mills in Belding, one produced silk thread, two produced various fabrics and the fourth manufactured sewing and embroidery silks of every description as well as a variety of crochet cotton. The Belding Silk Company was famous at the beginning of the 20th century and merged with the Hemingway silk company in 1925. The last mill in Belding closed in 1932.

Belding is a name that dates back to Anglo-Saxon time in Britain. It is derived from the old English personal name Bealding which itself was originally derived from the name Beald. During the Middle Ages the English language evolved and Belding had many spelling variations including Belding, Balding, Baulding, Bauldyne, Bolding, Baldyng, Beldyng and Baldinge among others. The first known Belding settlers in North America were Richard Belding who landed in Connecticut in 1653 and Samuel Belding who arrived in New England in 1661.

Scrib's mother was educated at a small school, Dana Hall, and wanted to go to Wellesley but her father thought it not proper for young ladies to go to college. She had always wanted to be a writer and became an editor of a small Chicago magazine started by the Junior League of Chicago. Based on her success there she was offered editorship of a magazine called Today that later became Newsweek and she moved to New York for about a year. In the mid-1930s when her husband's lumber business was having great difficulties the family moved to California where she went to work as a news editor for the San Francisco NBC radio newsroom and then became a writer for CBS and wrote a number of wartime dramas. She died of cancer of the colon at the age of 46.

Scrib was also named Hibbard after his godfather, Jack Hibbard, who had been the college roommate of Scrib's father and best man at his wedding. It was he who later introduced Scrib to the delights of fly fishing for trout, a sport that he continued to enjoy throughout his life.

Scrib's grandfather, Charles Ezra Scribner, was an engineer and inventor at Western Electric who had worked closely with Alexander Graham Bell and invented the multiple switchboard that made telephone exchanges possible. Thomas Edison described him as "the most industrious inventor I have ever known. His imagination seems boundless."

Carleton Scribner, Scrib's father, had been in the first graduating class in aeronautical engineering at Massachusetts Institute of Technology. He had flown in World War I as a flight instructor at Kelly Field and was a part time aeronautics inspector for the state of Illinois. In 1933 a local small airline was used to ferry people to the Chicago World's Fair and one Sunday the plane crashed about 20 miles south of Deerfield. Scrib's father was called to inspect the crash and took his 12-year-old son with him. The

sight remained a vivid memory with Scrib. His interest in flying was ampli-
fied by the fact that at a nearby farm there was a person who had a Curtis
JN-4 "Jenny" airplane that he used to fly people around the area for a $5
ride. Scrib was fascinated watching the plane take off because it was from
a small field and sometimes it only just made it over the trees at the end of
the field. As a result of his father's interest and these experiences, Scrib developed a lifelong interest in planes and flying

Scrib's father was in the lumber business with a retail lumber yard in
Morton Grove, about 10 miles south of Deerfield. In 1929 the family lost a
lot of money in the stock market and in the ensuing Depression the builders
who had bought lumber from him went bankrupt because they were unable
to sell houses. As a result the lumber company was virtually bankrupt too
and so in the mid-1930s the family moved to California where Scrib's father
died in 1941.

Scribner disliked his first name intensely because it was unique and
because his family called him "Bel" or "Elle" both of which sounded like
a girl's name. This was extremely embarrassing to a young boy and consequently, early on, he became known as "Scrib" by almost everyone.

Scrib was born in Chicago and grew up in nearby Deerfield, Illinois,
which at that time was very rural. As a child he suffered severely from asthma, hay fever and eczema and had to leave Chicago each fall during the
ragweed season and go to Wisconsin to avoid having asthma attacks. Being
sickly as a child and spending a lot of time in doctors' offices was one factor
that later led him to become a physician.

He attended an elementary public school in Deerfield but got behind
because of his medical problems and so in the second grade he moved to a
private school in Highland Park and then to another private school in Lake
Forest where he got reasonably good grades and enjoyed playing baseball.
This was where the shop teacher, Whitey Cannon, introduced him to "tin-
kering" and where he built his first radio. The same teacher ran a summer
camp in Temegami, Ontario and there Scrib learned canoeing and how to
live outside and he won the cooking contest baking cornbread in a reflector
oven but he was never interested in becoming a Boy Scout.

For high school, he won a scholarship to Fountain Valley School, a Colorado prep school that he later said was marvelous and that luckily it was "a private school. I'm one of those people who needed the shelter and protection of that environment. It wasn't the prestige. It was because I was insecure."

In 1937, at the age of 16, he spent his first year at university at Williams College in Massachusetts where he was taught freshman chemistry by Professor Paul Fong who was an incredibly imaginative teacher. It was here that he was introduced to the effects of osmotic force when Fong did an experiment in the 3-story stairwell of the chemistry building. He put copper sulfate, a blue-colored solution, in a very strong bag with a long tube, closed at one end by a semipermeable membrane that was submerged in water. The resulting osmotic force pushed the copper sulfate solution three stories up the tube during following week. It was experiments that like this that started Scrib's interest in chemistry.

In 1938 his family moved to California and Scrib transferred to the University of California in Berkeley, graduating with a Bachelor of Arts degree in 1941. It was here that he attended a course in microchemistry that gave him the skills he used later to develop bedside tests for electrolytes but even so he did not major in science. Rather he took the new general curriculum at Berkeley which provided a great general education. One of his advisors suggested he take English composition courses to learn to communicate. The professor teaching the courses was tough and a harsh critic of Scrib's compositions but he felt strongly that this resulted in his ability to write clearly and easily. He always felt this professor and Professor Fong were the important figures in his education before he went to medical school.

One reason Scrib went to Berkeley was that it was the only university on the West Coast with a Sigma Phi fraternity He had belonged to this fraternity at Williams and so had his father at the University of Michigan. At Berkeley he learned the hard way about politics. He played intramural sports and broke his leg playing football and so went out to be track manager to support his fraternity. He was a good track manager, worked hard, and the point came when a head overall track manager was to be appointed. Scrib lost out and discovered later that this was because the fraternity of this individual carried more political clout than Sigma Phi and that was the way such things were settled.

Almost all his subsequent life was spent on the West Coast and later he said "I always liked the West Coast. I had the sense there was more freedom there and a lot more chance to be an individual. I had to choose between Harvard and Stanford Medical Schools and I chose Stanford for that reason. It turned out to be the most crucial decision I ever made." Stanford was far less structured than Harvard and far smaller in those days, far more personal, and it turned out that he would have two important role models in medical school.

Scrib entered Stanford University School of Medicine in San Francisco in 1941, and graduated MD in 1945. He actually completed medical school in three years because with America's entry into World War II medical school was completed in three years with no vacations, and his fourth year was spent as a rotating intern at San Francisco County Hospital where George Barnett ran the medical services and became one of his role models. In December 1941, following Pearl Harbor, medical students had to join the armed forces and because he enjoyed sailing Scrib chose the Navy where he was ranked as an apprentice seaman.

In relation to his later career, it is interesting that his mentor in medical school was Professor Thomas Addis, a Scottish physician who was a world-renowned pioneer in both hematology and in the investigation and treatment of kidney disease. Having seen a postoperative patient die from fluid and electrolyte imbalance, Scrib worked with Addis on salt and water balance in patients. At that time, a method to measure chloride by titration had just been described and encouraged by Addis and by Dr.? George Barnett. Scrib took this and developed a bedside test to measure chloride in urine and blood to diagnose saline depletion in patients. Addis was so impressed by this that he paid for a special cart to be built for Scrib that he could wheel around the hospital in his white coat, as he said "looking like an ice cream seller."

While still in medical school Scrib's eyesight began to fail from a congenital condition called keratoconus and as a result was discharged from his obligations to the Navy. Fortunately, he was referred to an eye surgeon in New York, Dr. Townley Patten, who had founded the first eye bank in the United States and was a pioneer in corneal transplantation. Later, in 1951, Scrib had the first of several corneal transplants that he required at intervals during his life and that saved both his vision and his career.

Because of World War II, Scrib's fourth year of medical school was spent as an intern at San Francisco County Hospital. Following this internship, Scrib stayed on as a resident in medicine at the same hospital for the next two years. He had heard about the Mayo Clinic as a place to go to get good training to become a physician before going out into practice. At that time he had no intention to go into academic medicine, otherwise he would have gone to an academic institution. In June 1947 he became a Fellow in Medicine at the Mayo Clinic in Rochester, Minnesota, planning to continue his interest in electrolytes and kidney disease following his experience with Addis. It was here that he developed further bedside tests to measure bicarbonate, total base and urea in serum and published his first papers describing these tests.

His life changed one sunny afternoon in July 1950 when he was planning to play golf. One of his friends persuaded him to come to hear a talk by Dr. John Merrill from Boston about the rotating- drum artificial kidney and the treatment of acute kidney failure. This convinced Scrib that hemodialysis had a real future and that the artificial kidney would be an ideal research tool for studying fluid and electrolyte balance. Unfortunately, the Mayo Clinic did not share his enthusiasm and refused to purchase an artificial kidney. He went on and completed his fellowship in 1950 and stayed on at the Mayo Clinic for a further year as an Assistant to Staff while obtaining a Master of Science degree from the University of Minnesota.

Because his eye problems continued, it was while at the Mayo Clinic that he realized that he could become blind and decided to pursue an academic career rather than go into practice. At the Mayo Clinic he also had a corneal transplant. His eyes had been carefully managed by the ophthalmologist at Stanford with the result that his cornea was not scarred. But with time, the cornea bulged and got thinner and if it were to rupture it would cause scarring. Scrib was carefully followed and before he got to the rupture point he had another corneal transplant by Dr. Patten at the Manhattan Eye and Ear Hospital. Unfortunately on the 15th postoperative day a chair he was sitting on broke and he fell and the graft popped loose. However, it was reworked but that graft never worked as well as it should have and was re-done in 1978.

When Scrib left the Mayo Clinic he wanted to go into some sort of institutional medicine and had obtained a position at Memorial Hospital in New York in order to be near to Dr. Patten for when he would need a second corneal transplant. However, he and his wife Betty first wanted to take their then three children to meet their grandmother in Los Angeles. It was while there that he heard there was a new medical school starting from scratch in Seattle and there might be a job there. He could not afford a daytime flight and so took the red-eye to San Francisco and went to the University of California and to Stanford, saying he was interested in a possible academic position but a nothing was available. He found the same at the University of Oregon in Portland.

The following morning he met with Professor Robert Williams, chairman of the Department of Medicine at the University of Washington Medical School, in a tiny building where the medical school now stands. Also present was Professor Robert Evans who had just been appointed head of medicine at the new VA hospital in Seattle and who had been a young professor at Stanford when Scrib was a medical student. Evans wished to hire him on the spot because he knew of Scrib's abilities and said "Williams, if we get this guy it's going to be great." Bob Williams knew the people at Memorial Hospital in New York who had hired Scrib and according to Scrib "called his buddy at Memorial Hospital and talked him into letting me give up my commitment, and so we came to Seattle." By the end of the day Scrib was hired to fill the third staff position in the Department of Medicine at the Seattle VA Hospital.

## The University of Washington Medical School

The University of Washington Medical School was founded in 1946 and was the first medical school in the four-state area of Washington, Montana, Idaho and Alaska. Dr. Williams was appointed the first chairman of the Department of Medicine and was able to attract up-and-coming young associate professors from the most prestigious medical schools around the country to become heads of the various medical divisions in the new medical school. Initially, Harborview Hospital, established as the King County welfare hospital in 1877, was the site of clinical teaching, and in its earliest days the medical school was situated in huts close by. It soon became obvious that a partnership with a community hospital was not enough to ensure that medical students and young doctors received sufficient clinical experience and so, in 1950, the medical school began planning a new teaching hospital. In 1954 the first phase of construction of University Hospital was completed to provide office space and laboratories for the medical school's clinical staff, and the hospital itself opened in 1959 with eight floors, 291 beds and a nursery.

Scrib first was appointed director of general medical research at the Seattle VA Hospital and a University of Washington faculty member as a research assistant, as he described it "the lowest of the low." In December 1951 he was promoted to be an instructor in medicine at the University of Washington Medical School. In 1953, he finally persuaded the VA to buy an artificial kidney and he chose the reusable Skeggs-Leonards dialyzer because it had a small blood volume. Ultrafiltration to remove excess salt and water was achieved by raising the hydrostatic pressure in the kidney. Subsequently, the internal resistance to blood flow in the kidney was lowered so that an external blood pump was unnecessary. For the next three years he transported this artificial kidney to local hospitals in a panel truck to treat patients with acute kidney failure. In 1957, he began using disposable twin-coil dialyzers. During this time, he and his associate, Dr. Jim Burnell, were performing classic studies on sodium and potassium, in particular the effects of potassium in the body. Scrib was also refining his bedside kit to measure chloride, bicarbonate, sodium, potassium and urea, and was developing an educational syllabus that was used for many years to teach medical students about fluid and electrolyte problems.

In 1958, the University of Washington established a Division of Nephrology. Scrib, now an associate professor, was appointed as its first head and soon developed a program to treat acute kidney failure at the University of Washington Hospital. Also in 1958, he was awarded a prestigious Markle Scholarship from the John and Mary R. Markle Foundation that was established in 1927 "to promote the advancement and diffusion of knowledge...and the general good of mankind." John Markle was the son of a Pennsylvania coal mine operator, inventor and financier, and he took over the family enterprises when his father fell ill. When he and his wife moved to New York City in 1902 he also began to devote himself to philanthropy, becoming involved with the city's and nation's elite and their social, financial, industrial and charitable interests. The foundation's original interest was in traditional social welfare, but in 1936 it began supporting individual research projects in medicine. In 1947 it created the Markle Scholars in Medicine program to increase the number of teachers, researchers and administrators in U.S. medical schools. Grants were awarded to gifted practitioners planning to further their careers in academic medicine. Scrib elected to go to Hammersmith Hospital in London where he worked with Malcolm Milne, one of Britain's leading researchers in kidney physiology. While living in London, he and his family visited France several times and this was when Scrib discovered the wonders of French wines as well as meeting a number of the leading French kidney doctors who became close friends of his.

In Seattle, Scrib, Dr. Tom Marr, his first research fellow, and Jim Burnell had been experimenting with gastrodialysis. This involved having the unfortunate patient swallow a large stomach tube ending in a large cellophane bag that sat in the patient's stomach. Dialyzing fluid was pumped in and out of the bag and dialysis occurred with urea and other toxins moving from the stomach contents through the cellophane membrane. They reported on this work at the annual meeting of the American Society for Artificial Internal Organs in 1958, but the technique was too inefficient to be clinically useful. However, the equipment they made for gastrodialysis played an important role in the development of peritoneal dialysis a few years later.

As described elsewhere, in 1952, the U.S. Army had established an artificial kidney unit using a Kolff rotating-drum artificial kidney in an evacuation hospital near Pusan in Korea to treat battle casualties with acute kidney failure. Scrib was intrigued by reports from Teschan and surgical researchers there that using the artificial kidney more frequently, what Teschan called "prophylactic" dialysis, improved survival in these seriously ill casualties. As a result of reading about the benefits of this, in 1959, Scrib came up with the idea of using continuous hemodialysis for patients with acute kidney failure. For this he used a Skeggs-Leonards artificial kidney and a modified large Sears-Roebuck deep freezer to maintain the dialyzing fluid (the dialysate), cooled for 12 to 24 hours to retard bacterial growth. This became the routine treatment for acute kidney failure at University Hospital.

As described in the Introduction, the first dialysis that changed the treatment of patients who had irreversible kidney failure occurred on March 9, 1960. Although how successful it would be was still far from certain, dialysis would lead to saving the lives of patients around the world suffering from what previously had been a universally fatal disease. What led up to this remarkable development?

## CHAPTER 6

# Belding Scribner, Wayne Quinton, David Dillard and the Shunt: 1960

---

IN EARLY JANUARY, 1960, A patient from Spokane with what appeared to be acute reversible kidney failure was admitted to University Hospital for treatment with the artificial kidney. Scrib said that he was unable to "recall ever having seen a sicker patient survive on the artificial kidney." He was in uremic coma and heart failure, but a week or so later after several dialyses was up and about and feeling well. Ominously, he was not passing any urine and so a kidney biopsy was performed. A special needle was inserted through his back into one of his kidneys and a small piece of tissue was removed for microscopic analysis by a pathologist. Unfortunately this showed that in fact he had a chronic kidney disease that had utterly destroyed his kidneys.

To quote Scrib: "What to do? ... We did the only thing we could do. We had an agonizing conversation with his wife and told her to take her husband back to Spokane where he would die, hopefully without much suffering....He died quietly (at home) about two weeks later...The emotional impact of this case was enormous on all of us, and I could not stop thinking about it. Then, one morning I woke up about 4:00 a.m. and groped for a piece of paper and a pencil to jot down the basic idea of the shunted cannulas, which would make it possible to treat people like the Spokane patient again and again with the artificial kidney without destroying two blood vessels each time. And, indeed basically it was such a simple idea – just connect the tube (cannula) in the artery to the cannula in the vein by means of a connecting tube or shunt, and the blood would rush through without clotting and maintain the cannulas in a functional condition indefinitely. Then when an artificial kidney treatment was needed, we could simply replace the shunt temporarily with the blood circuit of the artificial kidney. The most amazing thing about this idea was that unlike most such ideas it worked right from the start."

Although Scrib did not know it at the time, this concept had already been tried by others previously. In 1949, Nils Alwall in Sweden reported studies on treating experimental kidney failure in rabbits using hand-made glass cannulas connected to siliconized rubber tubing, the cannulas being connected between dialyses with a glass capillary tube and the rabbit being injected with heparin every four-to-six hours to prevent clotting. He also began to treat patients with acute renal failure using the shunt or closing off the rubber tubing with short glass rods between dialyses and heparinizing the patients. After a couple of years he abandoned the shunt because of problems with blood clotting, bleeding or local infection. Similar shunting of the cannulas was attempted in the 1950s by Teschan in Korea and by Parsons and Blagg in Leeds, England, but with the plastic tubing used for cannulas at the time the same problems were seen.

The secret of Scrib's success was the availability of Teflon$^{TM}$ tubing. Teflon (poly-tetra-fluoro-ethylene) had been developed in 1938 and by the 1950s was available in many forms, including Teflon tubing. How Scrib heard about it is rather uncertain but he had been discussing his idea with Dr. David Dillard, a pediatric cardiac surgeon, and it appears that one of Dillard's colleagues, Dr. Loren Winterscheid, told Scrib to try Teflon tubing during a casual conversation in the stairwell of the hospital. This was being used for cannulas to monitor arterial blood pressure after open heart surgery because the blood did not clot in the tubing and it was also used to encase implanted pacemaker wires. Winterscheid told Scrib to visit Mr. Wayne Quinton, head of the hospital's medical instrument shop, which he did. Wayne thought the answer was simple and that "any self-respecting engineer would immediately suggest a quick connection device when faced with the need to repeatedly put new catheters in a patient for each dialysis." A meeting was arranged between Scrib, Wayne and Dave Dillard for the afternoon of the 23rd of February to discuss and approve Wayne's proposed design that used Teflon tubing.

What Wayne came up with became the original shunt. Tubing for the two cannulas was tapered at one end so they could be placed in the radial artery and a vein in the patient's forearm. Each cannula then ran in a sub-cutaneous tunnel, making a 180-degree turn toward the elbow and then a step so they emerged through the skin vertically through a tight-fitting puncture wound some distance from the site of the vessel cannulation. This design and route reduced the risk of infection. A stainless steel arm plate was devised to be attached to the forearm. The arm plate had an upright mounting, which held two specially modified "Swagelok" fittings – regular plumbing devices used to connect two pieces of tubing – and supported a thin plastic cover to protect the cannulas. The square cut ends of the two cannulas fit into the Swagelok fittings precisely. The bypass loop (shunt) was a U-shaped piece of Teflon tubing with some constriction at its center to restrict blood flow through the loop to 100 to 200 ccs per minute. Between treatments, the loop was connected to the cannulas by the Swageloks, and for dialysis treatment it was removed and the arterial and venous bloodlines to and from the artificial kidney were connected to the cannulas. The arm plate served to anchor the cannulas and also provided an easy way to change the external circuit from the bypass loop to the dialyzer circuit. Quinton also had developed the technique for tapering the cannula tips, a device to heat and bend the Teflon tubing to make the cannulas and shunt, and a device to cut the ends of the tubing square to allow better connections.

Thus, the shunt was developed as a result of the efforts of three people. Everyone knows Scrib, who came up with the concept, and Wayne Quinton who developed the technology, but the third important person in 1960 was Dave Dillard, the surgeon. Dave would spend between one and three hours carefully inserting the cannulas, and without his meticulous surgery it might never have been seen as the solution to treatment of patients with chronic kidney failure. Indeed, Scrib and Quinton showed the shunt and its preparation at a private meeting in Chicago during the annual meeting of the American Society for Artificial Internal Organs and several of those who took away the materials and placed shunts in patients had problems because they did not heed the admonition to ensure careful surgery that was in the published report on the shunt.

The original Teflon shunts would only last for a few weeks or months, and the original patients, including some with acute renal failure, endured several shunts in arms or legs until Quinton improved the design. However, the shunt did not require patients to be anticoagulated between treatments, in part because kidney failure results in the accumulation of various toxins normally excreted through the kidneys and that are associated with some impairment of blood clotting. The use of Teflon tubing was also important because experience with its use in cardiac surgery had shown that it was non-tissue reactive, and blood in a tube of Teflon did not clot easily. Of course, Teflon now also is well known domestically for its non-stick properties.

In 1960 there were no Food and Drug Administration (FDA) or device regulations, and so fortunately, unlike with Alwall in Sweden in 1949, there was no need to conduct animal experiments with the shunt before using it in patients. If these had been necessary, they would almost certainly have been performed in dogs, and later experience showed the difficulties in maintaining shunts in dogs because of clotting. In fact, the shunt was implanted first and used for one dialysis in one patient with acute renal failure and then on March 9th, a little over two weeks after the meeting with Quinton, the first patient with chronic renal failure, now often called end-stage renal disease or ESRD, was treated with the artificial kidney using the shunt.

## CHAPTER 7

# Wayne Quinton and David Dillard

———————

WAYNE QUINTON WAS BORN IN Salt Lake City, Utah, in 1921. His childhood was spent on small Idaho farms and helping in the family dry-cleaning plant. After graduating from high school he spent a year at Ricks College, (now Brigham Young University – Idaho), where he studied physics and advanced math before transferring to Montana State University. However, because of limited funds he took a job as a draftsman at the Boeing Company in Seattle in December 1941 and was one of six preliminary tool planning engineers on the B-29 bomber. He later transferred to the physical research department to work on guided missile design. His years at Boeing provided intense training in production methods. During this time he also completed a two-year course in machine shop practice in metal fabrication provided by the War Production Program. His next employment was at the University of Washington as an electronics technician where he developed heat measuring equipment for an important Arctic Study program and this led to his inclusion in Life magazine's list of the Nation's 25 Top Young Scientists in 1950.

In 1952 he was hired by the University Hospital and the University of Washington Medical School as chief medical instrument designer and maker. His role was to keep medical instruments in good repair and to develop new devices as required by staff physicians. "My job" he later recalled "was to build anything they couldn't buy." His motto was "Never let lack of knowledge and resources keep you from doing something that needs to be done." His many accomplishments at the University of Washington include working with Robert Bruce in developing the treadmill for cardiology, with Cy Rubin in developing a device for intestinal biopsy and with Scribner in developing the Teflon shunt and its modifications that made long-term dialysis possible.

His first contact with Dr. Scribner had been when he was asked to procure a refrigerated dialysis tank and a device to rewarm blood for use during hemodialysis for acute renal failure. Scribner had treated a wounded deer hunter from Montana who bled from his extensive wounds during his dialyses and had assumed that less heparin would be required if the blood was cooled in the dialyzer. Quinton modified a Sears Roebuck freezer to serve as a dialysate tank and to function just above the freezing temperature of water instead of its normal lower temperature in order to minimize bacterial growth. He also developed a simple water bath to warm the blood before its return to the patient from the dialyzer.

After leaving the University he founded the Quinton Instrument Company. This grew rapidly and among other products came to have worldwide sales of cardiovascular stress testing equipment, gastric intestinal biopsy devices, and blood access systems for treating patients with both hemodialysis and peritoneal dialysis, all based on his original work with physicians at University Hospital.

David Dillard, MD, was a pediatric cardiac surgeon who joined the University of Washington Medical School faculty in the late 1950s. In addition to working at University Hospital he also worked at Seattle Children's Hospital where he established the first pediatric cardiac surgery program and developed the use of hypothermia for open heart surgery.

In the early days of the University Hospital and the Health Sciences building, physicians used to meet in a cafeteria on the top floor of the building for lunch. It was at one of those lunches that Scrib talked to Dave about the concept of the shunt that he was anxious to develop. As mentioned previously, Dave then told Loren Winterscheid, a young vascular surgeon who worked with him and it was Loren who told Scrib about Teflon and suggested he talk to Wayne Quinton.

Dave performed all the access surgery for the early dialysis patients until Meredith Smith, another vascular surgeon, joined him. In time, a small number of other vascular surgeons became experienced in access surgery. It was obvious in those early days that meticulous surgery was required to insert shunts, and the lack of such care was one of the reasons some of the early dialysis programs had particularly poor results with their shunts.

Among other projects Dave worked on were aortic valve replacement studies with Loren Winterscheid and others. He also coauthored with Donald Miller an atlas of cardiac surgery in which many of the illustrations were done by Dave. In fact, Dave was a gifted amateur artist not only in illustrative art but in painting and sculpture as well.

## CHAPTER 8

# The First Two Patients: Clyde Shields, March 9th, 1960, Harvey Gentry, March 24th, 1960

CLYDE SHIELDS WAS A 39-YEAR-OLD machinist at Seattle Machine Works who had chronic kidney failure due to glomerulonephritis and who had been followed by Scribner as an outpatient in the Renal Clinic at University Hospital for several years. He remained symptom free until 1959 and by December of that year had to stop work because of weakness, vomiting and headaches. Following a brief hospitalization and changes in his diet, he improved slightly but his blood pressure increased. By the end of February, when he was being considered for dialysis, he was an invalid with constant vomiting, spending most of his time in bed. He was admitted to the hospital early in March, by which time he was barely able to walk to the bathroom and was judged to have only two or three weeks to live, although he did not know this at the time.

On March 9, 1960, with Quinton at the bedside to make a shunt of the right dimensions for Clyde's arm, David Dillard, the pediatric heart surgeon, implanted the first Scribner-Quinton shunt in Clyde's forearm. Quinton then connected Clyde to a Skeggs-Leonards artificial kidney using the Sears Roebuck freezer that he had modified previously to hold dialysate at 4° C to slow bacterial growth, a syringe pump borrowed from the laboratories of the Physiology Department to provide heparin for anticoagulation during the dialysis, and an old office sterilizer to rewarm the blood before it was returned to Clyde. That first dialysis continued for 76 hours, by which time Clyde was feeling much improved, had stopped vomiting, felt generally well and could walk more easily than he had been able to do for several weeks.

Over the next three days Clyde developed severe headaches, weakness, shortness of breath due to congestion in his lungs and his blood pressure became very high. He was treated by severe dietary salt restriction and 24 hours of dialysis weekly. With this regimen, he was able to live at home, and after several dialyses generally felt well between treatments although lacking in stamina because of anemia requiring transfusion of one or two units of packed red blood cell each week. However, toward the end of April he began to feel weak and to vomit in the mornings on the last day or two before his next treatment. This situation was improved by changing his treatment schedule from once a week to once every five days for 24 hours. Harvey Gentry, the second patient, was a 22-year-old shoe salesman who was found to have chronic glomerulonephritis at the age of 18 when he was rejected for military service because of protein in his urine. He began to feel ill in 1958, and was referred to the University of Washington Renal Clinic in July 1959. By December he was suffering from tiredness, breathlessness, muscle cramps, swelling of the ankles, nausea and loss of appetite, but despite these problems he continued to work through February 1960.

Early in March he began vomiting and became so weak and tired that he could no longer work and was admitted to the hospital for possible dialysis. He had a shunt placed in his right arm on March 23, 1960, two weeks after Clyde's first dialysis, and was started on dialysis the next day. At that time there was little thought about the long-term implications of this treatment as it was still unknown whether patients would survive for more than a few weeks or months. Harvey was started on treatment simply because he was a patient in the clinic and would have died without dialysis. He was treated four times over the next seven weeks, improving after each treatment. He felt better, his strength improved, he was no longer nauseated and his muscle cramps went away. Apart from dialysis, his only treatments were a moderately restricted protein and low-salt diet, and regular blood transfusions. On a regimen of 24 hours of dialysis once a week he was able to return to work and lead a nearly normal life.

In April, Harvey was the first patient to suffer complications from having a Scribner-Quinton shunt. After a clam digging expedition he developed redness and swelling of his forearm and drainage from the cannula exit sites. Despite antibiotics, his condition did not improve until he was admitted to the hospital and treated, but as the infection cleared the shunt clotted. It was removed, revealing a small abscess at the venous site. Two weeks later an attempt was made to place the cannulas back in the arm but scarring made this impractical and so the cannulas were placed in the left arm.

The initial experiences with Clyde and Harvey suggested that the lives of patients dying of chronic kidney failure could be prolonged and that the cannulation technique could provide access for repeated hemodialysis. Remaining questions following these brief experiences were how long such patients might survive and how the problems of nutrition and diet, high blood pressure and anemia should be treated.

## CHAPTER 9

# The Sixth Annual Meeting of the American Society of Artificial Internal Organs (ASAIO) 1960

---

THE AMERICAN SOCIETY FOR ARTIFICIAL Internal Organs ( ASAIO(ASAIO) was founded in Atlantic City, New Jersey, in 1955 after Pim Kolff, Peter Salisbury and Clarence Dennis discussed establishing a society to "promote the increase of knowledge about artificial organs and their utilization." At that time, experience with the early artificial kidneys was beginning to grow and heart-lung machines were just beginning to be used for some forms of heart surgery. News of this interesting idea spread to a number of other scientists and engineers, and 47 individuals were corresponding by mail by April 1955.

The first meeting of the ASAIO took place on the evening of June 4 and the day of June 5, 1955, at the Chelsea Hotel in Atlantic City. There were 67 attendees and 29 papers were presented, 13 on artificial kidneys and the others on heart and lung devices .as well as movies of open-heart surgery and heart-lung machines. Kolff was elected first president of the society.

At the meeting there was discussion about whether the American Society for Artificial Internal Organs was the best name for the organization. Other suggestions included The Society for Biomechanics, for Physiological Instrumentation, for Physiologic Engineering, for Organ Substitution, for Biochemistry, for Organology, for Substitute Internal Organs, for Development of Artificial Organs, for Artificial Viscera, for Synthetic Viscera, for Plasmogony, the Biomechanical Society, the Artificial Heart and Kidney Club, the Society for Open Hearts and Shut-Down Kidneys, and the Pumpers and Pissers. This discussion was repeated at many of the early meetings, but the original name, the American Society for Artificial Internal Organs, has continued now for more than 57 years.

Scrib was elected to membership in the society at the third annual meeting at the Conrad Hilton Hotel in Chicago in April 1957, by which time there were 92 members. The following year, as mentioned earlier, Tom Marr presented a paper on gastrodialysis in the treatment of acute renal failure, coauthored with Scrib and Jim Burnell, but the Seattle group did not present a paper at the 1959 meeting.

The 6th annual meeting of the ASAIO was again in Chicago on April 10 and 11, 1960, at the Pick-Congress Hotel. Clyde Shields' first treatment was on March 9th, and the ASAIO meeting was some four weeks later in April. The program was already set, the only paper from Seattle being one on continuous hemodialysis, but the shunt was working and so Scrib took Clyde and his wife Emmy and Wayne Quinton to the meeting. There followed two separate small group meetings with Kolff, who was now at the Cleveland Clinic, Drs. George Schreiner from Georgetown University in Washington DC, John Merrill from the Brigham Hospital in Boston, Paul Teschan from Brooke Army Medical Center in Texas, Lewis Bluemle from the University of Pennsylvania, Joe Holmes from the University of Colorado, and Jack Leonard from Western Reserve University – most of the dialysis "establishment" at that time. At a breakfast meeting Scrib presented Clyde to the group and discussed the experience to date with Clyde (32 days) and Harvey (18 days). He described their treatment and its problems and noted they were now living at home, Harvey was working part time and Clyde was active around the house, and neither had shown any relentless weight loss or mental deterioration. He stressed that the treatment provided an "unusual opportunity for clinical and basic research."

The second meeting was held that evening in Scrib's hotel room. Quinton had brought Teflon tubing and had prepared sets of the equipment to bend the tubing, pliers for cutting the tubing squarely and patient arm plates for each of the physicians present. He demonstrated to them how to bend the tubing and prepare the shunt and cannulas. Scrib meanwhile looked out of the hotel room window, musing on the fact that his father had driven down this road 39 years earlier to take his mother to the hospital for his birth. Paul Teschan said that at the time he was much more concerned at Quinton wielding the Bunsen burner as he thought the old hotel was a potential fire trap.

The only paper from Seattle that was on the program and actually presented to the Society as a whole was a description of continuous hemodialysis for the treatment of acute kidney failure, its theoretical background as an alternative to more frequent dialysis, the equipment used, and clinical experience over the previous six months. The artificial kidney used was a Skeggs-Leonards dialyzer because its internal resistance was low, allowing slow blood flow through the dialyzer driven by the patient's blood pressure and without the need for a blood pump. The dialyzer was connected to the patient by 20-foot plastic bloodlines ending in cannulas in an artery and a vein in the arm. Various pumps had been used to provide a slow infusion of heparin through a special fitting to the arterial tubing just beyond the arterial cannula to prevent blood clotting in the tubing and dialyzer during treatment. Three hundred liters of dialyzing fluid with an electrolyte composition similar to normal blood was contained in a modified Sears Roebuck 15 cubic foot deep freeze maintained at near zero degrees Centigrade to minimize bacterial growth and reduce clotting. The dialysate bath was changed every 24 hours and the blood circuit and dialyzer every 24-48 hours. The equipment, its set up and use were described in great detail. Over the previous six months, 18 patients had been treated by continuous dialysis over a period ranging from half a day to 14 days for a total of 68 days. The system was shown to be as effective in improving the patient's blood chemistry over 12-14 hours as conventional six-hour hemodialysis was using other artificial kidneys. No serious complications due to dialysis were seen, but four patients died during or soon after treatment, although no postmortem evidence was found that the deaths related directly or indirectly to dialysis. The advantages of this method were the simplicity of the technique, which was well tolerated by patients, and that dialysis could be monitored by a nurse rather than by a physician.

George Schreiner, who was editor of ASAIO Transactions, recognized the importance of Scrib's work and asked him to write two papers that were then published in the 1960 Transactions even though they had not been formally presented at the meeting. In 2005 these papers – "Cannulation of blood vessels for prolonged hemodialysis" and "The treatment of chronic uremia by means of intermittent hemodialysis: a preliminary report" were selected by the ASAIO membership as being among the 25 Landmark Papers published by the ASAIO during its first 50 years. They made possible the treatment of a previously fatal disease, were forerunners for many more developments from Seattle over the years, and led to more than two million patients with kidney failure being treated around the world today.

## CHAPTER 10

# The University of Washington and the First Four Patients 1960

---

TWO MORE PATIENTS WERE STARTED on dialysis in 1960. Rolin Heming was a 29-year-old man with chronic glomerulonephritis who began to have symptoms in late 1959. Unlike the first two patients, Clyde Shields and Harvey Gentry, by the time Heming was referred to the hospital in late April of 1960, he arrived in uremic coma and close to death. He remained critically ill after starting dialysis, and after about two weeks developed rapidly progressive damage to his nerves - peripheral neuropathy - which was known to be one of the complications of uremia. Even with intensive dialysis the nerve damage continued to progress and affected his chest muscles so that he had to be placed on a Drinker respirator – an iron lung – for several weeks while continuing to be dialyzed. It was discovered that his neuropathy was aggravated by hyperkalemia – a high blood level of potassium – and when this was controlled he was able to come off the respirator. He recovered from the nerve damage to some degree but required a wheel chair and was left with residual paralysis of his lower arms and legs. Eventually he was able to walk with a cane. As was the case with the first two patients, Rolin was put on a regimen of 24 hours of dialysis once a week and required one unit of packed red blood cells every other week to maintain his hematocrit in the low 20s. With Clyde and Harvey he lived to see the 10th anniversary of the first dialysis with the shunt in March 1970.

The fourth patient, Jack Capelloto, was a 47-year-old pharmacist who had been known to have polycystic kidney disease and severe high blood pressure since 1953 and who started to have angina and heart failure in April 1960. In June, he developed severe staphylococcal pneumonia and was admitted to University Hospital in uremic coma. With removal of salt and water with dialysis, his heart problems and high blood pressure improved and he too was established on 24 hours of dialysis once a week. On this regimen, he recovered sufficiently to be able to start work again as a pharmacist but was unable to find employment.

All four patients were prescribed a diet restricted in protein and salt (40 Gm. protein, 400 mg sodium) but this was followed rigidly by only two of them. The patients also tended to limit their fluid intake appropriately. This diet and fluid restriction helped to control production of toxins and helped control hypertension but it was also important not to lower protein intake too much. In addition, they all received vitamin supplements because water soluble vitamins were lost in the dialysate.

With once-a-week dialysis (once every five days in Clyde's case) the patients were developing tiredness, weakness, itching and poor appetite some 24-36 hours before their next dialysis, and a common complaint was that cigarettes began to have a bad taste. The level of potassium in the patients' blood rose between dialyses, contributing to the muscle weakness that developed before the next dialysis, and so Clyde and Jack also took small doses of an ion exchange resin to control their hyperkalemia. The patients themselves recognized that with less effective dialysis the symptoms returned earlier and also that eating extra protein accentuated the symptoms. As a result, in early 1961, it was decided to change the treatment to 12 or more hours twice a week. With this, the patients' sense of well-being improved and the symptoms disappeared except at times when dialysis became less effective because cannula problems reduced blood flow during dialysis.

During the first year of their treatment, both Harvey Gentry and Jack Capelloto suffered an episode of viral hepatitis, probably related to the many blood transfusions the patients required. Both recovered, as did one of the doctors caring for them who also developed hepatitis, presumably from one of the patients. Hepatitis was to become a major problem in dialysis units only a few years later.

Also during the first year the patients suffered from a number of other complications. Clyde experienced several episodes of very severe hypertension early on, but this was controlled by more intensive dialysis with fluid removal. Thereafter, the degree of hypertension varied and, as at that time suitable antihypertensive drugs without serious side effects were not yet available, blood pressure was controlled by a low-salt diet, some fluid restriction, and reducing extracellular volume by removing fluid by ultrafiltration during dialysis.

All of the patients suffered from severe anemia related to deficiency of production of erythropoietin (EPO) by the diseased kidneys. Transfusion requirements were some 2 to 4 units of packed blood cells per month, but even with this their hematocrits averaged only about 25, about 55 to 60 percent of normal. It was realized that if erythropoietin had been available, it would have relieved the anemia, but that was not to occur until almost 30 years later following years of research on the anemia of kidney failure by Dr. Joseph Eschbach at the University of Washington. Another problem that developed later as a result of frequent transfusions was the deposition of iron in the liver from the transfused red blood cells. However this did not become a clinical problem during the first year despite patients receiving a large number of transfusions.

In terms of nutrition, Clyde and Jack lost weight initially but soon their weight stabilized. Rolin, and particularly Harvey, were less conscientious about following restrictions in their diet and both gained weight after starting treatment. Rapid weight loss occurred when dialysis became insufficient because of cannula problems or when patients developed an infection, but weight was rapidly regained following treatment. Concern had been expressed at the ASAIO meeting that weight loss over a few months would be inevitable, but because of adequate dialysis the patients maintained their appetite.

All four patients had problems with peripheral neuropathy that usually affected the feet and legs, resulting in some loss of sensation, diminution of their reflexes and weakness. After the first few months on dialysis Clyde began to show insidiously progressive changes, including loss of sensation, muscle weakness and wasting, and a flapping gait. By the end of the year, he was being dialyzed longer hours to see if this would help relieve neuropathy. The changes were negligible in Harvey and Jack but, as noted earlier, were progressive and very severe in Rolin and took between two and three months to stabilize. Gradual recovery then began but at the end of the year he still required use of a wheelchair.

The two patients who were oldest, Clyde and Jack, suffered episodes fairly typical of gout with occasional attacks of acute joint pain, swelling, tenderness and slight redness involving wrist, elbow, and knee and toe joints. The attacks were not severe, responded to aspirin, and subsided within one or two days. Uric acid levels in the blood are elevated in chronic kidney failure but unlike classical gout symptoms this complication did not appear to be related to the uric acid level or to dialysis.

After a year, and apart from the 24-hour dialysis each week, Harvey felt well, working 40 hours a week as a shoe salesman and going bowling in the evening twice a week. Jack would have been able to work but was unemployed. Rolin and Clyde were disabled by neuropathy but Clyde could do light work around the house and could go for walks. All four patients were described as having made remarkable adjustments to the way of life of a dialysis patient and had shown no reluctance to continue in the program.

Based on experience during the first year of treatment of these four patients, it was felt that the ideal candidate for dialysis would be a young adult under the age of 35 who was unable to work because of the symptoms of uremia, who had stable or slowly progressive kidney disease with only mild high blood pressure and no evidence of cardiovascular disease, and who was emotionally stable and mature.

CHAPTER 11

# Technical Developments 1960-1962

————

THE MOST IMPORTANT TECHNICAL DEVELOPMENT with blood access during this time was development of the Silastic-Teflon cannula. The original all-Teflon shunts were rigid and generally only lasted for several months, primarily because arm movements were easily transmitted through the shunt so that the rigid cannula tips damaged the lining of the blood vessels.

This had been recognized early on, and Quinton had realized that inserting a segment of silicon rubber (Silastic) tubing between the Teflon tips would provide needed flexibility. The problem was that the Silastic tubing available at that time had a relatively rough internal surface that would induce clotting in the blood passing through it. Quinton tried various measures to solve this problem and in 1961 developed a technique to improve the surface finish of the extruded Silastic tubing so that it was smooth enough that it did not induce clotting.

These Silastic-Teflon shunts were superior to the original Teflon shunts in that they were flexible and easier to insert without damaging the vessel lining, easier to adapt to the various anatomical problems that might be found at surgery, reduced transmitted movement to the cannula tips, resulted in increased blood flow by allowing better alignment of the tips in the vessels and, most importantly, extended cannula life. During 16 months of using the original Teflon cannulas in the first four patients, the shunt failure rate averaged one every 4.3 months. The experience with Silastic-Teflon cannulas in the seven chronic patients improved the rate to one failure every 11.3 patient months. Once available, these cannulas were used for all patients with both acute and chronic renal failure treated at University Hospital.

Another development was the use of lower leg vessels for shunts. The lower leg vessels were used in Clyde when his forearm vessels were no longer accessible. A Teflon shunt in these blood vessels lasted for 8 months despite normal walking and then was replaced with the successful Silastic-Teflon shunt. Following this development, leg vessels were cannulated in another patient, with the only complication a slight swelling of the cannulated leg at the end of the day, a complication that continued to be seen if patients were on their feet most of the time. However, the use of leg vessels nearly doubled the number of possible cannula sites.

With time, the Sears Roebuck freezers used to contain the dialysate began to rust and were eventually replaced with stainless steel tanks. Fortunately the Sweden Freezer Company in Seattle manufactured stainless steel tanks that were used in machines to make soft ice cream, and the president of the company, Harvey Swenson, was an inventor and developed a dialysis machine that was based on a 380-liter stainless steel tank that was used for dialysis in University Hospital and will be described in more detail later.

Another important advance was the introduction of the Kiil dialyzer. Scrib was in Europe in 1961, and while visiting Claus Brun in Copenhagen was shown a Kiil dialyzer. This device was invented by Dr. Fred Kiil, a Norwegian urologist, and soon became known as a reusable flat-plate parallel-flow artificial kidney with low internal resistance that could be used without a blood pump. It had a surface area of $1M 2$ and consisted of three or five hard plastic boards made from epoxy resin, the two-layer or the four-layer Kiil dialyzer. The inner surface of the two external boards was grooved as were both sides of the central boards. Two sheets of cellophane resided between each pair of boards. Blood flowed between the cellophane sheets and dialysate flowed in the grooves on the outside of the cellophane in the opposite direction to the blood flow. The boards were separated by rubber gaskets and the dialyzer was held together by external clamps. The device was also intended to be used as a membrane oxygenator but soon became widely used as a dialyzer because it did not need a blood pump, and proved very useful in dialysis units and later for home hemodialysis.

At about the same time Cuprophan, a new version of cellophane treated with a cuprammonium process and that was thinner and more permeable than classical cellophane, became available. The Kiil was assembled for each dialysis with new Cuprophan sheets and tubing sets. It was approximately 39 inches long, 13 inches wide and 6 inches deep and weighed about 60 pounds. Scrib talked by phone with Kiil from Brun's office and an arrangement was made that Scrib could purchase Brun's Kiil dialyzer for $500 and Kiil would replace it. Scrib returned to Seattle via New York Idlewild (now Kennedy) Airport with the Kiil dialyzer upright in the clothes closet of the DC8. At Idlewild he was faced by a customs agent who did not know what a dialyzer was and thought Scrib was smuggling diamonds. He was suspicious about the rubber gaskets on the board faces and opened them all with a knife.

The problem then was to make Kiil dialyzers in the United States. Wayne Quinton tried unsuccessfully to make a similar unit from another molded polymer but failed. Fortunately Scrib had a friend in Los Angeles, Dr. Jack Meihaus, who suggested he talk about the manufacturing problem to Martin Headman, the chief engineer at the Western Gear Company. Headman suggested making the boards by milling slabs of polypropylene to tight tolerances and set up a process to make the boards in their Everett plant. Scrib received the first two Kiil dialyzers free from Western Gear for testing and quality control and after testing was completed they were used at University Hospital. The Sweden Freezer Company in Seattle bought the boards from Western Gear for a number of years and sold them around the world. The first of the two-layer Kiil dialyzers were used at the Seattle Artificial Kidney Center when it opened in 1962. As its popularity spread, rivalry developed with units using coil dialyzers in the United States and between Scrib and Pim Kolff who had moved to the Cleveland Clinic.

## CHAPTER 12

# The Origins of the Seattle Community Artificial Kidney Center: 1960 and 1961

---

AFTER THE INITIAL PRESENTATIONS IN hotel rooms at the ASAIO meeting in Chicago in April 1960, Scrib presented his results in September at the inaugural meeting of the International Congress of Nephrology in Evian-les-Bains, France. He was already seeing the potential of the treatment and had enquired of a major insurance company to try to get some idea of the number of potential patients. However, uremia was not listed as a cause of death and so no information was available.

He saw the need to establish a prototype dialysis center but the big problem was money. In July 1960 he wrote to the Seattle Foundation for support but was unsuccessful. He approached Senator Magnuson and was advised to turn to the NIH for funding but he was already receiving NIH grants to support research and the training of renal fellows and federal funds could not be used to provide patient treatment. In addition, the nephrology establishment at that time primarily consisted of kidney research physiologists who regarded dialysis as of little scientific importance. At the same time even those who were members of the ASIAIO and had heard Scrib's talks were still struggling to make the shunt work.

The other problem was space for treatment of patients. Scrib was alternating in his mind between using the University of Washington Hospital or establishing a community-based dialysis center. The plan was to treat more patients and to do clinical research to improve patient care and the technology.

With the failure to procure support from foundations, Scrib applied for an NIH grant toward the end of the year but was turned down for several reasons, including because he was not doing a randomized trial. He also approached the U.S. Public Health Service and was also turned down. Early in 1961 he did get some grant support but not enough for his needs.

In late 1960 he approached John Hogness, then Medical Director of University Hospital, requesting to expand the area he had been using for dialysis in the Clinical Research Center to be large enough to treat as many as 12 patients with chronic renal failure and to serve as a center for treatment of acute kidney failure. Hogness advised him to "slow down" and insisted the issue of funding had to be settled before additional patients could be treated. There would be a moral responsibility from the state to future patients and the hospital could not take on this responsibility unless a corresponding commitment could be made to continue treatment for as long as necessary, essentially for the duration of each patient's life. If the patients died because funding ran out the adverse publicity would be disastrous. However, Scrib was allowed to continue use of two beds for the next year after which the research progress with dialysis would be reassessed in light of other research needs. As a result of these problems no new patients were started on dialysis and he turned again to the idea of a community-supported dialysis center.

In July 1960 Scrib had informed the Board of Trustees of the King County Medical Society (KCMS) that he was petitioning the Seattle Foundation for support for a community dialysis center for King County and the Board had expressed their support for his request. However, the Foundation rejected Scrib's request as did several other possible sources of funding including the Avalon Foundation, the Markle Foundation, the Department of Health Education and Welfare and the U.S, Public Health Service. Consequently, in early 1961, he approached the medical society again and, fortuitously, the KCMS President now was Jim Haviland who had previously served as associate and later acting dean of the medical school before going into practice. Jim was a very effective bridge between academia and physicians in private practice, and was familiar with Scrib's work. Jim Burnell, a nephrologist colleague of Scrib's, was also a member of the KCMS Board of Trustees at the time. The Society agreed to consider the issue.

Three major problems needed consideration in planning for such a center. First, where should it be established? Second, how would it be financed? And third, how would patients be selected? The costs of setting up the center and treating patients would be considerable and most patients would be unable to pay for their treatments and so, while initial support could be from grants, support from the community eventually would be essential.

Several hospitals wanted to have an artificial kidney center and that would result in duplication of expensive facilities, each requiring highly trained personnel. Scrib was anxious to avoid a repetition of the problem seen in Seattle shortly before this when about a dozen hospitals acquired heart-lung machines, even though most had neither the staff nor the experience to use them. Consequently it was decided at the KCMS Board meeting on April 17, 1961, to request the chairman of the Hospital Commission to get representatives from the Seattle Area Hospital Council together with representatives from KCMS and Drs. Scribner and Burnell to consider on a community-wide basis where and how such a center should be established. A special meeting of the KCMS Board of Trustees was held on May 3rd where Dr. Burnell presented the recommendation that two members from the Board and one lay person be appointed to meet with representatives of the Hospital Council to consider this further. The Board appointed Drs. Mudge and Ramey as their representatives and Mr. Edward Rosling as the lay representative and suggested the problems of patient referrals and staff privileges at the selected hospital also be discussed by the proposed committee.

This lay-dominated committee with representatives from the KCMS Board and the Seattle Area Hospital Council decided to invite any interested hospital to submit bids to become the site of the one community dialysis center. Consideration was given to physical plant, location of the hospital, staff structure, existing equipment, ancillary medical facilities, and intangibles such as the attitude of the hospital administration. Three hospitals responded, and the committee reported back to the KCMS Board of Trustees on June 12th that after much deliberation Swedish Hospital was chosen to be the site for what was called the Kidney Treatment Center Program. The relationship was described as the Center being "attached to the Swedish Hospital of Seattle in a public trust arrangement as a research and demonstration project." On June 15th, the KCMS Executive Committee decided to move ahead and implement the proposals in the report, that Jim Haviland would meet with representatives of Swedish Hospital to work out details of the arrangement, and that the committee appointed by the KCMS and the Hospital Council would continue to follow progress of the Kidney Center Treatment Program. After discussions, the basement of Eklind Hall --what had been the Swedish Hospital's nurses residence-- was chosen as the site for the Center.

The second problem was to find funding support for the proposed center, and so on June 26, 1961, Dr. Allan Lobb, Swedish Hospital's new administrator, submitted an application to the John A. Hartford Foundation. This foundation was established in 1929 by Mr. E.P. Roy, founder of the Atlantic and Pacific Tea Company, to further medical research "especially the clinical aspect, in voluntary, nonprofit hospitals." Its particular concern was "to reduce the lag between findings in the laboratory and their application in the care and treatment of patients." On July 26, 1961, the foundation awarded $250,000 to Swedish Hospital "to implement a community hemodialysis center for research and treatment of chronic uremia and terminal renal failure" and to be payable in installments in 1961, 1962 and 1963. As a result, the Seattle Community Artificial Kidney Center was able to begin operations as a three-station unit in January 1962 as the world's first out-of-hospital, community-supported dialysis unit where dialysis was primarily provided by trained nurses rather than by physicians. From the beginning the plan was that the Center would become self-sustaining at some early date and become incorporated as a non-profit organization as soon as feasible.

The Center was affiliated with Swedish Hospital which provided services, food, heat and administrative support in the early years. This relationship was important as on at least one occasion when the center was $40,000 in the red the hospital "carried" the Center until it had worked out its financing. At a later date the hospital provided more space in Eklind Hall when the center needed to expand. Consequently as Jim Haviland said later, without Swedish Hospital "the Center could well have foundered almost before it was successfully launched."

The other important affiliation was with the University of Washington Medical School and the Division of Nephrology headed by Dr. Scribner. The Center's medical director, John Murray, came from this program. It was the general understanding of what was now called the Seattle Chronic Hemodialysis Project that research and development would be carried out primarily at the University and patient services would be provided primarily at the Center.

It is worth emphasizing that while the original idea of a community dialysis center was Dr. Scribner's, this would probably never been developed without the support of Dr. Haviland with his wide relationships and knowledge of local medical politics. Thus the center had two "fathers" – Scrib and Jim Haviland.

The third major problem faced during development of the proposed kidney center was how patients were to be selected when only a very few could be treated.

By late June 1961 it appeared the requested funding from the John A. Hartford Foundation would be forthcoming and so the committee appointed by KCMS and the Hospital Council began to discuss how to handle patient selection. They decided to establish a Medical Advisory Committee to set strict medical criteria for admission and an Admissions and Policy Committee to make the final decisions. The original Medical Advisory Committee consisted of six nephrologists (Dr. Scribner, chairman, and Drs. James Burnell, Emily Fergus, John Murray, Richard Paton, and Ben Uyeno), two urologists (Drs. Tate Mason and John McCormack) and three other internists (Drs. John Lindberg, Alfred Skinner and William Steenrod). The original Admissions and Policy Committee consisted of seven members: two bankers, a businessman, a housewife, a minster, a physician who was not a nephrologist and a physician from the State Division of Vocational Rehabilitation (DVR).

A memo was circulated to members of the King County Medical Society announcing the forthcoming center and inviting them to refer potential patients. It was estimated there would be between 5 and 20 ideal candidates per million population per year and this matched an estimate from the Metropolitan Life Insurance Company of 10 to 20 ideal candidates for treatment per million population annually in the United States. Thus, it was obvious from the beginning that the potential number of patients would overwhelm the proposed three-station unit which could only treat nine patients using twice-weekly overnight dialysis for 12-16 hours.

## CHAPTER 13

# Patient Selection and the Birth of Bioethics

THE MEDICAL ADVISORY COMMITTEE WAS the group that developed the strict medical criteria for admission to the program. Based on the death of the fourth patient at the University of Washington in early 1961 and who was the oldest patient and was known to have pre-existing cardiovascular disease, it was felt important to accept only the patients most likely to survive in order to prove that long-term dialysis worked. Thus the original medical criteria for acceptance were extremely strict:

1.  a stable, emotionally mature, adult under the age of 45 who is disabled by symptoms of uremia;
2.  absence of long-standing hypertension and permanent complications therefrom, particularly coronary artery disease and cerebrovascular or peripheral vascular disease;
3.  demonstrated willingness to co-operate in carrying out the prescribed treatment, especially the dietary restrictions;
4.  renal function should be stable or deteriorating slowly since any residual renal function simplified the therapeutic problem; and
5.  children and young adults who are not potentially self-supporting were excluded because of doubtful patient cooperation and concern about not being able to support normal growth.

Patients with diabetes and other non-renal diseases that were the cause of their kidney failure also were excluded. These restrictions were gradually relaxed over the next nine years as funding became more available.

Because there were going to be more medically acceptable candidates in the community than could possibly be treated in the planned center, the Admissions and Policy Committee was tasked to "attempt to develop for the final selection on a non-medical basis" and "to protect those in charge of the Center from pressure to take a given patient." This final selection committee was also intended "to represent the Center in the community" as "the future of the Center rests, in the large part, on assessment of its acceptability as a community service by this group." But this latter was difficult when the committee requested to be anonymous. Composition of the committee was intended to represent a broad socioeconomic spectrum of Seattle society with the intent of helping minimize any bias in favor of candidates from certain social backgrounds or occupations. Obviously, despite the intent, the committee was largely upper middle class, well-educated and of similar occupation, income and social background. Later this led to concern from critics about the possible biases of the group.

The original charge to the committee was "In arriving at final decisions this committee has been given the opportunity to investigate the candidates in any way that seems appropriate to them, but the candidates' names are not revealed." At first the committee relied on information from the patient's own physician and the Medical Advisory Committee, but it soon became obvious that the committee wanted to know everything possible about the patients. As a result, they were given help from a clinical psychologist and a psychiatrist and somewhat later from a social worker and a vocational counselor. At first it was arbitrarily decided to require six months residence in the Northwest (Washington, Alaska, Idaho, Montana and Oregon) before application could be made, but the committee soon decided that candidates would be restricted to residents of the state of Washington. This was because of the difficulty in justifying use of local funds for those outside the state and the difficulty in ensuring job stability and support of rehabilitation potential if the patient resided far from Seattle. Some of the sociological factors used by the committee originally included "type of employment, employer attitude, number of dependents, and economic status of anticipated survivors."

With limited facilities, limited financial backing and nowhere else to turn to for help, the committees had considered several options for patient selection. Strictly medical selection was regarded as lacking diversity of viewpoints, could have built-in prejudices if a patient was followed by a physician member of the committee, and could have exposed committee members to outside pressures. First-come, first-served could make the decision difficult and arbitrary if there were too many candidates. If no medical criteria were used this might result in very poor candidates being treated, so jeopardizing the project with limited facilities and finances and nowhere else to turn to for support. Treatment of all candidates would have rapidly overloaded the center and perhaps the fairest might have been selection by lot. This would have avoided difficult decisions by the committee, increased public awareness of the problems that would be faced as other expensive medical technologies were developed, and dramatized the difficulties for society in making such decisions.

The committee began meeting, making decisions on individual patients before all the ground rules were established. They requested not to know the names of patients or their physicians and agreed that if any members recognized an individual patient or the patient's physician, they would rule themselves out of the decision process. They knew that hemodialysis was not advertised and that some prospective patients who could have been saved were never considered by the committee, either because their physician was unaware of the center and dialysis or knew that no space was available and so did not refer them. When a place was available and there was only one prospective patient the decision was easy – accept or reject. The problem was when there were two or three candidates for one place. The process started with discussion of the pros and cons of each candidate as seen by the committee members. The final decision was made by consensus and not by a formal motion, but then members were each asked whether they concurred with the consensus.

The reaction to this committee among nephrologists was low key at first, but the Seattle Community Artificial Kidney Center and the process of patient selection became a very public issue when in the summer of 1962,

Life Magazine sent a young reporter, Shana Alexander, later to become a well-known author and television commentator, to write an article about what she called "the Seattle Artificial Kidney Center at Swedish Hospital" and the chronic dialysis program. She was fascinated by the situation, and spent considerable time in Seattle researching all aspects of the Center's program. This resulted in publication of the article in the Life Magazine issue of November 9, 1962.

Much to the surprise of Dr. Scribner and his team, the main thrust of the article was a discussion of the selection process and its implications, not the exciting new development that had turned a previously fatal disease into one that could be treated. The article was entitled "They Decide Who Lives, Who Dies" and was accompanied by a photograph of the committee members in silhouette that became famous. In the text she designated it as "the Life or Death Committee." Nowhere in the article did she refer to it as "the God Squad" as has been claimed since, but she did write that, "No matter who decides, aren't the real choices all shaky, all arbitrary, all relative? They depend not on a patient's unique worth, but on his comparable position in a particular slate of candidates. Who really is the more suitable patient under the present committee rules - the man who, if he is permitted to continue living, can make the greatest contribution to society; or the man who by dying would leave behind the greatest burden on society? On the basis of the past year's record, a candidate who plans to come before this committee would seem well-advised to father a great many children, then throw away all his money, and finally to fall ill in a season when there will be a minimum of competition from other men dying of the same disease."

Thus, the ethical dilemma was graphically presented to the public. Triage was something that had long been practiced in the military situation when all casualties could not be saved, but at that time the application of such a process in civilian practice, except following major disasters, was unheard of. The article was the longest article ever published in Life, and as Shana Alexander later noted, it "sparked a national interest in what you today call bioethics." The Life article was followed in 1965 by a TV documentary by the National Broadcasting Corporation entitled, "Who Lives?

Who Dies?" hosted by Edwin Newman, and Redbook published an article entitled, "The Rest Are Simply Left To Die."

John Darrah, who was chairman of the Admissions and Policy Committee for most of its existence, commented later that when he was approached and asked to be a member of the committee, he was told by one of the physicians, "We are not asking you to decide who will die. This is already determined. Without treatment, needy patients will die within a few weeks... We are asking you to help decide who will be given the opportunity of extended life." At that time "hemodialysis for everyone who needed it was utterly impossible. It was an absolute necessity to decide who would be accepted for the limited treatment available. We were not primarily interested in the past, but rather the present and prospect for the future... We requested not to know the names of patients or their physicians... We knew that some prospective patients who could have been saved by hemodialysis were never considered by the committee... Places were not held open in case a 'worthier patient' would be forthcoming. The demanding decisions were when two or three prospective patients were considered at the same time for the one available place... We did not make snap judgments, and were honest in trying to do the job assigned to us. Final decision was made by consensus, not by formal motion... I am still haunted by the question, 'When is the time for death with dignity?'" As one of the other members of the committee said later "None of us enjoyed what we were doing. We had responded to a request and need and, without guidelines or precedent, were striving to do an honest and honorable job."

Reactions by scholars to the developments in Seattle and the publicity surrounding this were primarily criticisms. Dr. George Schreiner, chief of nephrology at Georgetown University, said "We have never had such a committee in Washington DC, and never will have. We feel that this is a device to spread the responsibility to people who by experience and education are really less equipped to take responsibility than the physicians in charge of the case."

In the UCLA Law Review a law professor, David Saunders, and a psychiatrist, Jesse Dukeminier, criticized the Seattle deliberations as "polluted by prejudices and mindless clichés" and described the situation as "a disturbing picture of the bourgeoisie sparing the bourgeoisie... This rules out creative non-conformists who rub the bourgeoisie the wrong way but who historically have contributed so much to the making of America. The Pacific Northwest is no place for a Henry David Thoreau with bad kidneys." They noted that if a project is experimental "the use of broad discretion in selecting candidates who can demonstrate the validity of the project is not objectionable. Once the procedure proves its merit and passes from the experimental to the standard ... justice requires that selection be made by a fairer method than the unbridled consciences, the built-in biases, and the fantasies of omnipotence of a secret committee. Selection by a secret committee operating without explicit criteria is a grotesque conceit worthy of Franz Kafka." Saunders and Dukeminier recommended that choices between patients be made by some method that did not require or permit ad hoc comparisons of their social worth. Possibilities would be ability to pay, first-come, first-served, lottery, or random selection, and "rules announced in advance that are not unconstitutionally discriminatory." They noted, however, that "None of these methods is perfect; each has its defects. But any of these methods is preferable to selection by ad hoc comparative judgments of social worth."

An analysis of selection for "exotic life-saving therapy" by the philosopher Nicholas Rescher was the first bioethics article to be published in the philosophical journal Ethics. He believed an acceptable selection system must be simple and plausible in the sense that ordinary people should be able to see that it was justified. All of the component criteria should be reasonable and rationally defensible, and it must be fair. In terms of inclusion criteria, he thought there were three important factors: the constituency factor based on the geographic area served; the progress-of-science factor based on research interests in relation to the specific nature of the cases at issue; and the prospect-of-success factor with selection of those patients most likely to benefit. These factors all related to the element of limited availability. Further selection should then be based on the relative likelihood of success based on a case-by-case comparison, life expectancy, family role and dependence of the family, and the potential future contributions of the patient. "A civilized society has obligations to promote the furtherance of positive achievements in cultural and related areas." Past services rendered could also be important. "Biomedical factors are easy, but familial and social factors are difficult and involved intangibles. Even so, these must be taken into account from the ethical viewpoint, and largely based on the principles of utility and of justice." He believed lay people could and should play a considerable role in the process. Thus, his criteria for selection were to start with the criteria for inclusion, then to use a scoring system for the further criteria for selection, and then use random selection if needed. This would obviate automatic application of an imperfect system, make rejection easier for the patient to accept, and relieve staff of the ultimate and absolute responsibility. As he said, "Life is a chancy business, and even the most rational of human arrangements can cover this over to a very limited extent at best."

James Childress, a theologian at the University of Virginia, felt it was important to decide which standard should be used and who should make the decision. First, it was important to determine medical acceptability, but use of psychological and environmental factors should be kept to an absolute minimum. He felt the difficulties with prediction using social worth raised doubts about the feasibility and justifiability of using a utilitarian approach, and there was also difficulty in judging the consequence of present actions and which persons would fulfill their potential function in society. The choice inevitably involved guilt. He believed that in general there should be no exceptions to the criteria for selection. If any were suggested, a lay committee should determine whether "the patient was so indispensable at that time and place that he had to be saved even by sacrificing the values preserved by random selection. Such an exception is warranted, if at all, only as the 'lesser of two evils.'" The method of choice advocated by Childress was the use of randomness - first-come, first-served or a lottery. This provided equality of opportunity and was more in keep with human dignity, helped preserve the relationship of trust between patient and physician, and reduced the psychological stress if selection is not on the basis of social worth.

Perhaps the best and most detailed description of the Seattle situation and its relation to bioethics is in the book "Courage to Fail" by sociologists Renée Fox and Judith Swazey. This includes Dr. Scribner's comments following the criticisms. "All of us who were involved felt we had found a fairly reasonable and simple solution to an impossibly difficult problem by letting a committee of responsible members of the community choose what patients (should receive treatment) among those who were medically ideal... In retrospect, of course, we were terribly naive. We did not realize the full impact that the existence of the committee would have on the world. We simply could not understand why everyone was most interested in the existence and operation of the lay selection committee rather than in the fact that in two years we had taken a disease and converted it from a 100 percent fatal prognosis, to a two-year survival. Nor were any of us prepared for the very severe storm of criticism that was to be forthcoming at the annual medical meetings and in the scholarly literature."

Even so, Dr. Scribner was well aware of the ethical issues involved from early on and he discussed these in his presidential address to the American Society for Artificial Internal Organs in 1964. They remain among the most important ethical issues today - patient selection for dialysis, overt termination of treatment, patient suicide, death with dignity, and patient selection for organ transplantation. He emphasized that, "Scientists are also members of society, and have an obligation to become concerned about the effect of their discoveries on society."

Thus, the Seattle Community Artificial Kidney Center program and its novel selection process raised many questions for the first time. The impact was well summed up in a presentation by Dr. Swazey in Seattle in 1992 in a program entitled, "The Birth of Bioethics." "Patient selection was certainly the most visible and therefore most discussed issue posed by the limited availability of chronic dialysis in the early 1960s, but it was by no means the only troubling matter that this procedure raised for medical technologies. The Seattle group was struggling in a much more forthright manner than most medical groups at the time with a number of issues that at once were medical, moral and social, and would become the major foci of those who wandered in and became known as bioethicists. These topics included the available and appropriate ways of financing a costly medical technology, the prolongation and quality of life, and the termination of treatment by a physician or by a patient."

## CHAPTER 14

# Preparations for the Seattle Community Artificial Kidney Center and the First Patients; the Original Four Patients and the First Death: 1961

———————

KING COUNTY MEDICAL SOCIETY WAS responsible for the overall direction of the Center until it was incorporated in December 1963. It acted first through the committee appointed by the society and the Seattle Area Hospital Council in 1961, but once the Center opened on January 8, 1962, the Medical Advisory and the Admissions and Policy Committees reported directly to the Medical Society's Board of Trustees.

In the summer of 1961 remodeling began in the southwest corner of the basement of Eklind Hall located one block west of the hospital at the corner of Boren and Columbia Streets. The building had originally been the residence for Swedish Hospital nurses and nursing students. Placing the Center outside the hospital proper meant the space would be less costly. Sufficient space was obtained for a patient area, a laboratory for assembly and maintenance of dialyzers, chemistry and research laboratories and offices. The patient area was in the southwest corner and large enough to accommodate three beds and associated dialysis equipment "since one nurse can conveniently monitor three patients on dialysis."

Between August 1, and December 31, 1961, key personal were appointed to the Center. Dr. John Murray was appointed Medical Director on Scrib's recommendation and Dr. Murray, with advice from the three physicians caring for dialysis patients at the University Hospital (Drs. Robert Hegstrom, Robert Hickman and Jerry Pendras) selected Jo Ann Albers, a dialysis nurse from the Clinical Research Center at University Hospital, to be the first head nurse. Terry Pollard, a technician at the university, was selected as the Center's first technician. Jo Ann transferred to the Center and began working there in September 1961. Her first month was spent on a floor at Swedish Hospital to orient to the hospital and nursing services and to arrange supporting services, such as pharmacy, laboratory and house-keeping and to arrange the relationship with the King County Blood Bank. She also wrote all the procedures for the Center while Terry worked with hospital administration on ordering supplies and equipment.

Initially the Center was viewed as part of Swedish Hospital and op-erated as an outpatient facility under the hospital's license. Financial and administrative support came from the hospital as well as the other support services, and the staff was treated as employees of the hospital.

Scrib's experience at the University of Washington had shown for the first time that dialysis could be a nurse-technician procedure and this was essential for the new operation. At that time in the state of Washington, nurses were not allowed to start intravenous infusions or administer blood transfusions, and while dialysis patients were monitored by nurses, the pro-cedure was always started by a physician. However, it was planned that when the Center opened dialysis would be a nurse/technician procedure. Such a nursing responsibility for patient care and treatment management was almost unknown at that time.

Further personnel included two more nurses and a nurses-aide, two laboratory technicians and two further artificial kidney technicians. They were appointed early so they could receive training at University Hospital. This was considered to be sufficient to treat at least seven patients and the nurses were scheduled to work four eight-hour shifts a week and be on call for emergencies.

The first death of a Seattle patient occurred during the early summer of 1961. Jack Capelloto died in his sleep after twelve months on dialysis. He had a long history of hypertension and had developed angina and heart failure several months before starting on dialysis. An autopsy showed he died from hemorrhage into an atheromatous plaque in his right coronary artery and confirmed the diagnosis of polycystic disease. Interestingly, in addition to the expected vascular changes, his body also showed evidence of complications that later would be found to be common in long-term dialysis patients. These included enlargement of the parathyroid glands that control calcium and phosphorus in the body, calcifications in soft tissues, and bone changes. There was also evidence of the recent episode of viral hepatitis, probably related to repeated blood transfusions to treat the anemia of kidney failure. At this time there was no test for the hepatitis virus and in the next few years outbreaks of hepatitis affecting dialysis patients and staff were to become common in dialysis units. At the age of 48, Jack was the oldest patient in the initial series and his death was the major factor in the development of the original strict medical criteria required for a patient to be considered for treatment at the Center.

Meanwhile, three of the original four patients continued dialysis at University Hospital and, based on the experience from treating them, two principles were evolving that were described as facilitating rehabilitation of patients with terminal uremia: patients generally needed dialysis 12 to 16 hours twice a week to control the symptoms of uremia and any new patients should be carefully selected, preferably weeks or months before they needed to start dialysis.

During the last few months of 1961, a further four patients were started on dialysis at University Hospital to wait for opening of the Seattle Community Artificial Kidney Center. All had been followed as outpatients for some time, were felt to be excellent candidates for treatment and were approved by the Center's selection committees.

James Albers, a 27-year-old male graduate student in physics at Seattle University, had been known to have polycystic kidney disease for ten years and first began to develop symptoms of uremia in March 1959. He was managed conservatively with a low protein diet and liberal salt intake as his disease was causing salt loss in his urine. It was planned that he would be the first patient at the Center when it opened in 1962, but his condition deteriorated and he was unable to continue his studies until after he was started on dialysis for 10 hours twice a week at University Hospital on

August 23, 1961, replacing Jack Capelloto as the fourth University patient after Jack's death. He was married to the nurse, Jo Ann Albers.

The second new patient, the first female patient, was a 38-year-old white housewife, Kathy Curtis, who had had chronic glomerulonephritis since youth. She started to have uremic symptoms in September 1961 and deteriorated rapidly and had to be started on dialysis on October 2, 1961. Because she had some residual kidney function and was a small person she was dialyzed for 18 hours once a week. On this regimen she was able to resume her role as a housewife and live a relatively normal life.

Frank Smith was a 40-year-old male industrial engineer who also had been known to have chronic glomerulonephritis since his youth. He was found to have hypertension in 1957 and began to develop symptoms of uremia in 1960. These worsened gradually, and he was started on dialysis at University Hospital on December 4, 1961. He was moderately improved with weekly dialysis but soon was changed to 16 hours of dialysis twice a week and then was able to return to full-time work.

The fourth patient, John Myers, was a 37-year-old business man, also with chronic glomerulonephritis. His renal disease was discovered during a discharge physical from the military in 1946 but he remained well until 1960 when he developed headaches and was found to have hypertension. In September 1961 he was hospitalized for a short time with symptoms of uremia. Because his condition continued to worsen, he was re-hospitalized in December and was started on dialysis on December 27, 1961 at University Hospital. He began on a regimen of 20 hours of dialysis weekly, but this was soon changed to twice weekly dialysis because of persistent mild symptoms.

The Center opened for patient care in January 1962 and Dr. Murray wanted to start the first three patients in a staggered fashion over the first month of operation. John Myers, Frank Smith and Kathy Curtis were not considered university patients since the hospital was not allowed to accept any new patients in its program at that time and the three were being held very temporarily after approval by the Center's Admissions and Policy Committee. The first patient to dialyze at the Center was John Myers on January 17, 1962, following three dialyses at University Hospital. The second patient was Jim Albers because Kathy Curtis did not want to go to the Center and Jo Ann wanted her husband at the Center, and so he changed places with Kathy and first dialyzed at the Center on January 19, 1962. The third patient was Frank Smith who transferred to the Center on January 31, 1962.

## THE 1961 MEETING OF THE ASAIO

The seventh meeting of the ASAIO was held in Atlantic City, New Jersey, in April 1961. There were six papers on the program from Dr. Scribner's unit at the University of Washington.

The first was by Dr. Pendras, Mr. Cole, and Drs. Tu and Scribner describing improvements in the technique of continuous flow hemodialysis. Continuous flow hemodialysis was described at the 1960 meeting and since then the procedure had been simplified and improved to make dialysis largely a nurse-technician procedure. Dialysate was kept in a 300 L refrigerated tank at 0-24° C and changed every 24 hours. The program did between five and 12 hemodialyses a week, each lasting 20 to 72 hours. The major change in technique was replacement of the original six-layer Skeggs-Leonards dialyzers with two four-layer Skeggs-Leonards dialyzers arranged in parallel as suggested by Dr. Ed Leonards who had found that with six layers channeling occurred and the dialyzing surface area available was not fully utilized. Two four-layer dialyzers in parallel offered less resistance to blood flow and increased efficiency. The paper described the dialysis technique, the description and maintenance of the equipment and the preparation for dialysis.

The second paper by Dr. Sherris, Mr. Cole and Dr. Scribner discussed the bacteriology of continuous flow hemodialysis. One of the problems was that the dialysate contained glucose and later, during the dialysis, contained urea. The dialysate was agitated and oxygenated by a mixer and the system provided time and the conditions for bacterial growth. When prolonged dialysis was first tried, the dialysate tank was held at 37° C and it was soon found that colony counts rose high in the dialyzing fluid after 12 to 18 hours. Something had to be done to avoid this and the first step was to lower the temperature of the dialyzing bath to as near 0° C as practicable under operating conditions. Even so, high bacterial counts still occurred after 18 hours of dialysis. When freshly prepared dialysate was studied it was also found to contain a significant level of organisms and was being contaminated by the tank because of problems with the cleaning procedures. Attention was given to better cleaning and steril-izing the tank between runs and it was found that two or three minutes of exposure to 1: 1000 benzalkonium chloride solution destroyed the or-ganisms. Prevention of excessive bacterial growth depended on adequate decontamination of all the apparatus between runs and maintenance of a local low temperature. The benzalkonium solution was non-reactive, non-toxic to the patient, inexpensive and of comparatively high antibacterial activity. The methods were described in detail and further studies were being undertaken.

Dr. Hegstrom, Mr. Quinton, Dr. Dillard, Mr. Cole and Dr. Scribner presented a paper on one year's experience with the use of indwelling Teflon cannulas. It described in detail placement of the cannulas and the shunt, repair of clotted cannulas, prevention of infection, removal of cannulas, and placement of cannulas in children. The average duration of the most suc-cessful cannulation in each of the four original patients was approximately 6 ½ months and they were looking for ways this could be improved. Cannula failure resulted from clotting in all four patients, usually due to mechanical problems and the patients had four wound infections during a total of 42 ½ months of treatment. Only one infection resulted in cannula failure. The four patients had had indwelling cannulas for an average of 10.6 months without apparent cardiovascular complications and there had been no hem-orrhages from the cannula in any of the four patients between dialyses. In addition, 19 consecutive patients with acute renal failure had had Teflon cannulas, which remained functional until electively removed in all but six of the patients. Cannula failure in these patients was always due to venous insufficiency resulting from previously traumatized veins. The technique of cannulation was described in detail.

Mr. Quinton, Dr. Dillard, Mr. Cole and Dr. Scribner discussed possible improvements in long-term cannulation. Mechanical problems were the most important in terms of causing cannula failure as described in the previous paper. They had removed the plastic shield over the cannula described in the 1960 paper, eliminated the arm plate and shortened the subcutaneous tunnels to reduce cannula stress. The ideal cannula would have an inner surface that minimized clotting, the material would provide minimal tissue reaction on its exterior surface and yet allow attachment to the tissues in order to anchor the cannulas firmly in place. They described fashioning the middle segment of the cannulas out of Silastic rubber tubing as this had been reported to retard clotting even more effectively than Teflon but so far spontaneous clotting had occurred invariably in the system. They were studying how this might be overcome.

Doctors Murray, Hegstrom, Pendras, Burnell and Scribner described experience with the use of continuous flow hemodialysis and cannulas in the management of acute kidney failure. They reported their experience with 16 patients with acute renal failure over an eight-month period of time. Most of the patients were uremic at the time of admission and continuous flow dialysis was begun soon after the cannulas were placed. The 16 patients received a total of 39 dialyses (2.4 for a patient on average). Total dialysis time was 1621.5 hours and on average each patient spent 101 hours or 23% of the duration of acute kidney failure on the dialyzer. The patients were reviewed in detail and it was pointed out that questions were still being raised as to whether dialysis was necessary for survival in most cases of acute renal failure. Since dialysis by these methods was virtually without risk and significantly reduced cost and effort and since the risks of uremia were great, the question of whether dialysis was really necessary for survival was no longer pertinent.

Doctors Hegstrom, Murray, Pendras, Burnell and Scribner discussed the results of treatment of the four patients with chronic kidney failure who had started dialysis during 1960. There had been no deaths, and all patients lived at home and entered the hospital at 5-7 day intervals for 20-24 hours of hemodialysis using the continuous flow technique. A 40 g protein, 400 mg sodium diet was prescribed for all, but rigidly followed by only two. All received supplementary vitamins and two took ion exchange resins for potassium removal. The paper reported the continuing experience with these patients in great detail. Two patients had daily urine volumes of less than 100 ml and with 24 hours of hemodialysis every 5 to 7 days had not had progressive weight loss or mental deterioration. Clinical symptoms of uremia, if they occurred, began 24 to 36 hours prior to the next hemodialysis and consisted of lethargy, nausea, pruritus and vomiting. Severe anemia, requiring frequent transfusions of packed red blood cells, was unchanged by hemodialysis. Control of hypertension was achieved by sodium restriction and the reduction of extracellular fluid volume during each dialysis. Severe peripheral neuropathy occurred in the two patients with the least renal function and the cause was as yet unknown. Acute gout in the absence of a family history had been observed in the two oldest patients. One patient worked full-time and led a nearly normal life, two were capable of light activity, and one was crippled with severe neuropathy. All patients led relatively comfortable lives at home, coming to the hospital for regularly scheduled dialyses. Based on the experience so far, the ideal candidate for long-term intermittent hemodialysis should be a young uremic adult with stable or slowly progressive renal disease, who is emotionally stable and free of hypertensive cardiovascular disease.

CHAPTER 15

# What Was Learned Between 1960 and 1962?

THE GOAL OF THE CHRONIC dialysis program was to preserve patient well-being and avoid uremic symptoms, but this was not achieved in the first year using dialysis once every five to seven days as patients developed symptoms again 24 to 36 hours before the next treatment. As a result, patients were changed to a twice-a-week treatment schedule without necessarily changing the total weekly hours of treatment. Blood pressure was generally well-controlled by dietary salt restriction and removal of fluid at each dialysis. The three original patients had episodes of acute arthritis pain resembling gout that occurred in many joints, but not in the toes. This complication tended to occur when poor cannula function caused less effective dialysis. The first three patients also developed calcified nodules in their soft tissues, primarily close to various joints, that became quite large and unsightly. These appeared to be related to high levels of phosphate in the blood and possible changes in parathyroid function. Later it was found that oral antacids, which remove phosphate through the gut, relieved this metastatic calcification, which literally melted away.

Another problem seen in the first patients was nerve damage – peripheral neuropathy – leading to diminished leg reflexes and numbness in the feet and lower legs that made walking difficult. This too appeared to be an effect of inadequate dialysis and responded to more treatment. Anemia also remained a problem. Each patient required transfusion of two to five units of packed red blood cells a month because of the anemia of renal failure and also the loss of blood cells left in the dialyzer after each dialysis.

The first three patients gradually continued to gain weight and appeared relatively well-nourished with normal adipose tissue. However, whenever dialysis became less effective as a result of shunt problems, they tended to lose weight and at the same time their blood protein levels tended to decrease.

Most importantly, five of the first eight patients were able to carry out their usual work comfortably. These included all of the second four patients who had been more carefully selected with the potential for rehabilitation in mind. Physical activity ranged from moderate for the housewife with children, the industrial engineer and Harvey, the shoe salesman, to slight in the case of the student and the business man. Even so the impression was that a patient doing heavy labor probably could not have been fully rehabilitated. Clyde could undertake light exercise, such as long walks, but had not attempted to return to his job as a machinist and, as he was receiving total disability from Social Security, he had little incentive to seek retraining. The other surviving patient, Rolin, was still disabled as a result of the severe neuropathy that had affected him early in the course of his treatment.

What had been learned over the first two years was that sufficient dialysis was essential for patient well-being and that careful selection was important if patients were to be rehabilitated.

CHAPTER 16

# The Start of Peritoneal Dialysis in Seattle: 1961-1962

---

HEMODIALYSIS USES A SYNTHETIC MEMBRANE to separate blood from a dialyzing fluid so the uremic toxins that have accumulated with kidney failure can diffuse across the membrane and be removed from the body. The process of peritoneal dialysis is similar, but uses the living membrane that lines the abdominal cavity, the peritoneal membrane. Dialyzing fluid is instilled in the abdominal cavity, left for a time so toxins can cross the membrane from the capillaries lining the membrane into the fluid in the abdomen. This fluid is then removed and further fluid instilled.

As noted earlier, Necheles was the first to use the peritoneal membrane for dialysis although not in vivo. Rather he used gold-beater's skin, a commercial preparation of peritoneal membrane from calves, in a dialyzer he had devised and showed uremia in nephrectomised dogs was improved by dialysis.

Peritoneal lavage was used in the eighteenth century as a treatment for fluid accumulation in the abdomen due to liver disease, and in the nineteenth and early twentieth centuries the anatomy and physiology of the peritoneum were widely studied. In 1923, Georg Ganter in Wurtzburg, Germany, pointed out that it would be much simpler to use the peritoneum in the body rather than in a dialyzer as Necheles had done. He described experiments infusing saline into the abdomen of rabbits and guinea pigs made uremic by tying off their ureters and showed that the animals appeared to improve. He also reported infusing 1.5 liters of saline into a woman with renal failure secondary to ureteric obstruction from cancer and 3 liters into a diabetic patient and felt that both were improved by the procedure. Several other investigators performed peritoneal dialysis in a small number of patients over the ensuing years but the biggest problem was the frequency of infection and peritonitis. The first prolonged treatment of a patient with chronic renal failure using peritoneal dialysis was by Richard Ruben in San Francisco in 1959 where he successfully treated a female patient for six months.

Meanwhile, between 1951 and 1959, Fred Boen in Rotterdam in the Netherlands had been performing landmark research on peritoneal dialysis and had published a book describing this. As a result, Scrib invited Boen to join his group in Seattle to develop a peritoneal dialysis program. He arrived in January 1962.

The first patient Boen treated, J. R., was a 28-year-old man with renal failure due to glomerulonephritis who was started on hemodialysis at University Hospital on November 18, 1961, with the intention of transferring him to the Seattle Community Artificial Kidney Center when it opened. Unfortunately, he had a rare problem that caused clotting of his shunt after every treatment and would have run out of cannula sites within a short time. (Think what the effect might have been if he rather than Clyde Shields had been the first patient to be treated using the shunt!). Consequently, on January 22, 1962, he was started on chronic peritoneal dialysis using a modification of the closed system that had been developed at University Hospital in the late 1950s for the studies of gastrodialysis by Dr. Tom Marr. Boen had elected to use a closed system because one very frequent source of infection in peritoneal dialysis patients was the need to change bottles of the dialyzing fluid frequently and contamination could occur easily. The other problem was infection through the indwelling devices that were used at that time to enable repeated access to the abdominal cavity. J. R. was successfully treated by repeated peritoneal dialysis at University Hospital for many months, but eventually he died after repeated infection through the access device.

How Boen and Henry Tenckhoff, who joined him in 1964, worked at the University of Washington to develop the equipment and techniques that made peritoneal dialysis a safe and effective procedure will described later, together with the introduction of peritoneal dialysis to the Seattle Artificial Kidney Center.

## CHAPTER 17

# The First Year at the Seattle Community Artificial Kidney Center: The First Patients 1962

---------

THE SEATTLE COMMUNITY ARTIFICIAL KIDNEY Center, the first out-of-hospital dialysis center in the world and the first where dialysis was the responsibility of nurses and technicians without the continuous presence of a physician, opened its doors on January 8, 1962. It was established as an attempt to bring a new development in medicine into the community in an orderly fashion and was located in the basement of a building one block from Swedish Hospital. It consisted of a patient area, a laboratory for assembly and maintenance of dialyzers and related equipment, chemistry and research laboratories, and offices.

The patient area housed three beds but there also had to be space for a dialyzer, a dialysate tank and a rewarmer next to each bed, together with adequate space around the bed-dialyzer complex to allow ready access to the patient. The laboratory had space to store six dialyzers and six dialysate tanks and included a sink and counter for cleaning the dialyzers, a sterilizer, a steam line to sterilize the tanks, floor drains and several electrical outlets.

The first patients dialyzed twice a week during the day for eight hours until they were stable and then were transferred to overnight dialysis for 12 to 16 hours using a large Sweden Freezer batch-mix tank and a pumpless, low-temperature dialysis system and blood rewarmer. The system had only an imprecise thermostat to check the rewarming with only a single thermometer for a monitor – there was no audible or visual alarm and no fail-safe means of patient protection against any malfunction. An effluent pump was used to generate negative pressure for fluid removal and this was monitored using a large U-shaped mercury manometer. The dialyzers used were Skeggs-Leonards flat-plate dialyzers that were frustratingly difficult to assemble without leaks. Equipment was prepared by the technician and delivered to the patient's bedside where the nurse connected the patient to the dialyzer, monitored the run and detached the patient at the end of the treatment. No physician supervision was needed except in an emergency, and physician time was minimized as patients were seen only briefly during each dialysis unless there was a problem. A physician was on call by phone at all times to answer queries about the patient and the treatment. A complete patient evaluation was done just once a month.

With the long hours of overnight dialysis, a nurse was frequently alone caring for two or three patients with no one else in the building, but the patients were relatively young and without complications other than those associated with kidney failure. The nurses were also on call at all times to declot cannulas.

Three of the four patients who were started on dialysis at University Hospital during 1961 became the first three patients at the Center when it opened. During 1962, the first year of operation at the Center, the Medical Advisory Committee considered 30 patients, 17 of whom were judged medically acceptable based on the original strict medical criteria that had been established. All 13 rejected candidates died. Because community physicians had been told of the strict medical criteria, an unknown number of patients were not referred. The Admissions and Policy Committee then finally selected nine patients for treatment, including the original three, the decisions being based mainly on sociological and economic factors. This committee also changed its policy so that each candidate had to be presented twice, at least a month apart, so enabling better review of potential candidates.

By the end of the first year seven patients were being treated at the Center and by the end of January 1963 the maximum capacity of nine patients was reached. Dialysis was relatively uneventful, but because treatment was only twice a week patients often felt unwell for several hours after dialysis because of the large changes in fluid and electrolytes they had experienced. Because of this and the time needed to clean and resterilize the equipment, early activities were limited to one patient shift per 24 hours. With three dialysis stations and six days a week operation only nine patients could be treated. There was only one technical failure due to a dialyzer blood leak in the first of more than 400 dialyses. Emergency problems requiring immediate nursing attention occurred in about five percent of dialyses and emergencies needing a physician to come in occurred in only about one percent of treatments. Silastic-Teflon cannulas were used in all patients and there were no cannula failures. Two infections responded to antibiotics and there was one episode of cannula clotting.

Of the seven patients who had been treated longest, six were rehabilitated and had returned to near full-time work and their usual hobbies and recreation. Four were dialyzed twice a week and three who had more residual kidney function were dialyzed weekly at first. Dialysis was overnight for about 16 hours. The prescribed diet was 40-to-60 Gms of protein and sodium restriction, and blood pressure control was less satisfactory in those patients who found difficulty with the sodium restriction. Soft tissue calcification was less of a problem in these later patients, probably related to more dialysis, and episodes of acute gouty arthritis occurred in only one patient who had a family history of gout. Even with better techniques for returning blood from the dialyzer at the end of treatment, patients on average needed two blood transfusions a month, but no further cases of hepatitis occurred.

An early administrative problem occurred in February 1962 when Scrib proposed to the KCMS Board of Trustees that they provide financial support for his research. The Board declined, although it was willing to provide a testimonial for Scrib to use in applying to other sources of funding. This prompted discussion about the long-range financing of the Center and concerns about its continued existence and development. At this time the Board felt it could best perform its supportive function by helping the Admissions and Policy Committee in coordinating its activities attempting to obtain long-term support.

At its August 1962 meeting the KCMS Executive Committee discussed the continuing funding problems for the artificial kidney program again and developed an article for the KCMS Bulletin urging King County physicians to make the Center's committees aware of potential candidates for treatment far enough in advance to permit sufficient time for evaluation.

Later in the year, in November and December, the financial situation was again discussed by the KCMS Board when Dr. Burnell pointed out that the initial Hartford Foundation grant would expire on July 1, 1964. Jim Haviland raised the possibility of getting local rather than national financial support and it was agreed that Mr. Rosling, chairman of the Admissions and Policy Committee, would meet with Drs. Scribner, Mills and Haviland to consider and explore means of further financing. It was also urged that the American Medical Association be notified of the problem by a personal call and follow-up letter.

## THE 1962 MEETING OF THE ASAIO

The eighth annual meeting of the American Society for Artificial Internal Organs was held in April 1962 in Atlantic City, New Jersey. There were seven papers from Seattle.

Dr. James Albers, a physicist from Seattle University, presented mathematical models for predicting hemodialyzer performance. He discussed various models and compared the results with actual measured results with a Skeggs-Leonards dialyzer using the Seattle pumpless low-flow hemodialysis system. He showed that for a 300 L bath there was only a small gain in efficiency due to bath changes for periods of dialysis of less than 20 hours. The equations also indicated that dividing the bath into compartments resulted in less gain in efficiency than did a bath change. He also looked at the effect of blood flow rate and the source of preparation of the dialysate. He predicted that for patients with chronic kidney failure solute removal was best with a 300-to-400 L bath, two dialyses a week of 10 to 14 hours duration each, and no bath changes during the dialysis. Interestingly, the audience did not realize that Dr. Albers was the fifth patient to be started on chronic dialysis at the University of Washington in September 1961 and one of the original four patients transferred from there to the Seattle Artificial Kidney Center in January 1962.

Mr. Cole, Mr. Quinton and Mr. Williams, and Drs. Murray and Sherris from the Department of Medicine at the University of Washington, the Quinton Instrument Company, Seattle, and the Seattle Artificial Kidney Center, had developed a new modified Kiil-type hemodialyzer that greatly simplified the pumpless, low-temperature hemodialysis system. A new stainless-steel dialysis fluid tank also had been developed which made possible dialysis at 20° C. The tank was much easier to clean and maintain than the rusting "deepfreeze" tanks and could be used to measure fluid removed by ultrafiltration directly. Studies of the saline rinsing procedure at the end of dialysis showed that rinsing with the dialyzer in a horizontal position actually rinsed mostly plasma while the red cells remained in the dialyzer. By turning the dialyzer into the vertical position with the blood flow downward during the last 10 minutes of the dialysis and then rinsing with saline, the red cell loss could be reduced by as much as 50% and transfusion requirements, which then were averaging five units a month with twice weekly dialysis, could be cut by 50% or more. The overall technique of hemodialysis had been simplified and organized so that patients with chronic kidney failure could be hemodialyzed entirely by nurses, no physician time being required for the dialysis procedure itself.

Mr. Quinton, Dr. Dillard, Mr. Cole and Dr. Scribner from the University of Washington Departments of Medicine and Surgery reported on eight-months experience with Silastic-Teflon cannulas. At the 1961 ASAIO meeting they had shown the potential benefits of using cannulas in which the middle segment was made of silicone rubber (Silastic) but that these had problems with clotting. They had now improved the internal surface finish of the extruded Silastic rubber tubing to the point where clotting from this had been eliminated. They described the technique of insertion, the details of caring for the cannulas, and the importance of good care in preventing clotting. They also described the use of lower leg vessels for cannulation, as this nearly doubled the number of cannula sites available for long-term treatment. The Silastic-Teflon cannulas appeared to be superior to Teflon cannulas in a number of respects and were expected to last longer. It was hoped they would eliminate the cannula as a major factor limiting longevity in chronic kidney failure.

Drs. Boen, Mulinari, Dillard and Scribner from the University of Washington Departments of Medicine and Surgery reported on their experience with periodic peritoneal dialysis in the management of chronic uremia. A question had been whether periodic peritoneal dialysis would be of value in patients with chronic kidney failure. Studies in acute renal failure patients had shown similar kinetics for both hemodialysis and peritoneal dialysis although the clearance of peritoneal dialysis was lower. For the previous three months they had been performing periodic peritoneal dialysis in a 28-year-old male whose creatinine clearance was less than 2 ml/min and whose daily urine output was 200 to 400 ml. Nine hemodialyses had been performed on the patient from November 18, 1961 to February 22, 1962, and had needed separate cannulations in seven sites in the arms and one in the leg because clotting occurred after each cannulation for unknown reasons. On January 22, 1962, periodic peritoneal dialysis was begun 2-to-3 times weekly for 12 weeks. The patient had been restored to reasonable good health and otherwise would have died. They presented the biochemical results. A new access fitting had been developed that might make possible an unlimited number of dialyses, and in the first three months the fitting seemed to be sound from mechanical and bacteriological points of view. In addition, an automatic cycling machine that greatly reduced the amount of nursing care needed had been developed for use in peritoneal dialysis.

Drs. Hegstrom, Murray, Pendras, Burnell and Scribner from the University of Washington Department of Medicine and the Seattle Artificial Kidney Center reported on two years' experience with periodic hemodialysis in the treatment of chronic uremia. They described in detail the clinical results of this treatment in the original four patients and in four new patients who had been added to the program during 1961. The patients originally had Teflon cannulas and more recently had been changed to Silastic-Teflon cannulas. They lived at home and came to the hospital twice a week for scheduled dialysis. Composition of the dialysate was based on the anticipated need to remove extracellular fluid and potassium. Physician duties were limited to an interval history, a brief physical examination and orders. When there were occasional problems with the dialysis that a nurse felt she could not handle, a physician was called. One patient died as a result of an acute coronary occlusion after 12 months of treatment and five of the surviving seven patients had had a favorable response to treatment and were able to perform comfortably in their usual occupations. The other two were not working, although one led a comfortable active life despite the fact that he had been anuric for at least 20 months. During the second year of the program, symptoms of uremia had been eliminated and patients had had a greater sense of well-being as result of more frequent (biweekly) hemodialysis. The peripheral neuropathy that had disabled two patients was greatly improved with more frequent dialysis and would appear to be due to uremia rather than a vitamin deficiency. Two of the surviving patients continued to have symptoms of gout that appeared after periods of less effective dialysis. The same two patients had had problems with severe metastatic calcification. The importance of adequate dialysis and careful patient selection to achieve favorable rehabilitation was emphasized.

Drs. Hickman and Scribner from the Departments of Pediatrics and Medicine at the University of Washington School of Medicine described the application of the pumpless hemodialysis system to infants and children. Hemodialysis in small children using the twin coil dialyzer required elaborate precautions and continuous monitoring to avoid dangerous shifts of blood between patient and dialyzer and so they had applied cannulation and the continuous-flow dialysis technique to children. These techniques eliminated some of the dangers because there was no blood pump, the external circuit had a fixed volume, and the technique was simple enough that once begun the dialysis could be monitored by a nurse. They described the application of this technique to six pediatric patients aged between seven months and nine years. Five patients had acute kidney failure and one had so acute glomerulonephritis that then was shown to be irreversible and the patient was allowed to die. The simplicity of the technique and the importance of preventing the symptoms of uremia in the seriously ill pediatric patient were emphasized.

Drs. Murray, Tu, Albers, Burnell and Scribner from the Seattle Artificial Kidney Center and Swedish Hospital described the first community hemodialysis center for the treatment of chronic uremia. The Seattle Artificial Kidney Center was established as an attempt to bring a new development in medicine to the Seattle community in an orderly fashion. Three major problems required consideration in planning of the Center. First were the costs of both establishing the facility and its continuing operation. While initial costs would be borne by a grant, support by the community would eventually be required for continued operation. The second problem was that several major hospitals in Seattle wanted an artificial kidney center. This would have required duplication of expensive facilities and larger numbers of highly trained personnel. The problem was resolved with the aid of a lay-dominated committee appointed jointly by the Board of Trustees of the King County Medical Society and the Seattle Hospital Council. The third problem was the number of persons who might benefit from treatment and, following a survey, it was estimated there were between five and 20 ideal candidates per million population per year. As a result, a Medical Advisory Committee was formed composed of physicians interested in renal disease and a psychiatrist. This committee set up strict criteria for patient acceptance that have been described elsewhere. The presentation described the physical plan of the Center, how it operated, and how dialysis was instituted in new patients. At the time of the presentation, the Center had been operating for three months and had been trouble-free and appeared to be well-suited for further management of such patients.

## CHAPTER 18

# A Community Report of Experience in the Treatment of Chronic Uremia in the Pacific Northwest March 1960-January 1963

———

LATER DURING 1963 DR. SCRIBNER and representatives of the existing dialysis facilities in the Northwest put together the following report:

Our groups have now been treating patients who would otherwise die of end-stage kidney disease for almost three years. We presently have 15 patients under treatment and have accumulated 17.8 patient-years of experience, which represents roughly 1,500 hemodialyses. Except for two of the first three patients, all patients have been fully rehabilitated and have been leading normal lives. We estimate that we have been able to provide a total of over ten patient-years of full rehabilitation to date.

During the entire experience there has not been a serious technical failure and we have not lost a patient because of treatment failure. Three of the original four patients are, despite nearly three years of anuria in two of them, in better health now than at any time since entering the program. The fourth died at the end of a year of a myocardial infarction.

A brief summary of specific aspects of the program follows:

1. Cannulas: Since Silastic-Teflon cannulas were introduced in August 1961, cannula failures have been greatly reduced. Patient JA has the original set of Silastic-Teflon cannulas and they are still functioning well after 18 months. Since Dr. Murray opened the Seattle Artificial

Kidney Center in January 1962, he has not had a cannula failure. Cannula failure is no longer considered to be the factor limiting longevity. Adequate instruction of staff and patients in cannula care is considered an essential prerequisite to success.

2.  Hemodialysis technique: We have felt it essential that hemodialysis become strictly a nurse-technician procedure, and since this goal has been set we have been happily surprised to find that nurses, once they learn the technique, handle the procedure much better than physicians. Furthermore, the dialysis nurse has emerged as the most important medical person in the lives of the patients. The physician, of course, decides on the goals of dialysis, using it in the same way that the diabetic specialist would use insulin.

    Switching to the Kiil 2-layer dialyzer and improved design of all components of the dialysis system from connectors to dialysate tanks has made it possible to cut dialysis costs slowly but steadily. The latest cost-accounted figure for a fully operational center, including physical plant and equipment write-off and professional fees, is right about $100 per dialysis or $10,000 per year for two dialyses per week. The optimum size for a center seems to be multiples of five beds or 15 patients. With present techniques, going beyond a 10-bed, 30-patient center probably will not cut costs or improve the operation.

    Most of us working in this area feel that we are on the verge of further major improvements in technique, which will both cut costs and increase dialyzer efficiency, thereby shortening dialysis time from around 12 hours twice-weekly to 8-10 hours. Also, it may be possible to return some patients to a once-weekly schedule, thereby cutting costs in half.

3.  Sodium and hypertension: Control of sodium intake continues to be the most difficult problem for the patients and physicians to master. We find that it takes several months in some cases before patients really master the low sodium (20-30 mEq) diet.

Control of body sodium continues to be the key to control of blood pressure. We have encountered no exceptions and most of the investigators in other centers now concur. We continue to be impressed with the ease with which sodium overload precipitates severe hypertension. Then the vasculature seems to become rigid and removal of sodium difficult. As attempts are made to withdraw sodium, wide swings in blood pressure with periods of rather severe postural hypotension occur, which may result in several weeks of relative ill health. However, if sodium removal is continued, eventually the blood pressure stays down between dialyses and changes in blood volume no longer cause marked changes in blood pressure. In other words, sodium overload is a very difficult complication, which probably makes the vasculature rigid and thereby makes treatment more difficult.

4. Peripheral neuritis: If a patient develops neuritis it is because of being inadequately dialyzed.

5. Dialysis arthritis: A gout-like arthritis, which is responsive to colchicine, has occurred in some patients and is due to inadequate dialysis. The syndrome has been reproduced in two patients by putting urate in the bath and thereby maintaining a falsely elevated uric acid level in the blood. It takes several weeks of elevation before the attacks of arthritis begin, and several weeks of lower levels before they disappear.

6. Metastatic calcification: This seems to be due in part to a high calcium/phosphate product. When serum phosphate levels are controlled with modest doses of aluminum gel, metastatic calcium nodules disappear.

7. Peritoneal dialysis: Automatic cycling equipment and on-the-spot manufacture of fluid makes it possible to carry out peritoneal dialysis for around $70-$90 per dialysis, including hospitalization. However, since a minimum of three 12-hour dialyses a week are required by our technique, the cost is $210-270 per week, or

$6,200-$8,100 per year plus professional fees. In addition, in our one 10-month experience, a great deal more physician time was required than with any of our hemodialysis patients, so costs would be proportionately higher.

During the ten months that we had an ideal candidate under treatment, we were unable to rehabilitate him completely with peritoneal dialysis. The uncertainty of repeated complications, particularly abdominal wall infection and peritonitis, makes the technique unsuitable for routine use at this time. If the technique could be improved and moved into the home, then it might become useful as a routine procedure, but if the goal of therapy is complete and sustained rehabilitation with elimination of absenteeism from work, peritoneal dialysis, in our hands at least, will not accomplish this goal.

8. Selection of patients and institution of therapy: We continue to use the extremely rigid medical criteria listed herewith:

A stable emotionally mature adult under the age of 45, who is no longer able to work because of symptoms of uremia;

Absence of long-standing hypertension and permanent complications therefrom, particularly coronary artery disease and cerebrovascular or peripheral vascular disease;

Demonstrated willingness to cooperate in carrying out the prescribed medical treatment, especially the low sodium diet;

Renal function should be stable or deteriorating slowly, since any residual function simplifies the therapeutic problem;

Children and young adults who are not potentially self-supporting have been excluded so far.

Even using these criteria, there were 15 patients who fulfilled them in our area in the last 12 months. Only seven could be accepted for treatment because of limited facilities. This indicates an annual incidence of roughly 15 patients per million population per year, which is in the range we have been talking about. However, the figure cannot be relied upon as being accurate for a number of reasons.

Last fall, for the first time, we were able to begin to select patients well ahead of the time they needed to begin their hemodialysis therapy. Treatment has been started "early" at a time when they were still able to live sedentary lives at home. The severe terminal heart failure, hypertension and uremia that occurred in all ten earlier patients were avoided. Probably as a result of this difference, the latter patients did not suffer the usual permanent deterioration in renal function upon starting hemodialysis therapy. As a result, they required only one dialysis a week, despite the fact that one of them is the largest (85 kg.) patient in the series.

9.  Activation of new centers: Centers in Spokane, Washington, Edmonton and Alberta, Canada, Danville, Pennsylvania, and a pilot "shoestring" operation in Portland, Oregon, is now underway. The personnel of these centers have been trained in Seattle.

    The Spokane Community Center opened October 1, 1962, and has rehabilitated its first patient. The center is ready to accept 11 additional paying patients. The Spokane Center is operated by a group of internists who are in full-time private practice. On the basis of their experience, this group feels that any community can operate a center provided proper facilities are available and personnel, including physicians, are properly trained.

    The Edmonton Center has been open for two months and has two patients under treatment. There have been no technical problems.

    Although we don't recommend it, Portland has opened without adequate financing. They have only one patient and can't take more until funds are raised. They are operating under adverse conditions using obsolete equipment, which we have loaned them. Despite these conditions, careful attention to detail has resulted in complete and sustained rehabilitation of a young minister.

    Experiences to date suggest that the time required to train personnel is as follows: Physician 1-6 months (depending on background); Chief Technician 2-3 months; Nurse 1-3 months.

## Summary

We believe that the technique we have developed for the rehabilitation of patients with chronic uremia can be used by any intelligent internist who is willing to be trained and who has proper hemodialysis facilities, and most important of all, properly trained personnel to operate those facilities.

Periodic hemodialysis, using our technique, will fully rehabilitate properly selected patients 100% of the time. Careful attention to detail, especially with regard to cannula insertion, patient instruction and dialysis procedures are, we believe, essential prerequisites to success. It is important that a minimum of 3-4 patients be brought under treatment as quickly as possible because mutual emotional support is important.

Any change in technique of treatment invariably causes trouble at first: (when we switched from twin-4 Skeggs-Leonards dialyzers to Kiil dialyzers, all our patients suddenly became hypertensive because the ultrafiltration was less with the Kill). For this reason we make it a rule never to change our technique without first trying out the change on dialyses of patients with acute renal failure where minor technical problems are of no consequence. This rule applies particularly to changes in cannula technique.

On the basis of the many unfortunate experiences that have been reported to us from around the country, we feel that it is wrong to undertake the treatment of chronic uremia unless optimal conditions prevail. These include adequate financing, proper facilities and most important, properly trained personnel.

Facilities contributing to this report: University of Washington Hospital and University of Washington School of Medicine, Seattle, Washington, supported by National Institutes of Health research grant #AM-06741-01A1 (A portion of this work was conducted through the Clinical Research Center Facility of the University of Washington, supported by National Institutes of Health grant #OG-13); Seattle Artificial Kidney Center at Swedish Hospital, 1102 Columbia Street, Seattle, Washington, and the Spokane and Inland Empire Artificial Kidney Center at Sacred Heart Hospital, Spokane, Washington, supported by the John A. Hartford Foundation, Inc.; Portland

Artificial Kidney Center, Good Samaritan Hospital, Portland, Oregon; and University of Alberta Department of Medicine, Artificial Kidney Division, Edmonton, Alberta, Canada.

CHAPTER 19

# More Patients: The Second Year at the Seattle Community Artificial Kidney Center 1963

---

IN JANUARY 1963, THE CENTER expanded to four beds unexpectedly in an interesting sequence of events. Dr. Murray came into the patient area late one day and told staff the sad story of a woman with a young son whose husband, a Boeing employee, had just died unexpectedly. The woman had driven all the way back from Florida to Seattle and was now in Swedish Hospital dying from kidney failure and, unfortunately, there was no space available at the Center. Later that evening, when the Center was empty, a nurse and a technician rearranged the beds and put the tanks at the heads of the beds rather than between them. With this arrangement they could squeeze another bed in. They then called Dr. Murray to come and see what they had done. He was delighted and went straight to the hospital to cannulate the patient, Doris Boardman, who was in a coma. She was then put in an ambulance to bring her the one block to the Center where she was dialyzed by the nurse alone in the unit. This extra bed would allow a further two patients to be treated but, in fact, after Mrs. Boardman, no other new patient was started until later in the year.

The AMA had responded to the letter from the society and invited it to send a representative to appear at the meeting of the Committee on Scientific Activities of the AMA Board of Trustees in Chicago. It was decided to send either Dr. Scribner or Dr. Murray to this meeting. (In fact, it was Dr. Burnell who attended the meeting.)

102

The Board addressed several other noteworthy issues throughout its second year.

## CENTER FINANCING

The KCMS Board of Trustees continued discussions about funding and what role the society should play in operations of the Center, and in February it was reported that letters had been received from the AMA and the Department of Health, Education and Welfare declining to provide support. Dr. Haviland reported on a misunderstanding that had developed between Swedish Hospital and the Kidney Center regarding the space housing the unit in Eklind Hall.

In March it was reported to the KCMS Board that short-term fundraising efforts were being made. There were still problems between Swedish Hospital and the Center about space and concern about the Center's possible long-term financing and operations. The Board requested that the Kidney Center underwrite Dr. Burnell's recent trip to the AMA in Chicago, but if that were not possible the KCMS might provide some or all the necessary funds. It was noted there had been recent correspondence from the Secretary of the Department of HEW and from Senator Henry Jackson but no funding at this time.

Dr. Haviland reported at the April meeting that he had met with the Assistant Surgeon General regarding possible financing for the Center. There had been no change in local sources of funding. It was proposed that a Finance Committee be formed to guide the fund-raising efforts of the Center and there would be discussion with the Admissions and Policy Committee about recruitment of members to this new committee. There was also discussion of the obligations of the KCMS in relation to the financing the Center. The consensus was that the society should not engage itself directly in fundraising but should assist the Admissions and Policy Committee in establishing a community financing program.

By May the Finance Committee had been established and its first meeting had shown the interest and enthusiasm of the members. The consensus now was that the immediate cost of continuing operation of the Center would be met by a grant from either the John A Hartford Foundation or the Public Health Service. The greatest problem would be developing a long-range financing program.

Dr. Burnell had been supported to attend a conference on the treatment of chronic uremia in New York, and at the July Board meeting he reported on this and the issues of medical, moral and financial concern that were discussed. He also commented on the planning for future dialysis facilities by the Veterans Administration.

## PERSONNEL CHANGES AND EXPANSION

A request from the Center that Dr. Robert Wright, a psychiatrist, be added to the Medical Advisory Committee was approved. In July, Dr. Jerry Pendras started to work at the Center. At about the same time Dr. Robert Erickson joined Dr. Haviland's practice and he and Dr. Pendras began to share call with Dr. Murray at nights and weekends. Also, renal fellows from Scrib's program at the university began to rotate through the Center to get experience with dialysis for chronic renal failure. As a result, Dr. Dale Lindholm also worked at the Center and his calm nature helped immensely when problems developed among the staff. He went on to be Chief of Nephrology at Tulane University and later at West Virginia University.

At the August 1963 meeting the Board was informed that the Center was considering plans for expansion and that there was no new information on incorporation. However, at the September 9th meeting, there was discussion of proposed developments in the Kidney Center organization, including proceeding with incorporation and a suggested structure for the organization. This would include formation of a Board of Trustees for the Center that would be composed of two representatives from the Admissions and Policy Committee, two representatives of the Finance Committee, one representative from Swedish Hospital, one representative from the Medical Advisory Committee and the past president of the King County Medical Society.

Drs. Jerry Pendras and Robert Erickson were appointed to the Medical Advisory Committee on the recommendation of Dr. Murray. And in December, Dr. Haviland reported on the resignation of Dr. John Murray, medical director of the Center, (see Chapter 22) and that he, Dr. Haviland, felt the Center's various organizational problems would be worked out in time. The KCMS Board would be kept informed of progress.

## INCORPORATION

In May, Dr. Haviland suggested that once the Center was incorporated, the proposed trustees of the Center should be designated from representatives of the Medical Advisory, Admissions and Policy, and Finance Committees, and that for the present the KCMS would maintain its role of appointing the Center's Medical Advisory Committee. The KCMS Board expressed the feeling that KCMS should withdraw its active support of the Center after it was incorporated and that it would assist the Center with the administrative details of the proposed incorporation.

At the October meeting it was reported that the Center was drafting bylaws and was appointing a Board of Trustees for the incorporation consisting of Dr. James W. Haviland, Reverend John B. Darrah, Mr. Elmer J. Nordstrom, Mr. Robert S. Beaupre, Dr. James M. Burnell, Mr. Edward L. Rosling and Dr. Richard R. Paton.

At the December meeting of the KCMS Board of Trustees, Dr. Haviland reported on the recent incorporation of the Center as the Seattle Artificial Community Kidney Center and that the Center's Executive Committee would include a representative of the King County Medical Society.

## TECHNOLOGICAL ADVANCES

There had been new technological changes in hemodialysis equipment. The use of cold dialysate was changed to a system using warm dialysate at 40° C that had been sterilized using ultraviolet light. The dialysate was passed through the dialyzer once and then discarded ("single pass") using circuit as there was now no need for a blood rewarmer in the circuit before the blood was returned to the patient. This also reduced resistance in the blood circuit and allowed more efficient dialysis. In addition, the dialysate tanks with their noisy pumps were moved to an adjoining room about 50 feet from the patients and this resulted in a quieter environment in the dialysis room that allowed patients to sleep better during treatment overnight.

## THE PATIENT POPULATION

By the end of the second year, December 1963, there were eleven patients at the Center. Now all were being treated for 10 to 16 hours twice a week. No patient had died.

Generally there were no major changes in the clinical courses of the patients. Average cannula life was 11.4 months for both arterial and venous cannulas, at least one episode of clotting had occurred in eight patients, and most had had at least one cannula infection but these had responded to antibiotics. Episodes of acute arthritis were reduced by using an antacid to lower phosphate levels, as suggested to Dr. Scribner by local gastroenterologists. As for rehabilitation, the goal of the Center was "to maintain satisfied and productive patients who are able to play a continued role in society" and this was considered to have been achieved in nine of the patients. The other two were limited by peripheral nerve damage but were ambulatory and, because they were self-employed, were able to continue part-time work.

## THE 1963 MEETING OF THE ASAIO

The society's ninth annual meeting was held in Atlantic City, New Jersey in April and there were three papers from Seattle, one each from the Kidney Center and the University of Washington and one jointly from both organizations.

Doctors Lindholm, Burnell, and Murray reported on the first 13 months experience of treatment in the outpatient community hemodialysis center and they discussed patient selection. The Medical Advisory Committee had considered 30 candidates of whom 17 were considered medically acceptable. Many of the 13 rejected, all of whom died, would have made reasonably good candidates medically. The medically acceptable candidates were reviewed by the Admissions and Policy Committee that had been appointed by the King County Medical Society and made final selections based chiefly on sociological and economic factors. Of the 17 medically approved candidates, 10 were finally selected and were being treated. The report was confined to seven of the ten accepted patients because the last three had started on treatment only since February 1963. There was discussion of the cannulas and their function, operations at the center and the clinical results in some detail. In summary, based on their experience with the seven selected patients, cannulas were shown to be very satisfactory with no cannula failures. One episode of clotting and two minor infections had occurred in 60 patient months. With regard to the pumpless, low-temperature hemodialysis system, dialysis had been shown to be a safe and effective treatment as a simple nurse-technician procedure with only a minimum of physician time involved. The treatment had maintained patients free of uremic symptoms and made it possible to restore to self-supporting occupations.

Dialysis disequilibrium syndrome had been known for some years, occurring when a patient with a high blood urea level (BUN) was dialyzed with an efficient dialyzer. After one to two hours the patient would develop headache, seizures and various neurologic symptoms and alterations in the electroencephalogram (EEG) and might die. It was believed to develop because urea in the brain diffused more slowly into the bloodstream than from other tissues, resulting in a continuing high level in the brain tissues and swelling of the brain. Drs. Gilliland and Hegstrom from the University of Washington measured the effect of hemodialysis on cerebrospinal fluid (CSF) pressure in two groups of uremic dogs, dialyzing one group normally and in the other group using a dialysate with a high level of urea, so reducing the gradient for removal of urea from the blood and tissues including the brain. The initial CSF pressure in the two groups was about equal as was the blood urea level. In the group dialyzed with normal dialysate, the CSF pressure increased rapidly to an average of 114 mm within a couple of hours. Those dialyzed using the urea-containing dialysate showed no or only a slight increase in CSF pressure. This was consistent with the idea that during normal dialysis the slower removal of urea from brain tissues leads to an increase in brain water and brain swelling and a rise in CSF pressure.

Jack Cole for the University of Washington and Terry Pollard and Dr. Murray from the Center reported on the 2-layer Kiil dialyzer manufactured in the United States using polypropylene for the plates. They showed that its blood-flow resistance and effectiveness as a dialyzer were comparable to the European Kiil dialyzer but that its internal volume was smaller. They described a simple technique for returning blood to the patient at the end of dialysis that reduced the average blood loss from 140 ml to 35 ml per dialysis. As a result, the average hematocrit of patients rose from 23 to 27.5 and their average monthly blood transfusion requirements fell from 5 to 3.1 units of packed red cells. The dialyzers proved to be dependable and required little time for assembly and processing.

## CHAPTER 20

# Professor Albert Leslie "Les" Babb and the Development of New Dialysis Technology 1963-1964

————

LES WAS BORN IN 1925 in Vancouver, British Columbia, where his father was a pharmacist. He was an engineering student at the University of British Columbia specializing in chemical engineering and a graduate student at the University of Illinois. After graduation, Les became a research engineer at Rayonier Incorporated. In July of 1952 he had a letter from Professor Moulton, chairman of the University of Washington Department of Chemical Engineering, asking him if he would be interested in an academic position. He decided to accept the offer.

The Dean of Engineering at that time, Harold Wessman, was chairman of the Joint Committee of the American Society for Engineering Education and the Atomic Energy Commission whose objective was to study how nuclear technology could be applied in a peaceful manner. He told Les "to establish a nuclear engineering educational program on the campus and to start getting ready for it." As a result, Les spent the summer of 1955 at the Hanford site working with the process for separation of plutonium and uranium from fission projects. He continued to work with the Atomic Energy Commission through 1956 and was sent back to the Argonne International School for Nuclear Science and Engineering where he learned more about neutron physics, reactor physics and shielding design.

In 1957 Les went back to Argonne to learn how to manage a small reactor after the dean decided the campus needed a nuclear reactor for teaching and research. In 1958 it was decided to build a freestanding reactor on the University of Washington campus and by 1961 the Nuclear Reactor Building was completed and the reactor went critical.

Early in 1963 Professor Moulton called Les into his office as he had just had a telephone call from Scribner who wanted to know if there was a young faculty member who could work with him in reducing the cost of hemodialysis. The reason Scrib had called Moulton was because Moulton had been sick the previous year with acute kidney failure and Scrib had treated him successfully.

As a result, in June 1963, Les went down to University Hospital to a small room off the cafeteria where six physicians in white coats were sitting around. They explained to him the development of the shunt that had made it possible to connect patients to the artificial kidney repeatedly and described the equipment used to do hemodialysis. The dialyzing fluid was prepared from chemicals and water in a large stainless steel tank maintained at 4°C and the artificial kidney was the Kiil dialyzer that was about 30 inches long, 13 inches wide, 6 inches deep, and weighed about 60 pounds. The doctors then took Les up to the fifth floor of the hospital and showed him the tanks that had replaced the Sears Roebuck freezers when they had started to rust. This tank was made by the Sweden Freezer Company in Seattle, the first company to make soft ice cream. Each patient had a separate tank. The tank had two pumps to circulate the dialysate and to pump dialysate into the dialyzer outside the membranes; the patient's blood was pumped into the dialyzer by the patient's heart and flowed between the two layers of cellophane to remove toxins.

Shortly after Les had returned to his office in the nuclear reactor building Scrib called him again to point out that it cost about $20,000 per patient per year for two 12-hour dialysis treatments a week and he was interested in reducing the cost of treatment. Les then walked through the whole procedure for dialysis with a stopwatch, and it did not take him long to figure out that it was a very labor-intensive process. Too many people were involved. The tank had to be separated from the patient, pushed into an elevator, taken down to the basement, emptied and sterilized. Chemicals were weighed and placed in the tank that then was filled with water and stirred with a canoe paddle to dissolve the chemicals. The tank was then pushed back into the elevator and returned upstairs. It took three people to push the tank into the elevator and there were nurses hovering everywhere. Les realized that what they were actually doing was trying to remove urea and other metabolites from the patient and the process was not dissimilar from the Purex process used at Hanford.

He found it difficult to get over the fact that the technicians were weighing out the various salts and dumping them into the tank. Scrib had already contacted a company in Minneapolis who proposed that for each chemical they would provide a small screw feeder with a hopper from which the chemicals were poured into the tank. The screw feeders were designed in the right proportions to provide the correct composition of the dialysate when diluted with distilled water. Les's idea was to pre-mix the chemicals into a concentrated solution and continuously dilute this with treated water in the right proportion using proportioning pumps made by the Milton Roy Company in St. Petersburg, Florida. With this approach the individual tanks could be removed from each bedside and replaced with one large tank in which the dialysate could be mixed and then could be piped around the walls to the four patient stations in the dialysis room before being discarded into a waste pipe. The mixing system and other items could be in the corridor outside the hospital room, but when this was suggested the fire marshal would not allow it. Consequently, it had to be put in the patients' room, so ruining the elegance of the whole procedure. The device was dubbed "the Monster" and proved very successful. Les told University authorities that this technology might generate millions if not billions of dollars if the University patented it but was told that as an institution of higher education it was in no way interested in commercialization. The staff at Sweden Freezer began working on a similar device as did the Milton Roy Company.

In addition to working with the Division of Nephrology, Les had been very busy running the reactor and teaching nuclear and chemical engineering. Once the Monster was being used, it was realized that its cost was about half that of the individual tank system and the net annual cost for a patient was only about $10,000. Les's engineers then looked at the dynamics of dialysis using analog computer technology to model the process to attempt to optimize the treatment. As a result, they suggested three 8-hour treatments a week rather than two 12-hour treatments and convinced the medical staff to switch to this practice.

## Photos: Memorable Moments from the Early Days of Dialysis and Northwest Kidney Centers

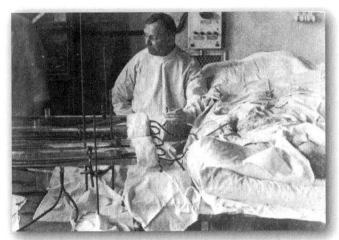

Dr. Georg Haas treats a patient. Haas performed the first human dialysis in Giessen, Germany in 1924.

Nils Alwall of Sweden produced the first dialyzer with controllable ultrafiltration in the 1940s.

Willem Kolff's original rotating drum artificial kidney
in 1943, the year he built it in Holland.

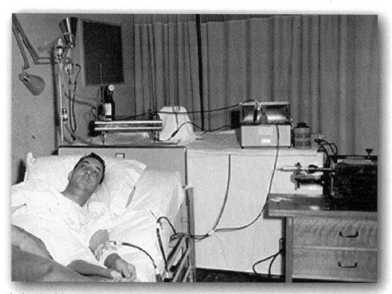

Clyde Shields, a 39-year-old Seattle machinist, was the first person to survive
long-term on hemodialysis. His first dialysis treatment was in 1960.

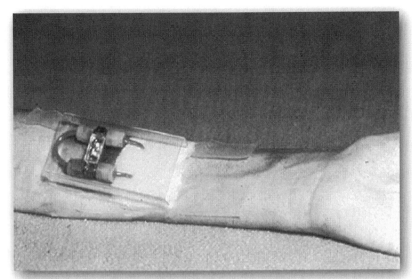

The original Scribner-Quinton shunt was implanted in 1960 in the arm of Clyde Shields. Its invention by Dr. Belding Scribner and Wayne Quinton enabled long-term survival on dialysis.

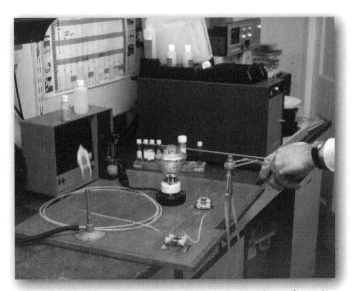

Bending Teflon to make cannulas and shunts in the early 1960s. A technician often did this at bedside, with the surgeon present, to get the correct shape for an individual patient.

University of Washington biomedical engineer Wayne Quinton, who joined Dr. Belding Scribner to create the arteriovenous shunt in 1960.

Dr. Belding Scribner, dialysis pioneer, inventor of the Scribner shunt and a founder of the Seattle Artificial Kidney Center, now Northwest Kidney Centers.

Dr. Fred Boen, working with Dr. Belding Scribner at the University of Washington in 1962, developed the first successful peritoneal dialysis technique to treat chronic kidney failure in the hospital. In May 1964, Boen sent the first patient home on long-term home PD.

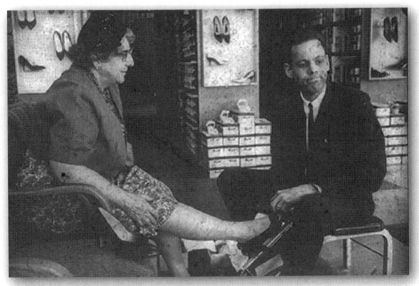

Between dialysis treatment days, patient Harvey Gentry worked as a shoe salesman. This photo is from 1961.

Who should get access to the limited resource of dialysis? In Seattle, the decisions were up to the kidney center's anonymous Admissions and Policy Committee – a labor leader, a housewife, a pastor, a banker, a surgeon, and two representatives from the state Division of Vocational Rehabilitation. A famous Life magazine article of Nov. 9, 1962 pondered the implications – giving rise to the formal study of bioethics. *Photo courtesy of Getty Images and photographer Lawrence Schiller.*

Eklind Hall at Seattle's Swedish Hospital in the 1960s. The basement of this nurses' dormitory became the home of the Seattle Artificial Kidney Center.

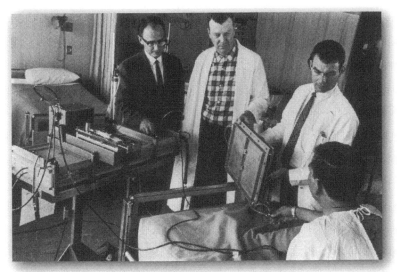

Early dialysis innovators: University of Washington professor Les Babb, who helped develop a 1960s dialysate delivery system dubbed "the Monster;" his PhD student Lars Grimsrud; dialysis engineer Jack Cole; and Ron Bull, the first patient in Seattle to have an arteriovenous fistula.

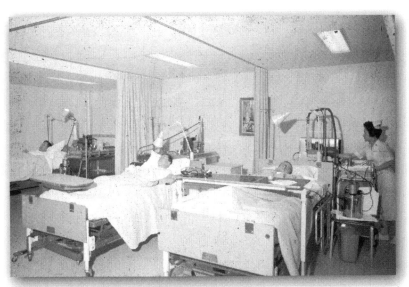

The first home of the Seattle Artificial Kidney Center was in the basement of Eklind Hall at Seattle's Swedish Hospital. There were three beds for treatment.

Members of the kidney care team in Seattle, 1962. Dr. John Murray, Dr. Belding
Scribner, Dr. James Burnell, Dr. Jerome Pendras, nurses Jo Ann Albers and Carol
Williams, James Albers, Dr. Robert Hegstrom, Dr. Robert Hickman and Wayne
Quinton. *Photo courtesy of Getty Images and photographer Lawrence Schiller.*

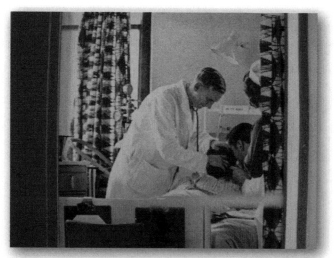

Dr. Christopher Blagg cares for a patient at a hospital in Leeds,
England in the early 1960s, prior to his move to Seattle.

In 1963 Professor Les Babb and University of Washington colleagues developed the Monster, a machine that mixed chemicals and water to make dialysate. About the size of a piano, this bulky, noisy machine was used in the University of Washington's four-bed dialysis room in the early 1960s.

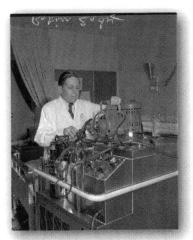

London medical student Robin Eady was near death from kidney failure when he flew to Seattle for dialysis in February 1963. He is photographed here after two months of regular treatment. Restored to health, he became a dialysis technician and later a well-known English dermatologist. The longest-living person with kidney failure, Dr. Eady received home dialysis care for 24 years, and has lived with a kidney transplant since 1987. *Photo courtesy of the Post-Intelligencer Collection, Museum of History & Industry, Seattle.*

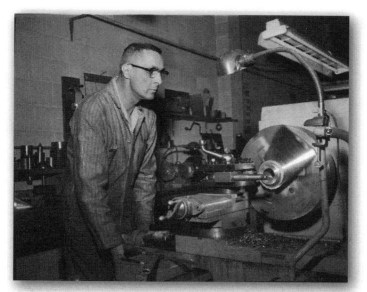

Clyde Shields was the first person put on maintenance dialysis when it was still experimental. He received 16-hour treatments at Seattle's University of Washington Hospital starting in 1960. *Photo courtesy of the Post-Intelligencer Collection, Museum of History & Industry.*

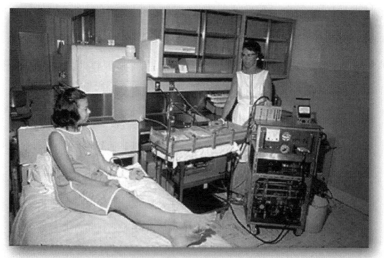

Seattle high school student Caroline Helm became the first person to use home hemodialysis in June 1964. Her mother, Susan Vukich, trained in caregiving techniques to keep her daughter alive.

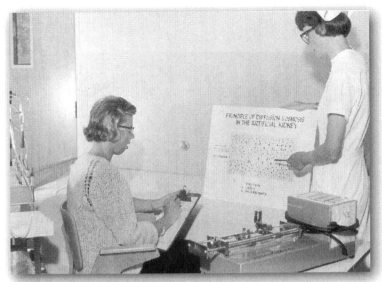

In 1964, Susan Vukich was trained at Seattle Artificial Kidney
Center to keep her daughter alive with home hemodialysis.

The Mini-Monster or Mini-I was invented in 1964 to enable Caroline
Helm to dialyze at home. This machine became the prototype for
nearly all single-patient hemodialysis machines in use today.

The Milton Roy company produced the first commercial portable
dialysis machine, seen here in 1965. Based on the Mini-I built for
Caroline Helm, it allowed patients to dialyze at home.

An article about the Seattle Artificial Kidney Center in the Seattle
Post-Intelligencer from 1965 shows Jim Albers, a dialysis patient
and husband of kidney center nurse Jo Ann Albers.

Dr. Belding Scribner leased space in the mid-1970s to create a home dialysis training center at the Coach House motel in Seattle. The staff included: Dr Suhail Ahmad; Mike Heron, dialysis technician; Bill Jensen, engineering technician; Mike Nelson, dialysis technician; unknown, secretary; Diane Heron, head nurse; Dr. Scribner; Jack Cole, division administrator, UW Nephrology; Joe Vizzo, chief dialysis technician.

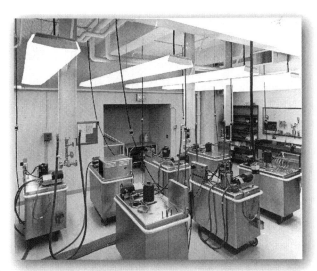

The lab at the Seattle Artificial Kidney Center in Eklind Hall, where dialysis machines were cleaned and prepared for use. The large metal containers, made by Sweden Freezer, are 100-gallon stainless steel tanks storing dialysate.

15-year-old patient Bonnie Parks with Dr. Fred Boen's home peritoneal dialysis cycler in 1967. Bonnie trained on PD at the University of Washington and later moved to home hemodialysis through Northwest Kidney Center.

The Kiil dialyzer, used primarily from 1961 to 1971, was a fixture in the home of Nancy Spaeth. Spaeth started dialysis at Seattle Artificial Kidney Center in 1966 at age 19. After 50 years of renal replacement therapy including four kidney transplants and years on dialysis, she continues to lead an active life.

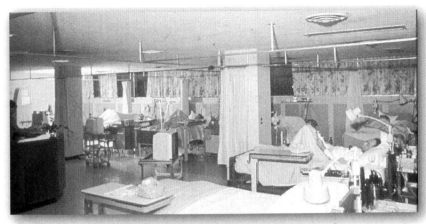

The Seattle Artificial Kidney Center in Swedish
Hospital's Eklind Hall, Seattle, 1960s.

Dr. James Haviland, president of the King County Medical Society, was a
driving force in creation of the Seattle Artificial Kidney Center. He chaired its
first board of trustees and served as senior counsel until his death in 2007.

Dr. Tom Sawyer began work at Northwest Kidney Centers in 1965, and became chief medical officer in 1971 when Dr. Christopher Blagg was named executive director. Sawyer's focus on clinical operations, dedication to patients and sense of humor made him popular with both staff and patients during his 27 years as chief medical officer.

Harvey Gentry, Clyde Shields, Dr. Belding Scribner and Rolin Heming. Gentry, Shields and Heming were the first three long-term dialysis patients in Seattle.

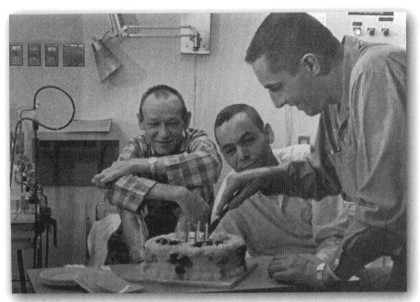

Rolin Heming, Harvey Gentry and Clyde Shields — the first three patients
— celebrate their 10th anniversary on maintenance dialysis in March 1970.

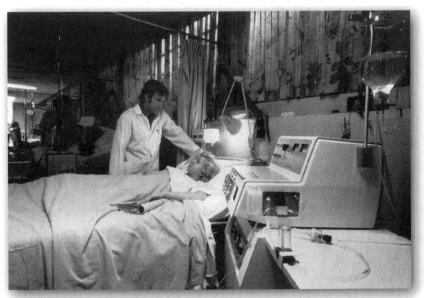

A 1971 Seattle Artificial Kidney Center patient in Eklind Hall gets
treatment using a Physio-Control peritoneal dialysis machine.

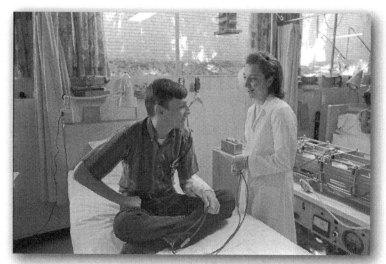

Jo Ann Albers, Seattle Artificial Kidney Center's first head nurse, with Pat Juhl in 1971. Albers served from 1961 to 1971, establishing the fundamental practice of outpatient dialysis performed without a physician. *Photo, also on the cover, is courtesy of the Post-Intelligencer Collection, Museum of History & Industry, Seattle.*

Marcia Clark, instrumental in founding the American Nephrology Nurses Association, became renal coordinator at Northwest Kidney Centers in 1971. For the next 18 years, she pushed nursing staff to bring best practices to the rest of the world.

Registered nurse Connie Anderson arrived at Northwest Kidney Centers in 1974, eventually becoming vice president of clinical operations. She has guided the organization to a holistic approach to patient care and developed innovations like case management and diabetes and infection control programs.

The 700 Broadway building in Seattle when Northwest Kidney Centers purchased it in 1977.

Northwest Kidney Centers' headquarters at 700 Broadway, Seattle, in the 1970s. In 2017, the building housed a dialysis clinic, specialty pharmacy, administrative offices, clinical research space and the organization's dialysis museum.

## CHAPTER 21

# Home Hemodialysis 1961-1966

———

THE FIRST MENTIONS OF HOME hemodialysis were at the 1961 meeting of the American Society for Artificial Internal Organs (ASAIO). In the discussion following presentation of a paper from Seattle detailing the survival of the first four patients using the shunt, Kolff complimented Scrib "for the work that he has started and just to show to what situation it will lead, may I present the picture made by cinematographer Mervin La Rue. Undoubtedly, we all want our artificial kidneys at home and this will happen if you are a little late." Following this, in his Presidential address, Charles Kirby, a cardiac surgeon, said, "Perhaps what we need is a home dialysis unit to be placed by the patient's bedside, so that he can plug himself in for an eight-hour period once or twice a week."

Credit for the first use of hemodialysis in the home for a patient with chronic renal failure goes to Peter Bent Brigham Hospital in Boston where Dr. Eugene Schupak, one of John Merrill's renal fellows, often traveled to work with one of his neighbors who was a patient who was being dialyzed at the hospital. Schupak thought that because both the patient and his wife were intelligent there was no reason why they could not be trained to do dialysis in their home. He put the idea to Merrill who thought the idea quite reasonable and arranged for Schupak to present his proposal to the whole renal team. They were not impressed and voted eleven to one (Gene Schupak was the one) against the idea. However, Merrill pointed out that he had not voted himself and as the chief he had twelve votes. As a result, a twin-coil artificial kidney was installed in the home of the patient in Framingham,

Massachusetts in late 1963. The group started two more patients on home dialysis in early 1964. At first, dialysis was performed in the home once a week and at the hospital once a week, the home dialysis being monitored by a physician and a nurse from the hospital. Dialysis was done for four-to-six hours and the dialyzer was primed with 500 ml of blood saved from the end of the previous dialysis and stored at the blood bank and with 400 ml of the patient's own blood. The artificial kidney was installed in a bedroom and water for making the dialysate was obtained from the bathroom and mixed with the appropriate chemicals in the tank of the dialysis machine. The dialysate in the tank was drained through the shower and replaced every two hours. Once stable at home, dialysis was started by a physician and the rest of the treatment was supervised by a nurse. With time, experience and increasing confidence in the technique, the patient's wife was trained to carry out the whole dialysis. By the time of the 1965 ASAIO meeting, Peter Bent Brigham Hospital had four male patients at home, three dialyzed by their wives and one, who was not married, treated by a private nurse. Two patients were still being seen by a physician at the start of their dialysis and two were not.

Early one Saturday morning in February 1964, Les Babb was awakened by a call from a distressed Scrib. A patient of his, a 15-year-old high school student, Caroline Helm, had been rejected by the Seattle Community Artificial Kidney Center because she was less than 18 years old and was suffering from kidney disease as a complication of lupus erythematosus, a generalized autoimmune disease. She would probably require dialysis in about four months' time. Scrib thought that although she had been turned down by the Center it would be quite legitimate to enroll her in a University of Washington research project funded from an outside source. For this, he wanted Les's team of engineers to miniaturize "the Monster," the device that made dialysate from concentrate using proportioning pumps and that had recently been installed in the dialysis room at University Hospital. This new device was to be used for a single patient and be portable enough to be taken to a patient's home. In effect, he was asking the engineers to design and build a portable, fail-safe, single-patient dialysis machine. Les was concerned about the time and effort this would require for his staff and himself but was convinced when Scrib said "Caroline's father is a good friend of yours." This was because Harry Helm, Caroline's father, was the local representative of a company that had provided some of the instrumentation in the recently constructed nuclear reactor on the University of Washington campus.

After the weekend, Les met with his staff and, following a discussion, they agreed to undertake the project. The magnitude of this effort was enormous. They would have to make many of the items required themselves and many of the instruments required would have to be modified. The technical phase would consist of designing the central logic unit, specifying the control and monitoring devices, designing the hydraulic system, specifying what should be monitored and how, and doing a reliability and safety analysis of the design. In addition, decisions had to be made about the degree of patient participation, the monitoring required for both patient and fluid system, the adaptability for use in the home, the operating costs, the bacteriology involved, and the adaptability for commercial production. The system had to be automated to minimize patient effort, be able to pasteurize itself with hot water at the touch of a button, produce dialysate of the right composition and temperature, and notify the patient when it was ready to be connected.

The engineers then began having frequent meetings with Scrib's medical group at the nuclear reactor. The physicians wanted a miniature of "the Monster" with additional monitoring to provide safe and reliable operation while the patient slept. The engineers wanted to make the machine as automatic as possible and so added design and programming of the system cycles to their tasks. The physicians began to refer to the device as the "miniature Monster" or the "mini-Monster" but because the term "monster" seemed inappropriate for a patient device for use in the home the name became "Mini-I." One of the principal aims was to develop a fail-safe device so that in the event of a major malfunction the machine would change automatically to a safe configuration.

Discussions were ongoing and frequent as solutions were worked out as to how to manage temperatures in the device and how to ensure valves in the hydraulic system would resist corrosion from the dialysate. Dual proportioning pumps were provided by the Milton-Roy Company. It was decided not to demineralize the tap water, as Seattle water from the Cedar River was chemically benign, but filters were used to remove particulate matter and a system was designed to de-aerate the dialysate. Appropriate gauges and other devices were procured and the safety analysis was concluded.

This unofficial, unfunded development process was being done at the nuclear reactor using academic and technical staff that had a great many other responsibilities and the relatively new nuclear reactor building was one of the Dean of Engineering's favorite places to visit to see what was happening and to show off to visitors. Consequently, staff established a "Dean watch," as anyone in the reactor's control room could see in all directions and would warn over the intercom if he saw the dean coming. The machine would then be hidden in a closet.

Mini-I measured two feet by three feet and weighed 150 lbs. and was delivered to University Hospital on June 1, 1964. Caroline and her mother began to train together under the direction of a physician from Scrib's team, Kingsbury Curtis, and two nurses, Barbara Fellowes and Susan Daly. The first dialysis in the home was done in July, and by November 1964 some forty dialyses had been done at home without any serious problems.

## PROTOTYPES FOR HOME HEMODIALYSIS MACHINES

By this time it was obvious that the Seattle Artificial Kidney Center (the name had been changed in April 1964) could not support more patients without further expensive expansion. Consequently, it was decided to formalize the technical specifications and drawings for Mini-I and then have the university go outside to bid for construction of five prototypes that were to be called Mini-II. The bid was won by the Milton Roy Company, the makers of the proportioning pumps used in the original "Monster." Meanwhile, the Sweden Freezer Manufacturing Company had also developed its own prototype home hemodialysis device based on a tank system. Both devices were designed to deliver a mix of tap water and premixed liquid concentrate at specified levels of temperature, pressure, flow rate and concentration, with appropriate back-up monitoring when necessary, require minimum maintenance, have short start-up and shut-down time, and incorporate pro-grammed sterilize-rinse-normalize cycles.

The prototype Sweden Freezer device was used to train the second Seattle patient (William McHargue, a Seattle insurance underwriter) at University Hospital also in the summer of 1964. The third home dialysis patient (M.K.S.), the 33-year-old son-in-law of a prosperous businessman in Madras, India, came to Seattle with his wife and his physician in September 1964. They were trained to use the first production model of the Sweden Freezer machine later that year and, after dialyzing in a rented house near University Hospital, returned to India to dialyze on the family estate in early 1985. This patient survived for a year or so and his widow, who did the dialysis, was still able describe in great detail to Dr. Blagg 45 years later how to manage the shunt, prepare the Kiil dialyzer and do the treatment. Scrib always said she was more competent than the patient's doctor.

The three patients used Kiil dialyzers and blood tubing assembled in the home, and disposable plastic connectors that had replaced the original Swagelok fittings on the shunt. After assembly, dialyzer and tubing were sterilized using 3% acetic acid and periodic formalin treatment. Initially, dialysis was done two-or-three times a week during the day and automated monitoring was not used when the patient or a family member was awake.

In October 1964, Dr. Stanley Shaldon in London was the first to use overnight home hemodialysis and he visited Seattle in December 1964 to describe this development. As a result, overnight three-times-a-week home hemodialysis began to be used in Seattle in early 1965. It used monitor-ing with appropriate alarm connections, including a blood leak detector for blood in the dialysate, a drip bulb pressure monitor as described by Shaldon, and a digital blood pressure monitor using a finger cuff.

Training was carried out in a separate area at University Hospital and covered both the theory and practical technique of doing dialysis. As the patient and family member became more confident and more skilled, professional support was gradually withdrawn. Training lasted for about two months. At home, the patient and family member were able to clean, assemble and test the dialyzer, prepare and check the dialysate, hook up the patient to the artificial kidney, monitor the patient during treatment, and take the patient off dialysis. Family responsibilities also included management of the dialysis, including adjusting dialysis-negative pressure to maintain body weight and control hypertension, performing simple chemical tests on the dialysate, measuring the patient's hematocrit, and deciding on the need for blood transfusion.

The two Seattle patients had serious complications. Caroline had systemic lupus erythematosus with complications requiring steroid treatment and William had severe peripheral neuropathy that impaired his walking considerably. Nevertheless, one continued as an honors student in high school and at the University of Washington, and the other continued almost full-time work. Thus, both appeared early on to achieve what was called maximum "potential" rehabilitation.

Estimates of the cost of treatment, predicated on having a larger more efficient home dialysis program, were that expendable material per dialysis cost about $11.00, the estimated monthly operational costs were $273, and the start-up, training and capital costs exceeded $9,000. Of course this did not account for the work of the family, which included the actual dialysis time and 10-to-12 hours a week to cycle the dialyzer, care for the cannulas, maintain and check the equipment, and also do simple declotting procedures and simple laboratory tests at home.

## HOME DIALYSIS IS THE FUTURE

At the time of Scrib's Presidential address to the American Society for Artificial Internal Organs in April 1964 there were still only somewhere between 50 and 100 patients in the U.S. living on dialysis or with a kidney transplant. The Seattle Artificial Kidney Center had shown that dialysis could be successfully carried out by nurses in an out-of-hospital setting at significantly less expense than dialysis in a hospital and he thought such units might be the way to treat the ever increasing numbers of potential patients with end-stage kidney failure. However, by 1966, when he spoke at the 3rd International Congress of Nephrology in Washington, DC, he believed it important to study the directions chronic dialysis should take "in the future if maximum progress is to be made and the greatest number of patients benefited at the lowest cost." His opinion now was that the future of chronic dialysis lay in the home. At that time there were a total of 46 patients dialyzing at home: eight in Boston; 12 in London with a further two dialyzing remotely; seven in Seattle with nine dialyzing remotely; and four in Spokane, Washington, with four more dialyzing remotely. In the two-plus years since it was first used in Boston, no single fatality had been reported as occurring in the home and only one patient had died while hospitalized.

Home hemodialysis had started as a desperate experiment to treat more patients, and all who had been involved had been amazed by its success. The most important advance had been the introduction of overnight home hemodialysis by Shaldon, as this allowed dialysis at night while the patient and family could sleep, resulted in savings of time and effort by the patient and family, and made the future for home hemodialysis very promising.

The disadvantages of the procedure included minor technical failures that affected family time and delayed dialysis, but improvement in equipment and technique would be forthcoming. However, home hemodialysis could cause considerable stress on some patients and their families and so not all patients would be candidates for home treatment. This raised the question of what should be done for these other patients. One possible answer was a dialysis unit operated by the patients themselves, doing self-dialysis with minimal professional support, as had been used first by Shaldon in the Royal Free Hospital in London in 1963. Despite these disadvantages, the advantages of home hemodialysis made it the best answer to the problem of providing dialysis on a larger scale.

In 1966, Scrib detailed nine advantages of home hemodialysis:

1.  Home dialysis will always be less costly, and technical improvements, whether intended for center use or home use, would help to reduce the cost further. The reduced cost is primarily due to dialysis being done by the patient rather than by a nurse or technician;
2.  A dialysis center has a limited capacity and eventually will fill up and require expansion, more staff, more equipment, and in the long run will be more expensive than home dialysis;
3.  Activation of a large dialysis center is a major undertaking, involving careful planning, capitalization, new construction and personnel training. A home dialysis program can be activated with much less effort, and planning and can even begin as a remote home operation involving a single patient based at an established center several hundred miles away;
4.  A center operating permanently ties down an ever-increasing number of highly trained medical personnel at a time when such personnel are badly needed throughout all of medicine;
5.  To permit normal work and leisure hours, maintenance dialysis must be accomplished at night. Hemodialysis through the night is relatively easy to do in the home with modern equipment. On the other hand, nighttime operation of a dialysis center is difficult because of unwillingness of the personnel involved to work mainly at night. Another advantage of home dialysis is the flexibility in scheduling afforded the patient as compared with the tight dialysis schedule demanded by efficient operation of a dialysis center;
6.  Hepatitis outbreaks and other infections have been a problem in dialysis units, and because of the separation of the patient at home, the risks of infection are decreased;
7.  Experience has shown that a physician practicing hundreds of miles away from the home dialysis training center, can successfully manage a properly trained home dialysis patient, provided the physician is given brief indoctrination. With home dialysis, the patients

themselves can be made entirely responsible for the dialysis procedure and receive their technical backup, when needed, directly from the technical staff at the center;

8.  Home dialysis can be more frequent and more intense than in the center, and even daily dialysis may become practical. More frequent and more intensive dialysis has uniformly improved patient strength and well-being and virtually has eliminated many of the medical complications, such as arthritis, neuropathy, pruritus, and metastatic calcification. More frequent dialysis makes it possible to eliminate protein and dietary sodium restriction and at the same time blood pressure control is improved because more frequent removal of sodium minimizes wide swings in extracellular volume;

9.  A patient on self-dialysis at home tends to develop a much healthier attitude towards their disease and their treatment than a patient on center dialysis because the patient, rather than the institution, is primarily responsible for his continued good health. Home dialysis stresses independence, while center dialysis fosters a dependent attitude that over a period of time can make some patients very demanding and overly anxious. Home dialysis also alleviates anxiety by teaching the patient to be totally familiar with all the technical aspects of the procedure. During training the patient learns about the kinds of technical and medical malfunctions that can occur during dialysis and how to correct them. This knowledge increases the confidence of the patient in the procedure and minimizes the anxiety felt by some patients who do not have such knowledge about dialysis.

The weight of evidence summarized in these nine points clearly suggests that if large scale hemodialysis is to become a reality, this goal can be achieved most rapidly and most easily in the home where dialysis can be done more cheaply, with the patient accepting full responsibility for the dialysis procedure itself.

## New England Journal of Medicine Article

By mid-1965, nine patients from Seattle and from California had been trained for home hemodialysis at University Hospital and the results were sufficiently convincing that a decision was made to train further patients at the University of Washington. These included 15 patients from Washington State, 14 from California, 16 from other states and seven from other countries, including Chile, Mexico, the Philippines, Singapore and the Sudan. These 52 patients were followed for between 6 and 64 months and described in a paper written by Drs. Blagg, Eschbach, Hickman and Scribner published in The New England Journal of Medicine in 1970. The results are summarized below.

There were 36 male and 16 female patients with ages ranging from 9 to 59 years, including three pre-pubertal children, two adolescents, 12 housewives, and 35 men. All the patients' dialysis programs were funded by research grants or privately, and this had to be confirmed before a patient began training. Three of the patients had diabetes, one had systemic lupus erythematosus, and the remainder had primary renal disease of various etiologies. All patients were accompanied by a family member who was also trained, and patients from outside the Seattle area were accompanied briefly by a physician who would be providing continuing care.

Training by a nurse, technician, and physician took seven to ten weeks in the Coach House, a motel unit simulating the home and situated a mile from the hospital. Patients spent the last two weeks practicing unattended overnight dialysis. All treatments were carried out three or more times weekly for a total of 24-45 hours a week. Kiil dialyzers were used, together with one of four different monitored fluid delivery systems: four patients used the Sweden Freezer device; 12 used the Milton Roy Model A device; six used the Milton Roy Model B device; and 31 patients used the new Drake Willock machine. During dialysis, 1,500 units of heparin per hour were infused by pump after a priming dose of 2,000-3,000 units.

Most patients stored and reused their dialyzers as many as six times before rebuilding was necessary, and blood tubing was stored and reused as often as 18 times. All patients used external Silastic-Teflon cannulas during training to allow ease of performing self-dialysis, although by the end of the study two patients were using arteriovenous fistulae.

By June 1970, 16 patients had died, a mortality of 31%. Most deaths were due to infections or to cardiac problems. Eight deaths occurred during the second year of treatment, but only two deaths occurred in the 19 patients who survived for more than 3 years on hemodialysis. Six patients received renal transplants after 23-55 months on dialysis.

Rehabilitation present before death was judged to be good in 43 patients (83%) as judged by a return to pre-dialysis occupation, school, or household duties, and partial in four, but poor in five who were incapacitated by medical complications of diabetes, avascular necrosis of the hips and knees following transplantation, chronic subdural hematoma, and nonunion of a fractured hip due to renal bone disease.

Complications due to uremia were less frequent than in patients on center hemodialysis because of the more intensive dialysis in terms of hours of treatment. At the time of the study, most center patients were still being dialyzed twice a week, whereas these patients got dialysis three times a week. Poor blood pressure control was seen in seven patients (14%), primarily because they were unable to restrict dietary salt intake. Clinical bone disease occurred in 11 patients, but only caused major orthopedic problems in one who had nonunion of a fractured hip. Nonvascular metastatic calcification occurred rarely since serum phosphate levels were kept below 8 mg/dl by adequate dialysis, supplemented as necessary with oral aluminum hydroxide treatment.

Anemia was treated by transfusion in only 11 patients (21%), usually one unit of packed red cells per month. Blood loss was minimized by infrequent blood tests and good dialyzer rinse techniques, but small unavoidable blood losses occurred with each dialysis, eventually leading to iron deficiency in many of the patients. This was corrected with oral iron unless antacids were being taken when parenteral iron was required.

Major medical problems were only indirectly related to uremia, but nevertheless, pericarditis occurred in six patients, five had severe effusions and three developed tamponade, causing death in one patient. Other problems included menorrhagia in five patients, duodenal ulcer in five patients, with serious bleeding in three of them, and a subdural hematoma occurring in one patient after 18 months of dialysis. Only two patients acquired hepatitis, one following exposure to an infected family member and the other was infected during center dialysis while away from home attending medical school. Malaria was the only other transfusion-related complication, occurring in the Filipino patient after an unnecessary transfusion before a return visit to the United States. Other complications included deafness due to antibiotic treatment in Singapore, unexplained intermittent metabolic encephalopathy with seizures, and intermittent psychosis.

Complications related to dialysis included anticoagulation issues, both with heparin used during dialysis and warfarin given with failing cannulas. These aggravated or caused serious problems in 25% of patients, with death resulting in four. Three of the five patients with duodenal ulcers had bleeding during or after dialysis and three patients had hemorrhagic pericardial effusion with tamponade.

Cannula survival averaged seven to eight months, although 11 patients (21%) had severe infections at the cannula site or required re-cannulation more than twice in one year. Many patients had minor staphylococcal infections at the cannula sites that responded promptly to antibiotics and did not require hospitalization.

Equipment malfunctions caused serious problems in only two patients, although in both, this occurred during dialysis in hospital. Major machine malfunctions occurred in 11 patients, although serious only in two who died. One of these related to copper toxicity due to exhaustion of a deionizer during dialysis in hospital, and the second was in a patient who nearly died of cardiac arrest resulting from dialysis against tap water while in hospital where a nurse had neglected to test the dialysate of the Travenol tank. Dialysis against tap water occurred in three patients using Drake-Willock equipment at home when the patients failed to change the concentrate line from rinsing tap water to concentrate, failed to activate the conductivity meter, and failed to check the dialysate with bedside chloride test. All recognized this problem promptly, stopped dialysis, and recovered without injury.

Home hemodialysis is potentially stressful, and severe stress with maladjustment was present in ten patients (19%), and most had occasional stressful episodes due to medical, technical, or cannula problems. The ability to adjust to problems depended on the emotional stability of the patient, the frequency of the problems that occurred, and the emotional support provided by family, friends, and physicians. In general, older patients adjusted more readily to the rigid schedule and time entailed by dialysis, whereas teenagers and young adults usually found this more difficult.

Although all but one patient was trained to sleep during dialysis, 16 were sleeping poorly. Eight of these were among the ten who had continued stress and poor adjustment to dialysis. Experience with the preadolescents suggested that growth may occur with thrice weekly overnight dialysis, but the numbers of patients were very small. Forty-one of the patients were being cared for by 35 physicians who had no previous experience with home hemodialysis and four physicians managed two or more patients. All physicians without previous dialysis experience spent one to seven days at the training unit learning the essentials of medical management of their patients. House calls were infrequent, but routine office visits were required every few weeks or months and took longer for these patients than for patients not on dialysis.

The conclusion from the experience with these patients was that full-scale integration of a home hemodialysis program with a renal transplant program is essential. The recommendation at the time of this study was that unless a well-matched kidney was available for transplantation, all patients should learn self-dialysis initially. Because of the larger patient pool, it should then be possible to provide matched cadaver kidneys for many of the patients ultimately. Thus, the future treatment of end-stage renal disease should be a regional effort, utilizing the services of local physicians, nephrologists, transplant surgeons, immunologists, and their associates.

CHAPTER 22

# Administrative Developments at the King County Medical Society and the Seattle Community Artificial Kidney Center 1961-1965

———

As NOTED EARLIER, WHAT WAS originally called the Artificial Kidney Treatment Center or the Community Kidney Treatment Center or the Artificial Kidney Center was set up in 1961 by Dr. Scribner, Dr. James Haviland, and the King County Medical Society (KCMS). From then until the incorporation of what was at the time called the Seattle Artificial Community Kidney Center (probably in error) in December 1963, the Center was under the guidance of the KCMS Executive Committee.

The problem of finding the original funding support for the Center had been solved in the summer of 1961 with a grant from the John A. Hartford Foundation of $250,000 to Swedish Hospital to be paid in installments in 1961, 1962 and 1963. Funding the Center beyond these years was to become a major consideration.

## The Question of Funding Arises Once Again
On August 8, 1962, Dr. Murray, the medical director of the Center, presented to the Admissions and Policy Committee a progress report that had been sent to the John A. Hartford Foundation about the Center's first six months of operation. One hundred and fifty dialyses had been done at a gross cost of $390 per treatment, but eliminating research costs the net cost per dialysis was approximately $200. Equipment was becoming available

and, projecting ahead to when the Center would reach its proposed capacity of seven patients in October with about the same number of staff, the cost per dialysis would be about $100, or $10,000 per patient per year. If suitable patients continued to be referred it might be possible to treat as many as nine patients.

Dr. Murray noted it was now time for the committee to consider the program as a practical though expensive method of treating patients and no longer as a feasibility study. He presented a proposal for enlarging and operating a ten-bed artificial kidney center in the basement of Eklind Hall that would allow treatment of at least 30 patients. First-year costs with 10 beds, an average of 20 patients and 1,500 dialyses were estimated to be $385,000 for personnel, hospital charges, lab supplies and miscellaneous equipment, and remodeling. Second-year costs were estimated to be $324,000 based on 30 patients and 3,000 dialyses.

The proposal was discussed at length by the Admissions and Policy Committee at its August 8th meeting. The cost per patient had been estimated as $10,000 per year and, even though further technical improvements might reduce this, treatment would still be expensive. Doubts were expressed that this much support could come from the local community and a national foundation would have to be approached. Scrib felt that as the Center was without precedent elsewhere and would have appeal, especially after the Life magazine article was published in November 1962 (see chapter 13), and it was still unique to Seattle and should be supported at least in part by local funds. The original John A. Hartford Foundation support would end on July 1, 1963, since the program would no longer be a feasibility study or a research project and the Center should then become a local responsibility. In the meantime, patients were dying and the only thing limiting expansion was money. After July 1963 it would become difficult to even support the patients presently being treated. One suggestion was to appeal to the United Good Neighbors (UGN) but it was pointed out that UGN did not have enough money to go around the various organizations it was already supporting. Another possibility was the Boeing Employees Good Neighbor Fund. The question then was raised about establishing a policy that patients be asked to finance their own treatment to the extent of their ability to pay, as two of the current patients would be able to contribute about half the cost of their treatment. One member felt strongly that if this were done, ability to pay should not be a criterion for selection and that this type of information should not be divulged or discussed until after selection. Apparently the patients themselves were concerned, but had no suggestions how the problem should be dealt with. The committee then unanimously adopted a policy whereby patients would be expected to pay to the extent of their ability to do so, this rule being applicable to both present and future patients.

Scrib then told the committee about his recent conversation with Dr. Donald Sparkman, director of the Washington State Division of Vocational Rehabilitation, who by his position was uniquely situated to gather financial-related data about the patients. If the committee wished him to do this he felt he should resign his position on the Admissions and Policy Committee. This was agreed to and his resignation was accepted.

In the spring of 1963, Scribner's group proposed to the National Institutes of Health that the federal government finance establishment of outpatient dialysis facilities around the country but the request was turned down. This led to the realization that the Hartford grant would expire on July 1st and the center would have to close. Scrib admitted later "that we were so busy making the center run well technically that we never even thought about money. We just assumed the Hartford Foundation would renew their grant, and suddenly we found out they weren't going to. They had done their job by providing research money to demonstrate the feasibility of a dialysis center." As a result the main front page story in the May 2 Seattle Times carried the headline "Seattle Artificial Kidney Center Faced with Closure, New Funds Needed to Keep Patients Alive" and showed the photographs of all the existing patients.

Soon thereafter, Dr. Murray requested renewal of the Hartford grant, admitting that the idea that the community would be willing fund the center had been overoptimistic. He asked for $410,000 for a further 3 years of support, about $100,000 to help cover treatment costs, the remainder to develop a more efficient artificial kidney and improvements in equipment and the dialysis procedure. The Hartford Foundation sent a copy of the application to Dr. George Thorn in Boston who replied by supporting the application but also suggesting cuts in the Center's budget. As a result, on May 21, the foundation approved an immediate $100,000 emergency grant and asked for a revised budget proposal. This was sent and on June 20 the foundation amended the May 21 award for an additional $210,342 to be payable in 1963, 1964 and 1965.

Murray also applied to the U.S. Public Health Service (USPHS) for full support of the Center for a year and partial support for the following two years. Concern that the Center might have to close led Senator Lister Hill, chairman of both the Senate Labor and Public Welfare Committee, which dealt with health legislation, and the Appropriations Health Subcommittee that funded legislation, to arrange a hearing in the spring of 1963 in order to put pressure on the PHS. Scrib testified at the hearing, describing possible patient numbers as between 1,000 and 5,000 a year and that keeping the number low would require "ruthless patient selection." He said, based on very conservative figures, of an incidence of 1,000 patients annually could mean an annual budget of $100 million a year in 10 years and urged research to reduce the costs of dialysis together with transplantation research and noted that if a transplant failed this would not be fatal as the patient would then just continue on dialysis. As a result PHS acted favorably on the Center's application for support to provide "a demonstration of community involvement and support in providing dialysis to those with chronic uremia" and by September 1963 a three-year grant of $330,516 had been awarded to Swedish Hospital for a "demonstration and feasibility study with the understanding that significant local community support would be forthcoming." There was an explicit understanding that the local community would raise $70,000 toward construction and remodeling costs. The grant was to fund operations at the Center at 100% for the first year, 50% for the second year together with support for new construction at the Center, and 25% for the third year. The funds from the PHS together with a grant of $50,000 from the Boeing Employees Good Neighbors Fund were used in 1964 to construct a new 10-bed center, later expanded to 12 beds in the courtyard area between the two wings of Eklind Hall, and the original site of the Center was closed.

At its November 19, 1963 meeting, the King County Medical Society Board of Trustees also discussed the concern about funding once the Hartford Foundation grant ended, and at the December 17th meeting Dr. Haviland raised the question of seeking funds locally.

## DIFFICULTY IN SELECTING PATIENTS FOR THE CENTER

As discussed earlier, one of the major problems was patient selection. The Admissions and Policy Committee had informed the Medical Advisory Committee following its early meetings in 1961 that they wanted to make no medical judgments and wanted to know everything possible about potential patients. The Medical Advisory Committee discussed the possibility of rating patients by some numerical score or other means to assist the Admissions and Policy Committee but decided against this and ruled that all patients referred to the Admissions and Policy Committee should be "medically acceptable." It was decided that apart from the previously established strict medical criteria no other definite criteria should be set up and that each case should be considered individually on its merits. In order to help the Admissions and Policy Committee obtain desired non-medical information, consideration was given to hiring a social worker.

At the October 1961 meeting of the Medical Advisory Committee it was decided that in order to obtain information on potential candidates, all physicians in King County should be informed about the operation of the Center and, in particular, the kind of patient most suitable for treatment and the referral procedure for such patients. The committee asked the help of the KCMS Executive Committee for advice as to how best inform the KCMS membership. As a result, a letter was sent to all physicians in the county describing the Center, hemodialysis treatment, the strict medical criteria, how to make a referral, and the selection process, and informing them there would be the potential for more candidates than places available when the Center opened in January 1962.

In fact, because of delays in completing renovation of the basement of Eklind Hall, the Seattle Artificial Kidney Center did not open until January 8, 1962, one week behind schedule. A month later, at the February 18th meeting of the KCMS Board, the issue was raised of the relationship of the Center with the University of Washington, the problems Scrib was having doing research at University Hospital, and his wish to do research at the Center. The KCMS Board was interested in the continued existence, development and financing of the Center itself, and felt that it could best provide support by helping the Admissions and Policy Committee coordinate activities related to long-term support. Even so, the Board also wanted to reassure Dr. Scribner of its continued interest and support, and its desire that the various efforts related to dialysis be coordinated.

At the July 18, 1962 meeting, the Medical Advisory Committee reviewed the fate of the last three patients who had not been accepted for treatment. At that time, since the Center opened six months earlier, eight relatively ideal patients had been rejected and had died or were about to die. The last three patients had been referred by nephrologists on the committee and one had been told that detailed study had shown his disease would not benefit from treatment. The other two were told that there was no room for further patients at this time. The committee also discussed an acutely ill patient recently admitted to University Hospital who was now on dialysis with a diagnosis of chronic renal disease. The view was that such a patient should not be considered a priority over someone who had been followed for some time and referred in the appropriate manner. It was noted that as soon as equipment and funds became available it might be possible to treat between 20 and 30 patients at the Center and that the KCMS Board of Trustees had intended a major role of the Admissions and Policy Committee to be to take whatever steps were appropriate in order to make the Center a community responsibility. However, the committee had not yet had an opportunity to study the economic factors involved in expansion.

## A New Center in Spokane

During the latter half of 1962 a second dialysis center in the state opened in Spokane. This was the Spokane and Inland Empire Artificial Kidney Center and was intended to serve patients residing to the east of the Columbia River. It was an in-hospital unit in Sacred Heart Hospital, Spokane, was directed by Dr. Tom Marr, a nephrologist in private practice who had been one of Scribner's first renal fellows, and was overseen by Scribner from Seattle. Like the Center in Seattle, it was a non-profit institution and also was initially supported by the Hartford Foundation that provided two years of funding at $42,000 a year. This center did not engage in community fundraising and was also supported by the hospital. It was the first outpatient dialysis facility directed by a private physician.

## Resignation of the Center's Medical Director

In November 1963, Dr. John Murray had announced he would be resigning as medical director. Apparently this related at least in part to differences between Dr. Murray at the Center and Scrib at the Division of Nephrology at the University that had become apparent during 1963. The cause appeared to relate to differing expectations of how the Center would function and the roles of the two institutions, changing perceptions of the role of a medical director, and growing philosophical differences related to how research involving Center patients would be conducted. In addition, Dr. Murray was starting to suffer from a progressive medical disorder that impaired his functioning. It had not been obvious at first that the purposes and primary goals of the two institutions differed, and while mutual cooperation would be beneficial to both, each was seeking overlapping but different objectives. The feelings generated by this rift unfortunately affected both institutions to some extent for several years.

Dr. Murray's intention to resign caused concern for both patients and the Center's staff and on December 10th both groups wrote letters to the new Board of Trustees in support of Dr. Murray. All nine patients urged the Board to attempt to persuade Dr. Murray to remain as medical director or, if not, that Dr. Jerry Pendras, Dr. Murray's assistant, be appointed his successor. They also suggested that a contract be developed clearly spelling out the medical director's areas of authority, that he be appointed as a member of the Board, and that the Board consider allowing patients to select a person of their choosing to directly represent them on the Board. The patients were also concerned that Mr. Harvey Swenson, president of the Sweden Freezer Company, not be appointed to the Board because of his potential conflict of interest. The letter from the 17 staff members expressed much the same views.

## OTHER BOARD ACTIONS IN DECEMBER 1963

There were several other major administrative events in December 1963. On December 6th there was the initial meeting for the incorporation of what was called the Seattle Artificial Community Kidney Center. Seven persons had indicated their willingness to be Trustees: Drs. Haviland, Burnell and Paton; Reverend Darrah; and Mr. Nordstrom, Beaupre and Rosling. Dr. Haviland was elected president and Dr. Paton secretary. The proposed articles of incorporation were accepted with minor modification and it was agreed the bylaws would be approved.

At the next meeting of the Board of Trustees on December 13th there was discussion and selection of other possible candidates for the Board of Trustees so as to reach a total of 21 members. Dr. Haviland appointed Dr. Paton chairman of a committee to outline the duties of the medical director and the administrative structure of the Center, and to take steps to find possible candidates for the position of medical director to replace Dr. Murray. Dr. Burnell, Mr. Nordstrom and Reverend Darrah were appointed members of a committee for the purpose of long-term planning, and Mr. Beaupre was appointed chairman of a finance committee. The representatives of the patients would be invited to attend the next meeting.

The Board of Trustees of the Seattle Community Artificial Kidney Center met again on December 20th but as only Mr. Lyle Guernsey, Drs. Haviland and Paton and Reverend Darrah attended there was no quorum and no official business was accomplished. The principles of the organization's structure and the general aims of the Board of Trustees were discussed with three of the patients, Mr. Albers, Mr. Smith and Mr. Myers. The patients wanted to express their extreme faith in Dr. Murray and in the current operation of the Center, and emphasized the importance of the psychological relationship of the present Center to their own personal well-being.

On December 22th, the Medical Advisory Committee sent an urgent memo to the Board asking for a decision with regard to a possible "holding action" because there were a number of "ideal" candidates who were going to die before the new expansion would be completed and operational. The Medical Advisory Committee felt it could organize temporary treatment to keep the patients going at a cost of between $1,000 and $5,000 a patient, and that these patients might be able to provide all or most of such funds. They noted that if such a holding program was developed there was need to consider the method of patient selection to be used in the future. They therefore proposed that the Admissions and Policy Committee be abolished and all patients who met the medical criteria should be accepted, that only residents of King County should be considered, and that out-of-county patients should only be accepted if they were full-pay. Scrib noted that a decision was important because the National Kidney Disease Foundation was planning a national publicity campaign starting on January 4, 1964, one of the aims of which was to force emergency legislation through Congress to implement a plan that had just been developed at a conference of the foundation in New York.

CHAPTER 23

# The Seattle Community Artificial
# Kidney Center 1964

––––––––

THE CENTER WAS INCORPORATED IN the state of Washington as the Seattle Artificial Community Kidney Center on December 23, 1963. Presumably the name was an error on the part of the Center's lawyer, as all the minutes of the January and February meetings prior to the first annual meeting refer to the Seattle Community Artificial Kidney Center. The name of the Center was changed from the Seattle Artificial Community Kidney Center to the Seattle Artificial Kidney Center and new articles of incorporation were signed on September 23, 1964.

On January 2, 1964, the Incorporating Trustees of the Seattle Community Artificial Kidney Center – Drs. Haviland, Burnell and Paton, Reverend Darrah, and Mr. Beaupre and Rosling (Mr. Nordstrom was absent) – met to discuss current operations of the Board, the medical director job description and candidates for that position, long-range planning, financial operations and fundraising. Plans were already underway to enlarge the Center using funding from the Division of Chronic Diseases of the U.S. Public Health Service and other support from Boeing Employees Good Neighbors Fund and from patients themselves. The Board approved this expansion under the direction of Dr. Murray, with grants to be held in the name of Swedish Hospital.

Acceptances to be a Trustee had been received from Renaldo Baggott, John A. Dare, Kenneth B. Colman, Myrtle Edwards, Dr. Jess B. Spielholz, Willis Campbell, Lawrence E. Karrer, M. L. Bean, Sr., and Ross Cunningham. Dr.

Charles Odegard and John Jewett had declined to serve. At the next meeting of the Incorporating Trustees on January 10th, Frank R. Kitchell had agreed to serve, and an invitation was sent to H. Sedge Thomson of the University of Washington.

The property title from the PHS grant was vested in Swedish Hospital and if transferred the hospital would have to refund support unless prior approval was obtained. The Hartford Foundation would require the recipient to have tax-exempt status and the Center would not qualify for this for a year unless the IRS would grant a tentative exemption. The problem of the rights of occupancy of Pacific Northwest Research Foundation space and the part of Eklind Hall that had been remodeled by the Center would be investigated. Eight to ten patients who would meet medical criteria and would die in the next six months were known to the Medical Advisory Committee, but the Board could not commit space at the time.

The Incorporating Trustees met again on January 24th and issued an invitation to James Sullivan of the Electrical Workers Union; acceptance had been received from H. Sedge Thomson. The full Board was to be invited to the annual meeting, members whose term expired in February 1964 would be re-elected, and no new members elected until 1965. Mr. Rosling suggested that at the annual meeting a motion be made to change the name of the organization to the Seattle Community Artificial Kidney Center from the Seattle Artificial Community Kidney Center. This would mean filing amended articles of incorporation. In addition, the feasibility of obtaining a waiver of the one-year existence for tax exemption would be investigated.

The Incorporating Trustees met on February 14th. The Board was now complete with acceptances from James Sullivan, Leonard Hitchman from the National Kidney Disease Foundation and Fred Huleen from the Boeing Company. The committees appointed were as follows: Finance: Robert S. Beaupre, chairman, Mrs. Lowell Mickelwait, H. Sedge Thomson, Renaldo Baggott, Willis Campbell, Frank R. Kitchell and Elmer J. Nordstrom; Long-Range Planning: Dr. James M. Burnell, chairman, Reverend John B. Darrah, Kenneth B. Colman, Elmer J. Nordstrom; Publicity: to be appointed; Medical Advisory: Dr. James Burnell, chairman, Drs. Robert Erickson,

Emily Fergus, John Lindberg, Tate Mason, Jr., John McCormack, John Murray, Richard Paton, Jerry Pendras, Belding Scribner, Donald Sparkman, William Steenrod, Ben Uyeno and Robert Wright. Admissions and Policy: unchanged and anonymous.


## First Meeting of the Board of Trustees

The first annual meeting of the Board of Trustees was held at 7:30 pm on February 19, 1964 at 1102 Columbia Street. The trustees and their terms of office were introduced. Individuals and their terms expiring at the 1965 annual meeting were: Mr. Bean, Cunningham, Huleen, Karrer, Kitchell, Sullivan and Thomson. Individuals and their terms expiring at the 1966 annual meeting: Drs. Haviland, Burnell and Paton, Reverend Darrah, and Mr. Beaupre, Rosling and Nordstrom. Individuals and their terms expiring at the 1967 annual meeting: Mr. Baggott, Campbell, Colman, Dare, Hitchman, Mrs. Edwards and Dr. Spielholz.

The Board membership, membership of the Executive Committee and the Medical Advisory and Admissions and Policy Committees were approved. A motion was passed to change the organization's name from the Seattle Artificial Community Kidney Center to the Seattle Artificial Kidney Center. The history of the Center was recounted and its operations described, followed by a tour of the facility. Problems for the future and responsibilities of the Trustees were outlined, followed by a question and answer period with extended discussion of the many problems confronting the Center with special consideration of the problems posed by the need for continuing financing.

Later, a publicity policy committee was formed with John Dare, Ross Cunningham and the medical director as members.


## New Committees Discuss Center Financing

At the February 28th Executive Committee meeting, Dr. Burnell felt the Long-Range Planning Committee needed direction from the Finance

Committee. Mr. Beaupre, chairman of the Finance Committee, provided information that with 30 patients the current fiscal year (July 1, 1963 to June 30, 1964) would show a surplus of $2,324, but that over the next three fiscal years the annual deficit would be $35,228, $69,825 and $129,000 respectively. He enquired about the use of Hartford Foundation research funds for the expected deficits in patient costs but Dr. Haviland pointed out this would only help temporarily and the question of continuing financing would not be solved. It was reasonable to obtain financial evaluations of the present patients with the expectation of defraying costs where feasible. The committee agreed to inform the KCMS Board of Trustees of the present status of the Center and to send them copies of the articles of incorporation, the bylaws and reports of the meetings of the Center's Executive Committee.

The Finance Committee had held its first meeting during March and had concurred with the Executive Committee's action to proceed with the building program and an annual budget of about $300,000. Elmer Nordstrom had been assigned to work with Swedish hospital staff to determine the ability of existing patients to contribute to the cost of their care, Willis Campbell was investigating the possibility of the Seattle Foundation providing funding for a business manager to plan community fundraising, Renaldo Baggott would investigate the availability of funds from private health insurance, Frank Kitchell would investigate funds available for patient care through governmental agencies, particularly the state of Washington, Sedge Thomson would investigate possible candidates and salary for the business manager position and Robert Beaupre would investigate the feasibility of a community-wide fundraising campaign.

At the May 8th Executive Committee meeting, Dr. Haviland reported he had discussed funding with a representative of the U.S. Public Health Service but, due to their restrictions, grant funds were budgeted quarterly rather than annually. The Center faced a deficit of about $2,000 a month from July 1st. The Finance Committee reported the Seattle Foundation did not have funds for hiring a business manager. Mr. Beaupre had talked to the Cumerford Foundation, a professional fundraising firm, about a feasibility study of community-wide fundraising for the Center, but such a survey would cost $3,000. Mr. Baggott had contacted an association of major life insurance company presidents in New York and they were surveying the insurance field and studying the possibility of it contributing funds but presently no major insurance carrier had a policy providing continuing benefits for kidney patients. He was also in contact with a local insurance association about the feasibility of a policy written specifically for this. Dr. Burnell added that Scrib had $8,000 promised that he might contribute to hiring a business manager provided the individual would spend half his time statewide developing support for the Pacific Northwest Division of the National Kidney Disease Foundation. Dr. Haviland summarized that no easy funds were in sight. The question remained which was the greater need, a fundraising survey or hiring a business manager?

Dr. Burnell reported that the Long-Range Planning Committee recommended that some of the beds be made available on a fee-for-service basis. A reasonable cost would be $10,000 for capital expenditure and $800 monthly, to decline as costs declined. Dr. Lobb from Swedish Hospital felt this would be inconsistent with the thought of continuing community support and that a proposed fund drive for Swedish Hospital would be attractive because the Center was seen as a part of it.

The Finance Committee was waiting for a proposed budget from the Long-Range Planning Committee after which they would be assigned to raise the necessary monies. There had been contact with a professional fundraiser, but as far as available funds there were no state funds, no insurance, nor any other source except through the community. Mr. Beaupre announced that Frank Kitchell would be taking over as chairman of the Finance Committee. Meanwhile the Long-Range Planning Committee would be meeting to draw up budget proposals for several alternatives for the Center through 1967.

## A Dilemma Concerning One Patient

The Medical Advisory Committee had considered a candidate, Mr. Chou Chen Yang, who would need dialysis shortly or a commitment for future care so that interim care being provided by University Hospital could be continued. Dr. Murray expressed concern about adding a patient unless the patient could meet the full cost of treatment but this patient did not meet the medical criteria in terms of age nor his size. It was suggested that for the next four or five patients the Center should be open on the basis not only of medical, social and geographic criteria, but also financial ability to pay costs ($10,000 plus $800 per month). Some felt adding a financial stipulation was contrary to the basic concept of the Center but others felt total patient welfare was more important. Dr. Lobb thought they were not facing up to the problem and this should be resolved now while a tenth patient still could be added rather than later. Dr. McCormack felt the Medical Advisory Committee should be directed to consider all candidates, regardless of financial standing, and suitable candidates should be forwarded to the Admissions Advisory Committee for a decision. The committee voted to refer this particular patient to the Admissions Advisory Committee for consideration on medical, social, geographic and economic criteria, stipulating that this was not optimal but in a sense desirable because of the patient's possible financial help to the Center.

The Executive Committee met again on May 15th to reconsider this patient. The Medical Advisory Committee had approved the patient by six votes to three and he had been accepted by a unanimous vote of the Admissions Advisory Committee. Mr. Yang had served in the Chinese diplomatic corps in the 1930s and 1940s, emigrating to the U.S. at the time of the Chinese revolution, and had developed a national reputation for his artistic photography. However, a problem had arisen: Mr. Yang felt he was not in a position to pay $10,000 up front, but wished to have it build up through his monthly payments. Dr. Haviland said that although the Board did not want to find itself in a position of extortion, it needed to be recognized that Mr. Yang would only be taken on the basis of full pay as the Center was not in a fiscal position to accept anyone who did not absorb the full cost. Mr. Victor Lawrence, Mr. Yang's attorney, had requested that he and Mr. Yang appear before the Executive Committee to discuss financial arrangements. Dr. Haviland felt this was appropriate in the circumstances, but that steps must be taken to avoid a like situation in the future. It was agreed the issue should be worked out by the proposed business manager and the medical director.

Mr. Rosling indicated that the Admissions Advisory Committee probably would not have approved Mr. Yang if the Medical Advisory Committee had not first considered the financial needs of the Center and the patient's ability to pay, but Dr. McCormack reported that Mr. Yang was given consideration from a medical standpoint and that was the most important factor in the decision of the Medical Advisory Committee. The committee had asked that the standards for admission be re-evaluated as there were four or five individuals presently who came close to meeting the "ideal candidate" criteria but could not satisfy the financial responsibility and so had not been presented. He asked that another meeting of the Medical Advisory Committee be held to evaluate these candidates. The opinion of the Executive Committee was that in future, although financing would have to be considered, the Medical Advisory Committee should not have to be concerned over this.

Mr. Yang and Mr. Lawrence then entered the room and were introduced to the committee. They were advised that concern had been expressed about the addition of one more patient with the present facilities, that the Center was not in a position to increase its deficit, and that Mr. Yang had been considered in the belief that he was in a position not to add to this. Mr. Yang then talked at length about his financial position. He had been unaware there would be a financial burden as Dr. Scribner had told him earlier that he would be accepted in the program as an ideal candidate. Later he had asked Dr. Scribner exactly what the financial conditions were and was told that care would cost about $8,000 a year and it was not until four days before this meeting that he was made aware of the expected $10,000 down payment. He had been prepared to make monthly contributions for his care and now, recognizing the need for capital participation, he therefore proposed annual payments of $1,000 in addition to the $800 monthly charges. Mr. Rosling proposed obligating Mr. Yang's life insurance policy to cover the $10,000. Mr. Yang and Mr. Lawrence were then excused.

The Committee then agreed to accept $800 monthly for operating expenses and $10,000 to be paid at the rate of $1,000 yearly to be secured by assignment of Mr. Yang's insurance policy. They also agreed that the note would not be cancelled in the event of his death prior to the end of the ten-year commitment. An agreement would be worked out with Mr. Yang's attorney.

Mr. Yang was the only patient ever to appear in person before the Executive Committee to discuss its finances and request for acceptance as a patient.

## More About Center Finances

It was decided to open a separate interest-bearing savings account for monies from Mr. Yang and others in the future, noting that the Center's application to the IRS for such contributions to be tax-deductible was still pending. Mr. Kitchell reported the Long-Range Planning Committee had met with Dr. Spielholz concerning funding from the state's Department of Health and he had said he would amend the department's budget to provide support for the Center and the Spokane Artificial Kidney Center at Sacred Heart Hospital but would need requests from both institutions within a week's time. Discussion of the amount to be requested followed. As it was estimated the present patients could cover 25 percent of their care and treatment costs it was felt that $250,000 for the Seattle Center would be sufficient, although Dr. Spielholz could revise this figure if he needed to. Dr. Spielholz also suggested the Center propose a bill to the state legislature requesting a special appropriation for patient treatment. This was agreed to and Mr. Guernsey was asked to draw up the proposed bill. The Board and other interested persons would introduce this bill to the community and legislators in advance of the January legislative session. The Committee agreed to follow up on both of Dr. Spielholz' suggestions and, in addition, a request had been made to the Seattle Foundation for $5,000 as supplemental salary for a business manager-fundraiser.

As the expanded Center was already running more efficiently than expected, Dr. Pendras felt another patient could be added. He also proposed that full-pay patients be asked to make a capital investment rather than specifying a particular figure. It was agreed that if this procedure was approved the patient's attorney and the Center's attorney should meet to discuss a patient's financial position before consideration of the patient by the Admissions Advisory Committee

At the October 16th meeting there was discussion of the importance of stating costs per month or per year rather than per dialysis. It was decided that because many patients initially started on once a week dialysis before moving to twice a week, first-year costs would not exceed $10,000; after that the patient would pay $10,000 per year. Also the Center would accept capital contributions of any specific amount. Mr. Kitchell reported the Finance Committee wished again to consider the Cumerford Foundation to raise funds for the Center. Their costs for a preliminary survey were still $3,000, but there would be substantial other funds required for them to actually fundraise. The Committee decided to engage the Foundation using Dr. Scribner's funds and the funds requested from the Seattle Foundation, but it was still hoped that a business manager-fundraiser could be found for the Center.

## A HOPED-FOR DÉTENTE

In an effort to establish a better working relationship between the University and the Center, Dr. Haviland, Reverend Darrah and Dr. Robertson had met Drs. Scribner and Murray four times since Dr. Murray had announced his resignation. However, Dr. Murray had met separately with Dr. Scribner and then talked with Dr. Haviland indicating he thought it would not be possible to resolve this issue. Since it was essential that the Center work harmoniously with the University and other similar organizations, Dr. Murray's resignation would be accepted. As to what would happen to funding and grants made to Swedish Hospital in Dr. Murray's name as principal investigator, Dr. Murray would stay on for perhaps two months so the granting agencies could be notified of his successor. As there was no contingency in the budget for an overlap with a new medical director, Dr. Scribner felt he would be able to cover the costs of this.

## A NEW MEDICAL DIRECTOR

Dr. McCormack had been appointed chairman of a committee of three physicians and two lay members to select a new medical director and the job description for the position had been reviewed and revised. The committee recommended Dr. Jerry Pendras be considered for the position. Discussion was ongoing about details as Dr. Pendras had expressed a desire to do some outside medical practice and had asked that Dr. Murray remain on the staff for a time to assist in working with the patients to help them accept the change. Salaries were discussed, and it was felt that Dr. Pendras should be full time at the Center, at least until the construction and remodeling was complete.

Dr. Pendras replaced Dr. Murray as medical director on August 1, 1964, and Dr. Murray left the Center shortly after this. Scrib had suggested someone else as medical director but the Center's patients expressed a strong interest in the decision because at that time all were followed medically by either the medical director or his assistant. They wrote to the Board pointing out that patient choice in selection of their physician was an important patient right and this no doubt influenced the selection of Dr. Pendras.

## EXPANSION OF THE CENTER

Dr. Pendras discussed the Center's financial position, noting that about $38,000 would be needed to operate the Center for next fiscal year with the patient load held at twelve. Mr. Harvey Swenson of the Sweden Freezer Company had offered to provide a device similar to the University's "Monster" (see Chapter 20) to serve 15 stations in the expanded Center and to use as a demonstration unit for other centers and this would be discussed by the Finance Committee. The new Center should be ready for occupancy by early September, but initially, as staff adjusted, efficiency would not be high. It should be ready to accept new patients in November, although that would be dependent on the amount of money raised.

## FINANCIAL ACCEPTABILITY OF PATIENTS

The Medical Advisory Committee recommended patients be placed under the care of the Center three to six months before starting on dialysis as this improved adjustment to dialysis. Home hemodialysis was just beginning at University Hospital and some patients at the Center might be transferred home in the future, allowing more patients to be treated. The committee asked the Executive Committee to authorize it to assess the potential for home dialysis for acceptance of patients in the future. It had voted to remove age criteria from the selection criteria and replace it with "physiologic" age.

The Executive Committee decided the Admissions Advisory Committee should make the final decision concerning financial acceptability of patients under consideration for acceptance.

At the September meeting it was agreed to assess the ability of existing patients to make financial contributions. As for fundraising, it was suggested that the state of Washington might be a possible source and efforts should be made to seek support through legislation. Dr. Spielholz of the state Department of Health should be contacted as this was the time state departments were preparing budgets for the next biennium. The possibility of a one-time request to the Seattle Foundation was also considered. The conclusion was reached that a business manager was needed, and fundraising should be his first responsibility. Such a position could work part-time for the Center and part-time for Dr. Scribner who had funds for support of such a position.

## HOME HEMODIALYSIS

The Medical Advisory Committee had been studying home hemodialysis and estimated that half the present Center patients could be changed to the home, the cost of which might be borne more readily by the patient. The Center would own the equipment and lease it to the patients. The cost of home dialysis was estimated as $2,500 a year, exclusive of equipment purchase and amortization, and three times a week dialysis would be better and give more opportunity for rehabilitation. As home dialysis could be considered research, funds for this might be available from the government or other groups financing research.

Dr. Pendras was asked to review the acceptance process as there was a need to develop an integrated selection program with the University. He also wanted to look further into the possibility of a "Monster," as the new center could readily be converted to use this and it would save money and personnel and so more patients could be accommodated.

Dr. Scribner had requested sufficient research funds from the Hartford Foundation for the home dialysis program at the University of Washington to support seven patients for three years. The Foundation was anxious there be no request for further funds for these patients at the end of the study and this would be discussed with the university. All patients admitted to the university's home dialysis program should meet the acceptance criteria for the Center, and it might be necessary to have backup space at the Center for the patients during the course of the study.

Patient credit reports on the twelve current patients showed that four could possibly pay in-full for their care, two could part pay, three could pay 20% of the cost and 3 could not pay at all. Based on this it was estimated that some $56,000 could be expected from the patients in the next year.

On November 27th, a meeting of the University of Washington Artificial Kidney Center Liaison Committee was held to discuss the proposed home hemodialysis research program and its implications for the Center. Dr. Scribner was planning on a total of seven patients over the next three years and admission to the program would be through the Center's process and committees. After completion of three years on the research program patients would become the responsibility of the Center for ongoing care and dialysis. The process would give an unusual privilege to the Center of control of the whole program. It was also agreed that once a patient was accepted into the home dialysis project he would remain permanently on home dialysis, barring major social or medical problems that might necessitate a change of modality. The three-year grant would allow Center staff to help the patient and family with future financial requirements. It was anticipated that the cost of ongoing home hemodialysis would be $4,000 a year. This meeting demonstrated that the two organizations could function as cooperating components of the same general community program.

## Patient Selection and Patient Costs

The proposed patient selection procedure resulting from discussion with the University of Washington also was discussed. The chairman of the Admissions Advisory Committee said that it should make the decision of which patient would better meet the economic, social, moral and ethical requirements when more than one patient was being considered for a position. The Long-Range Planning Committee reported on discussions on the working relationship with the university and that the Center felt all patients, including those on home dialysis, should meet the patient selection criteria. This posed some problems for the university.

## The U.S. Public Health Service

Meanwhile, the U.S. Public Health Service had $1,860,000 funds available for chronic disease research and in September 1964 provided its second dialysis treatment award to Downstate Medical Center in Brooklyn and Dr. Eli Friedman. The PHS was open to further applications for demonstration projects for treating kidney failure with the artificial kidney "in an operational setting in a community." The funds were only available for training, equipment, remodeling and renovation, and new construction, but in accordance with Federal policy could not be used to "finance direct care services to individuals."

## LEGAL ISSUES OF IMPORTANCE

The Center's attorneys reported on a number of issues that needed attention: the importance of setting up books that would enable tax reports to be filed and would help clarify corporate assets and the tax status of the employees; the question as to whether the Center needed a hospital license or not should be clarified; the need to establish a liability insurance program and a casualty insurance program as the Center developed assets; the relationship between the Center and Swedish Hospital would need clarification as would the Center's rights of occupancy of the premises, whether this was to be left on a month-to-month tenancy with or without rent, or whether there should be a long-term lease; the status of ownership of the equipment, inventory and supplies had to be decided and whether the Center wanted to own them; and a decision was needed as to what entity received the payments from patients. The Center was not covered by Swedish Hospital's liability and casualty policies and so had no coverage. This had to be dealt and so the situation would be further studied.

## A NEW POSITION: BUSINESS MANAGER-FUNDRAISER

Mr. Earl Rice, Jr. was interested in the position of Business Manager-Fundraiser and an interested medical social worker, Elizabeth Robinson, had contacted Drs. Haviland and Pendras about a part-time position to help patients with their social and financial problems.

## PUBLIC INFORMATION POLICY

A proposed Public Information Policy was discussed and approved. This made the medical director and the president of the Board of Trustees the principal spokesmen for the organization. It was also planned to develop an "information" brochure to be available to visitors.

## BOARD CHANGES DURING THE YEAR

At the March Executive Committee meeting Dr. Paton, who represented the Medical Advisory Committee on the Executive Committee, resigned for personal reasons and Dr. McCormack was appointed and approved as its new representative. At the June Executive Committee meeting Dr. McCormack was appointed secretary in place of Dr. Paton who had resigned earlier.

## DR. SCRIBNER'S PRESIDENTIAL ADDRESS, 1964

Dr. Scribner was president of the American Society for Artificial Internal Organs in 1964 and titled his presidential address, "Ethical Problems of Using Artificial Organs to Sustain Human Life." He explained some of the moral and ethical problems that had come up in connection with the use of the artificial kidney to rehabilitate persons who would otherwise die of end-stage kidney disease. He believed that there were five specific problems that would recur again and again as new, complicated, expensive, life-saving techniques were developed.

The first and in many ways easiest problem was the matter of patient selection. Some believed there was no need for selection, but in 1964 in the United States there were no more than 50 to 100 patients alive on kidney transplants or chronic dialysis, yet in the last four years since these techniques became available 10,000 or more ideal candidates had died for lack of treatment. Obviously rigid selection of one sort or another must have taken place. Data collected in England and Wales during 1962 showed that in the ideal age range of 15 to 49 there were about 25 deaths per million population per year, so about 5,000 a year in the United States. Consequently, the problem of selection was going to become more and more serious over the next few years. Because of the costs involved, the program in Seattle had been preparing to train its first patient in the technique of hemodialysis carried out in the home by the patient and the patient's family. If successful, the cost of treatment would be reduced considerably and selection might become "natural" rather than arbitrary; in other words, those who can learn to treat themselves would survive and those who could not would die. He did not want to discuss the question of how selection should be carried out as a group of dedicated and knowledgeable theologians, lawyers, psychologists and physicians had spent two days at a workshop the previous year deliberating on this subject.

The second issue, a much tougher and more unpleasant problem, overt termination of treatment, was so unpleasant a subject that many physicians would rather not even mention it. However, when dealing with an expensive treatment to sustain life by means of artificial organs, the question will ultimately arise. For example, if one of the Seattle patients suffered a severe stroke and had to be brought on a stretcher to the Center every week in a coma showing no signs of improvement, few in the audience would criticize the decision to stop hemodialysis. The problem was where to draw the line, what criteria to use and to whom should we turn to make such a difficult life-and-death decision. So far in Seattle this problem had not had to be faced but would almost certainly have to be in the future.

The third issue was the problem of the patient himself overtly terminating treatment, in other words, a form of suicide. To date, suicide had not so far been a problem in chronic dialysis, despite the ease with which it could be accomplished by a patient wearing an arteriovenous shunt. To his knowledge, there had been only two suicide attempts in the entire world-experience to date. If one examined the psychology of suicide, one would have predicted the suicide rate among patients on chronic dialysis would be extremely low. Studies had shown repeatedly that among persons whose lives were threatened by external factors, such as disease, famine or war, the suicide rate was extremely low and the greater the threat, the lower the rate. If this proved correct, then as the quality, security and safety of chronic hemodialysis improved and the threat to life from treatment failure became less and less, the suicide rate among patients might gradually increase – a paradox!

The fourth and probably toughest problem raised by development of a new treatment like chronic dialysis involved the question of "death with dignity," a question often raised in the early days by those who believed prolonging life by chronic hemodialysis was a fate worse than death. Actually the opposite problem existed because dialysis could be used to permit every uremic patient to die a most dignified death instead of dying the slow death that characterized terminal uremia. It would be more humane and less expensive to offer such a dying patient weekly hemodialysis for a limited period so he could live a relatively normal life right up to the end and die quickly without prolonged suffering. Such a maneuver, which would avoid much of the suffering and expense that characterized natural death from uremia, would be utterly impossible under existing moral, ethical and religious guidelines. He did not know what should be done about this.

The fifth and final problem was the question of donor selection for organ transplantation. On this subject he was speaking as a patient as well as a physician because he was looking at the audience through donated corneas and felt a personal debt to a society that permitted the development of eye banks and willed eyes, which made donation of corneas possible. The problem with donating other organs was greatly complicated by the fact that storage for most organs was difficult if not impossible at this time. Hence donation prior to the moment of death becomes a real consideration and introduces ethical, legal and religious complications. For example, in the state of Washington, it was illegal to obtain an autopsy permit prior to death and as a result the state's first kidney donor's husband and minister were forced to stand by her bed for 11 hours watching as the last spark of life ebbed away. When death finally came the kidney to have been to be donated had been severely damaged by the terminal events. Personally he thought the ethics of organ donation required further discussion. He felt ethical and legal guidelines should be devised to permit him and others to volunteer to donate one of their kidneys while they were well or when they had a fatal disease. He would like to be able to put in his will a paragraph urging that when his physician felt the end was near he would be put to sleep and any useful organs taken prior to death.

He felt the ASAIO was the one scientific organization that was uniquely qualified to attempt to solve some of these problems. The society was unique because its goal was the creation of the artificial organs that had created these problems in the first place. Its broad membership represented that segment of the scientific community that should be most concerned with the consequences of progress in the field of sustaining human life by artificial means. To those who argued that scientists should have no concern for the effect of their discoveries on society, he answered that scientists too were members of society and as such had an obligation to consider these concerns. He urged the membership of the ASAIO to take positive action to develop a code of ethics, a modern Hippocratic Oath, to guide in the use of artificial organs to sustain human life. He intended to appoint a special ad hoc committee on ethics to study these recommendations and take any course of action deemed necessary. He would like to see such a committee contact the appropriate groups in the fields of law, theology and philosophy and explore the possibility of a joint effort to find solutions to these vexing and urgent problems.

In closing, he noted that in the age of overpopulation, atomic war, space travel and artificial organs, it was becoming increasingly clear that moral and ethical guidelines handed down over the centuries were becoming more and more inadequate to govern our behavior. We often forget how morals and ethics were largely developed by societies that believed the earth was flat and the sun rotated around it. More in terms of technological advances, life control, death control, communication, etc., had occurred in the last hundred years than in all of prior recorded time. Consequently a new code of ethics was needed if we were to avoid destroying our population.

He had come across one idea recently which might prove helpful in the future. It was expressed by Sir Julian Huxley at a 1963 conference held in London on "Man and his Future." The essence of Sir Julian's advice was as follows: "Whatever we do, whatever we decide, let us temper our decisions with the thought that our overriding goal is that men will still be living on this planet with its natural resources intact 100,000 years from now."

## THE 1964 ANNUAL MEETING OF THE ASAIO

The 10th annual meeting of the ASAIO was held in Chicago in April 1964. The program included six papers from the University of Washington and two from the Seattle Artificial Kidney Center.

Doctors Babb and Grimsrud from the College of Engineering at the University of Washington described improvements in the membrane support in a dialyzer in order to control blood channel height to obtain maximum mass transfer rate while avoiding channeling effects. Using a nickel foam support and a dialyzer constructed for laboratory studies, they found that the total resistance to mass transfer was significantly reduced compared with the Kiil dialyzer and that blood and dialysate mass transfer resistances varied with dialyzer length. Their aim was to develop methods to predict dialyzer performance.

Doctors Lindholm and Murray from the Center described a method for regional heparinization during hemodialysis. Using a simple protamine titration test requiring no more than three ml of the patient's blood, they developed a formula to indicate the proper heparin and protamine dosages required by the patient. This made regional heparinization quite predictable, safe and easy.

Mr. Fry and Miss Hoover from Scribner's program described a system of single pass dialysate flow for the Seattle pumpless hemodialysis system. This used 37° C dialysate from a central tank, which was discarded after a single pass through the dialyzer. This technology was superior to recycling dialysate because of increased efficiency, improved bacteriology, and elimination of the need for a blood rewarmer. Single pass technique was a first step in development of a centralized dialysate fluid supply system.

Doctors Grimsrud and Babb had developed a mathematical analysis to optimize dialyzer design. They showed that for a dialyzer with a constant blood volume, mass transfer rate increased as dialyzer length decreased. In other words, a short multi-layer dialyzer is more effective than a long single-layer dialyzer. When the length of a dialyzer is known its mathematical formula would find the one distinct blood channel height to give maximum mass transfer. They also showed that mass transfer rate was essentially independent of dialysate flow rate if the dialysis flow rate was kept above a certain minimum critical value, which was generally about three to four times the blood flow rate.

Dr. Grimsrud, Mr. Cole, Mr. Lehmann, Dr. Babb and Dr. Scribner described a central system for the continuous preparation and distribution of hemodialysis fluid to a number of dialysis stations. The paper described in detail the apparatus developed for the University of Washington dialysis program that became known as the "Monster" (and is described in a previous chapter).

Doctors Mion, Hegstrom, Boen and Scribner described the substitution of sodium acetate for sodium bicarbonate in dialysate. The first "Monster" developed at the University of Washington required a third proportioning pump for bicarbonate since concentrated bicarbonate solution could not be mixed with the other concentrated salts, particularly calcium and magnesium. This pump could be eliminated and a single concentrate used if a soluble organic ion such as lactate or acetate could be used in place of bicarbonate in the dialysate fluid. They showed that substitution of acetate in concentrations of 35–40 mEq/L for bicarbonate in dialysate was effective in correcting the acidosis of both chronic or acute kidney failure. Using acetate to replace bicarbonate in dialysate made it possible to make a single concentrated salt solution for use in a centralized dialysis fluid supply system, thereby eliminating the need for a separate pump for bicarbonate concentrate.

Doctors Murray, Pendras, Lindholm and Erickson reported on 25 months experience at the Seattle Artificial Kidney Center. Eleven patients currently were being treated twice weekly for 10-16 hours and nine of the eleven were rehabilitated. Two were considerably disabled with peripheral neuropathy. So far in 15.33 patient years of treatment, no patient had died after starting in the program. Blood pressure control, transfusion requirements and serum chemical variations before or after dialysis were appropriate. Silastic-Teflon cannulas were used and the average cannula life was 11.4 months for both artery and vein. A standard declotting kit was used for clotted cannulas, and cannula infections were due to staphylococci and responded to vancomycin or methicillin. They also reported on their use of dialysate tanks placed in an adjoining room about 50 feet from the patient area and showed that hemodialysis using warm 40° C dialysate was more efficient than pumpless, low-temperature hemodialysis as it allowed elimination of 15 feet of blood tubing previously need for rewarming blood in the low-temperature system. This reduced resistance in the extracorporeal circuit resulting in a significant 15% increase in blood flow in the warm circuit over that in cold system.

Doctors Eschbach, Hutchings, Burnell, and Scribner and Mr. Meston reported on a technique for repetitive and long-term human cross circulation. This had been done in two pairs of patients in order to supply a normal organ via cross circulation to an individual suspected of having a reversible organ failure. One patient with hepatic coma was cured by this means, allowing time for liver regeneration to occur. The second patient with agranulocytosis showed no marrow regeneration despite provision of leukocytes via cross circulation and it was hoped that immunological tolerance might be achieved in the uremic partner. They described the technique in detail but noted that much more experience would be required.

Doctors Boen, Mion, Curtis and Mr. Shilipetar described long-term peritoneal dialysis using repeated puncture and an automatic cycling machine in two patients treated for nine and eleven months respectively. They described the technique of repeated puncture for access to the peritoneum that reduced the frequency of infection and the automatic cycling machine developed at the University of Washington. One patient previously described at the 1962 ASAIO meeting survived for nine months on dialysis but after four months had repeated infections resulting in adhesions. The second patient was a 28-year-old married woman started on peritoneal dialysis in November 1962. She had had one episode of peritonitis treated successfully with tetracycline, and after 11 months of once-weekly peritoneal dialysis was in good condition, completely rehabilitated, and enjoying a normal life on six out of the seven days of the week. They felt that the approach they had used promised the opportunity for long-term success with intermittent peritoneal dialysis.

## NATIONAL INSTITUTES OF HEALTH CONFERENCE ON HEMODIALYSIS AND THE UNIVERSITY OF WASHINGTON WORKING CONFERENCE ON CHRONIC DIALYSIS

On November 9 and 10, 1964, the National Institutes of Health held a conference on hemodialysis. The aim of the conference was in order to elucidate the technical aspects of hemodialysis in which improvements in efficient and satisfactory hemodialysis equipment and techniques could be discussed. The meeting had been organized by the NIH and by Dr. George Schreiner of Georgetown University and was by invitation only. The only person invited to attend from Seattle was Mr. Lars Grimsrud, an engineer who worked closely with Professor Babb at the University of Washington School of Engineering and with the Division of Nephrology at University Hospital. Subjects discussed included dialyzing membranes, basic design of the dialyzer, bath fluid and fluid circulation, perfusion of the dialyzer, physiological limits to dialysis, dialyzing center design, and novel and different approaches. The proceedings of the meeting show that most of the discussions related to technical developments in hemodialysis.

Dr. Scribner was incensed, feeling that the University of Washington dialysis program was being deliberately snubbed. Consequently, he developed a working conference on chronic dialysis that was held at the University of Washington, December 3-5, 1964, and sponsored by the Seattle Artificial Kidney Center, the Spokane and Inland Empire Artificial Kidney Center, the Puget Sound Chapter of the National Kidney Disease Foundation, and the University of Washington Division of Nephrology. There were many more participants then there had been at the NIH conference and most of Dr. Scribner's Division of Nephology was there, including renal fellows and ex-renal fellows, and dialysis nurses and technicians. The other participants were primarily those involved in clinical programs of dialysis throughout the United States. The topics discussed were cannula problems, hemodialysis technique, experience to date with home hemodialysis, conservative or predialysis management of chronic uremia, the role of peritoneal dialysis in chronic renal failure, the medical problems associated with chronic dialysis, other applications of cannula technique, interrelationships between chronic dialysis and transplantation, and the organization of the chronic hemodialysis center. The program covered experience in most of the dialysis programs in the United States. The discussion on home hemodialysis was particularly far-reaching and it was at this session that Dr. Stanley Shaldon from the Royal Free Hospital in London described the first use of home nocturnal hemodialysis in October 1964. For clinicians, this meeting was much more helpful than the NIH meeting. The proceedings were published by the University of Washington.

CHAPTER 24

# The New Center and the First
# Death at the Center 1964

─────────

THE NEW 10-BED UNIT OPENED in June 1964 and later that month Dr. Pendras reported that twelve patients were being treated. Of these, eight were rehabilitated to full-time employment and the others were partially rehabilitated in that they were ambulatory and capable of some employment but limited by peripheral neuropathy.

This unit had a machinery or "tank" room at the back so that individual dialysis machines no longer had to be at the patients' bedsides and the dialysate was pumped through the walls to the bed stations. Initially, dialysate was prepared in a separate tank for each station but this was soon replaced by the central proportioning system ("Monster') developed by the Sweden Freezer Company.

During 1962 a major technical improvement at the Center was replacement of the Skeggs-Leonards dialyzers with Kiil dialyzers. These were based on the one Scrib had brought back from Europe in 1961 and were being made by the Western Gear Company in Everett. The change was viewed as a miracle by the staff as the Kiil was so much easier to prepare than the Skeggs-Leonards dialyzer.

During 1962 a heated controversy developed between those in the west who used Kiil dialyzers and those in the east, particularly Kolff, who used coil dialyzers. Kiil proponents saw its advantages as low internal resistance so no blood pump was needed, although treatment took longer than with the more efficient coil dialyzers. Additionally, contained blood volume was less, blood was more easily and more completely returned to the patient at the end of treatment, and longer, slower dialysis meant patients had fewer problems recovering following dialysis. At a meeting where Scrib and Kolff argued the merits and disadvantages of the two dialyzers, Scrib offered to take one of Kolff's patients from the Cleveland Clinic to Seattle. The patient had deteriorated rapidly after starting dialysis and developed complications, including neuropathy, which in turn had led to drug dependence because of the analgesics prescribed for him. Kolff accepted the challenge and in January 1963 sent the patient, Mark Murdock, to Seattle.

Mark rapidly responded to intensive dialysis, medical treatment and social support and the results were described as "miraculous." When he had recovered he refused to return to Cleveland and so became a permanent patient of the Center. He met a woman who worked at the Pacific Northwest Research Foundation upstairs in Eklind Hall and they were married with many of the Center's staff and patients attending the ceremony. Thus it was ironic that as a result of a malfunction of the new Sweden Freezer Company's central proportioning system in April 1965 he was infused with a concentrated solution of sodium chloride and developed cerebral symptoms and a subarachnoid hemorrhage and died 24 hours later. Mark was the first of the Center's patients to die, some three and a quarter years after the Center opened and two and a quarter years after he moved to Seattle. He was also only the second of all Seattle patients to die, some five years after Clyde Shields' first dialysis.

As a result of this tragedy, design modifications were made in the equipment but later it was replaced by a central delivery system designed and manufactured by Frank Smith, an engineer, who had been one of the first patients treated at the Center when it opened. Frank went on to design two machines for dialysis of individual patients that he successfully marketed in the Midwest and eastern U.S. and in Holland. Unfortunately, he was a much better engineer than a salesman and his company failed, leaving him poor and unhappy. Nevertheless he lived for twelve tears on dialysis and was highly respected by the staff and the other patients.

## CHAPTER 25

# The Seattle Artificial Kidney Center and Reports from the ASAIO 1965

―――――――

NINETEEN SIXTY-FIVE WAS THE FOURTH year of operation of the Seattle Artificial Kidney Center and many issues that had been facing it since its opening continued. These included how to increase funding to continue treatment of existing patients and to start more patients on dialysis, and how to select patients for the funds available. At the same time a number of issues related to the internal operation of the Center and its external relationships had to be dealt with. All-in-all, 1965 was a busy year.

## THE SECOND ANNUAL MEETING OF THE BOARD OF TRUSTEES

The second annual meeting of the Center's Board of Trustees was held on February 17, 1965. M. L. Bean, Ross Cunningham, Fred Huleen, Lawrence E. Karrer, Frank R. Kitchell, James Sullivan and H. Sedge Thomson were re-elected to serve a three-year term as trustees. James W. Haviland, MD, was re-elected president, Edward M. Rosling was re-elected vice-president, Robert S. Beaupre was re-elected treasurer and John L. McCormack, MD, was re-elected secretary. The Executive Committee for the next year was designated as Renaldo Baggott, James M. Burnell, MD, Revered John A. Darrah, James W. Haviland, MD, Frank R. Kitchell, John L. McCormack, MD, and Elmer J. Nordstrom.

The following new staff members of the Seattle Artificial Kidney Center were introduced by Dr. Haviland: Jerry P. Pendras, MD, medical director, and Earl G Rice, business manager.

The president, Dr. Haviland, reviewed the developments and accomplishments of the past year. The Center had established closer liaison with the University of Washington in terms of a working agreement. The financial policies relating to patients had been discussed, including the present concept of "fully supported" patients. Present admission policies emphasized that the medical, ethical, sociological and financial aspects of each candidate be simultaneously evaluated with recommendations for final acceptance or rejection made by the Admissions Advisory Committee and the medical director. The current news media policy was also described. He thanked Swedish Hospital, Dr. Scribner and the Division of Nephrology at the University of Washington, the Seattle Foundation and the Sweden Freezer Corporation for their aid to the Center.

He also outlined the implications of the home dialysis program and the reaffirmation of the policy that the Center's program be confined completely to chronic dialysis.

Dr. Pendras reported that the Center had increased from a 4-bed to a 12-bed capacity during the past year and the patient load had increased from 11 to 17 patients. The efficiency of each dialysis had been increased by at least 100% as a result of the added efficiency of the staff and the use of a central dialysate unit. The projection was that expansion would allow a minimum of 36 patients to be cared for in the present facilities and the patient load was increasing at a rate of 2 patients a month.

Mr. Rice discussed the Center's finances and presented the working budget for the remainder of the fiscal year. The anticipated deficit was $20,359 but might change depending on the cost of supplies and possible added patient support. He also introduced the proposed budget for the fiscal year ending June 30, 1966, with an expected budget of $331,000, and described the anticipated revenue sources.

A spirited question and answer period followed. A motion to support with commendation the efforts and actions of the Executive Committee during the previous year was passed unanimously.

There followed a tour of the Center and refreshments.

## Revision of the Patient Admissions Procedures and Streamlining Patient Evaluation

In January, there was discussion about reactivating what was now known as the Admissions Advisory Committee and the need to integrate the whole admissions process. The acceptance of out-of-state patients had to be addressed, as well as what to do about patients who met the medical criteria but had little hope of acceptance because of other considerations such as finances, morals, useful citizen potential and so on. It was felt the Center should accept patients on a regional basis from Washington, Alaska, Idaho and Montana and probably Oregon. The Admissions Advisory Committee should consider the social and moral as well as the financial aspects of candidates, and should have the added function of evaluating other committees' findings regarding the applicant. They would summarize the findings and make a recommendation to the Executive Committee about the patient's acceptability. Mr. Rice was tasked to work out the integration of the financial evaluation into the admissions procedure so that no one admissions criterion appeared to be predominant.

There was need to keep the evaluation process of a prospective patient secret, and no information should be released to the patient until a final decision was made by the Executive Committee. The Medical Advisory Committee should recommend whether a patient was suitable for home or center dialysis and the candidate was then to be considered by the Admissions Advisory Committee for either home or center dialysis on the basis of financial condition, home situation and sociological aspects. Once a patient was committed to home dialysis, he or she had to stay on this treatment unless major changes of a medical or social nature developed. There was no University Hospital backup for these patients and the Center must provide them with backup services if needed.

Over the next month, the Admissions Advisory Committee discussed whether they needed to meet to discuss a medically acceptable patient when a space was available. However, it was agreed that as a mainly lay committee they should determine a prospective patient's moral, ethical and financial status for acceptability on the program. A complete financial evaluation with recommendations was now being given to the Admissions Advisory Committee as well as steps taken to acquire financial resources if funds were not readily available. There was discussion about the definition of "full pay" as this was not clear to outsiders and it was decided to change the term to "fully supported" as this allowed a more general meaning of how the patient's treatment was being supported and did not imply it was being paid solely by the patient.

The question of treating out-of-state patients had been raised again, but the committee reaffirmed that only patients from the five northwestern states were eligible for treatment at the Center. After discussion, it was agreed that when prospective patients were willing to completely move to Seattle in order to be considered for treatment, even though they would be taking a great risk in actually being accepted, they would have every right to be considered. Dr. Pendras was asked to work out the Center's future policy on considering out-of-state patient candidates.

The U.S. Public Health Service and Dr. Scribner wanted a letter to be sent to President Lyndon Johnson from the patients as a group. The purpose was to apply pressure where it could be more helpful in encouraging support for federally supported kidney centers. Dr. Scribner said that Shana Alexander of Life magazine would also get the letter published for extended publicity purposes. The committee agreed this letter might prove valuable and consented to it being sent.

In April, a question was raised whether the various patient selection processing committees were yet working satisfactorily together in obtaining the information necessary for considering the patient's acceptability. The most difficult part of the evaluation process was determining the financial status of a patient, particularly when there was a question of obtaining funds from the community in which the patient lived. Mrs. Robinson, the Center's part-time social worker, believed a patient's acceptability for treatment should be decided by the Admissions Advisory Committee before anything was done in the community to raise funds. The Executive Committee agreed that community contacts could be made by a Center representative when it appeared probable the particular prospective patient would be accepted for treatment. This approach would specifically state to these contacts that acceptance of the patient was likely and additional funds were needed from community resources. There was discussion about whether a financial commitment should be made when money from other persons or the community would be needed as part of the coverage of treatment costs but it was decided there was no way of knowing what amount of money could be raised in a given community and therefore financial commitments could not be made. A representative from the Center could be instrumental in organizing and offering guidance in community fundraising efforts but the family and friends of the patient would do the actual work. Communities such as Bainbridge Island and Vancouver, Washington, had indicated interest in helping the Center patients who lived in those areas and arrangements were being made to meet with them.

The Medical Advisory Committee had considered a change in the selection process to consider candidates in two categories: 1) a patient who was medically acceptable with no foreseeable complications; and 2) a patient medically acceptable with minor complications. The Admission Advisory Committee would not be expected to make any medical decisions. The Executive Committee approved these changes.

With regard to patient evaluation, it was decided in May that new referrals should go to Dr. Pendras to allow him to assess initial medical acceptability. Patients would then undergo psychological/psychiatric evaluation and financial-social study before referral to the Medical Advisory Committee for final medical acceptance. This would enable less frequent meetings of the committee and mean no time was wasted in initiating and completing the medical selection process. It was also felt that the Admissions Advisory Committee should consider whether a proposed patient could be rehabilitated to a near normal life and so patient psychological/psychiatric evaluations should include a statement of the potential for rehabilitation.

The Executive Committee at its June meeting discussed whether it should take specific action to finally approve each new patient. This would be more administratively correct and would spread responsibility from the other committees or any individual, and would ensure the Executive

Committee be properly informed of the Center's activities and problems. The committee also approved a statement about residence of future patients and that they must be domiciled in the five-state Northwest region for at least six months prior to submission of an application. The possibility of establishing satellite kidney centers was also discussed as the community of Longview might support such a project. This was to be discussed further.

In August, a patient had been approved by the Medical Advisory Committee whose socioeconomic position was doubtful. The Reverend Darrah, as a member of the Admissions Advisory Committee, thought that if there was a spot available, the committee would be inclined to accept any prospective patient. In order for the committee to vote for refusal, the reason would have to be very clearly stated in the patient's summary given to the committee. It was suggested that the referring doctor or a member of the medical staff attend the Admissions Advisory Committee meeting to give additional insight into the individual being considered. The moral impact of accepting this particular patient with a questionable social background and denying care to a later patient who filled all the requirements was discussed and it was pointed out that it was the Executive Committee that had the final say on acceptance or rejection.

In September, Dr. Haviland stated that the Admissions Advisory Committee had recently rejected a prospective patient on the basis of his being an unacceptable candidate for the program. This particular case had served the purpose of showing the function of the Admissions Advisory Committee in the selection process.

At the October meeting Dr. Pendras noted that a wealthy 65-year-old gentleman from the East Coast had indicated a desire to be treated in Seattle. The question was how this type of problem should be handled now and if it should occur in the future. The problem was that of an aged person from out of the five-state region requesting care with sufficient funds in his own rights to pay for treatment. Could this person be considered at all in view of his age being considerably above the present upper age limit of 45 years, or could an exception be made if an agreement was made for the person to pay for his care as well as contribute toward the cost of care of other patients without funds? This could amount to a great deal of money. During discussion, the committee agreed that this additional money would be desirable in terms of the ability to care for and finance other patients and possibly help support some research. Some procedure should be developed to follow in reviewing future cases of this nature. The discussion would be continued.

At the December Executive Committee meeting the Medical Advisory Committee reported having considered a change in the selection process to consider candidates in two categories: 1) a patient who was medically acceptable with no foreseeable complications; and 2) a patient medically acceptable with minor complications. This classification would only differentiate the more medically acceptable candidates. The Admission Advisory Committee would not be expected to make any medical decisions. The Executive Committee approved this change.

## MEDICAL-RELATED ISSUES

### PATIENT CENSUS

At the beginning of 1965, the Center was treating 15 patients and had committed acceptances for two further patients and by March, 17 patients were being treated. In August, 19 patients were being treated, one of whom would be returning to Vancouver, British Columbia after a three-month temporary treatment in Seattle because of an infection. One other patient was ready to start dialysis in the near future and three more patients had been accepted who did not yet require dialysis. Also in August the second patient death since the SAKC opened occurred when Sydney Selden died of congestive heart failure. The third death occurred in October when Mrs. Lois Owen, a patient who had been in the program for three years, expired. By the end of the year there were 23 patients being treated in the Center.

TREATING ACUTE KIDNEY FAILURE

Early in the year, the question of providing dialysis for patients with acute kidney failure at the Center was raised but there was neither staff nor equipment for this and a policy was set forth stating that these services were not available at the Center itself. It was thought it might be possible to work out an arrangement with Swedish Hospital for them to provide acute dialysis in the hospital using management by Center staff but not at Center expense. This had led to a report on dialysis for acute kidney failure in Seattle. Some physicians would like an alternative to University Hospital to treat such patients, not because of problems of quality, but because personal care at University Hospital by private physicians was too limited. Another consideration was economic as it was estimated that no more than 60% of patients with acute renal failure pay the full cost of hemodialysis care. Tax dollars were used to subsidize the care of these patients at University Hospital as a function of the teaching institution and whether a private hospital or the Center would be willing to subsidize this form of treatment was unknown. Opinion was divided as to whether the Center should set up such a program but it was pointed out that Swedish Hospital was prepared to backup such a program with participation of Center staff. This topic would be discussed again at a later date.

HOME HEMODIALYSIS AND PERITONEAL DIALYSIS

In June, Scrib reported that the home hemodialysis program at University Hospital, fully supported by the Hartford Foundation grant, was now treating four patients and had funds to treat three more. In addition, further patients could be treated if fully funded from their own resources.

He also reported that Drs. Boen and Tenckhoff at the University were ready to do a trial on long-term use of peritoneal dialysis in the home and asked whether the Center would underwrite this as it had done for home hemodialysis so that funds could be requested from the U.S. Public Health Service for treatment of patients. He thought they might fund a five-year trial as the treatment was expected to cost only $2,000 to $3,000 per patient per year. The question was raised whether the PHS would pay toward the cost of hemodialysis for the patients should peritoneal dialysis fail for some reason. Drs. Haviland and Pendras would discuss further details concerning establishment of a peritoneal dialysis program with Dr. Scribner and report back later. Scrib also noted that he would be testifying before a U.S. Senate Committee about funds for research and for establishment of artificial kidney centers.

At the July Executive Committee meeting, Scrib passed out copies of the "Outline for the Expansion of the Home Peritoneal Dialysis Program." This would involve only two patients who were fully funded from their own resources. This would be discussed further by Drs. Haviland and Pendras and Mr. Rice and brought back to the committee at a later meeting. Scrib also suggested the possibility of having two hemodialysis centers in Seattle: one for patients whose physical condition was marked by complications, such as leg braces, osteodystrophy or other serious illness, the other for patients with no apparent complications from their disease. Another possibility might be the "swapping" of such patients between the Center and University Hospital – to refer a patient with medical complications to the University and transfer a patient in good condition to the Center for treatment. This too was to be discussed further.

Two months later Dr. Scribner told the Executive Committee that in his view a patient could be expected to stay on home hemodialysis indefinitely and that this was a permanent arrangement. This would be discussed further.


PROVIDER TRAINING

Discussions were underway with the University and the Veterans Administration about setting up a training program at the Center to educate physicians, nurses and technicians as new dialysis units were now being established elsewhere in the country. By August, Dr. William Robertson at University Hospital had written to Dr. Pendras suggesting how to make advance preparations so such a training program could be developed. It was expected that after the NBC television documentary aired (see below) considerable pressure might be expected from other communities to obtain trained personnel and so a training program would be necessary.

SATELLITE UNITS

In June, the possibility of establishing satellite kidney centers was discussed, as the community of Longview might be interested in such a project. Later, in the fall, Dr. Haviland reported he had spoken at the Montana-Wyoming regional meeting of the American College of Physicians and also to a group in Virginia concerning satellite centers and other aspects of dialysis treatment. Both groups were very receptive to the material presented and hoped to work with the SAKC to establish centers in their areas. Dr. Pendras had talked with the Yakima County Medical Society about establishment of a satellite center there as a patient from there had already been accepted by the Center and would soon need dialysis. At the December Executive Committee meeting there was further discussion about establishing satellite units including those proposed for Longview and Yakima. Plans were being made for the training program to send a nurse and technician from Seattle to train the necessary staff in community hospitals, and Dr. Pendras was working with the U.S. Public Health Service for possible grant support for such a training project.

Scrib described the difference between remote units like the several University of Washington home dialysis patients who lived out of state and satellite centers in Washington State that might be established and administered from the SAKC. Cost estimates per patient after a satellite unit had been equipped for use were $14,000 to $15,000 per year compared with remote (home) units at $3,000 to $4,000 per year. Two physicians were thinking of establishing a dialysis unit in an apartment in Seattle and it was felt they should discuss this with the Center. The future of peritoneal dialysis was also discussed but there was little interest in establishing a separate unit to provide this treatment.

## CENTER EXPANSION

Early in the year, Dr. Pendras reported that plans were under way to install a "Monster" at the Center. The two possibilities were one from Sweden Freezer and one made by patient Frank Smith who was an engineer. Dr. Pendras described the process of bidding for the devices. The objective was to compare their effectiveness. In August it was noted that the Center had to consider the legal aspects of the proposed specifications for letting of bids to manufacture a Monster as there had been some pressure locally related to who was going to manufacture the machine. The specifications would have to be written in a broad, objective manner. Consequently, Drs. Babb and Lars Grimsrud, who had developed the original "Monster" for University Hospital, had prepared specifications. Once these had been reviewed by legal counsel, bids would be requested. This machine would be essentially the same as the old Monster but with added safety devices to ensure foolproof operation. Approximate cost for building such a machine would be $30,000 to $40,000.

By September, the Center had 19 patients and two patients who had been accepted; other potential patients were being evaluated. If these individuals were also accepted there would not be space for further patients for three to six months as equipment and space would be limited until installation of the Monsters.

By December, Center staff had met with the bidders for this new central dialysate supply system. Following this, it had been considered advisable to expand the patient bed space from the present 12-bed capacity to 20 beds as the central system was to be designed to handle a maximum of 20 patients simultaneously. Consequently, additional bed space would need to be made available and this could be obtained by remodeling the "old" patient and lab areas. The operation would be more efficient treating 20 patients at a time utilizing the central system and staff would not necessarily have to be increased except for an additional nurse aide for managing the expanded area as it was located away from the present patient area. The cost for the bed space expansion had not been projected but would include a $600 to $700 investment in each patient station for equipment alone. However, individual stations could be equipped as they became needed and it would be necessary only to prepare the area with appropriate drainage and remote control systems to allow for connection to the central system. The cost of the central system was estimated as $35,000 to $45,000. Scrib said that University Hospital could loan extra tanks to the Center if necessary and/or they might be able to provide a holding action on some patients who were admitted to the program while construction was occurring. The committee approved expansion to 20 stations and a central dialysate system to serve them.

## HEPATITIS

The Center reported the first outbreak of hepatitis in a dialysis unit. Four patients had contracted the disease and there had been three outbreaks, two of which involved a staff member and one patient, and the third involved a staff member and two patients. In all cases onset was relatively acute with nausea, vomiting and lethargy, followed by jaundice in two cases and elevated serum glutamic oxaloacetic transaminase levels in all. Recovery occurred over eight weeks. As a result, a program of prophylactic gamma globulin administration had been started in all patients. Hepatitis was assumed to be the result of infection from blood transfusions, as at that time tests for the hepatitis B virus had not yet been developed. Shortly after this, a number of other units in the United States and Europe had outbreaks of hepatitis, some with deaths among both patients and staff.

## THE NBC DOCUMENTARY "WHO SHALL LIVE?"

In January, the Executive Committee was told that arrangements were being made for NBC to film a TV documentary at the Center starting on June 16. Mrs. Lucy Jarvis, producer of the documentary, had previously filmed portions of the ASAIO meeting and a congressional hearing concerning artificial kidney centers. In July she attended the Executive Committee meeting and reported that the filming had been virtually completed. She said that "the documentary would bring out that: 1) the program of artificial kidney treatment was definitely a successful and positive means of prolonging a person's life; 2) because the treatment program was so effective, there should be more centers around the country so that others might be treated; and 3) the "prohibitive" cost of treatment was less significant for a rehabilitated patient as compared to keeping a completely invalid person alive. Special mention was made that different dramatic devices would bring out the financial costs in a positive yet light manner. The committee asked that the documentary show there were centers in other parts of the country and not only in Seattle. The one-hour program entitled "Who Shall Live?" narrated by Edwin Newman was scheduled for a Sunday afternoon at the end of October or November 1965. In an interview years later Mrs. Jarvis said that President Johnson had asked for a copy of the program to view at the White House and that he had asked Congress to look at how to fund more dialysis centers.

## THE CENTER'S RELATIONSHIP WITH OTHER INSTITUTIONS

Dr. Kingsbury Curtis attended the August Executive Committee meeting to discuss the relationship between the Center and the proposed dialysis unit in the Seattle VA Hospital. The program had been passed by President Johnson's Executive Advisory Group and funding approval now was in the hands of the Bureau of the Budget. The plans for the Seattle VA program had been cleared by the VA's administration and it was expected the unit would open in about a year after approval from the Bureau of the Budget. Some funds had been received for a training program, but none so far for construction or equipment. Senator Magnuson (D-Washington) was being kept informed about the development of the program in the hope he could be of assistance in expediting the allocation.

The fact that a patient was a veteran was an advantage as he or she could be treated at the Center and transferred to the VA unit when it opened. It was decided that Dr. Curtis should be involved in meetings of the Medical Advisory Committee and that the Center should think in terms of 18 months financing for a holding operation for veterans approved for treatment by the Center and Dr. Curtis.

There was further discussion of the Center's relationship to Swedish Hospital and the Pacific Northwest Research Foundation (PNRF). Dr. Lobb pointed out that while the PNRF did not have a lease on the whole of Eklind Hall it had paid for the addition to the original building. This would all require clarification. Also, the ownership of assets other than the building was unclear and some of the assets had been purchased under grants. This too needed clarification in order to establish the corporate books and so clarify insurance coverage. The hospital insurance did not cover the Center's equipment.

## FINANCES

### INSURANCE COVERAGE FOR THE CENTER

At the January 8, 1965 Executive Committee meeting, Mr. Earl G. Rice, Jr., a retired Navy Supply Corps Commander and the Center's new business administrator-fundraiser, was introduced. He was the only one of several applicants remaining when they were told that there was no money for a salary and that the recipient of the post would have to raise the funds to pay his or her own salary. His responsibility was to raise funds to replace the soon-to-be terminated grant support and make the Center self-sustaining. It was also announced that Mrs. Elizabeth Robinson would be joining the staff as part-time medical social worker, primarily to help patients put together their "financial package." Money was advanced for both Mr. Rice and Mrs. Robinson's salaries by Dr. Haviland and several other board members from their own pockets.

As the Center still did not have liability insurance, Mr. Rice was asked to look into this, to speak to Swedish Hospital about temporary coverage and to obtain fire insurance as soon as possible.

University Hospital had agreed to the terms for the Center to take eventual responsibility for patients in the University's home hemodialysis project. There was need for the Center to set up an initial set of books for accounting. Mr. Rice had completed an inventory of equipment and supplies and would be asking for rates for fire, casualty and liability insurance.

At the next meeting in February, Mr. Rice was still receiving bids on insurance and it was suggested he contact board member Willis Campbell, president of the General Insurance Company, to give him the opportunity to bid. Mr. Rice was still working on a financial report but it appeared that the Center deficits would be less than anticipated. There were now a total of 15 patients and two more committed acceptances and all new patients had funds available to pay the full cost of treatment. Professional liability insurance had been purchased for the Center as an entity but not for individuals.

A question was asked whether the Center would become liable in the case of accidental deaths of Center patients if double indemnity insurance payment for accidental death was requested by the family. It was suggested this be discussed with John Soderberg through whom the Center received its insurance and/or Mr. Kitchell.

Mr. Rice stated that in the case of prospective patients where sufficient liquid financial resources were not available, some type of insurance or other adequate resources should be assigned to the Center. In connection with the establishment of a reserve fund during the period of treatment covered by the Hartford Foundation grant, a specific question was raised concerning major medical insurance coverage being drawn on now to apply to actual care at a later time. The committee felt that the involved insurance companies should be contacted regarding their attitude to this type of situation.

FUNDING BY THE STATE

The county and state medical associations had been contacted by Dr. Pendras about helping with the state legislature and Reverend Darrah had already brought some legislators through the Center and it appeared they were favorably impressed. It was planned to have more visit the Center during the coming legislative session. However, at the next meeting on January 22, it was learned that the item that would have supported kidney centers had been dropped from the state budget. There was hope that funding for the Seattle and Spokane kidney centers might be reinserted in the state budget.

By the March Executive Committee meeting the state had said it could not provide support but might be able to do so in the future. The state Division of Vocational Rehabilitation had said it might have sufficient funds in fiscal 1965-1966 to consider new programs and, as some of the current patients were rehabilitated, this route would be worth exploring. However, the possibility of funding through the state legislature still existed, and the state health department was still interested and enthusiastic for the Center to obtain funds through its budget or through the legislature.

Several representatives of the Center went to Olympia taking with them patient Mr. Chou Chen Yang. Mr. Yang had served during the 1930s and 1940s with the Chinese diplomatic corps and had immigrated to the U.S. following the Chinese revolution. Since then he had distinguished himself nationally by his artistic photography, a former hobby. (See chapter 23, A Dilemma concerning One Patient.) Several of the legislators later accused the Center of bringing this man before them to "plead for his life" and they felt "blackmailed" and remembered this for years. Nevertheless the issue was resolved with a $125,000 award for the biennium July 1965 through June 1967 for use by the Center in treating needy patients.

PATIENT FINANCING FOR DIALYSIS

There was discussion of the financial commitments that home dialysis patients would be asked to make to the Center and the University of Washington. The conclusion was this should be $5,000 a year for the three-year study period ($15,000), payable monthly and with the condition that the rate would change to that of the Center if in-center dialysis was later required. There was divided opinion whether the amount of money paid in should be returned to the family if the patient died before it was used for treatment, but it was concluded that the patient was only obligated to the Center or the University of Washington for treatment up to the date of death.

A new patient who started dialysis on January 1 had made an arrange-ment with the Aetna Insurance Company to pay up to $24,000 for her care. This was the first time a major private insurance company had agreed to support dialysis.

In April the chief topic of discussion again was patient finances. The Executive Committee had concluded previously that home dialysis patients should make commitments to the Center to pay $15,000 over a three-year period to assure continued treatment, as well as to apply toward the cost of care, after the three-year Hartford Foundation grant ran out. Also, that the amount of money paid into the Center by the family would be returned at the patient's death after paying costs of care that might be due at that time.

## THE CENTER'S DEFICIT
In July Mr. Rice reported that the deficit for the fiscal year ending June 30, 1965, was $14,736.60.

## FUNDRAISING EFFORTS
The Finance Committee recommended that a fund drive be held in November 1965 as that would give time for it to be organized and would coincide more or less with airing of the NBC documentary. The local chap-ter of the National Kidney Disease Foundation had offered to help with a fund drive. The deficit expected by June 30 was still likely to be $20,000 and a bank loan might become necessary. There was discussion about whether patients from outside the Northwest who were willing to move to Washington might be considered for the Center; this was to be considered further. Discussion had also begun about whether patients who had to be held at the University before starting at the Center might be treated by peritoneal dialysis at the Center. There had been an unexpected bill for a further $8,000 for construction costs and this would be investigated.

Mr. Walter Schoenfeld was introduced as chairman of the fundraising campaign at the September Executive Committee meeting. He would be assisted by Monty Bean and Marvin Burke and by Mrs. Marjorie Lynch, Washington State representative from Yakima, who would serve as vice chairman. Governor Dan Evans would be asked to be honorary chairman and would probably participate in the Center's dedication. Senators Jackson and Magnuson had also indicated interest in participation.

Mr. Schoenfeld said that rather than a specific amount the target should be $10,000 per patient per year and with the "sky as the limit." The drive would be statewide to include the Inland Empire Artificial Kidney Center in Spokane. Mr. Rice had talked to Dr. Marr concerning its participation because the Spokane Center treated patients from Walla Walla and the Spokane areas and it was agreed that the Spokane center would receive contributions from these areas. This limitation would be for one year only. Headquarters for the drive would be in Seattle.

A follow-up meeting was devoted to discussions about the fund drive, review of the brochure that would be used and the Center's dedication. Several politicians including Vice-President Hubert Humphrey would be invited to the latter. Governor Evans had agreed to be honorary chairman for the fund drive which would begin on November 15. Plans were for the Center dedication to be held on November 8 and Senator Warren Magnuson had been asked to speak. It was also noted that Representative Brock Adams and Senator Magnuson were working on bills to allocate federal funds for artificial kidney centers.

By December, the fund drive had brought in $183,000 and would be extended until January 15, 1966. A suggestion had been made that a Women's Auxiliary might be established for the center.

## THE CENTER AS A RESEARCH PROGRAM

The question was raised whether the Center could be considered a research program as the current grant supporting the Center as such would be phased out completely as of July 1, 1966. It was suggested that if the program was still considered research, $45 million might be appropriated to continue operation for such purposes. Consensus was that the Center was performing clinical research on patient care in its operation.

# THE 1965 ANNUAL MEETING OF THE ASAIO

At the annual meeting in Atlantic City there were six reports on research from Seattle.

From the University of Washington, Dr. Curtis, Jack Cole, Barbara Fellows, Larry Tyler and Dr. Scribner reported on the first two patients treated by home hemodialysis in Seattle, one using the University of Washington "Mini-Monster" and the other using a prototype tank system made for home hemodialysis by the Sweden Freezer Company.

Drs. Boen and Tenckhoff recounted the first experience with peritoneal dialysis in the home.

Jack Cole, John Fritzen, Joe Vizzo, Winifred van Paasschen and Lars Grimsrud reported on experience with the central dialysate supply system (the "Monster") at University Hospital.

Dr. Jim Albers, who had been the fifth Seattle patient and started dialysis in September 1961 at the time when he was completing his PhD thesis in physics, gave a paper describing the first use of electrical conductivity to measure in-vitro dialysis performance and its use for this purpose with the Kiil dialyzer. Interestingly, most of the audience had no idea that Jim was a dialysis patient.

Richard Bell, one of Dr. Babb's research fellows, reported on a mathematical model using an analog computer to simulate the patient-artificial kidney system using a two-pool model to examine removal of BUN and creatinine. His stimulation studies showed that more frequent hemodialysis lowered the average concentration of low molecular weight solutes and could be used to plan the optimization of dialysis treatments. This was the first theoretical indication of the advantage of more frequent hemodialysis.

Drs. Pendras and Erickson from the Seattle Artificial Kidney Center reported on sixteen chronic kidney disease patients treated by chronic hemodialysis. A central unit developed by the Sweden Freezer Company had been used for about 400 dialyses over three months during which time there had been two malfunctions. One was a mechanical problem that shut the machine down for 45 minutes but on another occasion a combination of a personnel failure and a design deficiency resulted in a patient death – only the second in Seattle since the beginning of chronic hemodialysis in 1960 and the first death at the Center (see next section). As a result, design modifications were made. They also described less frequent cases of peripheral neuropathy with earlier and more intensive dialysis, renal bone disease with pathologic fractures that appeared to respond to treatment with vitamin D, and gout and arthritis with metastatic calcifications that responded to colchicine and phosphate binders: Basaljel and/or Aludrox. Other complications included four cases of septic pulmonary emboli, three of which followed a declotting procedure. All responded to antibiotics, and careful alcohol prepping of the cannulas eradicated this problem. Patients were receiving an average of 2.4 units of blood a month and iron overload was becoming a problem.

CHAPTER 26

# SAKC Annual Board Meeting and Executive Committee Meetings; ASAIO Annual Meeting 1966

———

THIS WAS THE FIFTH YEAR of the Seattle Artificial Kidney Center and again the organization was slowly growing in the numbers of patients treated. From the medical side the most important issues remained discussion on the potential of a home hemodialysis program at the Center and where it might be situated and the expansion of the Center itself to allow the treatment of more patients. This expansion would require purchase of a new and expensive central system to distribute the dialysate to all the stations in the Center. On the financial side, in 1965, the state had provided funding to the centers in Seattle and Spokane for the first time and the 1965 fund drive had been quite successful. During the year, the Washington State congressional delegation had continued to press the Congress for legislation to support kidney disease treatment in the United States, and the Bureau of the Budget Committee that was to report on the situation nationally had visited Seattle and other programs.

## THE THIRD ANNUAL MEETING OF THE BOARD OF TRUSTEES

The meeting was held on February 16, 1966. The by-laws were amended to add six more positions to the board, bringing the total number of trustees to 27, and to add two new positions to the Executive Committee to make a total of nine members. The reasons for the changes were to ensure that no more than one third of the total trustees' terms of office would expire at any one time and that it would permit an increase in participation by additional persons. New trustees were Mrs. Alice Micklewait, Walter Schoenfeld and Drs. David P. Simpson and Richard R. Paton, and existing members reelected were Robert Beaupre, Reverend John Darrah, Dr. John McCormack, Edward Rosling and Elmer Nordstrom, and Drs. James Burnell and James Haviland. New Executive Committee members were Walter E. Schoenfeld, Monte L. Bean, Sr. and Willis L. Campbell, who joined Reverend Darrah, Drs. McCormack and Haviland, Lisle Guernsey, Renaldo Baggott and Elmer Nordstrom. The officers elected were: James Haviland MD, president; John McCormack MD, vice-president; Monte Bean, Sr., secretary; and Robert Beaupre, treasurer.

Dr. Pendras reported that in February 1965, 17 patients were being treated and that now, a year later, 23 patients were under care. During the past year, three patients had died and nine new patients were admitted to the program. Six additional patients had been approved and would be admitted for treatment when that was found to be necessary. The total capacity the Center could handle was 32, not 36 which had been reported previously because a few patients were now being treated three times weekly. During the past year 30 applications had been received and processed.

Earl Rice provided a review of the organization and its administration. He noted that Ross Cunningham, a trustee, was most instrumental in the Center's obtaining funds through the state legislature. From the total amount appropriated for the biennium, funds now would be requested for the second year in addition to the funds requested for the present year. Patients were now contributing toward the cost of care after studies were carried out and agreements made for patients to pay what they could.

Mr. Baggott gave the Finance Committee report and noted that the Center had now received the fund drive money and would use it during the year current year. Currently, $195,000 had been committed to the Center, including $112,300 received in cash, $54,800 in pledges payable during the current year, a value of $17,600 in different securities held by the Center and $3,000 that was given to the Center by the Seattle Foundation to start the fund drive. It was anticipated that the final figure would be close to

$250,000. The fund drive had been a success in that it showed interest had been raised in the community to support the Center. Walter Schoenfeld and Mr. Rice were commended for their work with the fund drive.

Dr. Burnell reported that the Long-Range Planning Committee had not met during 1965 as it was felt the committee could not be useful until funds were available to the Center. Most recently, the committee had met to discuss the home dialysis program and its future. Dr. Francis Wood from the university also was invited to discuss his thinking on the use of the Clinical Research Center (CRC) at University Hospital to do research on particular patients from the Center. Patients at the CRC would need to be exchanged with patients at the Center, and the problem of finances was yet to be resolved.

Dr. Scribner expressed the opinion that, in the future, home hemodialysis programs were probably the way to go and Dr. Burnell noted that the Long-Range Planning Committee was in agreement that the Center should be thinking about integrating the home dialysis program into the Center's program.

Scrib said Seattle had shown the nation that the general public could be aroused to help fund a program for treating kidney disease patients. Congressman John Fogarty, the leading figure concerned with health care issues in the U.S. House of Representatives, had visited Seattle, and on his return to Washington was working with Senator Henry Jackson and Congressman Brock Adams to prepare a bill for funds to allocate to dialysis centers. The SAKC would not benefit from the bill as written, which only supported new centers, but training funds might be appropriated.


## Problem with the National Kidney Disease Foundation and Others

At the January Executive Committee meeting, Dr. Scribner reported that a major problem had arisen in the eastern United States where it was being said that chronic dialysis had not been proven in practice and therefore should not be supported other than as research. As a result, the National

Kidney Disease Foundation and other organizations had reported that they would not support patient care services, only research. Those involved were apparently unaware of the Seattle program and so the committee decided an approach should be made to the American Medical Association to urge a realistic and objective study of the Seattle program. A formal report would be made and should include particular discussion of the implications to the federal government. Dr. Haviland would contact Dr. Hugh Hussey, president of the American Medical Association.

## MEDICAL-RELATED ISSUES

### PATIENT CENSUS

At the beginning of the year the Center was treating 22 patients and in the next few weeks an additional patient was accepted for treatment. Dr. Pendras reported that by early April, 24 patients were being treated and 10 others already had been accepted for treatment, 5 of whom were close to needing to start. A request to accept a patient from the Portland Veterans Administration Hospital who was currently on dialysis but ineligible for VA support was considered. A home dialysis program was being developed in Portland, although progress was slow, and so it was decided the Center would not accept the patient in the hope of encouraging establishment of the program in Oregon as quickly as possible. By the end of the month there were 28 patients being treated, six waiting to start and six being processed. In view of the increasing number of patients, it was decided to establish temporary standby space for patients who started and could be treated until space became available in the basement. The Spokane dialysis unit was currently treating ten patients, was reported to have started a home dialysis program, and had received a three-year grant from the U.S. Public Health Service. By June, 32 patients were being cared for at the Center including one patient training for home hemodialysis. By November, the Center was fully or partly funding 28 patients, five other patients were fully funded through their own resources, and three patients were being trained for home hemodialysis. Eight patients did not yet need treatment. At the final Executive Committee meeting of the year, December 16, 1966, Dr. Pendras reported that two new patients had started dialysis, one a transfer from the University of Washington program and the other on a temporary arrangement with the VA for one year. Currently there were 29 patients dialyzing in-center, five at home and two who would be starting in the next month. There had been no referrals for the past three months but these were now starting again.

## Home hemodialysis and Center expansion

The third patient trained for home hemodialysis at University Hospital in Seattle was from Madras, India, where he was the son-in-law of the owner of India's largest newspaper, one of the richest men in India. He came to Seattle with his wife and personal physician for several months in the fall of 1964 for training. On his return to Madras in 1965, he was dialyzed very successfully at home by his wife – Scribner later said that she was much more competent in this regard than the physician. He died about a year later and Scribner attended his funeral. When Dr. Blagg visited Madras, now called Chennai, more than 40 years later, he visited the patient's widow at home, now well into her 80s, and was fascinated by the fact that she could describe in great detail how she performed the dialysis and managed the preparation and maintenance of the equipment.

This home hemodialysis almost halfway around the world proved so successful that the University of Washington decided to start training fully-funded patients from elsewhere if they were accompanied by a family member and a physician. Two more patients from California had been trained and were now dialyzing at home and plans were being made to expand this program to suitable patients from elsewhere in the United States and the world. Experience had shown that home dialysis could be performed by suitably trained, well-motivated patients using equipment with fail-safe monitors. This reduced costs (training was $12,880 and ongoing home hemodialysis was $4,150 annually), provided more independence and preservation of the family unit and allowed for greater availability, making home hemodialysis preferable to dialysis in a center.

In addition to this remote home hemodialysis program, the University had been funded by the John A. Hartford Foundation to undertake research studies into home hemodialysis using patients from Washington State.

A community dialysis center could develop such a program and this was actively being considered by the Center's Executive Committee. In light of the dialysate central system being so expensive (see below), the question was raised whether home hemodialysis should be the future direction for adding new patients to the program. It was thought probable that in the future most patients would have to be in the home program, with only problem cases dialyzing in-center, which would also serve as backup for home dialysis patients with problems. There was also discussion of the need to slowly convince present patients to go home, based on cost and convenience. The question was also raised about the effect kidney transplants might have on the program in the future. However, currently, kidney transplants had only a two-to-three year survival, although if the results of surgery became more successful most patients would have the opportunity to undergo a transplant.

The Long-Range Planning Committee had recommended the Center move as rapidly as possible to organize its own home dialysis program and Dr. Pendras had recommended the appointment of Dr. Robert Davidson as research director for the Center to direct the home hemodialysis program, and this was approved. The old lab area on the fourth floor of Eklind Hall at Swedish Hospital was being remodeled as space to train patients to do home dialysis and would have two beds and the ability to train four to six patients simultaneously. The training would encourage the patient to take responsibility for his or her own treatment, with the spouse acting only as an assistant. In the future, most new patients would be admitted directly to the training program and some of the current patients dialyzing in the Center might also transfer to home dialysis. Blue Cross medical insurance would not cover the costs of home dialysis but would pay for training at the

Center. Consequently, Mr. Rice was investigating the possibility of funds from the state Division of Vocational Rehabilitation to cover at least some of the treatment costs. The training room in Eklind Hall would be ready by June and the first patient (Mrs. Rena DeKoning) had been selected and would start training within a few weeks. Dr. Eschbach said that training at the university took about two months and it might take an extra two or three weeks to train a patient to sleep overnight on dialysis. He believed that this was ideal treatment if the patient could do it, as it was safe and allowed for a more normal life during the daytime. The expected cost of training would be about $2,000 plus $2,400 for supplies and personnel. Currently, the machine cost $10,000. He felt that as the university program primarily was concerned with research and development, it was important the two programs be interrelated and work together closely. The university wanted to increase its home dialysis research patient load and so would like to take some of the patients processed by the Center. However, the university had no funds for service cases and had no way of raising funds for patients and so the issue of the Center raising funds for both institutions would have to be considered.

Following discussion about a possible home dialysis agreement with the university, it was agreed that the Center would assign five patients to the university to complete the 12 patients funded in its home dialysis research program. The costs of dialysis treatment for the five patients and any back-up dialyses required would be covered by the Center.

At the October meeting, recommendations from the Long-Range Planning Committee were discussed: that the Center not consider expansion for at least three to six months while the effect of home dialysis on the in-center patient load was seen; that efforts should be made to accommodate Class II patients who currently were being rejected because of a shortage of staff to manage more complicated patients; and that patients accepted for treatment should be limited to residents of the state. Without expansion, the current 17 beds could treat a maximum of 51 patients with two additional beds for home dialysis training. If only Class I patients were accepted, this should be sufficient for 12 to 18 months. The recent patient load had been reduced with one patient going to the VA unit, one going home and one transferring to Portland for home dialysis training. After discussion and consideration that more patients would be going home in the future, it was concluded there was no current need to plan for expansion. The Center's first patient had gone home and three patients were being trained for home hemodialysis. It had been proposed that the university should train all out-of-state referrals for home dialysis who would have to be fully funded and have local medical support, and that the Center would not provide backup or funding for out-of-state patients.

## THE IDEA OF "KIDNEY TOWERS"
There was discussion of the concept of "kidney towers" where patients would live and could assist each other with treatment. This would reduce costs because of sharing of equipment but it appeared that patients would prefer not to live together because of interpersonal relationship problems and the desire to have a more normal life. However, the idea of bringing patients together to do their own treatment could be a possibility but would raise problems with equipment maintenance and other issues.

## AN ACUTE DIALYSIS CENTER?
There was further discussion about the possibility of establishing an acute dialysis center in Seattle for treating private patients so that community physicians could follow their own patients. Dr. McCormack reported that the Long-Range Planning Committee had met about this issue of acute dialysis outside the University Hospital. Its recommendation was that the Center should act only as a consultant on the issue and the question of acute dialysis should be referred to the Seattle Area Hospital Council and the King County Medical Society for their consideration and recommendations. The Executive Committee unanimously agreed with this.

New classification system for patients seeking dialysis
By June, 32 patients were being cared for at the Center including one patient training for home dialysis. The Center was almost at capacity and the selection process would need to be more selective as, recently, more than the expected two patients a month had started treatment and some of the existing patients had developed problems. It was suggested the Medical Advisory Committee divide acceptable patients into two classes: Class I – patients who meet all the criteria; and Class II – patients who meet all the criteria but were older than 45 years. Recently, the Admissions Advisory Committee had not had to be as selective and had expressed the opinion that if a space was available there was no reason to turn down someone who had been approved by the Medical Advisory Committee. There was also further discussion about whether patients should be limited to those from Washington State but it was thought that this would be undesirable and that other states should be encouraged to develop centers.

By a month later, an all-time high of 34 patients were under treatment even though two patients had died. Both were considered "risk" cases from the time of admission and both died of problems other than their kidney disease. As a result of the number of patients, there was discussion about limiting new patients to only two Class 1 (ideal) patients a month. However, there was concern as to whether this decision would be legal and so the Long-Range Planning Committee was asked about the possibility of additional space to treat more complicated, sicker patients so as to keep a separate complication-free environment for the majority of reasonably healthy patients. The Center would be opening a further seven beds within a month's time. Davidson reported that the Center's home dialysis program now was training two patients with another one possible. The program could expand if equipment became available. The Center had been discussing with the university the prospects for home peritoneal dialysis (PD) and while the Center could not support the university research of this treatment it would consider providing it when it had been proved successful.

In September problems had developed related to space occupied by the Center. The Pacific Northwest Research Foundation needed to increase its lab space and owned the space it had been renting to the Center. This meant the Center's lab would have to move to the new home dialysis training unit and that unit would have to be relocated to space on another floor. This issue was to be discussed further and with Swedish Hospital. Pendras pointed out that the Center was now at the point where some limitation would need to be placed on patients accepted for treatment. He suggested that as the recent fund drive had been limited to Washington State only potential patients living within the state should be considered. The Executive Committee agreed this would be advisable because of the limitations of funding and consequently the only out-of-state referrals to be accepted should be fully financed candidates for home dialysis.

By November the Center was fully or partly funding 28 patients, five other patients were fully funded through their own resources, and three patients were being trained for home dialysis. Eight patients did not yet need treatment.

A NEW CENTRAL DIALYSATE SYSTEM

A major issue during the early months of 1966 was the ongoing discussion about a new central dialysate preparation system for the Center. Bids were due by February 14 and the choice would be based on cost, design and reputation of the bidder. It would take three months to build the system and a further month to ensure adequate and proper operation. The "old" patient and lab area would be remodeled to accommodate the central system and to extend the Center's bed space, and until the new system was installed the number of patients would be limited to a maximum of 30.

Initially, 6 of the 16 companies approached were interested in bidding to provide the new system but eventually only two bids were submitted, probably because the project was more complicated than appeared at first sight. The bids were for $75,000 and $100,000, higher than the projected cost of $35,000 to $45,000. In addition, the cost of remodeling the patient and lab areas would be $15,000 to $25,000. The additional costs for remodeling could be requested from the Boeing Employees Good Neighbor

Fund, which might be more likely to support capital improvements than patient care.

A question had been raised as to whether all the monitoring and safety devices were needed on the central system, but Pendras said these were necessary to avoid any accident such as had occurred the previous year when a patient died as a result of a machine malfunction ( see Chapter 14). A suggestion was made that for the present, the Center might purchase a number of the Mini-2 single patient machines that were being made by the Milton Roy Company that were based on the Mini-1 that had been made for the first home patient at the university. When a new central system was installed these machines could be sold to home patients. It was also suggested that the Sweden Freezer Company might donate part of the cost of the central system but caution was expressed about this. Other equipment at the Center would soon need replacement and the options would be whether to expand the present patient area, to go into home dialysis or to operate a Center providing both in-center and home dialysis patients. Pendras preferred the latter. As a result of these discussions, Pendras and Rice were authorized to plan on the Center becoming involved in the home dialysis program and to work out the details of the space that would be needed for training, equipment and support of home dialysis.

These discussions continued into March when Pendras reported he had been continuing investigating further the central system that patient Frank Smith had been working on for three years, supported through the Center's Hartford Foundation fund. This machine would actually be the Center's property. It would cost about $9,000 to build and would cost far less to operate than the machines proposed by the outside bidders. As a result, the Executive Committee authorized Pendras to engage a consulting engineer to evaluate Frank Smith's machine and that a decision on the received bids would be postponed until after this evaluation.

A NEW KIDNEY TRANSPLANT PROGRAM

Scribner noted that Dr. Tom Marchioro would be coming from the University of Colorado to the University of Washington to start a kidney transplant program in July 1967. He would be performing as many transplants as possible for a cost of about $10,000 per transplant. To date, transplants were lasting for up to three years. These were related donor transplants and research was continuing on non-related transplants. With the addition of Marchioro, Seattle would have an overall program for the treatment of patients with chronic renal failure.

## The Bureau of the Budget Committee

The federal Bureau of the Budget Committee headed by Dr. Carl Gottschalk, a nephrologist from the University of North Carolina, had visited the University of Washington and the Seattle Artificial Kidney Center and reports on its visit had been very positive. The committee was visiting the main dialysis and transplant programs across the United States in order to report on kidney disease and its treatment in the country. This was because there was concern that an excessive amount was being requested of the federal government to support dialysis and kidney transplantation. The committee would eventually report to President Lyndon Johnson with recommendations as to whether and how the government should become involved.

## Center Finances and Fundraising

## State funding

Glen Rice reported in February that Ross Cunningham had been most instrumental in getting funding from the state legislature in 1965 and that patients also were contributing toward the cost of their own care. The greatest potential source of funding for patients could be through medical insurance and Glen was working with James Sullivan to arrange coverage through the unions of patients. Several auxiliary groups had contacted the Center about their willingness to serve in fundraising. A plaque had been placed on the wall of the Center listing major donors.

## Finance Committee and the fund drive

The Executive Committee had approved the request that the chairman of the Medical Advisory Committee should attend its meetings. It also approved a proposed budget for 1966 and noted that a Capital Reserve Fund had been established to handle unforeseen costs that might arise. The committee approved the motion that in the future all securities received by the Center should be sold upon receipt and also recommended that Walter Schoenfeld be fund-drive chairman again.

There had been discussion as to how the fund-drive money should be spent and that these funds were primarily solicited for patient care rather than capital improvements unless specified for the latter. There also might be funds forthcoming from the U. S. Public Health Service to the Center to provide training for physicians and staff from facilities elsewhere in the country. The next fund drive would be planned for April or May of 1967. Rice was authorized to retain a consultant from the Cumerford Corporation for two weeks to organize the next fund drive.

The world premiere of "Namu, the Killer Whale" was going to be held in Seattle in August with all benefits going to the Center. The movie was based on the story of Ted Griffin, owner of the Seattle Marine Aquarium (not to be confused with the contemporary Seattle Aquarium) who had purchased, displayed and performed with the orca, Namu, in 1965. He was the first person ever to swim with an orca. What was not generally realized was that Ted's sister, Nancy Spaeth, was a patient of Scribner and would need to start dialysis at the Center sometime in 1966.

By November, the 1965 fund drive had raised $220,000 and appeals in local communities for individual patients had been well received. Since January no patient had been rejected for financial reasons. The 1966 fund-drive goal of $512,900 was composed of $367,900 for patient care, $100,000 as an emergency fund and $45,000 for capital improvements. It was projected that the Center would add 42 new patients in the coming year who would be treated by either in-center or home hemodialysis and the new seven-bed expansion was now being served by Frank Smith's central dialysate system at much less cost than if one of the outside bids had been accepted. Mr. Clayton Nielson from the Cumerford Corporation reported that he had found the Center's fundraising campaign the most appealing of all that he had been involved with. He thought stress on saving individual lives was very appealing and that it was important that members of the board and Center staff participate actively in the drive. There would be a kick-off banquet on November 9, 1966, and the drive would officially start on January 10, 1967. The fund-drive chairman would be Greg MacDonald who then spoke on his plan for the campaign. Spielholz noted that it was time also to consider what financial support the Center would request in the state budget in 1967.

In December, Mr. MacDonald reported that organization of the fund drive was complete, the positions of division chairmen had been filled, and the services of Mr. Nielsen to the Center were being completed. Advance gifts to the fund drive were being solicited, with $42,000 received and pledges of more than $15,000. Nielsen recommended follow-up, including solicitation of board members, consideration of campaign leaders as future board members, and establishment of a national fundraising organization in Seattle. There was lack of experience and knowledge at the National Kidney Disease Foundation and its offshoot, the National Dialysis Committee, and so the Center got many requests for information. There were now ten or twelve community dialysis projects established in the country, mostly supported by the U.S. Public Health Service, although this would soon phase out as this funding was time-limited. The Center's support from the USPHS had already ended within the last year and community funds had become the Center's main support. While the board was supportive of an organization such as the National Dialysis Committee, the Center should not be involved other than becoming a member.

## A New Far-Reaching Development

The Peter Bent Brigham Hospital in Boston had been involved with dialysis since John Merrill started the program there in the late 1940s to treat patients with acute kidney failure using a modification of Kolff's rotating drum dialyzer – the Kolff Brigham artificial kidney. The hospital was also famous because it was there that Dr. Joseph Murray performed the first successful identical twin donor kidney transplant. For this he shared the Nobel Prize many years later together with Seattle's Dr. Donnell Thomas who did the first successful bone marrow transplant. Although the Brigham had done the first home hemodialysis a few months before the University of Washington in 1964, by 1966 the hospital was seeing increasing numbers of patients who were unable or unwilling to go to dialysis at home. As a result of the burgeoning transplant program and the increasing number of dialysis patients, it became necessary to ask Harvard and the Brigham to expand dialysis at the hospital. The Brigham had no wish to become a large outpatient chronic dialysis facility serving all of New England and so, like the University Hospital in Seattle, it declined to expand the number of stations. Consequently, Drs. Ted Hager and Constantine "Gus" Hampers went to the Massachusetts Department of Public Health for help but were advised to set up a committee like the one created in Seattle to ration care and decide who would live and who would die.

Hager had come to know the owner of an extended-care facility, Normandy House in Newton, Massachusetts, and like Scribner realized that to set up out-of-hospital dialysis stations there would be a cost-effective answer to their problems. Merrill was positive about the idea as it would relieve pressure on the hospital's transplant program and Merrill's chief, Dr. George Thorne, agreed and supported Merrill and Hampers in discussing the issue with the hospital board. At the same time, the Massachusetts Department of Public of Health and the Public Health Commission approved the concept.

As a result Hampers and Hager opened a six-station outpatient hemodialysis unit and began treating their first patients at Normandy House in 1966. They set the charge per dialysis at $160 at a time when the charge at the Brigham was $360 and by this time at least some private insurance companies were covering the costs of dialysis. It did not take long before the unit's capacity became inadequate and it also had the problem that it was situated in the Boston suburbs while many of the patients lived in central Boston. As a result, in early 1968, Hampers and Hager began to look for a new and larger facility and enlisted the help of a small investment firm to establish a private company to obtain the money to finance this. David McNeish raised the first $1 million in seed money to invest in an extended care facility (ECF) that was being constructed, convincing potential investors that Hampers and Hager would be the medical directors of a dialysis unit in the new ECF and that this would be the prototype for other out-of-hospital dialysis centers throughout the United States. After various trials and tribulations the new company, National Medical Care (NMC), was established. The final decision was to develop the combined ECF/dialysis unit on Babcock Street in Brookline, Massachusetts, and to acquire real estate options in New Orleans and Miami and other major cities. Construction began in January 1969. Meanwhile the state government was being encouraged to allow the new out-of- hospital dialysis unit to bill for its services through the state Department of Public Health. This became effective in 1970. NMC proved very successful and eventually raised some $12 million that enabled opening of ten dialysis centers by the end of 1971 in Boston, New York, Washington DC, Philadelphia, Tampa, Miami, Dallas, Los Angeles, Beverly Hills and Pittsburgh.

Eugene Schupak, who by this time was in New York where, with the assistance of NMC, he raised the capital to start the Queens Artificial Kidney Center and a new Corporation, Bio-Medical Applications, Inc. (BMA) that eventually was merged with NMC. The Queens Artificial Kidney Center differed from the NMC operation in Boston in that it was a simple, dialysis only, outpatient, storefront facility, easily accessible for patients and staff and located close to Elmhurst Hospital, the backup hospital. This became the model for the dialysis centers that proliferated across the nation that developed following the establishment of Medicare coverage for end-stage kidney disease on July 1, 1973. At the time the Queens Artificial Kidney Center was developed, Hampers, Hager and Schupak had no idea that within five years Medicare would be funding support for an entitlement program providing most of the costs of care for almost all U.S. patients with end-stage renal disease (ESRD) and that as a result for-profit dialysis would increase rapidly.

## THE AMERICAN SOCIETY OF NEPHROLOGY (ASN)

This specialty society was founded in 1966 by 18 nephrologists assembled at a meeting of the Kidney Section of the New York Heart Association that included Drs. Robert Petersdorf and Scribner from the University of Washington. The purpose of the ASN was "to advance the knowledge of nephrology and to foster the dissemination of this knowledge 1) through national scientific meetings, 2) through cooperation with other national societies of nephrology, and by other means approved by the members on recommendation by the Council."

The first annual meeting was held in October 1967 in Los Angeles and attracted 1,250 attendees. Dr. Blagg presented a paper on uremic neuropathy.

## THE 1966 ANNUAL MEETING OF THE ASAIO

At the 1966 meeting of the ASAIO in Atlantic City, two papers from the Center and two from the Division of Nephrology at the University of Washington were presented.

From the Center, Drs. Erickson, Williman and Pendras reported that patients who formed clots in their shunts more frequently had higher levels of some clotting factors in their blood.

Drs. Pendras and Smith reported on the Center's experience with the new Silastic-Teflon arteriovenous cannulas and how, with careful attention to detail, an average cannula survival of 12 to 14 months was attainable. However, in discussion following this paper, Dr. James Cimino from the Bronx first reported on the use of the arteriovenous fistula for blood access for hemodialysis. Over the next few years this technique almost completely replaced the use of cannulas, and Scribner later said how much he wished he had thought of the idea.

From the University of Washington, Drs. Anderson, DePalma and Halloran showed that passage of blood through a dialyzer had no effect on the platelet count in the blood but that adhesion of platelets to foreign surfaces was increased, possibly accounting for the risk of clotting in dialysis cannulas.

Drs. Eschbach, Wilson, Peoples, Wakefield, Babb and Scribner described experience with eight patients successfully treated by home hemodialysis, four of whom were performing overnight hemodialysis in the manner reported by Shaldon from London when he spoke in Seattle in December 1964.

## CHAPTER 27

# Annual Board Meeting and Executive Committee Meetings; the ASAIO Annual Meeting 1967

---

THE YEAR 1967 WAS THE sixth year of operations at the Seattle Artificial Kidney Center and was the first full year since establishment of the Center's home hemodialysis training program. Efforts were underway to send home as many of the patients who were dialyzing in the Center as possible in order to allow more patients to be treated with the limited funds available. There were continuing discussions regarding patient acceptance into the program. It was also the year in which Dr. Thomas Marchioro came to the University of Washington and made preparations to start the state's first kidney transplant program.

## THE FOURTH ANNUAL MEETING OF THE BOARD OF TRUSTEES AND REVIEW OF 1966 ACTIVITIES

The meeting was held on February 15, 1967. Trustees whose terms were expiring were re-elected except for Mrs. Harlan Edwards who had recently resigned. Current officers and Executive Committee members were re-elected for a further year.

Dr. Pendras reported that in 1966 the Center had expanded from 12 to 19 beds, two of which were used for home hemodialysis training, and the training unit had been relocated to the second floor. The Center was using the central dialysate system made by patient Frank Smith, as it was considerably less expensive ($10,000 to $12,000) than the systems proposed by dialysis equipment supply manufacturers ($75,000 and $100,000). The Center had a current contract with the U. S. Public Health Service to develop a training program for physicians, nurses and technicians from outside. A proposed satellite center in Longview had been discontinued as unfeasible because of the few potential patients.

The Center had changed its future main emphasis to home dialysis as this was seen as being the best method to treat more patients at a reduced cost. Dr. Davidson reported the Center's home dialysis program had been established in mid-1966 following the successful program at the university. Presently five patients were treating themselves at home: one in Ellensburg; one in Lake Stevens; and three in Vancouver, Washington. Two others were fully trained and waiting for equipment. For each patient, a local physician was trained regarding the unique problems with home dialysis. The program was becoming integrated into the Center so that patients dialyzing in-center could see it.

Mr. Rice reported that medical health insurance companies had become quite cooperative during the last year and even more would be participating in the future, although coverage for home dialysis was less satisfactory to date. Swedish Hospital no longer had to subsidize the Center.

Dr. McCormack reported that the Long-Range Planning Committee had discussed the process for classifying patient acceptability, the home dialysis program for expanding the Center's program and the decision that only Washington State patients would be accepted in the Center's program. These issues had been resolved. They were still discussing the issue of establishing an acute dialysis program outside of University Hospital.

Scrib reported that during the previous year the university had developed a technique for sterilizing and reusing blood tubing and the dialyzer, and patients had successfully reused equipment up to six times consecutively at home. This saved $5 per dialysis for the tubing and reduced patient work in preparing the dialyzer. There had also been testing of a new prototype dialyzer developed by Drs. Grimsrud and Babb. He felt that Dr. Marchioro joining the university's Department of Surgery later in the year would help integrate the process of dialysis and transplantation and would be a great step forward for Seattle.

Dr. Haviland announced that the Stewardess Emeritus volunteer group would hold a fashion show on February 28 at the Seattle Center with proceeds going to support the Seattle Artificial Kidney Center.

The meeting ended with a tour of the Center.

## Patient Numbers and Activities Throughout the Year

At the January Executive Committee meeting, Dr. Pendras reported there were now 34 patients in the program: 29 dialyzing in the Center; 5 dialyzing at home; and two more expected to start treatment in the next week and another within a month. There were also three patients being considered for acceptance, making the case load close to the Center's current capacity of 40. Home dialysis was moving slowly because equipment was not readily available, even though there was money for this now and Dr. Scribner stressed that maintaining an inventory of home equipment was essential. To date there had been a total of nine deaths in patients accepted by the Center. The first death had been the result of equipment failure, and since then eight Class II "risk" patients had died. Discussion continued about the Center only taking referrals from within the state while out-of-state funded patients would go to the university. This was approved unanimously.

By March, six patients were on home dialysis and 32 were being treated in the Center and it was expected that many of these would eventually go home. Federal funds had become available to construct a new dialysis unit at the Seattle VA hospital and the three service-connected VA patients currently being treated at the Center would be transferred there when the facility opened.

At the June meeting, Dr. Pendras reported that one patient had died because of complications other than kidney disease and that her adjustment to dialysis had been difficult because of her family situation. Three new patients had been started, bringing the patient population to 51. Forty-four patients were dialyzing in-center where the estimated capacity was 51 patients. A subcommittee was looking at the possibility of establishing a rehabilitation evaluation committee.

In July, Dr. Pendras reported that 42 patients were dialyzing in-center, including three new patients, and that a further five patients were being processed. He estimated that all but 15 of the current patients dialyzing in the Center could be sent home eventually. The current death rate was one patient dying every three to four months.

By September, there were still 42 patients on dialysis in-center, four recently accepted patients who were waiting to start treatment, and three patients were starting the selection process. There were 12 patients on home dialysis, four or five patients were ready to start home dialysis training but the problems with lack of equipment or finances persisted. One patient had died from a combination of complications.

In October, there were 43 in-center patients and twelve home dialysis patients. Two applicants had been accepted, one of whom was being dialyzed at University Hospital as she was eight months pregnant.

By the November meeting there were 41 in-center patients, 17 home patients and three patients in training. Five new patients had been accepted and a further seven patients had just begun the selection process.

In December, there were 39 patients dialyzing in-center, 21 on home hemodialysis and three in home hemodialysis training.


## HOME HEMODIALYSIS

In January, Dr. Davidson reported that the home hemodialysis training program was moving slowly because the necessary equipment still was not readily available. Initially the reason for not acquiring needed equipment was because the necessary funds were unobtainable, but now that funds had been set aside, the equipment distributor was not able to furnish the equipment as needed. Dr. Scribner again stressed the necessity of maintaining an inventory of home equipment. A suggestion was made that the Sweden Freezer Company be contacted to see what equipment they could supply.

However, this was considered inadvisable inasmuch as their equipment had not proven to be satisfactory for the purposes of home hemodialysis.

In March, Dr. Davidson reported that more funds were becoming available to support the home dialysis program and three patients dialyzing in-center would be going home shortly. He also reported that the Center's first home dialysis patient had developed serious unforeseen medical complications after going home and currently was being treated in the unit and was unlikely to return to home hemodialysis.

In June, no one had gone home from training in the previous month and the reasons for this included medical complications and the unavailability of the necessary equipment.

There was discussion of the management of patients trained elsewhere on inexpensive equipment. The Center's current policy for assuming responsibility for dialysis of patients who had been trained for home hemodialysis on equipment outside of Washington State was that the Center's only responsibility should be to give emergency care. If a situation arose where the patient could no longer use his or her own equipment, the Center's responsibility would cease unless the patient were eligible for the Center's program under the existing admission criteria. Following discussion, a motion was made to approve this policy of the Center providing only emergency care for patients utilizing equipment obtained from out of state. This was accepted unanimously.

In July, Dr. Davidson reported that not as many patients were going home as anticipated, the current total being ten. It was now the Center's policy to accept only patients who were potential home patients because of limitations of space for Center dialysis. At the time of acceptance, patients had to agree that they would go home if at all possible. Current limitations were still the unavailability of equipment and finances, and unexpected medical complications. The cost of outfitting a patient's home for dialysis had been reduced from $8,000 to $5,800. Discussions were underway with Madigan Army Hospital and the Seattle VA Hospital for them to provide backup dialysis and support for military dependents and service-connected veterans after they were trained for home dialysis at the Center.

The question had been raised whether patients rejected because they were unable to be trained for home dialysis (mainly because they were single) would affect the image of the Center. Mr. Rice said he would like to publicize the basic facts that the Center was operating with inadequate funding and therefore having to limit patients acceptable for the programs offered. It was probably advisable that the Center take the initiative before it was misinterpreted. No action was taken on this suggestion.

Dr. Haviland recalled that about a year previously the decision was made that the Center would not expand further in its bed space at that time because it was felt the home dialysis program had a real future in providing needed treatment for patients with kidney failure. Now there was again the question whether the Center should consider the possibility of expanding. Dr. Scribner agreed that something needed to be done to provide care for the increasing number of patients requiring treatment. He suggested the possibility of a new type of center where patients who otherwise would not qualify for the home dialysis program could assist in treating each other and in one location, probably an apartment. This "center" would be completely operated by the patient themselves with all responsibility lying with them also. The cost for such a facility would approximate that of home dialysis.

By mid-September there were 42 patients dialyzing in-center, 12 patients on home hemodialysis, four or five patients who were now in the home training program as well as several patients ready to start training but unable to do so because of lack of finances or lack of equipment.

The Center had negotiated with Swedish Hospital to rent two rooms for home hemodialysis training at $25 each per day as experience had shown that it was inadvisable to train patients for home hemodialysis in the same area used for in-center dialysis. Home patients had to be stimulated to care for themselves and not rely on staff to deal with problems. The training program lasted for eight weeks and for the first six weeks the patient and spouse used the training room during the day, three days a week. The last two weeks the room was used overnight. Two rooms on a six-day per week basis could handle four patients, and at the seventh week two more patients could start training. The Center anticipated taking over two further rooms at Swedish Hospital once the training program really got going. Dr. Sawyer, as the replacement for Dr. Davidson, would take responsibility for the home dialysis program and Dr. Eschbach would be attending the weekly meetings to plan for the home training unit. It might be possible to pool resources and personnel with the University of Washington home hemodialysis program. There were also four patients in the university home training program that would transfer to the Center on October 31 when the research support from the Hartford Foundation grant would end. Dr. Pendras reported that the Army was interested in taking over the financial responsibility for the home training of two in-center patients who were dependents of military personnel.

## PATIENT ACCEPTANCE AND OTHER MEDICAL ISSUES

During the course of the year, a number of issues were discussed related to patient numbers and acceptance by the SAKC. The Admissions Advisory Committee had questioned its role, as it felt that with beds available it could not reject any patient referred to the committee. This would be discussed further and reports would be made available to the committee about progress with patients they had accepted, and especially the degree of rehabilitation attained.

At the February meeting, Scrib questioned the recent rejection of Class II patients, particularly those without financial support, and said something should be done about this as more Class II patients without funds would be presenting than those with funds. Dr. Pendras reviewed the classification: Class I patients were ideal candidates; Class II patients were those with medical complications and/or psychological problems and/or over 45 years of age; and Class III patients were medically unacceptable. Most Class II patients accepted by the Center had been very poor and were costly to treat because of their medical problems. It was suggested that Class II patients be divided into acceptable Class II and unacceptable Class II patients related to their anticipated medical risk if accepted. There was concern about rejecting patients because of lack of funds and that the public should be made aware of the need for support. It was also suggested the John A. Hartford Foundation might be approached to provide funds to treat high-risk patients on an experimental basis after its existing support phased out in June 1967. The U.S. Public Health Service could also be approached to provide such funds.

A suggestion was made in March that the rehabilitation potential of patients should be included in the selection process and that a Rehabilitation Evaluation Committee be set up but no decision was made as to who might do this. Rehabilitation was defined as being able to return to a patient's former occupation or work comparable to his ability as limited by his condition. Some felt that all patients should be given the "benefit of the doubt" but the majority view was this would be better evaluated by psychologists, psychiatrists, social workers and vocational rehabilitation counsellors. If this committee were to be established, their reports would go for review to the Admissions Advisory Committee.

Also during the year concern was expressed about the image if the Center rejected patients who were not able to go home, and that they should take the initiative to talk publically about this. Three such patients had been rejected over the previous three months. There was discussion of the attitude taken by rejected applicants, their families and their doctors. Patient and family responses varied from pleading to hostility but they were told about the shortcomings of treating patients with serious problems and the discomfort that may ensue. Patients were not told a great deal about dialysis as they started the selection process so as not to build up their hopes. There was agreement that physicians needed more education about dialysis so they might refer patients earlier. Dr. Haviland pointed out that 12 months earlier the decision had been made not to expand the Center further because it was felt that the home program would provide treatment for many patients. However, now was the time to consider expansion.

Dr. Scribner again raised the concept of developing a patient-run program in an apartment as the cost would be similar to that of home dialysis. He also commented that as of July 1, Dr. Thomas Marchioro had begun organizing a transplant program at the University Hospital and within a year or so this should be taking patients away from dialysis, although dialysis would still be needed if the transplant failed. The estimated cost of a kidney transplant was $12,000 to $15,000.

It was reported that the Spokane Center was full but was hoping to be able to take more patients in the near future. The Portland Center could take patients from the Vancouver area, although Dr. Richard Drake, the medical director, had just been drafted into the Army. With all of this in mind, Dr. Haviland said there now was a need for the Center to expand to provide continued treatment in-center and backup for home dialysis and the transplant program. The Center would need an additional physician and nursing personnel. Until the expansion was complete, the university might help by training patients for home dialysis who had been accepted by the Center. This issue was to be discussed further.

With regard to accepting patients who were not fully funded, the Center continued to take such patients who were medically acceptable and quite often they later became funded by insurance companies or could be supported at least in part from community fund drives. Dr. Pendras expressed concern about taking patients without resources, as new capital was needed for improvements and to purchase home dialysis equipment as the number of applicants continued to increase. Dr. Haviland said it would appear that the Center now had to survive on its own, supported by the fund drive, and could continue to accept applicants as in the past, although the policy would be reviewed each month. Plans were being developed to coordinate the university's transplant program with the Center.

In September it was reported that in the case of the three patients who had been rejected for treatment in the previous three months a letter was sent to the referring physician, signed by Dr. Haviland, informing the physician that after careful consideration of all the information presented to the Admissions Advisory Committee, they were unable to recommend the patient's admission to the Center's program. A discussion ensued pertaining to the attitude taken by the public regarding rejected applicants. Dr. Haviland said that occasionally he was contacted by a patient's physician and Mr. Rice commented that he had seldom been approached by the public regarding a rejected patient. Dr. Pendras said that his contact was usually with the applicant and his family. Their reactions varied from one of pleading on behalf of the applicant to hostility toward the staff. These people were then informed as to what the shortcomings would be of treating this type of applicant and the degree of discomfort the patient would experience on hemodialysis. Dr. Scribner believed the selection process should not be changed at that time because it sufficiently diffused responsibility and Dr. Haviland agreed saying this was also the consensus of opinion concerning the function and value of all the various Seattle Artificial Kidney Center's committees.

The Rev. John Darrah inquired as to what the attitudes were of the patient and family upon being accepted to the program. What were their expectations? Dr. Norton, the psychiatrist, made the comment that when applicants came to him for psychiatric evaluation they had only a very vague idea of what hemodialysis was all about. Dr. Pendras explained that during the initial contacts between the patient, his family and the Center's staff, they were not told too much so as not to build up their hopes. They were given to understand, however, that the Center could not guarantee anything. Discussion ensued as to the various means by which the public might be educated as to what artificial kidney treatment was. Dr. Pendras said that on occasion he had spoken to doctors at hospital staff meetings and had met with an enthusiastic response. The committee agreed that educating physicians should be the first step. Dr. Scribner said he felt this would prove most beneficial as physicians would then realize the importance of an early referral. Dr. Haviland said that one method might be to send out letters to all physicians and that physician education was one area in which a public relations committee could work something out.

Mrs. Profant from University Hospital was asked if the university's transplant program would call for backup dialysis assistance from the Center. She replied the university was presently formulating policy with Dr. Marchioro and that she would keep in touch with Dr. Haviland and Mr. Rice as to possible involvement of the Center in the transplant program.

In November there was again discussion of accepting applicants who lacked full funding. Mr. Rice said that the Center was continuing to accept such patients if otherwise qualified for acceptance. Many times such patients became funded by a medical insurance policy or following a community drive for them. These patients might well have been denied the opportunity to live because at the time of application the financial picture was bleak. The Center was now carrying approximately 40% of the patient's costs.

Dr. McCormack suggested that the public be notified that due to lack of funds the Center might have to turn down applicants who had no funding, as had been suggested before. Dr. Pendras was concerned that it was extremely dangerous to accept unfunded patients when the Center's accounts payable figure was so close to the accounts receivable figure. The Center needed capital to make improvements and to buy new equipment for the home program. He believed that the operation of the Center should be scaled down to one that was more economical to run. As previously suggested, a self-care unit where dialysis patients could help one another with their treatment would help.

To sum up, Dr. Haviland stated that from all appearances the Center must continue to survive on its own, supplemented by the fund drive. The committee had to decide whether to limit acceptance to those who were fully funded or to continue as in the past. The committee decided to continue the existing policy but to review the situation every month.

Dr. Haviland had attended a meeting at the University of Washington Hospital with the administrative personnel regarding the transplant program and the Center's possible involvement in this program. Present plans were to have a Northwest regional chronic uremia program. This would be the first project of its kind in the United States. Plans and details were being developed for later presentation to the executive committee.

At the December meeting Dr. Haviland asked the committee if its decision to continue accepting applicants, with or without funds, was to remain in status quo through the month, until the January committee meeting. He also asked if the committee felt the results of the fund drive would be sufficient for the Center to continue its present operation. It was agreed the Center should continue as it had done for another month and, regardless of the activity of the 1968 fund drive, the policy should be reviewed every month.

## Acute Renal Failure

There was further discussion of the possibility of setting up acute dialysis services at hospitals other than University Hospital. Dr. Pendras estimated the costs as being $6,000 for equipment and $150 for space to maintain the equipment but this did not include the costs and time of training staff or the costs of actually providing hemodialysis. It was decided it was not feasible to do this yet as University Hospital only treated 25 to 30 patients with acute renal failure annually from the entire Pacific Northwest. Drs. Pendras and Haviland then met with Seattle Area Hospital Council representatives to discuss this issue further and to inform the council that the Center could provide training for interested personnel, but each hospital would have to provide and maintain the equipment and provide dialysis. Following discussion, the council was of the opinion that it would be impractical for other hospitals take on acute dialysis at this time in view of the small number of patients requiring it each year.

Even so, a few months later, Dr. McCormack wondered if it would be practical for the SAKC to treat patients with acute renal failure at Swedish Hospital and raised the question whether some of the Center's patients might be transplanted there. However, Dr. Pendras pointed out that the Center got an average intake of four patients a month and so it was necessary for four Center patients to go into home training each month.

## Finances

In September, Mr. Rice reported that the Center had $65,000 cash on deposit at 5% interest, mostly held in trust for individual patients. The Center had met its payroll but was two or three months in arrears to other creditors. Swedish Hospital had been paid through June. There was $147,000 in accounts receivable, money from medical insurance companies, etc.

A month later there was $67,813 on deposit in five savings trust accounts. Accounts payable totaled approximately $115,000; accounts receivable, $152,000. Mr. Guernsey inquired if it was possible to acquire a list of organizations and firms that had committed pledged financial aid, including grants, to worthy institutions. It was suggested that Mr. Clayton Nielson of the National Kidney Foundation and Dr. William Robertson of the University of Washington Medical School might be of some assistance with this inquiry.

By November, there was $80,000 in savings accounts and $11,000 in checking accounts. Accounts receivable was $141,000, of which $106,000 was collectible from patients and/or their insurance companies, and $27,500 was due the Center from the U.S. Public Health Service training contract. Accounts payable was $135,000. It was requested that a financial statement be prepared every month and mailed to committee members prior to each Executive Committee meeting. Dr. McCormack asked about what financial support would be coming from the government and Scrib reported the picture was dismal as the Gottschalk Report had been submitted to the Bureau of the Budget but was being ignored (see below).

At the December meeting, it was noted that the Center was operating at a deficit of about $2,000 a month and that it was hoped that the next fund drive would raise $300,000. It was pointed out that insurance companies on the eastern seaboard were slower in processing payments than were the local companies. The committee also reviewed accounts payable and it was pointed out that until the previous year Swedish Hospital had absorbed many of the laboratory and blood bank costs, so subsidizing the Center. During the previous year Swedish hospital's cost of doing business had increased as had the Center's staff salaries, medical supplies, etc. The need to explain to major donors where the money was going was important – capital improvements, equipment, maintenance, etc. It was agreed that the policy of accepting patients without finances would be continued and reviewed at monthly intervals.

The general feeling of the Finance Committee was that the financial status of the Center was such that a study should be made to see what could be done to improve the operation. Mr. Campbell felt the Center should look at its expenditures to see if there were or had been extravagant spending. Dr. Haviland then requested Mr. Baggott, chairman of the Finance Committee, to have his committee study the Center's operation and report to the Executive Committee in January 1968.

STATE FUNDING

In February, it was learned that funds to be appropriated by the state through the Health Department for dialysis treatment were again in the new Omnibus Budget bill at $125,000, and legislators had been approached about acquiring additional funding. There would also be likely support from the state Division of Vocational Rehabilitation "for outfitting, training, and some six months supplies, service and support for eligible patients undertaking home hemodialysis. The Minnesota Division had supported patients for at least a year but the state office in Olympia was not enthusiastic. The breakthrough came with a phone call at Sen. Jackson's urging, from President Johnson's office to the Regional Administrative Office in San Francisco."

In November it was learned that the $160,000 to $170,000 proposed state funds for dialysis treatment that had been allocated to the state Health Department and the Division of Vocational Rehabilitation in the proposed state budget were held up by a technicality and their fate was uncertain.

FUND DRIVE

At the beginning of the year, Mr. Earl Rice reported that Advance Gifts for the fund drive had been solicited and were slowly being received and that Special Gifts and Clubs and Organizations would start as of January 25.

The National Kidney Foundation (NKF) based in Washington D.C. recently had released two TV films for publicity to raise money nationally and he was concerned that they were capitalizing on the Center's widespread publicity, particularly in the Pacific Northwest. The films said the NKF was accepting contributions for patient care even though until recently they had stated they only requested funds for kidney research. Mr. Rice had contacted the NKF to try to prevent further exposure, particularly in Washington State and during the Center's fund drive. No cooperation had been received so Mr. Rice would work with the local TV stations.

In February, the fund drive had received about $85,000, less than projected and inadequate for present operation of the Center. The shortfall might relate to the delay that had occurred in organizing the fund drive. The Finance Committee emphasized the need for informing the public about the Center's financial status and Mr. Rice was to contact KING TV, radio personnel and local newspapers. It was agreed that patients themselves could best interpret the meaning of this life-saving program.

In March, Mr. MacDonald, chairman of the fund drive, was concerned the drive was going slowly and only had reached $108,000. Unless this accelerated, the Center might have to turn some patients down. He noted that not all members of the board had contributed yet. Two ongoing efforts were a radio publicity endeavor to bring attention to an 18-year-old girl in Everett who had no financial resources and a "Race for Life" to be held at the Kent Pacific Raceway on April 16 to raise funds.

By June, the fund drive totaled $152,339 and a few small community drives outside of Seattle were still being undertaken to support local patients. For the next drive it was suggested the public be approached directly through media publicity and this should include requests for smaller contributions rather than just from businesses. In addition, NBC had been approached about making a follow-up documentary timed to the coming year's fund drive.

The fund drive by July had raised $175,000 and about $34,000 had been pledged from five other counties. There was also $147,000 in accounts receivable. It was decided to start the 1968 fund drive in November 1967, as the Boeing Employees Good Neighbor Fund fund drive would be over by then and there would be an advantage in having the drive cover the end of the tax year.

A meeting was planned to be held at the Washington Athletic Club on December 11 to report to 400 people on the status of the Seattle Artificial Kidney Center and give them a general idea of the problems the Center faced.

In December, Mr. Schoenfeld said that fund donors, especially large fund donors, were interested in knowing what applications donations were used for, such as capital improvements, equipment, maintenance, etc. He suggested donations be acknowledged with a statement of intended use as, for example, "40% of your donation will be spent on capital improvements." The committee agreed that all major donations would be acknowledged in a like manner, with information to the subscriber showing the intended disbursement of his grant.

## THE ARTIFICIAL KIDNEY FOUNDATION OF AMERICA

Mr. Nielsen from the National Kidney Foundation reported the incorporation of the Artificial Kidney Foundation of America on March 17, 1967, with the primary purpose of assisting the establishment of kidney centers elsewhere in the United States, including advising on financial support. The foundation was headquartered in Seattle and the president was Earl Rice, the vice-president was Lisle Guernsey and the secretary was Clayton Nielsen. This foundation would not be fundraising in Washington State because of conflict with the Center's fundraising efforts. The plan was for the foundation eventually to run a national fund drive for the benefit of all dialysis centers.

In June, Mr. Nielsen reported that some money had been donated to the Artificial Kidney Foundation of America and that some commitments had been made for the foundation's second and third years. Solicitation would be nationwide with the exception of Washington State and the SAKC Executive Committee recommended that this information should be included in the letter of solicitation. The SAKC Executive Committee hoped that the foundation eventually would combine with the National Kidney Foundation.

In fact, experience soon showed there was little interest in this foundation from potential developers of dialysis units and it was soon folded into the National Kidney Foundation.

## PERSONNEL CHANGES

In January, Dr. Pendras recommended that Dr. Christopher Blagg, who had recently returned to Seattle from England and was currently working with Dr. Scribner at University Hospital, be approved as a member of the Medical Advisory Committee. This was approved unanimously.

In September, Dr. Tom Sawyer replaced Dr. Robert Davidson and would take on responsibility for the home patients, and Dr. Joseph Eschbach from the University of Washington's home program was attending meetings at the Center. There was thought of joining the training programs at the Center and the university.

## THE GOTTSCHALK COMMITTEE

In 1966, prompted by the White House Office of Science and Technology Policy, the Bureau of the Budget had formed a committee to review dialysis and kidney transplantation in the United States and what the role of government should be. The committee was headed by Carl Gottschalk, a nephrologist from the University of North Carolina. The Gottschalk Report (see Chapter 34 on Politics from 1960 to 1973) had been submitted to the Bureau of the Budget but had been "put on the shelf" because of other financial problems including the Vietnam War and had not been published. As Scrib said, it was in limbo.

## THE 1967 ANNUAL MEETING OF THE ASAIO

At the 13th Annual Meeting if the ASAIO in Chicago, three papers were presented from the Center and four from the University of Washington.

Dr. Pendras presented a paper about experience at the Center with an Archimedes screw central dialysate production system devised by Mr. Frank Smith, a patient who was an engineer. It was relatively uncomplicated to use but required more automatic monitoring systems to show when blood leaks into the dialysate occurred and to follow pressure in the blood lines.

Drs. Davidson and Pendras discussed integration of a home hemodialysis training program into an existing dialysis center, so providing an integrated total hemodialysis program for the treatment of chronic uremia. This was illustrated by a description of the first eight patients trained for home dialysis at the SAKC.

The same two authors also presented the first two acute deaths ever reported in dialysis patients that were related to cardio-respiratory failure occasioned by hypercalcemia – a high blood calcium level. One case appeared to be related to tertiary hyperparathyroidism and might have been prevented by removal of the extremely overactive parathyroid glands; the second appeared to relate to an excessive vitamin D level in a patient who was a food faddist and taking vitamin D and calcium supplements. They discussed the diagnoses in detail.

From the University of Washington, Dr. Lars Grimsrud and Dr. Babb's group gave a classic talk on the safety aspects of hemodialysis and hemodialysis equipment and the necessary precautions.

Terry Pollard and Dr. Scribner's group described a technique for storage and reuse of the Kiil dialyzer and its blood tubing. This had been developed to ease the problems of Kiil dialyzer assembly in the home and enabled patients to rebuild their Kiil dialyzer only once every two weeks. Longer reuse was to be avoided because of the accumulation of deposits on the membranes and weakening of the cellophane with frequent cleaning, but the blood tubing could be reused for a longer time. Reuse reduced the supply costs for home dialysis and reduced patient time and effort required for dialysis.

Dr. Tenckhoff and colleagues reported on 31 patients treated by hemodialysis for as long as seven years and the nerve damage that could occur in some patients as a result of uremia and which, if it developed in motor nerves, could cause serious disability. They showed that development of this neuropathy related to inadequate dialysis and required intensified treatment to improve or at least stabilize the problem.

Drs. Yutuc and Tenckhoff also reported on the use of sorbitol in peritoneal dialysate rather than glucose. Using sorbitol avoided caramelization of the glucose during sterilization by autoclaving, and simplified the process at only minor extra cost.

## CHAPTER 28

# The Annual Meeting and Executive Committee
# Meetings; ASAIO Annual Meeting 1968

---

IN THE YEAR 1968, PERITONEAL dialysis was a major subject of discussion by the Executive Committee but nothing was finally decided. The home hemodialysis program continued to grow slowly but steadily, there were adjustments to the details of patient acceptance and the financial situation was still a cause of concern.

## THE FIFTH ANNUAL MEETING OF THE BOARD OF TRUSTEES

The meeting was held on February 2, 1968 at Eklind Hall. The Nominating Committee's recommendations were unanimously approved. The new president was John L. McCormack, MD, vice-president, Lisle Guernsey, secretary, M. L. Bean, Sr. and treasurer, Renaldo Baggott. Members of the board for a three-year term were James W, Haviland, MD, M. L. Bean, Sr., Lisle R. Guernsey, Ross Cunningham, Fred Huleen, H. Sedge Thompson, James M. Burnell, MD, Lawrence E. Karrer and James Sullivan. To fill the vacancies on the Executive Committee, James W. Haviland, M. L .Bean, Sr., and Lisle R. Guernsey were appointed, and Charles Anderson was appointed to the board for a term expiring February 1969 to replace Edward Rosling.

Dr. Sawyer reviewed medical activities during the previous year. Twenty-eight new patients had been accepted and 17 had been trained for home dialysis. There had been 6 deaths in the past year: four related to heart problems, one of whom died before starting dialysis; one related to a calcium metabolism problem; one due to an electrolyte abnormality related to infection; and one of unknown causes. There were no deaths directly attributable to dialysis.

During the year the decision had been taken that all new patients would be placed on home hemodialysis. This was done because experience at the university had shown home hemodialysis to be better treatment than Center dialysis as it provided safer dialysis with reduced blood requirements and decreased incidence of nerve injury from uremia. Patients enjoyed a greater sense of well-being and independence and the cost of treatment was reduced considerably. The University of Washington had helped train additional staff for the Center's home dialysis program and three rooms in Swedish Hospital were now being used to train home patients. Because of the similarity of the Center and the university home programs it was planned to combine the units so that when the patient census in the Center was sufficiently reduced a combined training program would be housed in Eklind Hall.

The training contract with the U.S. Public Health Service to train physicians, nurses and technicians would be continued for a further year. During the previous year four physicians, eight nurses and five technicians were trained in dialysis. The Seattle program was one of the only two such programs in the U.S.

Mr. Rice reviewed administrative activities. Costs per treatment in the Center had risen over the previous year from $96.50 to $133.00 per dialysis and the cost of home dialysis was about $4,000 a year after initial outfitting costs of $6,000. The Center was currently in arrears $110,000 on accounts payable and portions of the accounts receivable were not accessible. The current 1967/1968 fund drive totaled $59,316.07 with another $2,500 promised. Five new patients had been affected by the present financial situation. One had been referred to the Seattle VA unit, two had finally been funded from insurance and other sources, the fourth was in process of being funded, and one patient was without resources. Coordination with all news media would be used to inform the public about their plight. Dr. Haviland commented that the Center started with dialysis in the unit in 1962 and now, with the emphasis switched to home hemodialysis, more attention was being paid to rehabilitation and increasing a patient's sense of reliance. This represented a change in philosophy from the early days of the Center. The Center's experience now represented 170 years of life for otherwise unsalvageable patients. It was important that the news media be informed that home dialysis did not preclude the need for funding support.

Dr. John McCormack was installed as the second president of the Board of Trustees and chairman of the Executive Committee. He described the importance of Dr. Haviland's role in establishing the Center through the King County Medical Society, establishing the present structure of the Center and attracting community leaders to serve on the Board of Trustees.

In the question and answer session, Drs. Burnell and Simpson reported that Dr. Thomas Marchioro's current results with kidney transplantation at the University of Washington were that there was a 90% chance of a kidney from a blood-related donor functioning for one to two years and with cadaveric donors the chances decreased to 60% to 40%. All patients had to take immunosuppressive drugs continuously to prevent rejection and these carried certain inherent hazards. Dr. Sawyer was asked about moving more of the current Center patients to home dialysis and pointed out there were continuing problems with funds to buy equipment for home dialysis and a shortage of experienced personnel to train the patients. Combining the university's and Center's home dialysis programs had allowed better utilization of personnel. The plan now was to put all new patients into home training as soon as their medical condition stabilized and to reduce the in-center population by two patients a month. It was anticipated that by July 1968 the in-center census would be down to the mid-twenties. Most patients should be able to go on home dialysis, at least technically, but this did not take into account the philosophical and psychological difficulties encountered in individual patients.

## Patient Activities

In January 1968 there were a total of 67 patients: 37 dialyzing in-center, including three new patients; and 26 home hemodialysis patients of whom 15 had been trained at the Center, three were new patients and seven had been transferred from the University of Washington home dialysis research study. Four patients were in training – two at the Center, one in Portland and one at the university. Nine patients were accepted and awaiting treatment and four applicants were pending.

By March, there were 36 patients dialyzing in-center and seven not yet started on dialysis, two patients approved by the Admissions and Advisory Committee were waiting for funding, and three new applications had been received. Two patients had been transferred from the Center to home training in each of the last two months, and if this rate could be maintained the Center census would be reduced by eight. Currently, nine patients were training and 24 were at home. The goal was for home patients to be followed by outside nephrologists with the Center physicians as consultants.

By late April, there were 31 patients dialyzing in-center, down from 45 in July 1967 and 35 on January 1, 1968. Six outpatients were awaiting cannulation and five applicants had been accepted pending funding. There were 27 patients on home dialysis and 19 in training and four patients had completed and five had started training since the last meeting. During the previous two years an average of two patients had been accepted each month and since January this had increased to three patients a month. Two months later, there were 24 patients dialyzing in the Center, 34 had completed training and were on home dialysis and seven patients were waiting cannulation. If two patients a month continued to go to training, the Center population would be at an irreducible minimum of ten patients by January 1969.

At the time of the August meeting there were 17 patients in the Center compared with a year earlier when there were 47, and the expected stable in-center patient census was 14 patients. Forty-six patients had completed home dialysis training and 12 were in training. Seven funded patients were awaiting cannulation, two had been transplanted, and five more applicants were waiting for funding. By the September meeting there were 16 patients dialyzing in the Center, 50 who had completed home training, 11 who were in training (five at the Center and six at the University of Washington's Coach House Home Training Unit), seven funded patients awaiting treatment and two applicants who were awaiting funding, for a total of 84 patients accepted for treatment. At the October meeting it was reported there were now 11 in-center patients and 58 home hemodialysis patients, eight of whom had completed training in the previous month. Nine funded patients were awaiting treatment and four applicants were waiting funding. Two patients had been transplanted and one was scheduled for transplantation in October. The original estimate that 12 patients would remain as Center patients had been reduced to between four and six.

By the end of the year there were 14 patients dialyzing in-center, 64 patients dialyzing at home, and eight patients in home hemodialysis training.

## CHRONIC UREMIA COORDINATING COMMITTEE

Dr. Scribner described the proposed Chronic Uremia Coordinating Committee that would include the University of Washington, the Seattle Artificial Kidney Center, the Seattle VA Hospital and the King County Hospital. Its purpose would be to coordinate the approach to providing services to patients with chronic kidney failure, to exchange information and to discuss problems of interest to more than one institution. Patients presently on dialysis would receive priority for transplantation, and patients who were not acceptable for dialysis would not be accepted for transplantation. Patients accepted for transplant at this time would be restricted to those who had related donors. The referring center would be responsible for long-term care and other forms of backup. This committee was never established.

## HOME HEMODIALYSIS

The cost of renting space from Swedish Hospital for home training was prohibitive and so consideration of merging with the university's home program was being considered. In addition, because of the cost, reconstruction was being undertaken in Eklind Hall so that the home training unit could transfer back there. It was anticipated this would be completed by September but by the end of August the home hemodialysis training unit had completed its move back to the Center, so reducing the costs somewhat.

PERITONEAL DIALYSIS

Dr. Tenckhoff in Dr. Scribner's unit at the University of Washington now had several years of experience using home peritoneal dialysis. In April he came to the Executive Committee meeting to discuss peritoneal dialysis in the home as an alternative to hemodialysis. This treatment had become much simpler with his recent development of an indwelling peritoneal catheter with which patients could treat themselves at home and which ultimately became the peritoneal dialysis catheter used worldwide. He was working on an improved fluid delivery system and estimated that when such a system was developed the cost for treating a patient with home peritoneal dialysis would be about $2,000 a year (excluding initial equipment costs). He wanted the Center to consider integrating this alternate form of treatment into the SAKC program. The method was simpler, the patient could do it alone, the training time was shorter, and dietary restriction might be less. It was decided that Drs. Tenckhoff, Pendras and Sawyer would put forward a proposal based on this recommendation.

By June, the University of Washington's peritoneal dialysis (PD) program had treated nine patients, of whom seven were still on PD dialyzing at home 36 hours a week. He estimated the current cost was similar to that for home hemodialysis because the new fluid supply system was not yet available. Dr. Tenckhoff asked if the Center would be available for backup hemodialysis in the event peritoneal dialysis failed in a patient, but it was pointed out that by that time the patient might have exhausted his or her funds. Consequently, no agreement was made and such patients would be considered for hemodialysis through the regular channels of admission to the Center.

In August, Dr. Tenckhoff again asked for help from the Center in finding funds for peritoneal dialysis patients and if this was agreed to it would not make the Center responsible for patients for whom no funds could be found. Dr. Haviland suggested that this issue be re-evaluated after Mr. Rice worked on the financial aspects of the one current in-center hemodialysis patient who was recommended as now requiring peritoneal dialysis.

By September, Dr. Tenckhoff reported there were eight patients in the University of Washington peritoneal dialysis program now, six of whom had been rejected for hemodialysis because of medical problems. Patients dialyzed two or three times a week for a total of 30 to 36 hours. After 170 patient months of treatment the only problems had been two episodes of infection as a result of faulty technique. Cost was about $5,000 a year for twice-weekly dialysis and this was expected to fall to $2,500 to $3,000 when the new peritoneal dialysis fluid delivery system became available. Dr. Eschbach said that some patients were better treated with peritoneal dialysis and that physicians should have the option of treatment choice. Dr. Scribner felt the basic problem was the same with all modalities of dialysis and if a patient was trainable he could not justifiably be turned down for lack of funds. Dr. McCormack appointed a committee of Drs. Tenckhoff, Pendras and Sawyer and Mr. Rice to review the issues.

Dr. Tenckhoff noted that he felt integration of home peritoneal dialysis into the overall dialysis-transplantation program of the Center would have several advantages: It would avoid separate fund drives for PD patients; the training period was shorter and less expensive; the cost of treatment eventually should be the least of any modality; and home PD appeared to be particularly suitable for patients who lived alone, those with shunts that were difficult to maintain or who had run out of cannula sites, and those waiting for a related donor kidney transplant for whom the equipment could be rented. The total cost would be less than for in-center hemodialysis or the first year of home hemodialysis with the higher training and set-up costs. In the ensuing discussion, Dr. Pendras thought there was a place for PD through the Center but that it should be limited to patients unsuitable for hemodialysis and who could be rehabilitated. Mr. Schoenfeld suggested that it might also be applicable to patients who could not raise the full cost of hemodialysis. Dr. Scribner said that the Center was becoming a chronic uremia treatment center and that all methods of treatment should be available. Dr. Eschbach suggested that the charge be the same for each form of treatment. Mr. Campbell asked if there was any difference in the quality of treatment between the two methods and Dr. Pendras said that generally hemodialysis was more successful. However, Dr. Tenckhoff disagreed and said that with certain exceptions the results were equally good and the advantages of PD were that there were no cannula problems, no need for blood transfusions and it was easier for patients to do at home. The Executive Committee moved that the issue of the Center providing peritoneal dialysis be discussed further. In fact it was not until about 9 months later that the Center had its own first home peritoneal dialysis patient.

## Patient Selection Issues

At the March Executive Committee meeting the Reverend John Darrah was appointed chairman of the Admissions Advisory Committee and was requested to organize a review of the patient selection process and plan for re-orientation of the committee.

Mr. Rice had asked the Finance Committee to define "a fully funded" patient in order to comply with the Executive Committee's directive that only such patients should be accepted until the present financial crisis was past. The Finance Committee recommended the figure be set at $11,000 to help cover the first three months of home hemodialysis training and the equipment; after that, the patient must have $250 per month for continuing care in the home program. The committee also recommended that the burden of credit be lifted from the Center by having patients purchase all supplies directly from the manufacturers. The report was accepted for discussion.

In April, the Medical Advisory Committee noted that as more patients were being transferred to home hemodialysis they would come under the care of private nephrologists. The committee therefore suggested that, except for funding issues, the responsibility for patient selection should pass to the Medical Advisory Committee, which would base its decisions on medical, sociological and psychological factors with professional help from social workers, psychologists and psychiatrists. The Committee would like to try this approach for six months. This proposal was to be discussed further. Shortly thereafter it was realized that the recent Medical Advisory Committee proposal that it should make the treatment decisions (with the exception of funding) – because patients now would be followed by community nephrologists – would lead to elimination of the Admissions Advisory Committee. This was discussed further but no decision was reached.

Patient selection was reviewed in August. From the medical viewpoint patients were divided into three classes:

Class I – ideal patients with no serious medical complications or psychological problems;

Class II – patients with some problems but in whom it was not possible to predict to what degree these would interfere with treatment. Some would do as well as Class I patients and others would develop more problems than predicted;

Class III – patients who were rejected for medical or psychological reasons. Sometimes these patients might be deferred for further testing if the committee felt this might be helpful in making a decision.

Class I patients would be given the fullest support in raising funds but Class II patients would be given no help in fundraising and would be left to their own devices.

Since February 1968, only fully funded patients were being accepted. Patients with problems included: those without adequate funds who very likely could be saved by treatment; those who required dialysis to survive until it was ascertained whether adequate funds were available; those who were being treated and had run out of funds; and home patients who had deteriorated medically and could no longer be dialyzed at home. Dr.

Eschbach was concerned with how long a holding action should be while funds were being raised and, if the patient could not raise the funds, who would pay paid for treatment during the holding action? Mr. Rambeck from University Hospital was concerned that patients held there might increase in numbers so as to overwhelm the hospital and he expressed concern about the moral obligation to continue treatment once it was started. He suggested that a simultaneous medical and financial decision would help. Mr. Rice said that he was hoping to initiate financial studies at the time of application. Mr. George Irvine from the University of Washington suggested another simpler classification: trainable or untrainable. He also suggested that a prospective patient be told what the amount of money they had available would cover in terms of equipment, training and support for "x" number of years based on the present cost of treatment. After that, the cost would be solely the responsibility of the patient. Dr. Scribner suggested the Center enter a financial partnership with insurance companies and state and federal governments so that physicians would only be concerned with medical issues. A bill might be introduced in the state legislature to allow solid funding for all dialysis patients so that the Center could get away from the problems of individual patient funding. Mr. Rice reviewed the various sources of funding but noted that there was still much to do and that the understandable desire to treat all patients had to be tempered with realism.

By September, the Medical Advisory Committee was still concerned about selection issues and was to meet with the Finance Committee about the financial aspects of selection. Dr. Haviland's view was that all dialysis patients should fall under the same acceptance and admission procedure and then be allocated to the most appropriate treatment for the patient. He also urged that the procedure come to a final decision at one particular moment so that no individual factor seemed to be the cause for rejection. Putting a limit of time of three to five weeks on the process should be sufficient. Since Mr. Rice said that funds could be raised for almost anyone if enough time was taken, Dr. Pendras suggested that during the holding period patients could begin training at the University of Washington's training unit at the Coach House to reduce the time involved. However, Dr. Eschbach said that the university would not go along with such a plan and Dr. McCormack pointed out that the Executive Committee's decision that a patient must be funded before acceptance would preclude training before acceptance.

The Medical Advisory Committee asked for clarification of the residency requirement for patients at the October meeting. Must a patient have been a state resident for six months prior to needing dialysis or six months prior to acceptance? An applicant had moved to Washington recently but the move was not related to kidney disease. The Executive Committee consensus was that each case should be considered individually.

Dr. Pendras pointed out that holding a patient while arrangements were made to assure adequate funds was sometimes necessary and that in most cases a funding prediction can be made. If the prediction was favorable, it could be possible to start the patient on home training. If there appeared to be no resources, the patient could be referred to the welfare agencies for support. He therefore suggested that new financial criteria be developed that would allow the medical and financial decisions to be made simultaneously. This would be discussed with the Finance committee.

## PERSONNEL CHANGES
Dr. Pendras would become half time in July 1969.

## FINANCES
Previously, the King County Blood Bank had prohibited solicitation of blood specifically for dialysis patients but in January the new director of the blood bank had revised this policy. The charge for dialysis now was increased to $133 per treatment. Accounts receivable was $136,000 and accounts payable was $182,000. The Executive Committee had met in closed session and approved Dr. Pendras' salary and the right for him to have a limited private practice and office space for this.

Martin LeGronsky of CBS Television nationally was interested in making a program on selection of patients for kidney transplantation and it was decided this would be possible provided the Center was compensated for time and inconvenience.

In February, the Finance Committee reported on its need to work more closely with Center administration for cost control and budget purposes. Mr. Rice would have administrative charge and also responsibility for fundraising and public relations, for working with insurance companies, and for working with the executive and legislative branches of the state government on problems relating to the Center.

The Center was preparing an application to Boeing's Employees Good Neighbor Fund but it was also suggested that the Center get out of fundraising as soon as possible. Dr. Scribner commented that the Center would become more committed to home dialysis and that eventually its in-center operation would be phased out except for backup of home patients. As a result the need for funds would gradually diminish.

At the March meeting, Denver Ginsey was appointed to succeed Renaldo Baggott as chairman of the Finance Committee and was also appointed to fill a vacancy on the Board of Trustees and to serve on the Executive Committee. In April it was noted that the 1968 budget indicated that $209,000 was necessary to operate the Center for the year but this figure was misleading as approximately $100,000 of the funds raised currently was used for 1967 expenses and budgetary variations might increase operating costs by $50,000. The budget suggested that only 17 patients would remain in the Center at the end of 1968. Dr. Haviland suggested that the Finance Committee report be modified to read that "the patient should have available $11,000" (not "must') and that it should be accepted that unusual circumstances would allow some variation from the recommendations. The current fundraising total was $133,000 of which $48,000 was raised in March and $35,000 in April.

As of July 31, the Center was $70,000-$80,000 in arrears and unless an additional source of funds was found the problem would be compounded the next year. A broader and more permanent source of funds was essential and the appeal to the governor should be pushed. The office space on the fourth floor was being remodeled and the cost would be offset by selling some cabinets to Swedish Hospital. Funds from the state Division of Rehabilitation had been fully used to move Center patients home. Mr. Rice was given permission to apply future funds from the Division of Vocational Rehabilitations to new applicants who were not fully funded.

STATE FUNDING

A committee was appointed to act on Scrib's suggestion that Governor Evans be approached for funds to make the Center solvent, facilitate home training and support kidney transplantation. It had been proposed to establish a Chronic Uremia Coordinating Committee to work on the dialysis-transplant relationship in the state. Senate Bill 2882 would provide funding for transplants and kidney centers but appeared unlikely to pass.

In September, Dr. McCormack reported that he had met with Mr. Howe, state Director of the Budget, who was anxious to help but pointed out that state funds must go through a state agency, which meant that the director of the agency had to initiate a request to the governor who would then appeal to the legislative committees. The Center's original request two years previously was through the Department of Health and Welfare but the Center had since been transferred to the Division of Vocational Rehabilitation (DVR), as this allowed for federal matching funds to be included. Mr. Howe suggested the Center wait for the next legislative session and try for an increased appropriation through DVR and try to increase the ratio of matching funds. He also suggested the Center keep legislators involved with the budget. Mr. Rice noted that the DVR had increased the matching ratio, which in the first year of the appropriation had been two federal dollars to one state dollar for a total of $187,500. Dr. Leahy pointed out that the ratio was three to one this year and was expected to rise to four to one in the coming year. Because of the change in the matching ratio and a carry forward of $20,000 from the previous year, the DVR funding for 1968 was $260,000. One million dollars had been requested for the programs in Seattle and Spokane. These funds could not be used for direct medical care but were restricted to training, outfitting and stabilizing patients at home for six months and efforts were being made to allocate part of the funds to the kidney transplant program. There must also be a strong infrastructure in place to assure patient support in the home and to foster patient independence and self-motivation.

FUND DRIVE

In January Jim Phillips reported that the fund drive began on December 11, 1967, and the goal was $290,000. It was moved and passed that the Northwest Artificial Kidney Fund be made a functional entity of the Seattle Artificial Kidney Center.

In March, Walter Schoenfeld was appointed chairman of the Fund Drive Advisory Committee. At that time, the fund drive total was $114,000 and as the drive would end on May 3 the goal of $270,000 would not be reached.

By June the fund drive had raised $178,780 although it had been hoped to reach at least $200,000 by the time the drive ended officially on June 1. A request for support from the Boeing Employees Good Neighbor Fund had been made, asking for $30,000 for current unfunded patients and $70,000 for such patients in the coming year but this request was not expected to pass. In the current year unfunded costs would be $145,739, and with the Center's existing deficit of $53,250 there would be a need for $198,989. Contributions received so far were $115,900 so the balance to be raised was $83,089. Since the next fund drive was not planned to start until December, consideration was given to approaching the Office of the Governor for at least $100,000 but it was decided to wait on this. The Fund Drive Advisory Committee recommended a coordinator for political activity, a permanent chairman to deal with public relations, and that future fund drives should start immediately after the end of the Boeing Good Neighbor fund drive.

By the end of July, Rice reported that returns from the fund drive totaled $188,000, but would reach $200,000. Accomplishments included development of a strong leadership and organization, establishment of a strong Public Relations Committee, and increased personal solicitation of major donors.

By October, $38,000 had been contributed to the Center since the previous fund drive ended, including $9,000 from the Boeing Employees Good Neighbor Fund and a $13,000 bequest.

## The 1968 ASAIO Annual Meeting

The 1968 meeting of the ASAIO was held in Philadelphia, where four papers from the University of Washington were presented. Babb and co-workers described how to determine membrane permeability and the rate of diffusion of solutes during dialysis in patients, information that could be important in comparing different dialysis membranes and dialyzers.

Drs. Tenckhoff and Schechter described what later became known as the Tenckhoff catheter, a bacteriologically safe peritoneal access device that soon became the standard access in the United States and Canada and is still used worldwide for peritoneal dialysis. This had been tested for as long as four years in patients. It used Dacron cuffs below the skin and outside the peritoneum in the abdominal wall to anchor the catheter in place. Interestingly, Tenckhoff had embedded pieces of Dacron in his own abdominal wall to show that tissue grew into the Dacron and would anchor it in place.

Dr. Orme and colleagues described one of the first successful pregnancies in a patient with moderately severe chronic renal failure who did not yet require dialysis at the time when she became pregnant. Starting at the 30th week of pregnancy, the patient was dialyzed for eight hours five times a week. No episodes of fetal distress occurred and the patient delivered a healthy female infant weighing 5lb 9oz at 37 weeks. The patient had sufficient remaining kidney function that she no longer required dialysis after the pregnancy.

Drs. Taves and colleagues from Rochester, New York, and Dr. Scribner examined the effect of fluoride in the municipal water supply in normal subjects and in dialysis patients in whom fluoride moved across the membrane from the dialysate to the blood. This was an important and timely study as municipalities were just beginning to fluoridate water supplies to help reduce tooth decay. The study showed that in normal subjects much of the fluoride was excreted by the kidneys but that blood levels were increased in dialysis patients. They expressed concern about the possible toxic effects of fluoride on bone in dialysis patients and this eventually would lead to the use of deionizers to remove fluoride from the water used to prepare dialysate. (The introduction of fluoride into Seattle's water supply is recounted in the next chapter).

## THE FIRST ANNUAL CONTRACTORS CONFERENCE OF THE ARTIFICIAL KIDNEY PROGRAM OF THE NATIONAL INSTITUTE OF ARTHRITIS AND METABOLIC DISEASES

The meeting was held in Bethesda, Maryland, on January 23- 24, 1968, and a copy of the proceedings of the meeting was sent to members of the ASAIO later in the year. The meeting was chaired by Benjamin T Burton, PhD, associate director for Program Analysis and Scientific Communication, National Institute of Arthritis and Metabolic Diseases and chief, Artificial Kidney Program The meeting presented a partial overview of the multi-disciplinary research and development effort funded by the NIH Artificial Kidney Program in 1967 in pursuit of its mission – the development of improved dialysis apparatus and methodologies and of related maintenance treatment for patients with chronic kidney failure, and attainment of better rehabilitation and a comfortable and productive life for such patients. During the conference, each project reported its negative and positive findings briefly to all other active contractors. Each presentation was followed by open, informal discussions intended to provide intercommunication and cross-fertilization of ideas from a large number of the participants and consultants to the program, coming from diverse biomedical and technological disciplines. This would create an environment in which new original ideas might evolve.

The opening session provided overviews of the Artificial Kidney – Chronic Uremia Program by members of the NIH staff. This included reviews of membranes, of dialyzers, of cannula and non-thrombogenic surfaces, of toxic components, of the Artificial Kidney Registry, the Kidney Disease Control Program and contract administration. The second session included 51 reports from contractors on membranes and mass transfer, hardware, cannulae and materials, and toxic factors. The section on membranes included a report from the Battelle Memorial Institute in Seattle on the development of improved hemodialysis membranes, and from the University of Washington on fluid mechanics, mass transfer and optimization studies of hemodialysis. The section on hardware also included a report from the University of Washington on fluid mechanics, mass transfer and optimization studies of hemodialysis. The section on cannulae and materials included papers from the University of Washington on cannula research and on the development of a bacteriologically safe peritoneal access device. Attendees from the University of Washington included Mr. Jack Cole and Drs. Bill Leith, Charles Maurer, Belding Scribner, Henry Tenckhoff and George Thomas. The third session comprised summary statements on cannulae, membranes, dialyzers and toxic factors. There was also a report from the Research Triangle Institute on the proposal to establish a medical registry and systems analysis of chronic intermittent dialysis.

## CHAPTER 29

# Annual Meeting, Executive Committee Meetings and ASAIO Annual Meeting 1969

———

THE YEAR WAS ONE OF continuing important changes and stresses for the Seattle Artificial Kidney Center. The number of home hemodialysis patients was steadily increasing and in November exceeded 100 for the first time, and in July the Center started its first home peritoneal dialysis program and was treating four patients by the end of the year. Also by the end of the year 11 of the Center's patients had received kidney transplants at University Hospital and the Center had discussed its policies about transplantation. There was considerable discussion of the process of patient acceptance and related issues. Mr. Del Ruble, the management consultant who had been studying the Center, made his report in March. Finances were improving over the year and the 1968-69 fund drive had raised $330,000 but there were problems with state funding. Mr. Earl Rice, the business manager, retired and there were several changes of personnel as a result. This was also the year the City of Seattle passed a measure to fluoridate the water supply starting in January 1970.

## THE SIXTH ANNUAL MEETING OF THE BOARD OF TRUSTEES

The Nominating Committee recommended by-law amendments to increase the number of trustees from 27 to 45 with three-year terms, and 15 members' terms to expire each year, and that the president of the organization be an ex-officio member and chairman of the Executive Committee. Nine members were elected to terms expiring in 1972: Charles Anderson, Robert S. Beaupre, the Rev. John Darrah, Denver Ginsey, John L. McCormack, MD, Mrs. Lowell Mickelwait, James Phillips and Walter Schoenfeld. David P. Simpson, MD and Richard Bangert were elected trustees with terms ending in 1971. The Rev. John Darrah, Denver Ginsey, Walter Schoenfeld and Richard Bangert were elected to the Executive Committee. Officers for the year were: president, John L. McCormack, MD; vice president, Willis Campbell; secretary, Lisle R. Guernsey; and treasurer, Renaldo Baggott. The motion to recommend was passed unanimously.

Dr. Pendras gave the medical review. A year previously, the Center had 19 Center beds in the basement of Eklind Hall for in-center hemodialysis and three training rooms in Swedish Hospital. Since then the training rooms in the hospital had been phased out and a section of the Center renovated to accommodate five training rooms and a nursing office. All this was accomplished with money donated by the Boeing Employees Good Neighbor Fund. Presently, there were only ten in-center beds. During the previous year there had been a change in philosophy so that the main function of the Center had become to train patients for home hemodialysis. Thirty-two patients had been accepted over the year and the Center now had 98 patients, 78 of whom were at home or in training. Three patients had received a kidney transplant and were doing quite well. It was anticipated that 50 new patients would be accepted over the coming year.

Mr. Rice reported on the Center's financial status. Due to an increase in costs, various charges had been revised: home dialysis training had increased from $133 to $189 per dialysis; the charge for equipment at home had increased by $640 to $6,640 that included preparation of the equipment, three visits to the home by a technician and a six-month warranty from the Center. The average yearly cost per patient for treatment in the home, including recannulation, declottings of the cannula and other problems, was $3,900. At the start of 1968 the Center had been behind in paying its bills in the amount of $110,000. At the start of 1969 the bills had been liquidated except for bills from Swedish Hospital and there were sufficient assets from the Public Health Service contracts to pay these off, leaving the Center completely current. The major financial hurdle for the coming year was the need to buy equipment to deionize the water supply for the Center and in patients' homes as fluoridation was coming. The Center was researching possible equipment. Funds set aside by the Center for specific patients had grown to $152,000 and the earnings from these funds during 1968 would support patient funding in accordance with the policy established by the Executive Committee.

Dr. McCormack introduced Dr. Allan Lobb, director of Swedish Hospital, Miss Roberta Schumann from the state Division of Vocational Rehabilitation and Clyde Shields, the world's first chronic hemodialysis patient who started treatment in March 1960. Certificates of appreciation were given to the Boeing Employees Good Neighbor Fund, the Stewardess Emeritus Association, Jack Schwartz, chairman of the Public Relations Committee and the members of that committee, and a plaque was presented to James Phillips, chairman of the Northwest Artificial Kidney Fund campaign. A birthday cake was presented to Clyde Shields who was celebrating his tenth year on dialysis.


## PATIENT ACTIVITIES AND HOME HEMODIALYSIS

At the beginning of 1969, the Center had a total of 97 patients: 14 in-center patients, 8 of whom were awaiting a vacancy in the home dialysis training program; 64 patients who had completed home training and 8 patients who were being trained; and 11 funded outpatients who had not yet started treatment. With the increasing numbers of home hemodialysis patients, the number of backup dialyses performed in the Center was increasing and might require adjustments in the capacity of the Center facility. Backup dialysis in a hospital had been suggested as an alternative but was not necessary so far. It was also suggested patients could take their own machine to the hospital but it would be very expensive to move the machine. The cost of peritoneal dialysis was still being studied.

By April there were 7 patients in home dialysis training, 81 patients at home, 12 in-center patients, 10 outpatients and 10 accepted pending funding. Two deaths had occurred in the previous month: one an anesthetic death and the other an unexplained death at home. Dr. Pendras asked for a directive from the Executive Committee regarding "problem" patients in home training. When a patient was poorly motivated, of borderline intelligence or had emotional problems, it was more difficult to teach the techniques involved in home dialysis. The Center had taken the attitude that as great an effort as possible be made but after a certain point the patient would be transferred home, even though the Center knew the patient was not fully capable of handling the ramifications of home dialysis and might have a shorter life expectancy. He wished the Executive Committee to either approve this policy or to provide guidelines for changing it. The committee confirmed that all new patients were accepted for home dialysis training with Center facilities only available for backup. A patient, once trained, must leave the Center. The policy of the Center would continue to be to reduce the in-center patient population.

By the end of June there were 83 patients in the home, 13 dialyzing in-center, eight outpatients and ten in home training (six at the Center and four at the University of Washington's Coach House facility). Seven patients had been accepted and were waiting funding before starting treatment. There had been two kidney transplants from live related donors and in May two from cadaveric donors. Three were doing well; one was marginal. There were two deaths during the month: one a newly accepted patient who was quite sick and the other a longtime patient with severe heart disease. Neither death resulted from dialysis treatment. It had been decided that the home hemodialysis training program could be improved by involving a professional educator and so a Ph.D. candidate in education had been hired to evaluate the program from a teaching standpoint and "teach how to teach." This would be supported by a $5,000 grant from the University of Washington.

A month later the Center was supporting a total of 132 patients. Eleven were outpatients being followed until their need for dialysis; eight were dialyzing in-center, and five had been accepted and were waiting funding. Ninety patients were at home, four having been discharged to home since the last meeting, and ten patients were in home training, two of whom were being trained at the Coach House facility. One patient had received a kidney transplant, making a total of eight transplants so far. There had been one death during the month. New plumbing was being installed in the Center and the central delivery system would be eliminated to make the Center environment as similar to the home training situation as possible.

At the June meeting Dr. Pendras proposed that patients for peritoneal dialysis now should be accepted by the Seattle Artificial Kidney Center. He made the following points:

1. There are certain medical, social, psychological, and economic reasons in certain patients that make peritoneal dialysis preferable;
2. Peritoneal dialysis has been demonstrated to be an effective, safe treatment. Patients appear to be happy and rehabilitated on this program. Dialysis failure has been limited;
3. Only a limited number of patients would require this form of therapy rather than hemodialysis;
4. The decision as to who would require peritoneal dialysis would rest with the referring physician and the Center's medical director. Approval by the medical director would be mandatory;
5. Initially, peritoneal dialysis would be performed by either University Hospital (Dr. Tenckhoff) or the Veterans Administration Hospital (Dr. Curtis).

It was moved and seconded to accept Dr. Pendras' proposal. In the discussion, it was noted that each patient presented for the peritoneal dialysis program would have to meet the same financial requirements as candidates for hemodialysis, i.e., three years of funding, at whatever level, to be accepted. Five patients were now on peritoneal dialysis at University Hospital and acceptance of these patients would make things easier for all concerned since there were no facilities for financial evaluation or fundraising at the university. These five patients would be submitted to the Patient Admissions Committee for evaluation. The motion passed unanimously.

At the August Executive Committee meeting, Drs. Pendras and Sawyer reported there were twelve outpatients waiting prior to their need for dialysis. Eight patients were dialyzing in-center, seven in home dialysis training, six had been discharged to the home since the last meeting, and four patients had been accepted who were on home peritoneal dialysis. One patient had died during the last month. Of the all-time high census of 47 in-center patients, only five now remained in the Center and three of these five were scheduled to start home training in September. The Center had nearly reached its goal of using its beds for stabilization of new patients before training and for backup dialysis for home patients needing in-center dialysis for one reason or another. Willis Campbell said staff should be complimented for their efforts in accomplishing this much under such difficulties.

By the end of September there were ten outpatients who had not yet been cannulated and ten in-center patients, seven of whom had their initial cannulation during the previous month. In home training there were five patients who started in the previous month and three who had gone home. At home there were now 98 patients on hemodialysis and five on peritoneal dialysis.

At the October 24 meeting of the Executive Committee, Drs. Pendras and Sawyer reported there were now twelve outpatients who had been accepted and were waiting until they needed dialysis, and nine in-center patients, four remaining from the long-term patient population and five stabilizing before starting home training. Seven patients were training, one had gone home during the month and two had started, and 99 patients were at home on hemodialysis and five on peritoneal dialysis. There were two deaths during the month, one a patient accepted by the Patient Admissions Committee who died before treatment started and one an elderly patient, who died from problems unrelated to dialysis. There had been two kidney transplants, one cadaveric with uncertain function currently and one related donor transplant with no problems. Five patients were currently scheduled for living related donor transplants and eight were tentatively being processed for cadaveric transplants. Discussion followed about transplant funding. Mr. Phillips assured the committee that a comprehensive plan would be formulated and presented for consideration. This would include some variation in the acceptance procedure to allow the Center more control. Dr. McCormack asked the Rev. Darrah to have his committee explore the mechanics of scheduling future transplants for SAKC patients and report to the committee. He also requested that Dr. Marchioro, head of transplantation at University Hospital and Mrs. Profant, an administrator, be invited to Executive Committee meetings when transplants were to be discussed.

By early December, the Center had ten outpatients being followed before their need for dialysis, eight patients dialyzing in-center, six in home training, 103 at home on hemodialysis and four at home on peritoneal dialysis. During the previous month there had been two kidney transplants, making a total of 11 SAKC patients who had received kidney transplants. There were three deaths: one, a patient who had been accepted but was unwilling to keep outpatient appointments; one, a Vancouver man who died of a subarachnoid hemorrhage; and the third a young man who died from hyperkalemia.

## PATIENT SELECTION AND THE MEDICAL ADVISORY COMMITTEE

In April, Dr. Eschbach reported that in the last year 64 applicants had been processed by the Medical Advisory Committee, six of whom were rejected without further review. Of the 58 processed, three were rejected, leaving 55 new patients over the year. Twelve were still waiting to be funded. The Center was getting eight to nine applicants a month; almost all were trained for home dialysis, and few medical complications contraindicated dialysis. Dr. Eschbach pointed out that the crucial problems for patients are social, psychological and financial. The Medical Advisory Committee asked for consideration of a proposed Patient Selection Committee. Dr. McCormack appointed a committee to be chaired by the Rev. John Darrah with Drs. Haviland and Eschbach and Lyle Guernsey to review this and report back.

Dr. Pendras asked for clarification of the residency requirement for applicants. The Executive Committee had previously advised the Medical Advisory Committee that each applicant's residency could be handled individually. If it appeared an applicant had moved to Washington for reasons unrelated to kidney disease and if it appeared the individual intended to establish permanent residence in Washington, the applicant could be processed at the discretion of the Medical Advisory Committee. Dr. Pendras presented two applications received during the past month that did not fit into the above category. In each case the applicant was traveling through Washington when his kidney disease was diagnosed and neither had a permanent residence. The Executive Committee agreed that the previous policy was broad enough to allow processing these patients.

In May, Dr. Haviland reported on the recent meeting of the Patient Selection Committee that had suggested that the Executive Committee support an alternative proposal to that of the Medical Advisory Committee:

1. The Medical Advisory Committee remain the same and process applicants from a medical standpoint;
2. The Admissions Advisory Committee composition be changed to the administrator of the Center, the medical director and an Executive Committee member;
3. The referring physician submit a report on the patient as part of the information to the Admissions Advisory Committee;
4. The director of Patient Finances be present at the Admissions Advisory Committee meeting to provide information but would have no vote;
5. The chairman of the Medical Advisory Committee be present to report its recommendation and to report back to it but would not have a vote.

The committee also recommended that the tentative three-month patient acceptance by the Center proposed by the Medical Advisory Committee be rejected.

The motion was made and seconded. However, Dr. Eschbach said that the Medical Advisory Committee was not pleased with this alternative as its recommendation had meant more active involvement of the physicians caring for the patient. The Medical Advisory Committee now was more of a rubber stamp since medical issues were of much less importance in the selection process. They suggested instead that:

1. The application be reviewed initially by the Medical Advisory Committee chairman and/or the medical director and if there were medical issues the Medical Advisory Committee be convened;
2. The Admissions Committee would be composed of the administrator and medical director of the Center, a Medical Advisory Committee member and an Executive Committee member;
3. Pertinent information would be presented by the social worker, the psychiatrist, the referring physician and the patient financial manager. They would be present but would not vote;
4. A motion to refer the issue back to the Patient Selection Committee to discuss the overall philosophy of patient selection and patient care provided by the Center passed unanimously;
5. The following month, the Rev, Darrah gave the Patient Selection Committee report. The ad hoc committee had discussed the proposal of the Medical Advisory Committee concerning patient applications for treatment at the Seattle Artificial Kidney Center and recommended the following:
   a. The applications received will be referred directly to the medical director of the Center, who will then instigate appropriate workup. The Medical Advisory Committee will continue in existence for at least six months, to be convened at the request of the medical director, the Medical Advisory Committee chairman, or the patient's physician. Upon the request, the Medical Advisory Committee would meet and give its recommendations concerning a particular case to the Patient Admissions Committee. Otherwise, upon approval of the medical director of the Center, the applications will go directly to the Patient Admissions Committee;

   b.  The Patient Admissions Committee will be composed of the administrator of the Center, the medical director of the Center, the Medical Advisory Committee chairman, and two Executive Committee members;

   c.  Pertinent information would be presented by the social worker, the referring physician, the psychiatrist, and the patient financing manager. They would be present for the meeting but would not have a vote;

   d.  A favorable vote of three is necessary for the acceptance of an applicant;

   e.  If the referring physician is a member of the committee, an alternate will take his place on the committee. In no case would the referring physician have a vote.

The Rev. Darrah moved approval of this proposal and the motion was seconded. It was noted that since the social worker charged the center for her time, and since her presence was not crucial, it was recommended that her report is submitted with her presence not be required. The psychiatrist presently was supported by a grant from the University of Washington, but it was also recommended that his presence not be required. It was moved, seconded and passed that point 3 of the proposal the amended to read: "the pertinent information concerning the applicant will be presented by the referring physician and the patient financing manager. (They will be present for the meeting but will not have a vote). A report from the social worker and the psychiatrist would be read at a meeting as part of the information to be considered concerning the applicant." It would be optional, at the discretion of the committee, as to whether or not to invite the psychiatrist and social worker. Walt Schoenfeld moved that since it was necessary to have an affirmative vote of three for acceptance of an applicant, the proposal be amended so that alternate members of the executive committee might be called by Dr. McCormack to attend the meeting. This was seconded and passed. The proposal as amended passed unanimously. Dr. McCormack appointed the Rev. Darrah and Denver Ginsey to serve on the committee. The Rev. Darrah will be co-chairman.

In July, The Rev. John Darrah reported there had been two meetings of the Patient Admissions Committee, primarily to establish ground rules and criteria for patient acceptance. There still was no clear-cut decision as to financial acceptability. At the last meeting, data were given on three patients; of these three, one died prior to the meeting, one was accepted, and one was deferred for consideration at a later date. A major problem was the semantic question of what "acceptance" meant to the Center and to the patient. The Patient Agreements may be changed to read "treatment may commence" rather than "accepted for treatment." However, an attempt would be made to establish a policy eliminating expensive holding actions at the university, as the committee would try to make an educated guess as to potential funding. Center staff would put as much financial information together as possible in the two-week period before each meeting.

A month later the Rev. Darrah gave the Patient Admissions Committee Report. The committee had now established meetings on the first and third Thursday of every month. At the first meeting of the last month, one applicant was accepted and one was deferred; of the four peritoneal dialysis patients considered, two were accepted, one rejected, and one referred back to the University of Washington. At the second meeting of the month, two patients were accepted and one deferred. The current procedure for consideration of an applicant was much the same as before. The referring physician gives a brief medical report on the applicant and the psychiatric, social, and financial reports are mailed to committee members four days before the meeting. The committee will need more experience before changing any of the present criteria for patient acceptance.

In September, the Patient Admissions Committee had met twice in September and the Reverend Darrah gave a brief summary of each applicant and the action taken. The moral commitment of the Center toward patients who have been "accepted" was discussed and all agreed that legal counsel would be appropriate at this point. Walt Schoenfeld moved that the president of the Board of Trustees authorize the expenditure to obtain legal services for the Center and the motion was seconded and passed unanimously.

It was agreed legal services would begin with rewriting the Patient Financial Agreement and investigating the Center's role and obligation to patients upon acceptance.

There were two meetings of the Patient Admissions Committee during the next month, one a special meeting on October 6 to consider an applicant who subsequently died, the other on October 16, at which four applications were considered; two were accepted and two were deferred.

In December, the Rev. Darrah reported that at its last meeting the Patient Admissions Committee considered seven applications and all were accepted. Each acceptance was contingent upon the fulfillment of a restrictive clause, different in each case. Recent questions regarding acceptance criteria had made the Patient Admissions Committee's role difficult.

Dr. Eschbach reported on the special meeting of the Medical Advisory Committee. He recounted briefly the discussions of the past six months. Because physicians in the community felt that medically anyone could be treated by hemodialysis and because patients would be trained at the Center for home dialysis and returned to the care of the community physician, the Medical Advisory Committee was serving no purpose. The Admissions Advisory Committee was limited in that it was composed only of SAKC personnel. As a result, the Executive Committee had adopted the Patient Admissions Committee to replace the two-committee process. The Medical Advisory Committee special meeting was to consider recent developments and special problems: the increasing availability of kidney transplants with their attendant successful survival rate; the present solvency of the Center; and the question of criteria for patient selection. The Medical Advisory Committee therefore recommended that:

1.  The name of the Seattle Artificial Kidney Center be changed to the Seattle Kidney Center;
2.  Transplantation from a related donor is the best mode of therapy for selected patients;
3.  In view of our past inability to predict rehabilitation, that dialysis or transplant should be made available to every medically acceptable patient if funds were available.

## Kidney Transplantation

In December, Dr. McCormack asked that Dr. Pendras present the Seattle Artificial Kidney Center's transplant proposal (see below) before discussing the Medical Advisory Committee's recommendations, since the proposal had direct bearing on the committee. This noted that since related donor kidney transplants were becoming the preferable mode of treatment, the attached proposal compared the cost to the Center for unfunded patients treated by hemodialysis and transplant for a three-year period. The figure of ten patients was estimated on the basis of 50 anticipated new patients, 40 percent of whom would require SAKC funding (20 patients), and predicting that 50 percent of these would have well-matched related donors for transplantation. These estimates were on the high side. The proposal also estimated the cost of three cadaveric transplants for unfunded patients versus home training and home hemodialysis. It was moved and seconded that the transplant proposal be accepted by the Executive Committee.

In discussion, it was pointed out that since some patients may not adapt well to home hemodialysis, Center-funded transplant would be a mechanism to enable the Center to accept without reservation all medically acceptable applicants, if funds were available. Also, in certain cases, a kidney transplant would be the preferred medical treatment of renal failure. The fact that using state money for funding patients raised questions about the legality and morality of a selection process, and the fact that the ability to predict patient rehabilitation was poor, precluded the philosophy of patient "selection." With the ability to choose either home hemodialysis or transplantation, the Center would be able to care for any medically acceptable patient with terminal kidney failure if funds were available, regardless of vaguely predicted personality problems or unclear social history. All patients considered for transplant that required Center assistance in funding would be presented to the Patient Admissions Committee. The motion was passed unanimously.

PROPOSED TRANSPLANTATION POLICY

The following numbers of patients to be transplanted are those in whom public funds, i.e., DVR, state health service money, or fundraised money, would be necessary for their support.

1. As many as ten patients with related donors could be transplanted per year;
2. No patient would receive a cadaver transplant who is unable to perform home dialysis, either home peritoneal or home hemodialysis;
3. A total of only three cadaver transplants would be performed in the next year.

COMPARATIVE COSTS: THREE-YEAR TRANSPLANT COSTS VS. THREE-YEAR HOME HEMODIALYSIS COSTS

In 1970, it was estimated there would be 50 new patients, 20 (40%) of whom would require total funding from the Center. Of these, it was estimated that a half (10) would have a well-matched related donor for transplantation and so 10 new patients could receive a cadaveric donor transplant as the primary form of treatment. Based on this it was estimated that the comparative costs over three years between transplantation and home hemodialysis were as follows:

Ten related donor transplants at $9,000 per person in first-year costs would cost $90,000. The estimated ongoing care for ten transplanted patients in the second and third years would be $6,000 per person per year for a total cost of $120,000. With an estimated 20% transplant failure rate requiring a second kidney transplant, the additional cost would be a further $18,000. The total three-year commitment for ten patients would therefore be $228,000.

In addition, it was estimated that three unfunded patients, (either new patients acceptable for home dialysis or patients currently on dialysis in the Center) would require cadaveric transplants during 1970. Problems with cadaveric transplants include a higher failure rate of approximately 50%, the cost of holding a patient on dialysis until a suitable donor becomes available and the possibility of multiple re-transplants and related holding action. For purposes of estimation, the following over-conservative assumptions were used: all cadaveric transplants would fail after six months and all patients would be held on dialysis for six months awaiting each transplant. Thus, the total three-year commitment for three patients receiving a cadaveric transplant was estimated to be $117,000. For comparison the first-year cost for ten home hemodialysis patients was estimated to be $135,000, including the cost of training, with second and third year ongoing care costs of $35,000 each year. The total three-year commitment for ten home hemodialysis patients was estimated to be $205,000.

Thus, the one-year commitment for ten patients receiving a related donor transplant would be $90,000 and for three patients receiving cadaveric transplants would be $48,000 for a total cost of $138,000, compared with a first-year cost for 13 patients on home hemodialysis at the cost of $13,500 per person or a total of $175,500.

The three-year commitment for ten patients receiving a related donor kidney transplant would be $228,000 and for three patients receiving cadaveric kidney transplants together with holding dialysis would be $117,000 for a total of three-year cost for 13 transplanted patients of $345,000. The three-year cost of 13 patients on home hemodialysis was estimated to be $266,500.

## FINANCIAL ISSUES

In January, the Finance Committee hoped that by the end of the fiscal year the Center would break even or might even eliminate some of the deficit. Holding actions were the problem causing the most inefficiency in operations and the committee had suggested that if home hemodialysis training could start once it appeared that funds could be raised for a patient a reduction in expenses could be achieved. However, Mr. Rice felt this would be detrimental to the fundraising potential of a given patient. The committee passed a motion that Mr. Rice be given more flexibility and, if in his opinion, funds would be available, the patient could be accepted for training.

Mr. Thompson distributed copies of the recently completed audit and pointed out that while "cash-restricted" funds for a given patient was not a legal restriction it was a moral one and the funds should only be used for the patient for whom they were intended. He also pointed out that without the substantial help received from the state Division of Vocational Rehabilitation and from the fund drive, the financial picture of the Center would be grim. He hoped every effort would be made to continue these sources.

In April, Renaldo Baggott presented the Finance Committee report. They committee recommended the salary schedules proposed by Del Ruble and so moved, but this was not seconded and Dr. McCormack asked the Executive Committee members to study the proposed schedules. Lee Harvey noted that there was $68,000 in the checking account and the accounts receivable balance was $280,000.

At the May 23 Executive Committee meeting, Dr. McCormack announced that he had agreed to the center participating in the care of a patient with acute kidney failure at Swedish Hospital because space was unavailable for the patient at the University hospital.

The Finance Committee reported there had been progress in collecting accounts receivable. The Center had selected one of the two proposals to provide deionizers for the Center. The Center's laboratory had been closed and patients were receiving their laboratory tests at Swedish Hospital. This would result in savings to the Center of approximately $400 a month. Currently there was $180,000 in uncommitted funds and $87,000 committed for specific patients. The fund drive would end on June 30, 1969.

In June, Denver Ginsey gave the Finance Committee report. The Puget Sound Blood Bank had been paid $13,156, representing the final payment, as after a two-year period of discussion this figure had been established as being equitable. The accounts receivable was still about $315,000. The committee had agreed that the 60-to-90 day accounts receivable would be acceptable; however, the Center was still in a situation of catching up from past receivables.

In July, Denver Ginsey gave the Finance Committee report noting that $32,000 more had been billed in the current year compared with the previous year. The quarterly statements would be mailed after review by the auditor. In addition, $59,000 in uncommitted funds was available. The new fund period would start August 15, 1969.

Mr. Ramsey gave the Finance Committee report in August. A cash flow statement for the month representing resources and how they were spent was distributed to the committee. The statement showed that $99,148.03 was received and $60,085.36 in cash was applied to accounts. The balance currently in checking accounts was $62,992.27 and would be used to pay the remainder of the July bills. Since the last meeting, patients had received the first quarterly statement showing the charges incurred, the amount credited to the account by contributions, the amount paid by insurance, and the amount owing or written off. Monthly statements would now be sent out showing charges for the month.

The guests were excused and the Executive Committee met in closed session where it was moved, seconded, and carried that as SAKC employees became eligible, they would be given the option of joining the Swedish Hospital Retirement Program. It was also moved, seconded, and carried to combine the position of administrator and fundraiser and to attempt to recruit a qualified person to assume this responsibility.

The Finance Committee met on August 27, 1969, and the tentative budget was accepted. This was given to the Executive Committee for its review.

Mr. Ramsey reported for the Finance Committee that the balance in checking accounts as of October 23, 1969 was $51,816.30, accounts payable had a balance of $135,000, and accounts receivable had a balance of approximately $300,000.

In December, Mr. Ginsey reported that the Finance Committee had met and had agreed that now there was better control of accounts receivable with the monthly billing. However, lack of a contractual agreement with patients presented a hardship to the Center when billing accounts, and so the

Finance Committee recommended that the Center be permitted to retain legal counsel. The preliminary audit showed a net income of over $200,000, a substantial portion of which was restricted funds to be used for stipulated patients' future care. These funds were not free for use on operational expenses and so the figure as it appeared in the audit report was misleading. However, the Finance Committee agreed that the Seattle Artificial Kidney Center was financially sound at the present time. In the ensuing discussion of the Finance Committee report, it was noted that there had been a difference of opinion concerning how the restricted funds would appear on the audit report. The report had been delayed as Jim Thompson, the auditor, felt that listing restricted funds as such on the audit might initiate potential problems with the Internal Revenue Service. It was suggested that a Receipts and Disbursements statement might be preferable to an audit report.

STATE FUNDING

In January, Mr. Rice reported that a patient funding crisis was occurring. Because of reduced federal funds the state DVR funds available had been reduced by 20 percent – a cut of $59,689, leaving only $9,542 available to the Center until July 1, 1969. This would make it difficult to meet the obligations to patients already accepted. DVR expected additional money to become available in May or June that might be enough to help four or five patients at that time but until July 1 the situation was potentially a serious problem both for patients already accepted but not started on training and for new applicants.

In April, Dr. McCormack asked Dick Bangert, a new board member and Executive Committee member, and Jack Schwartz to consider means of maintaining contact with the legislature.

In May, he announced that the Washington State Legislature had passed the $300,000 appropriation for the care of dialysis patients in the state; the remaining $128,000 necessary to complete the budget was put in a supplemental budget bill that did not pass. The Center had recently formed a political action committee that would follow this more closely.

In June, Dr. McCormack reported on the Olympia meeting where representatives from the Spokane Artificial Kidney Center, the University of Washington and the Seattle Artificial Kidney Center had met with representatives of the Department of Health and the Division of Vocational Rehabilitation to discuss guidelines for the $300,000 that had been appropriated by the legislature. Any state money spent for transplantation must go through either the Seattle or the Spokane Centers. A plan for DVR distribution had to be worked out and this probably would be earmarked for training and equipment. DVR would like the kidney centers to buy the machines and lease them to the state. Dr. McCormack had appointed Walt Schoenfeld, Willis Campbell, Dick Bangert and Tom Siefert to meet and discuss the leasing of kidney machines. The Executive Committee would be kept informed of the discussions on dividing the appropriations between the two centers.

In July, Dr. McCormack reported that the monies the Center hoped to obtain from the Division of Vocational Rehabilitation had been drastically reduced from $700,000 to $425,000 or less. This was a direct result of economies in Washington, D. C. over which the state had no control. The Center had agreed to divide the $300,000 appropriated by the state legislature on a 60-40 basis ($180,000-$120,000) with Spokane receiving 60 percent. This division was agreed upon since the original representation had assumed that Seattle would receive the larger share of DVR funds. It would be stipulated by the state Department of Health that each center's remaining funds would be reviewed in January 1970. This had the advantage of giving the Center factual data to present to the special session of the legislature. Dick Bangert, Walt Schoenfeld, Jack Schwartz, and Tom Seifert had met and were exploring avenues of possible liaison with the state legislature. Recommendations would be made at a later date.

FUND DRIVE

In April, Earl Rice reported that the fund drive presently stood at $130,000 in uncommitted funds and $35,000 in committed funds.

At the meeting of the Executive Committee on July 25, 1969, Dr. McCormack announced that KAPA (Kidney Auxiliary for Patients' Assistance) would have its grand opening July 21 through July 27. This venture was started by interested citizens in the community to assist in fundraising for patients at the Center.

In August, Tom Seifert reported on the 1966-67 fund drive when 3,000 gifts resulted in contributions totaling $168,000. The "Let Leslie Live!!" campaign resulted in 2,500 gifts. The 1967-68 drive received 1,800 gifts totaling $201,000. In 1968-69, 2,445 gifts totaled $330,000. These figures included committed and uncommitted contributions. The 1969-70 fund drive chairman would be Dr. Richard Philbrick; Harry Machenheimer would head the Major Gifts Division, Roger Jones the Special Gifts Division, and Larry Pint, the New Gifts Division. The Public Relations Committee was preparing for a November 10 kick-off of the fund drive.

Mr. Phillips reported on the fund drive: the Major Gifts list was complete and would be returned to the Major Gifts chairman and the Special Gifts list was being completed. Television, radio and newspaper material was being worked out to publicize the Christmas card sale. Dr. McCormack mentioned that solicitation by the Board of Trustees was entirely voluntary.

In October, Mr. Phillips reported the 1969-70 Fund Drive would begin November 7 with a kick-off breakfast at the Washington Athletic Club for volunteers and drive chairmen. The committee was given a tentative list of planned activities involving the fund drive.

## REPORT OF MR. E. D. RUBLE, MANAGEMENT CONSULTANT

A closed session of the Executive Committee was called on March 18 to discuss the report of Mr. E.D. Ruble, management consultant, who had reviewed the organization of the Seattle Artificial Kidney Center. Lyle Guernsey felt that more time was necessary to work out the various problems and asked that an evening meeting be held to get down to the basic implementation of the recommendations in the report. It was decided to hold a dinner meeting early in April.

Dr. McCormack reviewed the attached report and the reorganization called for in the organization chart and asked Dr. Pendras to discuss the report from the medical director's standpoint.

Dr. Pendras said that one of the problems at the Center had been that there were no clear-cut lines of responsibility in dealing with members working for and with the organization. He felt the proposed organization chart would be of considerable help within the organization. Dr. Pendras also said that he would not be able to assume the responsibility of full-time medical director.

Mr. Ruble pointed out that, if working within the framework of this proposed organization, it was important to have a full-time medical director and a very strong financial manager.

An alternative plan was suggested, to have a full-time director-financial manager in charge of the Center. Mr. Ginsey asked if the committee thought it possible for a non-medical man to function over the medical field of the Center. Dr. Haviland stated the plan deserved some thought by the committee as the medical side had never faced up to the fact that the Center was not an open-ended project. Bringing in a businessman might make things run more smoothly.

The consensus was to leave the decision open for further investigation as to whether the executive head of the Center should be a physician or a businessman. Dr. Haviland moved acceptance of the concept that administration of the Kidney Center follow along the lines of the organization chart with a full-time executive head. Mr. Guernsey seconded the motion and the motion was passed.

During the meeting of May 23, the committee met in closed session and after considerable discussion the salary schedule presented by Mr. Del Ruble was accepted and would be re-evaluated annually.


PERSONNEL

At the Executive Committee meeting of April 25, Dr. McCormack introduced Dick Bangert, a new board member and Executive Committee member, Del Ruble, management consultant and Tom Seifert, new administrator of the Kidney Center.

At the June 27 meeting of the Executive Committee, Dr. McCormack announced that Earl Rice had submitted his resignation effective as of July 1 because of medical disablement. He welcomed Dr. Richard Philbrick, cochairman of the current fund drive, and noted that the firm Stokes & Company had been engaged to audit the books of the Center.

At the Executive Committee meeting on September 26, 1969 Dr. McCormack announced that James W. Phillips, a former newspaperman and freelance writer with a background in communications and the author of the book "Washington State Place Names" had assumed the position of executive director of the Seattle Artificial Kidney Center on September 15, 1969, and that Terry Pollard, chief technician, had taken on additional administrative responsibilities. Tom Seifert who had been acting administrator for three months would be leaving the Center to accept a position with the University of California at Berkeley and had submitted a report on the re-organization accomplished and that remaining to be done. Dr. McCormack would have this report disseminated to the Executive Committee and asked all members of the committee to give this report their attention.

Mr. Phillips expanded the business department and established a separate public relations and fundraising department with Mr. Clint Howard as director and Mrs. Lucy Ransdell as his assistant.

## CORPORATE RESOLUTION

A corporate resolution to be adopted by the Executive Committee was moved and seconded: The Seattle Artificial Kidney Center Board of Trustees, hereby resolve that effective November 1, 1969, the registered office of this corporation shall be at 1102 Columbia Street, Seattle, King County, Washington, 98104, and that the registered agent for this corporation shall be Mr. James W. Phillips, whose business address is 1102 Columbia Street, Seattle, King County, Washington, 98104, and all previous designations of registered office or registered agent are hereby revoked and terminated. The motion passed unanimously.

## Visitors
The Executive Committee meeting of August 22 was attended by Drs. John Pierce and Robert Levine, Warren Thompson and Lillian Weikel from the renal unit of St. Mary's Hospital in Grand Rapids, Michigan.

## Fluoridation of the Water Supply
In 1969, the City of Seattle voted approval of a plan to add a small amount of fluoride to the Seattle water supply as a prophylactic measure to reduce the incidence of dental caries. Implementation of this plan would begin on January 12, 1970. Some of the surrounding communities that obtained their water from the Seattle system would be similarly affected, since the addition of fluoride was to be at the Seattle water source. Fluoride was to be added in a concentration of 1 part fluoride per million parts of water by weight (1 ppm). This concentration was that long recommended by the United States Public Health Service and the American Dental Association. Even considerably larger amounts of fluoride occurring naturally in many areas of the United States were not known to produce any ill effects in normal people.

Fluoride in excessive amounts, as with almost any substance, could be harmful and the effects could be either acute or chronic and cumulative, depending on just how excessive the dose was. The only known condition in which the addition of 1 ppm of fluoride to the water supply could be potentially harmful to health was in persons dependent for a long time period on an artificial kidney for survival. This was because such patients are exposed to the fluoride in a large volume of water used to make the dialysate so that during dialysis the patient would absorb 50 to 250 times the amount of fluoride he or she would receive from the water they drank each day. This was compounded by the fact that with normal kidney function, approximately

60 percent of the ingested dose is excreted by the kidneys; but in a patient on the artificial kidney who has no significant kidney function this large dose becomes even more significant.

Although no acute toxic effects had been reported using water with 1 ppm fluoride to make dialysate, chronic bone changes had been reported to occur after a number of months of such dialysis. Therefore, it was generally felt that the fluoride should be removed from water used to make dialysate for patients on regular maintenance hemodialysis. It was therefore recommended to the Center that fluoride should be removed from the water. This policy was further supported by information from the United States Public Health Service.

Since there was no evidence there were any harmful effects to bone occurring with the amount of fluoride a patient would receive with dialysis using fluoridated water for at least six months, the Center had the advantage of this grace period to install the deionizing equipment necessary to defluoridate the water. The Center would contact individual patients dialyzing at home to make an appointment for installation of the equipment.

Complete removal of fluoride from water containing only 1 ppm can be readily accomplished, though is relatively expensive. An estimate of the cost for a home hemodialysis patient was $396 for the first year for installation and maintenance of the deionizing unit and $204 a year thereafter for recharging and maintenance. There would probably be a small additional expense, at least initially, to process water samples to verify the effectiveness of the deionizer. The Center had investigated existing equipment and worked with a manufacturer to develop a specialty deionizer that would function at optimum efficiency at the lowest possible cost.

Several potential avenues to cover the cost of de-fluoridation were being explored. However, at least at the onset, the cost would have to be borne by the patient through his or her own insurance or other resources. The Center would financially assist those who could not provide for the equipment and service themselves, just as it helped fund the cost of other equipment, supplies and services to patients who cannot afford them.

# The 1969 Annual Meeting of the ASAIO

At the meeting in Atlantic City, there were only three Seattle papers from the University of Washington. Dr. Henry Tenckhoff and his staff described home peritoneal dialysate delivery systems that replaced the use previously of sterile dialysate delivered to the patient's home in 40 L glass carboys. With the Tenckhoff catheter having proved to be a safe peritoneal access device the new systems removed the final obstacle to wider use of home peritoneal dialysis. Peritoneal dialysate requires pure water, and experience had shown that filtration to prepare pure water was rather difficult, unreliable and more expensive than distillation. They described two means of preparing dialysate using a large stainless steel tank to sterilize the water for use in a proportioning system or to sterilize premixed dialysate. The proportioning method used sterile proportioning of pure water from the tank with sterile concentrate at a ratio of 20:1 by means of a roller proportioning pump. However, compared with the batch method, the equipment was more complex and costly and cost more to use because of the pumps and the need for a conductivity measuring device. Consequently, they had developed a batch system using the large pressure boiler system to sterilize premixed dialysate solution. The glucose in the dialysate was replaced with sorbitol to avoid caramelization of the glucose during the heating process. The prototype tank was made by the Cobe Company of Denver to sterilize 160 L of dialysate. Experience showed that 80 L was required for one treatment. The procedure was completely automatic after initial filling of the tank with dialysate, which was then heated up over about 3 hours to 124° C at a pressure of 18 p.s.i. at which point it was maintained at this temperature and pressure for 45 minutes. This had been shown to kill all heat-resistant organisms, molds, spores and viruses. The patient connected to the tank when it had cooled down to a dialysate temperature of 38° C ± 1° C at which temperature it was maintained until the end of the treatment. The device had been tested clinically in the hospital and had performed very satisfactorily for dialyses lasting 10-18 hours. It was planned to use this method in the home.

Dr. Bill Leith, an engineer from Dr. Babb's group, Dr. Blagg and others from Scrib's program had studied the optimal characteristics for an ideal dialysis cannula system including factors affecting pressure drop and blood flow through the cannulas and through their tips. The study suggested the optimal diameter for cannula bodies should be between 0.125 to 0.50 inches diameter, with suitably shaped cannula tips and tip material that was stiff and allowed little wall damping. This would allow high blood flows with minimum boundary layer separation at the tip-vessel junction and would help prolong cannula life. Of course, this came at the time when the benefits of the routine use of the arteriovenous fistula for blood access were beginning to be seen and would shortly reduce the use of shunted cannulas to almost nothing.

Dr. George Thomas, a Seattle vascular surgeon, described his development of a large vessel shunt for dialysis based on principles of vascular surgery. These were to eliminate vessel stenosis by eliminating all foreign bodies from the vessel lumen, to get good healing by applying graft material at all vessel junctions and permitting continued blood flow in the host vessel to eliminate the risk of thromboembolism. The device consisted of a Dacron applique bonded to Silastic tubing that was sutured to the wall of the femoral artery and a soft Silastic tip that was advanced into the saphenous vein and had a proximal Dacron cuff that was attached to the vein wall. The two lines were then brought through the skin and connected. Dialysis was achieved by disconnecting the two tubes and connecting them to the artificial kidney. He reported preliminary animal studies in 34 dogs and successful use in 10 patients. Early follow-up was very encouraging, (but see the January 1970 report from the Center in Chapter 30).

## Second Annual Contractors Conference of the Artificial Kidney Program of the National Institute of Arthritis and Metabolic Diseases

This conference was held at the NIH in Bethesda Maryland on January 22-24, 1969. Like the previous Contractors Conference, the program consisted of reports on each of the contracts that had been worked on in 1968, together with open informal discussions.

Dr. David Hathaway, deputy chief of the Kidney Disease Control Program (KDCP), a division of Chronic Disease Programs of the Regional Medical Program Service, began the meeting by reporting on the program that had been in existence for approximately three years with the overall mission of reducing morbidity and mortality resulting from kidney disease by supporting applied research. The program had funded both in-center and home-training dialysis programs and, in addition, projects dealing with epidemiology, therapy and prevention of renal disease in its earlier stages.

Starting in 1963, under authority of the Community Health Services and Facilities Act, funding was initiated for development of hospital-based chronic dialysis centers. Over the ensuing three years, 14 centers were developed and about 450 patients had been partly supported with Public Health Service (PHS) monies. In-center chronic dialysis costs ranged from $15,000-$25,000 per patient per year and so in 1967, 12 home hemodialysis training centers also were funded by the PHS in order to test the medical feasibility of home hemodialysis, to collect uniform medical and cost data from a variety of units and to stimulate financial support for the units locally. At no time was the primary aim to provide direct support for patient care. The project was specifically designed and administered such that cost, medical and survival data would be generated and the applicability of dialysis as a means of rehabilitation tested. In the first year and a half of this program, the 12 facilities had trained about 180 patients for home dialysis, with only 12 deaths. First-year costs, including purchase of equipment, training, home renovations and supplies had ranged from $11,000 to $14,000 and the cost for 12 months of treatment at home ranged from $5,000 to $7,500. It was anticipated several factors would help reduce these costs over the next few years. Improved managerial methods and staffing patterns should affect a 20 to 30% reduction in training costs, an increasing number of small hemodialysis programs throughout the country would increase demand for equipment and hopefully production and marketing costs would be reduced, and continuing research on dialyzers together with more widespread reuse of dialyzers might substantially reduce supply costs. Dr. Hathaway's view was that there could be a 10 to 30% reduction in first year costs to $9,000 to $11,000 and ongoing annual costs to $4,000 to $6,000.

In addition, the KDCP had sponsored medical and paramedical training programs in which 71 nurses, 44 technicians and 37 physicians had been trained. In addition, numerous other practicing physicians had received partial or complete training in the management of dialysis patients. Program training manuals were being developed and would be available shortly.

Evaluation of home hemodialysis supply systems was being conducted by an industrial consulting firm to assess safety, reliability and performance factors and the results would be made available to the medical community and industry in anticipation that improvement in techniques and equipment could result. Because of the difficulty in soliciting local funding support for the 14 in-center dialysis programs, the KDCP was undertaking an analysis of funding resources for the treatment of end-stage patients, with particular emphasis upon the extent of insurance coverage and its potential role in developing a more comprehensive treatment program for the country.

With regard to kidney transplantation, KDCP had developed a contract to perform a cost and functional analysis of transplantation programs. Systems analysis would assist in prediction of the amount of dialysis support required to maintain a transplant program, information that would be crucial in planning future comprehensive programs for patient care. The KDCP was also developing demonstration cadaveric organ procurement that might serve as models for organized organ procurement efforts various locales throughout the country.

The KDCP was also involved in studies to improve understanding of epidemiology and management of the early renal and urinary tract diseases. These included studies on the pathogenesis of hyperimmune diseases, the etiology and control of urinary tract infections and improvement of diagnostic detection techniques. The control of kidney and urinary tract diseases required greatly increased emphasis on prevention and early control and as a result staff was preparing a comprehensive sourcebook describing for each state the facilities and treatment programs for this.

On the basis of death certificate review it was estimated that about 60,000 patients per year died with terminal kidney failure. Of these 60,000, 7,000 to 9,000 were considered acceptable medical candidates for either dialysis or a kidney transplant. An additional 10,000 would benefit from dialysis or transplantation but their long-term results would be unpredictable due to other systemic diseases such as diabetes, coronary artery disease, lupus erythematosus, etc. Although considerable progress in technical developments had been made since 1960, the record of actual treatment was less impressive. Since 1960 in the United States, about 2,600 patients had been maintained on hemodialysis, with about 500 of such patients starting treatment in 1968. In the same eight-year span an estimated 64,000 acceptable medical candidates would have required dialysis. Thus, less than 5 percent of deserving patients had been treated through the current health care delivery system, The current estimate was that there were no more than 1,800 patients being maintained on chronic hemodialysis in the United States and a maximum of 400 of these were being treated by home dialysis and about 50 percent of the latter were being supported through demonstration projects receiving PHS funds.

It was imperative that funding for dialysis and transplantation be assumed by agencies other than those of the federal government. Analysis of patient support as of January 1, 1968, revealed that 52 percent of all patients on chronic dialysis were receiving some degree of federal government support, and the remaining 48 percent were funded by private or local means. Of the 52 percent, 31 percent was supported from PHS grants and contracts, and 20 percent was funded through the Veterans Administration (VA). The remaining 1 percent were beneficiaries of Military Health Services. In addition to PHS, VA and military funding, many states had been successful in implementing Title XIX coverage, but unfortunately this usually required a patient be nearly economically destitute to become eligible for support. Also, during the previous year, 33 states had agreed to provide limited support through Vocational Rehabilitation Agencies but this was usually for only several months at most. Finally, eight states had specifically appropriated money for the treatment of kidney disease, most of which had gone into dialysis programs. Amounts ranged from less than $100,000 to several hundred thousand dollars a year.

There was no doubt limitation of resources was the primary obstacle to implementation of a comprehensive treatment program for patients with end-stage kidney disease. Only cooperative application of resources from all available federal, state and local resources could combat the problem of kidney failure successfully. Transplantation would assume an increasingly important role but planning would be critical delivery of this treatment. The development of demonstration model systems of integrated dialysis and transplantation programs, supported by improved detection and diagnostic measures and an increasing number of trained personnel, must have priority if effective management of kidney disease was to be realized.

The remainder of the meeting was devoted to presentations from the various contractors. The four sessions were: hardware and mass transfer, chaired by Dr. Babb; membranes, chaired by Dr. Donald Lyman; toxic factors, chaired by Dr. Louis Welt; and cannulas and materials, chaired by Dr. Scribner. In the first session, Drs. Babb, Scribner, Blagg, Leith, and Christopher reported on their progress with mass transfer studies and development of protocols for membrane evaluation, hemodialyzer design and evaluation, optimization studies and red cell dynamics; in the second session, Dr. Babb and Mr. Popovich reported on their contract to study diffusion and ultrafiltration performance in dialyzers; in the third session, Dr. Tenckhoff reported on his contract to develop a simple and inexpensive home peritoneal dialysis delivery system; and in the final session, Drs. Scribner, Thomas, and Parker and Mr. Cole reported progress with their cannula research contract to develop an animal experimental model, a permanent Dacron-Silastic AV shunt for dialysis, a quick-connect cannula coupler and cannulas with Silastic tips. These were followed by the final session that attempted to pull the entire program into perspective during which the session chairman from the four sessions presented a summary for their session.

On this occasion, in addition to 21 members of NIAMD staff, there were 129 participants of whom nine were from Seattle. These were Mr. Cole and Mr. Popovich, Drs. Babb, Christopher, Leith, Parker, Scribner, Tenckhoff and Thomas.

## CHAPTER 30

# Board and Executive Committee Meetings and the ASAIO Annual Meeting 1970

————

THE YEAR 1970 WAS ONE in which the transition to home hemodialysis as the Center's main treatment option continued to grow in order to allow the acceptance of more patients. Kidney transplantation and peritoneal dialysis also continued to grow. There were continuing discussions on the patient acceptance process and the role of patient income and with the state of Washington with regard to state funding for the treatment of chronic kidney failure. Altogether this was a most successful year.

## THE SEVENTH ANNUAL MEETING OF THE BOARD OF TRUSTEES

The meeting was held on February 18, 1970. A resolution was proposed, seconded and passed unanimously that Article 1 of the Center's bylaws be amended to change the name of the Seattle Artificial Kidney Center to Northwest Kidney Center.

Elected to three-year terms as trustees were Renaldo Baggott, Willis L. Campbell, Mrs. Grace Collette, John Dare, Elmer J. Nordstrom, Jess B. Spielholz, MD, Emery P. Bayley, Bruce Baker, John Kennedy, MD, Richard Philbrick, DDS, Del Ruble, Jack Schwartz and Evans Wyckoff. Elected to two-year terms were Nicholas Bez Jr. and Robert Burns. James W. Nolan Jr. and Mrs. Frankie Frydenlund were elected to a one-year term. Offices elected were president: John L. McCormack, MD; vice-president: Willis L. Campbell; secretary: Lisle R. Guernsey; and treasurer: Renaldo Baggott.

The following were elected to the Executive Committee: Renaldo Baggott, Willis L. Campbell and Elmer J. Nordstrom.

The various reports that followed provided a summary of activities at and related to the Center throughout the previous 12 months.

Dr. Pendras gave the Medical Director's Report. The current patient treatment facility was essentially unchanged over that in 1969. The Center had three home training rooms, ten Center dialysis beds used primarily for new patient stabilization and backup hemodialyses, and an additional two beds that could be used for home hemodialysis training or in-center dialysis. The medical objective of the Center was as far as possible to provide home dialysis for all patients. Over the previous year, ten of the Center's patients were transplanted at the University of Washington and the Center took on five peritoneal dialysis patients. Overall there were now 107 patients on home hemodialysis, six in training, fifteen in-center dialysis patients, of whom four were awaiting transplantation, and seven who were awaiting home training. Medical staff had remained unchanged with four home hemodialysis training nurses, four home dialysis technicians, four center dialysis nurses, two center dialysis technicians and two physicians. Despite the medical load, the staff had performed excellently and with expedition.

Dr. McCormack read Dr. Joseph Eschbach's report on the Medical Advisory Committee. The patient selection process had been altered and now had a more representative and comprehensive Patient Selection Committee. With advances in treatment, almost all patients currently being referred to the SAKC were acceptable for treatment and did not need to be discussed by a group of nephrologists. The new committee, established in July 1969, had functioned well and could now undertake its role of being advisory to the Center. Over the preceding six months, the committee had recommended that renal transplantation be considered a funding responsibility of the Center, that pre-pubertal children be considered for treatment based on the same criteria as adult patients, and that "artificial" be eliminated from the Center's name as the scope of treatment provided had changed. Dr. Eschbach was encouraged to know the Center could continue to respond to the changing needs of patients and physicians and that much progress had been made in the past year.

Mr. Ginsey gave the Financial Committee Report. The average cost per patient had been reduced over the previous three years as a result of the emphasis on home dialysis. In 1966, the budget was $456,999 with 45 patients at an average cost of $10,000 per patient. Corresponding figures in 1967 were $673,000, 69 patients and $9,700; in 1968, $954,981 with 97 patients at an average cost of $9,800; in 1969 the figures were $1,021,000 with 150 patients at an average per patient cost of $6,800. The 1970 budget was expected to be $1,268,000 with 205 patients and an average cost per patient of $6,185. Mr. Phillips reported on the fund drive. Between November 7, 1969 and February 7, 1970 public solicitation had garnered $139,727 in undesignated funds and an additional $58,880 had been received in designated funds for a total of $198,607, mainly from King County. The goal was $230,000. The newest innovation had been establishment of county chapters of the Northwest Kidney Center Fund Drive. The Pierce County Chapter, co-chaired by Dr. John Kennedy and James Mattson, currently had an ongoing fund drive with a target of $30,000 and the Yakima County Chapter, chaired by local TV personality James Nolan, was aiming to raise $16,000. Dr. Philbrick and his chairmen would be leading the next fund drive.

Dr. McCormack, in his President's Report, thanked all those individuals and organizations that had helped during the preceding year. He noted the change in attitude at the Center. Originally established to demonstrate how a chronic hemodialysis program could be successful in a nonuniversity environment, it became obvious after a few years that this had been achieved. The Center now had recognized other forms of treatment in order to provide the best possible care, including home hemodialysis, peritoneal dialysis and kidney transplantation, and was working closely with the University of Washington transplant team. The second development had been reorganization of the Center thanks to the efforts of Mr. Del Ruble who had presented a proposal that was made operational under the direction of Earl Rice and Del Ruble in the spring of 1969. When Earl retired, the Center was fortunate to have Tom Seifert spend four months at the Center to continue the reorganization and to recruit James Philips as executive director. He had also recognized the abilities of one of the technicians, Terry Pollard, and had advanced him to take up some administrative responsibilities. Another change was the Admissions and Policy Committee becoming the Patient Admissions Committee, chaired by the Reverend John Darrah, so making the process of patient selection much more efficient.

He also discussed the Center's relationship to the two health-related departments of the state of Washington. The Division of Vocational Rehabilitation had been most helpful in clarifying regulations and defining the basis for patient acceptance for their program and he noted the great assistance of Miss Roberta Schumann over the last two years. The other source was the Department of Health whose director, Dr. Spielholz, was a member of the Center's Board of Trustees. The department had been most helpful in aiding provision of funds for patient care. The Center was also grateful to the state senators and representatives who had made these appropriations possible. However, state dollars only accounted for about 20% of the Center's total funding, roughly equal to what the Center received from fund drives and public solicitation. He hoped the Center would be able to continue its present policy of doing its utmost to provide funds for all patients who required treatment for end-stage renal disease, whatever the form of treatment that might be.

Margo Marsh, president of the Stewardess Emeritus group, presented a $5,000 check to the Center. Dr. McCormack presented plaques to Emery Bayley who had headed up the successful 1968-69 fund drive and to Trevor Evans who had been invaluable in the field of public relations. He presented certificates of appreciation to Jack Schwartz who had chaired the Public Relations Committee for two years, to George Toles, Ken Hatch and Nancy Tarbox of KIRO who had arranged the public radio and TV spots during the fund drive, to Raymond Keitel, president of the Boeing Employees Good Neighbor Fund, and to Jim Kelly of KING radio who had helped prepare a slide presentation for the Center.

## PATIENT NUMBERS

In late January 1970 it was reported that 12 patients had been accepted over the last months, six of whom had been cannulated and started treatment. Ten patients were dialyzing in-center, 105 were at home and seven in home hemodialysis training. Five patients were on peritoneal dialysis for a total of 127 patients on dialysis. Eleven of the Center's patients had been transplanted. Two patients had died, one from a heart problem and the other from infection in a Thomas femoral shunt. The latter device, developed by Dr. George Thomas, a Seattle vascular surgeon, had been used for patients who had run out of vein sites for regular cannulation in their extremities. Several patients elsewhere who had Thomas shunts had also developed infections and the Seattle patient was the second to die. The problem was that infection of a shunt in the large femoral vessels could spread rapidly throughout the body. A small number of deaths due to hemorrhage had also been reported from elsewhere and so the decision was made that the Thomas shunt would no longer be used by the Center and patients would instead have an arteriovenous fistula placed.

Six months later, 14 outpatients were being followed prior to their need for dialysis and four patients were dialyzing in-center, three of whom were new patients. Three patients were being trained and three of the four in-center patients would be starting training for home hemodialysis. There were nine patients at home on peritoneal dialysis and 120 at home on hemodialysis. Thus there were 136 total dialysis patients and 19 patients had been transplanted, for a total patient population of 155. In the last month eight patients had been trained for home hemodialysis and three patients, all on home hemodialysis, had died: one from internal hemorrhage; one from heart failure; and one from a stroke and bleed into the brain.

By early December, the Northwest Kidney Center (NKC) was responsible for 184 patients, including 20 who had been transplanted and 14 outpatients who were being treated prior to their need for cannulation or transplantation. One hundred twenty-seven of the patients were at home on hemodialysis, of whom six had been trained and discharged home in the previous month, six patients were being dialyzed in-center to be medically stabilized so they could enter home hemodialysis training, six were being trained for home hemodialysis and eleven were on peritoneal dialysis at home. There had been two deaths during the previous month.

## Activities Elsewhere in Seattle

In August, reports were made on current activities at other hospitals in Seattle. The Veterans Administration Hospital had received funds to establish a home hemodialysis patient training program. Additionally, the hospital was now able to take all veterans, instead of just those with service-connected renal disease. This would be extremely helpful in lifting some of the burden from the Northwest Kidney Center. Until the VA's patient load decreased so they had available beds for home hemodialysis patient training, the Center would train VA patients, with the VA assuming the cost.

Children's Orthopedic Hospital had agreed to abide by the decisions of the Center's Patient Admissions Committee on the selection of children for dialysis. They would continue to provide hospitalization, on-going costs, and kidney transplantation and the Center would be responsible for home dialysis training costs and equipment.

Group Health Hospital was considering a change in policy to cover dialysis costs. At present, they would pay training costs, excluding equipment costs and other hospitalization costs. They would also cover the cost of transplantation.

George Irvine reported that the University of Washington Coach House was attempting to get federal support for renal disease and dialysis-related research. The application was pending but they could not be sure of support, and so they proposed that if in the future the Center could count on the Coach House unit to perform 300 to 400 backup dialyses per year there could be a reduction in equipment and staffing at the Center which could save some money. If the Center could in turn pass some of these savings along to the Coach House in the form of an operating subsidy, perhaps $20,000 a year, it could go a long way toward solving its financial crisis. Elmer Nordstrom questioned whether in light of this financial situation the Coach House research might be conducted at the Kidney Center instead. Dr. Eschbach answered that much of the research was performed by University of Washington academic personnel and students. Additionally, other departments such as engineering assisted in some of the research. While the NKC was staffed for patient care, it was not staffed to handle research as well as patient care. Dr. McCormack referred the proposal to NKC staff for further consideration.

## PATIENT ACCEPTANCE

In the previous year the system of patient acceptance had been modified. Now there was the Medical Advisory Committee and the Patient Admissions Committee. In January one of the patients referred to the Medical Advisory Committee had been deferred because it was a child and as a result the committee met to discuss a recommendation as to the minimum age for acceptance. Medical concerns in treating children were uncertainty about whether the child would develop physically and sexually, and the psychological effects on the family. Also, the state Division of Vocational Rehabilitation did not provide financial support for children. The University of Washington had trained four children for home hemodialysis under a grant that no longer existed: one had died; one had a congenital problem that made growth unlikely; and two were doing well. Since excluding children was discriminatory, the Medical Advisory Committee had recommended that children be accepted for treatment at the Center. It was agreed to discuss this further with Dr. Robert Hickman, the nephrologist-pediatrician at University Hospital. Following discussion, this was approved at the May meeting of the Executive Committee.

The Patient Selection Committee met on May 9 and recommended that: 1) the Medical Advisory Committee remain the same and process applicants from a medical standpoint; 2) the Admissions Advisory Committee be changed to consist of the administrator and medical director of the Center and an Executive Committee member; 3) the referring physician would submit a report on the patient as part of the information to be considered by the Admissions Advisory Committee; 4) the director of patient finance would be present at the Admissions Advisory Committee meeting to present information, but would not have a vote; and 5) the chairman of the Medical Advisory Committee would be present to report the recommendations of the Medical Advisory Committee and to take back information to the Medical Advisory Committee but would not have a vote. The committee also recommended that the tentative three-month patient acceptance proposed by the Medical Advisory Committee be rejected by the Executive Committee. Dr. Haviland moved that the Executive Committee accept the recommendations of the Patient Selection Committee and the motion was seconded by Willis Campbell.

Dr. Eschbach said he had discussed these recommendations with the Medical Advisory Committee and they were not pleased. The main purpose for proposing a different selection process was to involve the physicians caring for patients more actively in the decision making. Keeping the Medical Advisory Committee unchanged perpetuated the problem of a rubber stamp. Since the Medical Advisory Committee had little information about the patient other than medical information, and since medical problems had become of minor importance in patient selection, the Medical Advisory Committee felt that to continue the present function of their committee would serve no purpose to the Center, themselves, and the community. They suggested instead that: 1) applications received be reviewed initially by the chairman of the Medical Advisory Committee and/or the medical director of the Center and in the event of a medical problem needing discussion or other opinions the Medical Advisory Committee would be convened. Otherwise, after this initial screening, the application would go directly to the Admissions Committee; 2) the Admissions Committee would be composed of the administrator and the medical director of the Center, a member of the Medical Advisory Committee and two members of the Executive Committee; 3) the pertinent information would be presented by the social worker, the psychiatrist, the referring physician and the patient finance manager who would all be present at the meeting but would not have a vote. Mr. Schoenfeld moved that the motion be referred back to the Patient Selection Committee for further discussion. The motion was seconded and passed unanimously.

It was also suggested that this committee discuss the overall philosophy of patient selection and patient care provided by the Center. At the June meeting the Reverent Darrah reported that the ad hoc committee discussing the Medical Advisory Committee's proposal concerning patient applications for treatment now recommended the following: 1) applications received would be referred directly to the medical director of the Center who would then institute appropriate workup. The Medical Advisory Committee would continue in existence for at least six months, to be convened at the request of the Center's medical director, the Medical Advisory Committee chairman, or the patient's physician. Upon the request, the Medical Advisory Committee would meet and give its recommendations concerning a particular case to the Patient Admissions Committee. Otherwise, upon approval by the medical director, applications would go directly to the Patient Admissions Committee; 2) the Patient Admissions Committee would be composed of the administrator and medical director of the Center, the chairman of the Medical Advisory Committee and two members of the Executive Committee; 3) pertinent information would be presented by the social worker, the referring physician, the psychiatrist and the patient finance manager who would all be present at the meeting but would not have a vote; 4) a favorable vote of three would be necessary for acceptance of an applicant; and 5) if the referring physician was a member of the committee, an alternate would take his place. In no case would the referring physician have a vote. The Rev. Darrah moved that the Executive Committee approve this proposal. The motion was seconded.

Over the next six months the Patient Admissions Committee held nine meetings and considered 32 applications, nine of whom were deferred for a few weeks in order to obtain further information. Thirty one of the applicants were eventually approved, including two for related donor kidney transplants and one applicant was rejected.

## PERSONNEL CHANGES

At the August meeting of the Executive Committee, Dr. McCormack announced that Jim Phillips, the Center administrator, was recovering from a heart attack and should be back at work in about six weeks. In addition, Dr. Pendras had elected to retire as medical director in September but would be available to work for NKC for approximately 12 hours a week. A search would commence immediately to find a full-time medical director and Dr. Tom Sawyer, NKC chief staff physician, would serve as acting medical director as of September 1. After Dr. Pendras's request that a full-time medical director be sought for the NKC and Executive Committee approval, Dr. McCormack had appointed a committee consisting of Dr. Joseph Eschbach, chairman, Dr. John Kennedy, Tacoma nephrologist, Dr. William McKee, Wenatchee nephrologist, Dr. Robert Hegstrom, nephrologist at the Mason Clinic and John Dare, administrator at the Mason Clinic, to review the functions of the medical director and his staff. They suggested that to attract and hold a medical director, he receive a salary more in line with what other nephrologists earn and what other institutions offer, be able to stimulate research and give incentives for preparation of medical papers, and be given health, disability and life insurance and retirement benefits similar to those offered other Center employees.

It was moved, seconded, and carried unanimously to announce Dr. Pendras's resignation as medical director and Dr. Sawyer's assumption of the duties of acting medical director. Dr. Pendras was unanimously elected to the Board of Trustees for a term ending in February 1973.

At the September Executive Committee meeting, Dr. McCormack announced that Dr. Jerry Pendras had resigned effective September 7, 1970, and Dr. Tom Sawyer now was serving as acting medical director. He also announced that Jim Phillips, the Center's administrator, was expected back at NKC on a part-time basis on October 5. However, at the October meeting, Dr. McCormack announced with regret that Mr. Jim Phillips was resigning as administrator of the Center because of continuing health problems following his recent heart attack. Terry Pollard who had been appointed assistant administrator by Mr. Phillips would serve as acting administrator. He also announced with regret the resignation of the Rev. John Darrah from the Executive Committee and the Patient Admissions Committee because of his move to Richmond, California.

Following Dr. Pendras's resignation, the Center carried out a nation-wide search for a new medical director. This including solicitation of recommendations from prominent nephrologists across the country and several interviews of potential candidates. At the December meeting, Dr. McCormack introduced Dr. Christopher Blagg as the new medical director of the Northwest Kidney Center. Dr. Blagg had been renal fellow with Dr. Scribner from 1963 to 1964 and returned to the University of Washington in 1966 as an assistant professor and member of the Nephrology Division staff. Although selected as the medical director in late 1970, he did not assume the position until January 1971.

At the same time, Dr. McCormack announced the appointment of Terry Pollard as administrator of the Center. He also introduced Jim Anderson, the assistant administrator at University Hospital, and announced that a nominating committee would be appointed to propose a slate for election at the 1971 Annual Meeting of the Board of Trustees.

## Name Change

In January, Mr. Phillips, the Center administrator had suggested the board change the Center's name from the Seattle Artificial Kidney Center to Northwest Kidney Center. The Medical Advisory Committee had suggested that "artificial" be removed from the name so that it would more accurately reflect the Center's activities. The Public Relations Committee had recommended the name be changed to Seattle Kidney Center to broaden the base for public support and to develop a uniform and identifying logo, and the Center's chapters in Pierce, Yakima and Snohomish counties had objected to "Seattle" in the name. The Center was now really the "Northwest" Center and in the future a new center might be established and use Northwest in its name, so limiting this Center to Seattle. It was moved, seconded and carried unanimously that the board change the name to Northwest Kidney Center at the Board of Trustees meeting in February. In May 1970 the dark mauve "K" logo was adopted.

In November it was moved, seconded, and passed unanimously that effective December 8, 1970, the registered office of the corporation should be at 1102 Columbia Street, Seattle, King County, Washington 98104, and that the registered agent for this corporation should be Mr. Terrance Pollard, whose business address was 1102 Columbia Street, Seattle, King County, Washington 98104, and all previous designations of registered office or registered agent would be revoked and terminated.

## FINANCES

### THE CENTER'S FINANCES

In January the Center had $150,000 in savings that had not been raised in the name of specific patients and, as there was adequate cash on hand, the Executive Committee authorized $75,000 be transferred from working capital to patient funding.

In May, the Finance Committee had looked at two contracts to furnish patients with deionizers to deal with the issues raised by the fluoridation of the Seattle water supply and a company had been selected. This resulted in a savings to the Center of approximately $400 a month. There was $30,000 in DVR funds that must be spent by June 30, $180,000 in uncommitted funds and $87,000 for specific patients. A new practice of presenting the Finance Committee with a monthly figure representing the amount available in uncommitted funds would be helpful in holding action cases.

In July, copies of the audit for fiscal year July 1, 1968 to June 30, 1969, prepared by Stokes and Company, were distributed and Denver Ginsey noted that although the audit was self-explanatory, Executive Committee members should remember that the recommendations made represented suggestions for the previous year, and almost all had been dealt with already. The Budget Report showed that the actual expenses for the first half of 1970 were $18,677 over budget. Depreciation of $12,936, did not represent funds spent, so actual expenses over budget were about $6,000. The yardstick for patient income was discussed. To be fair and consistent to all NKC patients, a guideline was sought to indicate how much of a patient's resources should be used to finance their care at the NKC. After consulting many sources and studying many guides it was determined that: 1) assets contributing materially and substantially to patients' livelihoods, residences and first cars would be excluded from calculations. Other assets (boat, summer house, investment property, etc.) the patient would be asked to convert to cash to finance their treatment; 2) income would be calculated in the form of the revised Illinois scale as "excess income over expenses." Expenses for a moderate budget, as determined by the federal government, subtracted from actual income, represented excess income. The moderate budget expenses took into account family size, location (urban, rural, etc.), age of children and all other contingencies affecting family finances. The excess income figure would determine the patient's cash payment, and cash payments would be calculated with insurance benefits in mind. In extenuating circumstances, the "flexibility range" might be applied. If the circumstances were such that the flexibility range was inapplicable, the executive director, administrative assistant, and manager of patient processing might set payment, if any, outside the flexibility range. The Patient Income Yardstick would be implemented immediately with all incoming patients, and as soon as possible with the present patient population.

The proposed budget for calendar year 1971 was considered by the Finance Committee at its September meeting. The budget figures were predicated on a continual flow of new patients, 75 anticipated for 1971, and a total patient population of around 200. Although there was some concern about funds from the state and DVR being forthcoming, the Finance Committee recommended Executive Committee approval of the budget. This was so moved, seconded, and passed unanimously. The Finance Committee also recommended $230,000 as the 1971 Fund Drive goal.

Dr. Scribner had asked that NKC consider a proposal to provide $20,000 to support the research activities at the University of Washington's

Coach House. The second review of the NIH research grant request would be in February, and Dr. Scribner felt the review group might give a favorable response if it noted the support of NKC. Dr. McCormack referred the proposal to NKC staff, with the request they present recommendations regarding this proposal. After meeting with Dr. Scribner to discuss his request for funds to assist research activities at the Coach House it was agreed there was no need for official action at this time.

At the December meeting of the Executive Committee the accountants presented the following resolution: "The Northwest Kidney Center considers itself to have a moral obligation to continue to finance, to the extent possible, treatment of its patients in the event of termination of their other financial support. Since this obligation could constitute a substantial liability to the Center, it is proposed that a reserve fund be set aside on the balance sheet to reflect the contingent obligations. Resolved: That a special fund shall be established to be known as a 'Board Designated Fund,' or some other appropriate terminology, which shall consist of such funds as the Board designate as a reserve for future treatment of patients. The Board shall, from time to time, transfer funds to said Fund from the General Fund, or to the General Fund from said Fund, as in its judgment, shall best serve the needs of the Center." Mr. Ramsey suggested a starting fund of approximately $150,000. The "Board Designated Fund" would not change the income statement, but would earmark banked funds as being restricted to patient care. This, according to Jim Thompson, would more accurately reflect the true situation on the fiscal year's financial statement. Dr. Sawyer pointed out that the budget was calculated on a steady flow of new patients and that most income is from new patients (through state and federal funds for home dialysis training and equipment and insurance billings). As insurance is depleted and if state and federal funds are not forthcoming as requested, it would be vital to have a fund set aside. The resolution was referred to the Finance Committee for further consideration.

Walter Schoenfeld recommended the Center establish an endowment fund. It was moved, seconded and passed unanimously that the principle of an endowment fund be established. The details of such a fund would be presented at a future meeting.

Dr. McCormack appointed the following committees: a committee to review salaries and policies pertaining to non-management staff: Mr. Ruble, chairman, and Mr. Wyckoff, Mr. Burns and Mr. Bean, members. Mr. Pollard and Dr. Sawyer would serve as non-voting members. A Compensation Review Committee: Mr. Baggott, chairman, and Mr. Burns, Mr. Ginsey, Mr. Ruble and Mr. Thompson, members, to review salaries of management staff annually or more often as needed; a Renal Transplantation Committee: Dr. Eschbach, chairman, and Drs. Burnell, Pendras, Blagg and Sawyer, and Howard Anderson and Allan Lobb, members, that was to investigate the possibilities of renal transplantation outside the University of Washington and the Center's current capability to assist in renal transplantation.

## THE CENTER AND THE WASHINGTON STATE LEGISLATURE

In December 1969, representatives of the state Department of Health had met with representatives of the SAKC (now called the Northwest Kidney Center) and the Spokane unit. The SAKC reported that if the fund drive was successful and the funds from the Division of Vocational Rehabilitation were continued the SAKC would not seek additional funds from the 1970 special session of the legislature. There was also discussion of patient acceptance criteria now and in the future and whether selection was still necessary. The group would meet again in mid-Spring.

In the fiscal year ending June 30, 1970, the Washington State Division of Vocational Rehabilitation had expended $284,114 for the Northwest Kidney Center and 56 patients had received assistance from DVR funds. DVR reported funds available for the fiscal year ending June 30, 1971, would be $267,483 to NKC (or 80% of the total allotment of $334,353) and $66,870 to the Spokane Center (20%). The percentage ratio was based on experience in the previous year. DVR cautioned that the amount could be affected by the federal government curtailing its allotment to Washington

State, by the state recalling some DVR money, or by Spokane's spending more than 20%. NKC spent $82,000 of state Public Health funds during fiscal year ending June 30, 1970, $22,000 in excess of the original $60,000 allotment that came available from excess funds allotted to the Spokane Kidney Center. Twenty-seven patients received assistance from these funds. Funds for the current fiscal year ending June 30, 1971, totaled $100,000 for both Washington State kidney centers. A contract for the amount would be written by the Attorney General's office. The Public Health Department would conduct a review of both centers' expenditures in January, 1971.

In September, the state Interim Legislative Budget Committee meeting would be hearing a report on fiscal aspects of artificial kidney programs in the state and Dr. Sawyer and Terry Pollard from NKC, Dr. Scribner and George Irvine from the University of Washington, and Mrs. Hansen from the Spokane Center would be attending. Dr. Scribner had prepared a statement for distribution at this meeting. At the meeting a request for funds prepared by NKC staff and approved by the NKC Legislative Committee and the Finance Committee, was presented to the state Interim Legislative Budget Committee. That committee had recommended continued support at the same level for kidney programs in the state. At a separate luncheon meeting, Mr. Walter Howe, state budget director, was apprised of the anticipated funding problems of the next biennium and that NKC and Spokane Center staff would be meeting with Dr. Lane, Department of Health, and Mr. Ryan, Division of Vocational Rehabilitation, to present the NKC budget for the 1971-73 biennium and request additional funding from the state. Suggestions from the Executive Committee were that the request to the legislature should include the present cost per patient per year compared with cost five years earlier and that figures be represented on graphs for visual impact and demonstration purposes. After the coming election, Mr. Bangert, chairman of NKC's Legislative Committee, would try to get local senators and representatives more involved with the Center.

A meeting followed in which Northwest Kidney Center and Spokane Kidney Center representatives had met in Olympia with Dr. Lane, Dr. Leahy, Dr. Spielholz, and Mr. Ryan to present to them the recommendations previously made to the Interim Legislative Budget Committee. An effort was made to justify the amounts requested. Current information suggested the present allocation in the governor's budget was to be the same dollar figure as in the last biennium. However, the Legislative Budget Committee would recommend the same percentage as last biennium, resulting in a higher dollar figure to take care of an increased case load. The current budget from NKC showed both appropriations to be inadequate to care for the expected patient load.

THE FUND DRIVE

During the previous year a Pierce County Chapter of the Northwest Kidney Fund had been established and its current fund drive had a target of $30,000. All money raised would only be used to support patients from Pierce County where there were currently 18 patients. A Yakima County Chapter had also been organized and efforts were being made to establish chapters in Snohomish, Grays Harbor and Kitsap counties. The chairmen of these groups would be nominated to the Center's Board of Trustees.

The fund drive report presented in July showed the income total for Undesignated Funds to date was $178,204 and for Designated Funds $112,393, for a total of $290,597. Fourteen thousand dollars had been contributed for capital improvements. All board members had been sent names of people who had not responded to this year's fund drive and any board member who knew anyone on the list was asked to contact them. Upcoming activities included the International Sports Car Race on July 2 and a Western International League-sponsored baseball game at Sick's Stadium. The baseball game tickets, $2 for adults and $1 for children, with very little expense involved, could be an important fund raising event for NKC.

In August it was reported that the Public Relations and Fund Advisory Committees had met with Jim Phillips and Terry Pollard to discuss plans for the forthcoming fund drive. It was agreed: 1) To open the drive on November 9, 1970; 2) to title the drive the "1971 Fund Drive," rather than use a dual-year title as in the past; and 3) to change solicitation procedures from past years by utilizing volunteers for key donors, potential donors and those who had not responded in the past. Those who had donated regularly would be sent letters, as would clubs and organizations. Two chairmen had been appointed to assist Dr. Philbrick, the 1971 Fund Drive general chairman: Mr. Groth and Mr. Gardener, who would chair the $100 and over division. All money collected up to September 30 would be credited to the 1970 fund drive; all money collected after that date would be credited to the 1971 fund drive. As of August 27, 1970, $188,633 had been received in Undesignated Funds and $115,701 in Designated Funds, for a total of $304,334, and $14,600 had been donated restricted to capital improvement. While the Undesignated Fund total had not reached the goal of $230,000 the Designated Fund total was much higher than anticipated.

The fund drive books were closed on September 30 and all contributions after that date would be credited to the 1971 drive. On September 25, there were undesignated funds of $193,678, and designated funds of $118,255, for a total of $311,933. The annual Stewardess Emeritus fundraising ball was to be held at the Washington Plaza Hotel on October 24.

In December, the 1971 fund drive total to date since the beginning of the drive in November was $64,973.71, of which $ 62,925.71 was Undesignated Fund donations and $1,148.00 was Designated Fund donations. This total represented a 13% increase over the previous year's total at the same time. The increase in part may have been from increased activity in the county chapters that were formed during the last year. Public solicitation from this year's drive so far was $12,000. The Open House was not as successful as was hoped in introducing NKC to new potential contributors although there were seven legislators among the guests.

There had been meeting with individuals in Alaska to consider starting a fund drive there and to establish procedures for payments to the NKC for Alaskan patients through the Alaska Division of Vocational Rehabilitation and Public Health.

## Other Items

In August, Dr. McCormack submitted a proposal to the Executive Committee to authorize funds for three NKC personnel to attend the Western Dialysis and Transplantation Society meeting in September at Las Vegas. Requested funds totaled $630.00, $210 each for three people, with round trip air fare $156, hotel $34, and expenses $20. Elmer Nordstrom moved that funds be authorized for the meeting and the motion was seconded and passed unanimously. The Executive Committee requested a formal report be given on the effectiveness and overall benefit of the meeting.

In September Mr. Pollard reported on the first annual meeting of the Western Dialysis and Transplantation Society held in Las Vegas, September 12-13, 1970. NKC staff members attending were Terry Pollard, Bruce Duncan, chief dialysis technician, and Gail Simmons, dialysis nurse. Topics ranged from medical, social and technical to financial. Mr. Pollard felt the meeting was worthwhile and beneficial to the staff. Of particular interest were comparisons in costs of operating dialysis equipment between other centers and NKC. Walt Schoenfeld suggested a paper be written, possibly for distribution as part of the fund drive literature, showing NKCs lower equipment operating cost.

## The 1970 Annual Meeting of the ASAIO

At the 16th annual meeting in Washington, DC, there was one paper from the Center and four from the University of Washington.

Dr. Pendras and Mr. Pollard reported on eight years' experience at the Center. The Center had been established to show the feasibility of developing a community-based dialysis center with a financial base independent of the United States Public Health Service and that could supply community needs for chronic dialysis treatments. As of December 31, 1969, these goals had been met. The Center's $1.03 million budget came from sources other than any federal or private dialysis granting agency and all the community needs for dialysis now were supplied by the Center. Some of the support came from the state of Washington, patient resources (including insurance) covered 60 percent of expenses, federal and state government 20 percent, and contributions 20 percent. The organization of the fundraising efforts was described including a description of the Northwest Kidney Center Foundation. The Center served a population of about 2.5 million people and in the first eight years of operation had started 175 patients on dialysis. During 1969, 58 new patients were added, a rate of about 25 new patients per million population, and at the end of 1969 the Center was treating 135 patients: 104 on home hemodialysis, four on home peritoneal dialysis, eight in home hemodialysis training, 12 who had been transplanted and only seven on in-center hemodialysis. There were few patients older than 55 years. Over the years, admission criteria had evolved to the point there was now minimal patient selection except for serious medical and other problems. Rehabilitation potential was a major factor in patient selection and currently all patients were expected to train to do home dialysis. The current home program and patient training for home dialysis were described. Patient survival was 90 percent at one year, 85 percent at two years, 75 percent at 3 years, 61 percent at 5 years and 55 percent at 5 to 8 years. In patients 55 years and older, survival was not as good and was only 40 percent at 2 years. Seventy-three percent of patients were regarded as fully rehabilitated and only 5 percent were regarded as not rehabilitated at all. The commonest causes of death were related to atherosclerotic cardiovascular disease and congestive heart failure or to cerebral hemorrhage.

Drs. Tenckhoff and Curtis described the University of Washington peritoneal dialysis program in detail. Nineteen patients deemed unsuitable for hemodialysis had been treated for periods of up to four years for a total of 25 patient years and 3,001 peritoneal dialyses. Sixteen of the 19 patients performed self-dialysis at home. Morbidity was low. There had been 16 infections, all of which were cured – an infection rate of 0.59 percent of all dialyses performed with indwelling (Tenckhoff) catheters. There were three deaths. In general, patients were well and rehabilitated although three were limited in physical activity by preexisting severe heart disease. Peritoneal dialysis was an acceptable alternative to hemodialysis and might be considered preferable for patients who lived alone, those with severe cardiovascular disease, children and, since blood transfusion was not required, might be preferable for those patients who refuse transfusion and those awaiting a kidney transplant.

Drs. Ramos, Christopher, Maurer, Scribner and Babb had a paper discussing slowly dialyzed molecules and, in particular, phosphate. They had made an experimental Dialyzer Testing System for Large Molecules which they used in experiments to provide data for mathematical calculation of the transfer of such molecules across a dialyzer membrane. They used the system to examine phosphate movement across the membrane and the effect of pH on this. The system would have obvious use for studying transport of other larger molecules across dialyzer membranes.

Drs. Lindner and Tenckhoff had looked at nutrition in six stable peritoneal dialysis patients, measuring daily protein and nitrogen intake and output under strict metabolic control. There had been concern that amino acid and protein losses in the peritoneal fluid would lead to poor nutrition but they had showed that a high protein diet could compensate for the losses and in some patients the administration of an anabolic steroid appeared to have some benefit. However, further research on this was needed.

Dr. Bob Atkins, Mr. Vizzo, Mr. Cole and Drs. Blagg and Scribner described experience with the "artificial gut" used to provide parenteral nutrition to patients with chronic bowel disease causing malnutrition. They had first tried infusing nutrients through Scribner shunts and arteriovenous fistulas but the concentrated nutrient solution was irritating to the vessel lining. Consequently, they went on to look at infusing the solution into the superior vena cava, the large vein in the upper part of the body that returns blood to the heart. They developed a catheter specially designed for this purpose that would avoid the complications with all previous catheters used in this way. The catheter they developed and described, the Broviac catheter, needed further studies. Eventually this became the Hickman catheter. This catheter and its modifications still are used worldwide for parenteral nutrition and for infusing sclerosing drugs into cancer patients and others.

CHAPTER 31

# Annual and Semi-annual Board Meetings and Executive Committee Meetings; ASAIO Annual Meeting 1971

———————

THE YEAR 1971 WAS THE tenth year of operation of the Northwest Kidney Center. From the treatment point of view the use of home hemodialysis continued to grow, peritoneal dialysis was in process of being moved from the university to the Center and kidney transplantation was growing steadily. With funds from the Regional Medical Program, the Northwest Kidney Center developed a regional cadaveric kidney retrieval organization program for Washington, Alaska, Idaho and Montana.

## THE EIGHTH ANNUAL MEETING OF THE BOARD OF TRUSTEES

The meeting was held on February 23, 1971. Dr. McCormack opened the meeting by making the following recommendations: that the following individuals be elected to three-year terms as members of the board, terms to expire in 1974: Richard Bangert, M. L. Bean, James Burnell, MD, Ross Cunningham, Lisle Guernsey, James Haviland, MD, James Sullivan, H. Sedge Thomson, Gerald Grinstein and Lem Tuai. Dr. McCormack asked for nominations from the floor; there were none. The nominations were approved unanimously. That the following individuals be elected to one-year terms as members of the Board of Trustees, terms to expire in 1972: Rabbi Earl Starr (to fill unexpired term of the Rev. John Darrah), Walter Hubbard (chairman, Yakima County Chapter),

William McKee, III (chairman, Apple Valley Chapter), Charles Savage (chairman, Mason County Chapter), Dale Smith (chairman, Snohomish County Chapter), Mrs. Frankie Frydenlund (representative, Stewardess Emeritus Association). Dr. McCormack asked for nominations from the floor; there were none. The nominations were approved unanimously. That the following be elected officers of the Board of Trustees: president: Denver Ginsey; vice president, Dr. Richard Philbrick; secretary, Renaldo Baggott; and treasurer, Robert Burns. Dr. McCormack asked for nominations from the floor; there were none. The nominations for officers were approved unanimously. That the following be elected to the Executive Committee, terms to expire in 1974: Dr. John McCormack, Richard Bangert, Dr. James Haviland, and the following to be elected to the Executive Committee, terms to expire in 1972: Dr. Richard Philbrick (to fill unexpired term of the Rev. John Darrah), James W. Phillips (to fill unexpired term of Walter Schoenfeld) and Robert Burns (to fill unexpired term of Lisle Guernsey). Dr. McCormack asked for nominations from the floor; there were none. The nominations were approved unanimously.

Dr. Blagg gave the Medical Director's Report and noted that as medical director for only less than two months most of the work he was reporting on was the result of the efforts of others. The medical objectives of the Center remained the provision of the most appropriate treatment in the form of either dialysis or transplantation for all patients in Western Washington who needed this treatment. During the year ending December 31, 1970, 75 new patients started on treatment, bringing the grand total since the Center opened to 250. Seventy-five new patients fitted well with the projections of 75 to 100 new patients each year for the next few years. During the past year, 24 patients died, a mortality of 11%. This compared favorably with published reports from other centers. The total number of patients now in treatment was 193 and during last year 54 were trained for home hemodialysis, for a total of 129 patients on home dialysis; nine were transplanted, bringing the total to 20; 11 were on peritoneal dialysis: 16 patients were either in home training or being dialyzed in the Center for holding or backup purposes, and 17 patients remained outpatients. The NKC had 5 percent of all the patients on hemodialysis in the United States and 10 percent of all the patients on home hemodialysis.

The staff was the same as in the previous year – two doctors, eight nurses and seven technicians, and it was due to their efforts that the results were so outstanding. During 1970, training time for home hemodialysis had been shortened from eight to six weeks and with the opening of a fourth training room NKC could train four patients at a time. This had enabled NKC to cope with the current patient load. A new development to improve patient care was the appointment of Paul van der Voort to head up a social work department. He would function to help patients during training and to coordinate various services such as DVR that they might need from time to time.

The important development of the past year had been the improving re-lationship with the Division of Nephrology at the University of Washington. Dr. Scribner and his group had been responsible for many of the techniques and much of the equipment used in hemodialysis and during the last two years maintenance hospital hemodialysis had been phased out of the uni-versity program. As a result, the division needed patients willing to undergo research to assist in development of new equipment and new techniques. In view of this, 91 of the patients living in the area had been asked if they would consider taking part in research projects. Sixty-one replied, of whom 56, or 92%, were willing to take part in such a project. The patients would need to give their consent and, in addition, the permission of their own physician and of Center staff would be needed. Such research would be of benefit to the university, the Center and all patients.

Peritoneal dialysis, which had proved to be a successful form of treat-ment for some patients, would be moving to the Northwest Kidney Center from the university.

One of the most pressing needs was for expansion of the transplant pro-gram, and particularly the cadaveric transplant program. Transplantation was the treatment of choice for children and for many patients up to the age of 45, but many of these did not have a related donor and so it was essential to be able to harvest organs from other sources. Secondly, as the Center's selection criteria had become more liberal, it became obvious there were some patients who had multiple problems, either from medical or psychosocial reasons who would benefit from early transplantation. This would benefit the Center, too, by reducing the costs of treating such patients. NKC was studying the prospects of developing a cadaveric retrieval program during the coming year. The treatment of end-stage renal disease was still not a static process and in the next few years there would be continuing improvements, both in selection of the most appropriate treatment for patients with kidney failure and in the methods by which they were treated.

Terry Pollard gave the administrator's report. Under the guidance of Jim Phillips, 1970 had proved to be a year of change and improvement for the Northwest Kidney Center. His direction provided the administrative groundwork for development of an efficient, financially sound and economical organization and the fruits of his efforts were realized in nearly all aspects of the operation. The total operational expenses for 1970 amounted to $1,243,000, more than $25,000 less than last year's budget. With increased efforts in collections and better administrative tools, accounts receivable was reduced by $16,000 compared to 1969, even with the addition of 75 new patients. The relationship with other hospitals in Seattle had been greatly improved and sharing agreements with the Veterans Administration Hospital and Children's Orthopedic Hospital had provided broader medical and financial coverage for a substantial portion of NKC patients. Financial agreements with the University of Washington Hospital and U. S. Public Health Service Hospital allowed greater flexibility in the use of patient resources. Advancements had been made and more were being negotiated with Group Health Hospital to broaden its coverage to include home dialysis.

The most successful fund drive in the Center's history occurred during the previous year, reaching a combined total of $330,000 in Designated and Undesignated Funds. This was due in part to increased publicity and generous support from all the news media and in part to the fund organization headed by Dr. Philbrick.

The 1971 budget target was $1,648.000. The Center expected to start 85 to 90 patients in the coming year as long as sufficient funds were available. New patient numbers had increased steadily; in 1967, the Center had 29 new patients; 1968, 39; 1969, 58, and last year, 75, and it was generally accepted there were 35 treatable cases per million population per year. Western Washington had a population of nearly 2.5 million, and using incidence rate as a guide, 87 new patients would require treatment in 1971. One hundred and seventy-five patients were now receiving treatment and by 1976, adjusting for deaths and transfers, some 422 patients would be receiving treatment by either dialysis or transplantation. Similarly, budget projections could be made and, barring revolutionary changes in treatment and their related costs, the 1976 budget would be in the neighborhood of $3 million.

The average cost per patient had again decreased over the preceding year. In 1966 it was $9,923; in 1967, $9,761; in 1968, with the advent of home dialysis, the cost dropped to $9,363; and in 1969, when the true benefits of home dialysis were realized, the cost was $6,945. In 1970, the figure dropped to $5,919. This trend was expected to continue. The cooperation and team approach of all departments and dedicated efforts of individual staff members had made this trend possible and allowed extension of treatment to nearly all who need it.

Clint Howard reported that the 1970-71 fund drive had been very successful and had raised $140,000 to date, 18% ahead of last year thanks to Dr. Philbrick, the General Fund Drive chairman. The drive was running about $23,000 ahead of last year but was still $90,000 short of the goal for 1971. The increase compared with the previous year was due to many factors, including three checks totaling $29,300, two checks for $10,000 and one for $9,000. Public solicitation had produced more than $34,000, almost exactly double last year's total.

In those areas of the community where funds had been solicited by letter and personal contact, the drive had raised about $60,000 in comparison to $54,000 last year, and the county chapters contributed $18,000, $10,000 more than last year, and most were still just beginning their fund drives. Memorials and bequests were also becoming a major source of income and had raised $18,000 compared to last year's $4,000. An interesting aspect of the 1970 drive had been the attitude of contributors – cash or not at all, with only one or two people making pledges. The response to solicitation had been, "We'll contribute if we have the money and if we don't, we won't." People were not sure enough about the future of the economy to pledge or promise to pay later. Another $90,000 was still needed. A new approach to raising money in the future would be through the establishment of a Northwest Kidney Center Foundation which would be part of the answer to the annual fund drives. The Center would be requesting $1.5 million from the state; currently, the governor had budgeted $900,000 for kidney treatment during the next biennium and it was hoped to get another $600,000 appropriated. The situation looked very favorable for getting the full budget request.

Dr. John McCormack gave the President's Report. He noted the overall reorganization of the Center began two years previously when Tom Siefert temporarily assumed the responsibilities of director and worked with Mr. Del Ruble to propose the reorganization. When Mr. Siefert left, Mr. Jim Phillips joined the staff as executive director. Dr. McCormack deeply regretted receiving a letter from Mr. Phillips dated September 28, 1970, stating, "On medical advice, I will not be able to return to work in the foreseeable future." His loss was felt by the entire staff and necessitated taking steps to reorganize the management of the Center. This was further complicated by the decision of Dr. Jerry Pendras to leave the Center for full-time private practice of nephrology. Both Dr. Pendras and Mr. Phillips gave to the Center that extra effort which made their contributions so outstanding and made it so difficult to find replacements. The Center was indebted to each for his contribution. Fortunately, with the help of many interested people in academic positions and a selection committee of the Board of Trustees, the Center was able to accomplish the reorganization. The first position filled was that of a full-time medical director, Dr. Christopher Blagg. Dr. Blagg took his medical training in England at the University of Leeds School of Medicine and was a member of the Royal College of Physicians of London. Subsequently he came to the University of Washington and for the past eight years had been working very closely with Dr. Scribner in the Division of Nephrology. The Center was grateful to Dr. Scribner for encouraging his right-hand man to assume the position of medical director.

Dr. McCormack commended Dr. Tom Sawyer who had assumed the responsibilities of medical director during the search and had continued to work with the patients in the Center. He was extremely grateful to Dr. Sawyer for his devotion to the patients in the Center and to the work he was doing.

The administrator, Terry Pollard, had been with the Center since 1961 and advanced from the position of chief dialysis technician to assistant to Mr. Jim Phillips. When Mr. Phillips was forced to retire because of illness, he strongly urged the Board to engage an expert to work full time in the solicitation of public funds and to guide the Center in its representation before the state legislature. Mr. Clinton Howard was hired for that position. He had thirteen years' experience in the public relations field and was a graduate of the University of Washington.

Dr. McCormack said he was always amazed to look back through the minutes of the monthly Executive Committee meetings and see what had happened. He would like to report that all of the problems presented to the Center during the past year had been solved, but this would not be true. Many decisions and policy changes had been made, but from previous experience it should be obvious to all that some of the immediate problems would not be easily solved and there would be a future that was impossible to speculate on. However, he would review certain aspects of what has transpired and perhaps make a suggestion or two for the continued operation of the Center.

Perhaps the most encouragingly thing that had happened during the past year had been the selection of Mr. Denver Ginsey as the incoming president of the Board of Trustees. He would receive the same wonderful cooperation from all associated with the Center that it had been Dr. McCormack's pleasure to receive.

When passing out accolades it should be recalled that the chronic hemodialysis program was initiated by Dr. Belding Scribner, professor of medicine and director of the Division of Nephrology at the University of

Washington in March 1960. Not only do the 200 patients in the Center program recognize a debt of gratitude, but all who have had the privilege of working with the Center through the years would always keep in mind his brilliant contribution to the management of chronic renal disease. In somewhat the same vein and speaking on behalf of the Board of Trustees of the Kidney Center, Dr. McCormack wished again to express appreciation to the board of the Swedish Hospital who had made it possible for the Center to continue to function in pleasant and medically superior surroundings.

He had alluded earlier to the wonderful cooperation he had received during his term as president. He felt compelled to mention by name several committees that had been exceedingly active during the past year. Denver Ginsey had been chairman of the Finance Committee whose members met faithfully and had contributed so much to the Center's financial stability. He was grateful to Dick Bangert and the members of the Legislative Committee who had taken the necessary steps to impress our state legislators and he was sure they would continue to function. He also wished to thank Del Ruble and his Personnel Committee who had met to review the needs of the people working in the Center on behalf of the patients. Another committee that had been working constantly for betterment of the Northwest Kidney Center was the Public Relations Committee and its chairman, Jack Schwartz. Mr. Schwartz had been faithful in attending the meetings and was most knowledgeable about the needs of the Center. All were indebted to the Patient Admissions Committee which was charged with the tremendous responsibility of selecting patients for continued care. Until last fall this committee had been chaired by the Rev. John Darrah. His loss had been deeply felt. Regretfully, the Northwest Kidney Center was not yet in a position to accept all patients with chronic renal failure. Its original motto was "Who Shall Live." Over the past eight years the medical facilities had been extended and the selection criteria widened so that many more patients were now being taken into the program. It was his opinion that a strong a selection process would be needed in the future. The task of selection was not easy and he congratulated the committee for their past courage and devotion and sincerely hoped this committee would continue to function as well. Finally, he wished to extend his personal thanks to the members of the Medical Advisory Committee, chaired by Dr. Joe Eschbach, for their continued support in assuring competent guidance on the medical problems which arose from time to time.

Because of the efforts of the Legislative Committee and Clint Howard, he was happy to report a distinct change in the attitude of state officials in Olympia, both those elected and those who were employees of the state. It was very gratifying to hear that representatives of the Center were being greeted without reserve by the floor leaders of both the House and Senate. During the past year we had also received excellent cooperation from others whose interests in our efforts were important for our wellbeing. Among them he mentioned particularly Mr. Walter Howe, director of the Budget, who had become most solicitous of the financial needs of the Center. The Center also received excellent cooperation from Drs. Lane and Spielholz from the Department of Public Health and Dr. Leahy from the Division of Vocational Rehabilitation. Unfortunately, cooperation did not always lead to funds and so the efforts of the personnel of the Center would continue to be exerted on the members of the legislature to assure appropriation of adequate funds to continue the program.

The Congress authorized the Regional Medical Program several years ago as an aid in the treatment of people suffering from heart disease, stroke or cancer. In the last session of Congress patients with end-stage renal disease were added to the program and the NKC became involved in an effort to use these funds to assist in training patients. Dr. Scribner and Dr. Curtis had been working on this but without success to date.

The Center had recently established a reserve fund to set aside any dollars in excess of the Center's immediate needs for the ongoing care of patients. NKC had never accurately defined its future responsibility to patients but he felt that once a patient was accepted there was a continuing responsibility to the patient for as long as the Center was in existence. Most of the Board of Trustees shared this concept of future responsibility.

It was only fourteen months previously that the kidney transplantation program began at the university with Dr. Marchioro. It had proved extremely successful and would be continued for the benefit of the Center's patients. As part of the program, the Center was looking at instituting a cadaver kidney retrieval program for the area using funding from the Regional Medical Program. It was also hoped to generate funds to support clinical research at the Center.

Dr. McCormack expressed his thanks to the citizens of the state of Washington who had so generously contributed funds to the ongoing medical program of the Northwest Kidney Center, to the wonderful staff of the Center – the nurses, technicians, secretaries, bookkeepers, etc., and to the patients themselves for their understanding of the Center's problems and their willingness s to cooperate in every way possible to allow the functions of the Center to continue.

Dr. McCormack then turned the meeting over to Mrs. Mickelwait, who presented certificates of appreciation to the following groups for their support and assistance during the year: Beta Sigma Phi (JoAnn Mellott); East Side Auxiliary (Roxine Brown); J. Garth Mooney Auxiliary (Karen Forslund); Queen City Auxiliary (Eva Osawa); Somerset Auxiliary (Beth Allott); and Stewardess Emeritus Association (Loretta Elderkin). The Stewardess Emeritus Association presented a check to the Northwest Kidney Center for $2,000, a result of its fundraising efforts. Dr. McCormack presented certificates of appreciation to: James Mattson, Jr. (Pierce County Chapter), John Kennedy, MD (Pierce County Chapter ); William McKee, MD (Apple Valley Chapter); James Nolan (Yakima County Chapter); Ex Ulsky (Snohomish County Chapter); Jeannette Murphy (representative KIRO TV); Mr. and Mrs. Jerry McManus (Washington State Fraternal Order of Eagles and Auxiliary – donation of display van); Larry Pinnt (Special Gifts Chairman); Muriel Smith (volunteer, fund office); Lawrence Karrar (Board of Trustees, 1964-1971); Fred Huleen (Board of Trustees, 1964-1971); and Boeing Employees Good Neighbor Fund (Mr. Clint Randolph accepting). Plaques were presented to: Fred Milke (photography for NKC slide show); Richard Philbrick, DDS (Fund Drive chairman 1969-71); Walter Schoenfeld (Fund Drive chairman, 1965-66, Executive Committee chairman, Fund Drive Committee, 1966-71); The Rev. John

Darrah (founding member of the Board of Trustees, Executive Committee and Patient Admissions Committee); and William Werrbach (designer of NKC symbol).

Dr. McCormack then turned the meeting over to the new president, Mr. Denver Ginsey who presented Dr. McCormack a plaque of appreciation on behalf of the Board of Trustees and the Northwest Kidney Center.

## SEMI-ANNUAL BOARD MEETING

At the April Executive Committee meeting, Mr. Ginsey suggested the possibility of quarterly Board of Trustee meetings to stimulate interest and enthusiasm among board members. Mr. Campbell suggested starting with a semi-annual board meeting, possibly before the beginning of the fund drive and the traditional February meeting. The Executive Committee agreed that a Board of Trustees meeting be held in September. In June, Mr. Pollard said that to get board members more involved with NKC a Board of Trustees meeting had been scheduled for September 15. There would be a brief business meeting with committee reports (dispensing with awards and presentations), followed by cocktails and dinner. Cost would probably be $10 per person with no-host cocktails and around $12.50 per person with cocktails. Mr. Phillips suggested October rather than September might be more appropriate, as it was closer to the opening of the fund drive. Dr. Philbrick suggested the meeting be held at Eklind Hall. The feasibility of this would be investigated and a report made to the Executive Committee.

The First Semi-Annual meeting of the Northwest Kidney Center Board of Trustees was called to order by the president, Denver Ginsey, on September 15, 1971 in the board room of the First Interstate Bank of Washington. Mr. Ginsey introduced new board members: Mr. Gerald Grinstein; Mr. Charles Savage; Rabbi Earl Starr; and Councilman Liem Tuai.

Mr. Ginsey briefly re-stated the history of the Northwest Kidney Center and the changes that had occurred during the past year: Dr. Christopher Blagg was appointed full-time medical director after Dr. Jerry Pendras resigned to go into private practice. Mr. Terrance Pollard assumed the duties of administrator after Mr. James Phillips became ill. Mr. Ginsey said the financial position of the Center was stable, with internal systems improvement in purchasing, accounts payable and accounts receivable. Exciting medical changes had occurred and the Center currently was a well-functioning program. The Northwest Kidney Center, the first maintenance dialysis program in the world, was still the largest and the best.

Mr. Pollard illustrated the continued progress of the Center by citing the number of patients able to be served. The number of new patients starting each year had steadily increased from 7 in 1962, to 76 in 1970, and 67 of the projected total of 90 had been accepted so far in the current year. In two more years it was anticipated that more than 500 people would have been treated who only 10 years previously had no alternative to their disease but death. With a projected budget of $4 million for the next two years to provide for the anticipated patient load, only a well-managed operation motivated by sound business principles would maintain the balance of funding currently being experienced. Systems improvements were underway; purchasing inventories, accounts receivable and accounts payable were being revamped. Budgeting would reflect unit costs rather than function, with greater emphasis on variable costs. Cost analysis would be a by-product of improved budgeting. Fees, which had not been adjusted for four years, would be realigned to be consistent with the needs and goals of the Center.

Dr. Blagg gave the medical report. One important revision had been in the area of training patients to care for themselves in their own homes. With funds from the Boeing Employees Good Neighbor Fund, a core curriculum had been established containing the essential information necessary for successful home dialysis. This had been programmed into videotapes, thus freeing nursing time for more intensive teaching where needed. Training time had been shortened from six weeks to three weeks with these new techniques. There was a new, closer association with the University of Washington research team, which would bring changes and improvements in equipment, techniques, etc. In the next two or three years many changes were likely to occur, such as shorter dialysis, smaller equipment, and more efficient dialysis. The Regional Medical Program, with federal funds for kidney disease, would support organizing a kidney retrieval program for an expanded cadaver kidney transplant program and it was expected that Northwest Kidney Center would be closely associated with this program.

Mr. Howard reported on Northwest Kidney Center Foundation. This would enable the Center to solicit funds normally not available to it, e.g. deferred giving, bequests, etc. The foundation needed to be developed because of increasing demands of the Center for funds and to relieve the pressure for specified annual amounts for the fund drive. The foundation solicitation would not interfere with the fund drive because there would be no publicity for the foundation – funds would be solicited by direct contact. The foundation would be a separate organization with its own Board of Trustees, and would be so filed with the Internal Revenue Service. If a national health care plan funded treatment of kidney disease in the future, the foundation would be dissolved. The proposed by-laws and articles of incorporation for Northwest Kidney Center Foundation were distributed. It was moved, seconded and passed unanimously that the Board of Trustees approve the recommendation of the Executive Committee and authorize the Executive Committee to take action as necessary to cause the Northwest Kidney Center Foundation to be established.

Dr. Philbrick reported on the fund drive. The cost of fundraising at the Northwest Kidney Center was less than ten percent and the raised money was spent locally on local citizens. County fund drives had been established and were very successful. In the last year, major gifts increased from $46,000 to $64,000, special gifts from $17,000 to $22,000, and public solicitation increased from $22,000 to $48,000. There were 111 charitable foundations in this area that could give to NKC, and they would be solicited during the next fund drive. Dr. Philbrick introduced the new fund drive chairman, Mr. Kirby Torrance, who said the next year's fund drive goal would be $270,000. The campaign would run November 15, 1971 through February 14, 1972 – a shorter time than previously, but with more intensive effort planned.

## Medical Activities

At the January 22, 1971 meeting of the Executive Committee, Dr. Sawyer reported the current patient census was 17 outpatients not yet needing to start dialysis, 8 patients dialyzing in-center, 7 in home hemodialysed training, 12 on home peritoneal dialysis, 131 on home hemodialysis and 21 transplanted, for a total of 196 patients. There had been one kidney transplant in the previous month and two deaths.

Dr. Blagg reported that at present time the social worker at the Center was employed on an hourly basis and performed initial patient application interviews, as did a psychiatrist. The social worker also provided short-term help to patients under treatment. He proposed that Paul van der Voort, the present social worker, be hired now on a salaried basis at three-quarter time, and that the psychiatric interview be deleted from the routine applications. With experience gained it had been found that with a good social and medical history most new patients did not require psychiatric assessment, which in many cases may be affected by the patient's biochemical problems at the time of application. The scope of the social worker's function would be increased by: 1) continuing the initial social service interview with applicants prior to acceptance; 2) providing acute and short-term or crisis intervention services to patients in training and at home; 3) assisting staff in understanding patients' psychosocial problems; and 4) maintaining necessary collateral contacts with DVR representatives and others. He would attend medical staff meetings involving patient care. The 1971 budget had provisions for a social worker's salary, and there would be savings realized by deleting the psychiatric interview. It was moved, seconded, and passed unanimously that Paul van der Voort be hired on a three-quarter-time basis at $13,500 and that the psychiatric evaluation of applicants be left to the discretion of the medical director.

In February the current patient census was 20 outpatients, 3 center patients, 8 home training patients, 13 home peritoneal dialysis patients, 134 home hemodialysis patients and 24 transplanted patients, for a total of 202. There had been 11 new patients since the last meeting; three patients had been transferred to other centers, there had been two kidney transplants and two deaths.

By late Match there were now 132 patients in the home on hemodialysis, 2 having been trained since the last meeting, and 6 now were in home training. There were 8 patients in the Center, 7 of whom were newly admitted patients and 6 of these had arteriovenous fistulae rather than cannulas, reflecting a change in philosophy of access to the circulation. There were 14 patients on home peritoneal dialysis, 17 outpatients awaiting dialysis or a kidney transplant, and 25 patients who had received transplants. There had been one related donor transplant during the last month. The total patient population was 202. There had been three deaths: a 24-year-old man who had been on the program 10 months; a 56-year-old woman on the program three months, who had an undiagnosed fatal disease prior to her admission to NKC; and a 51-year-old man, Clyde Shields, the first person in the world to be treated by long-term maintenance hemodialysis for terminal chronic kidney failure and who had been on the program 11 years.

At late April there were now 131 patients in the home on hemodialysis, 5 having been trained since the last meeting, and 7 now in home dialysis training. There were two patients in the Center, one awaiting a related donor transplant and one awaiting home training. There were 17 patients on home peritoneal dialysis, and 28 transplanted patients, 3 having been transplanted during the past month. Nineteen patients were being followed as outpatients prior to their need for dialysis or transplant. Two deaths had occurred: one, a 57-year-old man, the husband of an NKC employee, who had been on the program for five years; the other, a 59-year-old man, on the program for seven years, who was one of the first home hemodialysis patients.

Dr. Blagg discussed newspaper accounts of papers presented from Seattle at the annual conference of the American Society for Artificial Internal Organs held in Chicago on April 19 and 20 (See the 1971 ASAIO Meeting below). The papers discussed current research in dialysis therapy in progress at the University of Washington and implied that a new form of treatment would become available in the future at greatly reduced cost.

This was not the case, as the form of therapy being tested was still only a hypothesis to be proved or disproved. However, because of this publicity, it was necessary to explain to the legislature why the reduced costs would not be forthcoming, at least during this biennium. Briefly, the hypothesis stated that in addition to the molecules of urea and creatinine which accumulated in a person's blood with kidney failure, there might be other larger molecules, as yet unidentified. Over the last ten years, evidence had accumulated that these larger molecules might be more important than the smaller ones in the genesis of many of the complications of uremia. Engineering studies, both theoretical and practical, had shown that while the removal through an artificial kidney of the small molecules was dependent mainly on the blood flow rate and dialysate flow rate through the artificial kidney, in the case of the larger molecules, the limiting factor was the membrane itself. In effect, therefore, the important factors in removing large molecules were the surface area of the membrane and the duration of time during which blood was exposed to the membrane; in other words, the square meter hour. Slow flow dialysis was derived from this hypothesis. By reducing the dialysate flow rate from 500 ml per minute to 100 ml per minute, the removal of small molecules such as creatinine and urea was reduced by ten to twenty percent; however, because the surface area of the dialyzer remained constant, the removal of large molecules was unaffected. Therefore, if large molecule accumulation is important in the manifestations of uremia, reducing dialysate flow rate should have no effect on the level of large molecules. Reduction of dialysate flow rate in this fashion resulted in a saving of some $500 to $600 a year because dialysate is one of the most expensive items for the patient in the home. Another corollary of the hypothesis was the possibility of going to frequent very short dialysis. For example, by using a dialyzer of very large surface area the number of hours of dialysis during the week could be diminished considerably. If a dialyzer with a functioning surface area of three square meters were used for dialysis one hour a day, seven days a week, this would produce the same effect as using a standard Kiil dialyzer three times a week for ten hours. These ideas were still hypothetical and remain to be proved. The slow flow experiment intends to treat some six to nine patients for at least a year before we would feel justified to expose all new patients.

By the end of May there were 130 patients in the home, 4 having finished training since the last meeting. There were 5 patients in home training, 8 in the center, 6 of whom were new, 17 on peritoneal dialysis, 1 new, and 18 outpatients being followed prior to their need for dialysis or kidney transplantation. There were 29 transplanted patients, 2 having had related donor transplants in the last month; 1 transplanted kidney in a 23-year-old girl had failed. There had been five deaths: one, a 60-year-old patient on home dialysis died in the Public Health Hospital of an undiagnosed febrile and mental deterioration; a 58-year-old man on home dialysis died of pneumonia; a 28-year-old mam on home dialysis who had stopped taking anticonvulsant medication without his physician's knowledge fell and struck his head and died of intracranial bleeding; a 54-year-old man on peritoneal dialysis died of a heart attack; and a 55-year-old man not yet on dialysis died of liver disease.

Dr. Blagg discussed reorganization of the medical department. With both the current head technician and nursing supervisor leaving, their positions would be combined into a "unit manager" and replaced with one person, as yet to be hired, who would be responsible for both nurses and technicians.

By the end of June, Dr. Sawyer reported there were now 129 patients in the home, two having finished training since the last meeting. There were 5 patients in home training, 13 in the Center, 19 on peritoneal dialysis, 18 outpatients and 30 patients transplanted, for a total patient population of 214. There had been one related donor transplant in a 22-year-old girl, and two deaths; a 56-year-old man who died of heart failure and a 61-year-old man who committed suicide. In late August there were 130 patients at home on hemodialysis, 7 having been trained since the last meeting, and there were 5 patients in home dialysis training; 20 outpatients being followed; 16 Center patients; 15 patients on peritoneal dialysis; and 35 patients who had been transplanted, for a total patient population of 221. In the last month there had been four related donor transplants and two cadaveric transplants and six deaths. In September there were a total of 228 patients being followed by the Northwest Kidney Center: 23 outpatients, 15 patients in the center, 1 patient in home training (3 more patients would start), 13 patients on peritoneal dialysis, 135 patients on home hemodialysis, and 41 patients who had received a kidney transplant. In the last month there had been four cadaver transplants and two related-donor transplants and two deaths: one death three weeks post-transplant from pneumonia and one death attributed to heart failure. By late October, 233 patients were being followed by NKC: 134 in the home on hemodialysis and 14 on peritoneal dialysis; 27 outpatients; 9 Center patients; and 44 transplanted patients. Five patients had completed home training, including one trained on peritoneal dialysis at NKC. There had been one related donor transplant, two transfers to other dialysis centers, and one death: a patient on dialysis for five years who died from a cerebral hemorrhage.

In early December, Dr. Sawyer reported the Center was now responsible for 236 patients: 15 outpatients; 8 patients dialyzing in the Center; 16 home peritoneal dialysis patients; 6 patients in home dialysis training; 131 at home on hemodialysis; and 60 patients who had transplants. Seven patients had started treatment this month and seven were trained for home hemodialysis. Five patients received kidney transplants, two related donor transplants and three cadaveric donor transplants. There were four deaths: a 65-year-old man with diabetes who was blind, on dialysis for four months, who died of pneumonia; a 47-year-old man on dialysis eight years, who died of a cerebral hemorrhage; a 55-year-old man who died post-transplant of a heart attack; and a 59-year-old man on dialysis for one and a half years who died after an accident with his cannulas. Six groups of patients had completed the new three-week home hemodialysis training program and the staff was extremely pleased with the results.

HOME HEMODIALYSIS

In February, Dr. Blagg discussed a proposal to evaluate the effects of the new home hemodialysis training program. This was included in the Center's original proposal to the Regional Medical Program. As these funds were not made available, a similar proposal had been submitted to the Boeing Employees Good Neighbor Fund and it would meet in April to consider the proposal. In the meantime, the Executive Committee was asked to approve expenditure of funds to hire Mr. Gerald Stinson, an educational consultant, at a salary of $4,000 for three months, and to rent equipment at $250 per month. This expenditure would cease with approval of the Boeing Employees Good Neighbor Fund proposal or in three months. Mr. Stinson would establish a core curriculum of the knowledge necessary for the patient to be taught to do safe home hemodialysis, would standardize the training course, and would develop audiovisual teaching aids, particularly videotape instruction, to free NKC instructors from the role of teaching to one of observing and correcting the patient in training. He would also train NKC staff to develop new teaching programs and audiovisual aids. It was proposed to purchase the audiovisual equipment and hire Mr. Stinson for six months if the Boeing grant was approved. It was moved, seconded, and passed unanimously that Dr. Blagg's proposal be authorized.

By June, Gerald Stinson was reorganizing the home hemodialysis training program, and with funds provided by the Boeing Employees Good Neighbor Fund, was making videotaped teaching programs and rewriting the training manual. Previously, patients had been trained over a six-week period, with dialysis three times per week. Part of the reorganization would be to try three-week training, perhaps with daily dialysis. As this would affect training charges and costs, it would be studied further and more details reported later.

Three months later, the home training program has been shortened to three weeks through the use of revised training material, videotapes and other audiovisual aids, and intensive instruction, and it appeared that it might be possible to shorten to eleven days for younger, more intelligent patients.

In October, Dr. Blagg and Dr. Sawyer updated the Executive Committee on the home hemodialysis training program. In April, 1971, with the assistance of a Boeing Employees Good Neighbor Fund grant, televising of the home dialysis training program teaching was begun. Forty hours of programs had now been developed. These programs had gained interest in other parts of the country and representatives of the National Institutes of Health were very impressed. In addition, a core curriculum was established. The training time using the new teaching materials and televised programming had been shortened from six to three weeks, and the training staff had been reduced from three nurses and three technicians to two of each. Three groups of patients had been trained using the new program, and the results were most encouraging. It was suggested that in two or three months' time the Executive Committee should convene in the home training area to view firsthand some of the videotapes and methods for training patients to do home hemodialysis.

By the end of the year, six groups of patients had completed the new three-week training program and the staff was extremely pleased with the results.

PERITONEAL DIALYSIS

In February, Dr. Blagg noted that the peritoneal dialysis program, as developed by Dr. Tenckhoff at University Hospital, had proved an effective form of treatment for certain patients. At present, patients accepted for this were treated and trained for home peritoneal dialysis at the University Hospital. His proposal was to move the training facility to the Northwest Kidney Center in the next few months, thereby decreasing peritoneal dialysis training costs to the Center. It was moved, seconded, and passed unanimously that the peritoneal dialysis training program be transferred from the University Hospital to Northwest Kidney Center.

KIDNEY TRANSPLANTATION

Regular meetings to discuss transplantation had been held with representatives from Virginia Mason, Swedish, University of Washington and the VA hospitals, the Regional Medical Program and Northwest Kidney Center.

These meetings had been very successful in establishing communication between these institutions.

In February, Dr. Eschbach gave the Transplant Committee report. The committee had been appointed by Dr. McCormack in December 1970 to investigate the possibility of renal transplantation being done elsewhere than at University Hospital and what the Center's involvement should be. Historically, Dr. Thomas Marchioro, University Hospital, had done all transplants in Western Washington and the survival figures for related donor transplanted kidneys were better here than the rest of the country and for cadaver kidney transplants the figures were also good. For patients not doing well on dialysis and who did not have a relative who could donate a kidney, cadaver transplantation was the only solution. The Transplant Committee therefore submitted the following statement: We recognize that there is and will continue to be an increased need for kidney transplantations in Western Washington. In order to expand the present transplant program with the future likelihood that kidney transplantation will be done elsewhere than at the University Hospital, we recommend that Northwest Kidney Center begin efforts to undertake a cadaveric kidney retrieval program and to determine the funding and personnel needs of such a program. We also urge that authorization be made for the hiring of necessary personnel for this program. It was moved, seconded and passed unanimously that Northwest Kidney Center institute the steps necessary to investigate implementation of a cadaver retrieval program. Dr. Blagg would present cost estimates to the Executive Committee at the next meeting.

In March, Dr. Blagg reported that the Regional Medical Program was reasonably certain to receive funds to develop a cadaver kidney retrieval program and Northwest Kidney Center would be the most appropriate site for the collection and preservation of kidneys in the Northwest. A scientist with the Pacific Northwest Research Foundation in Eklind Hall was an organ perfusion expert and had space in his laboratory for such a program. When more information was available concerning possible Regional Medical Program financing, the possibility of a research grant for Dr. Ward would be investigated. The Northwest Kidney Center would work closely with the University Hospital transplant program so that the entire program was cohesive, with optimal opportunity for success.

In July, Dr. Blagg reported that the Regional Medical Program had now received that funding for the kidney disease portion, although not the amount requested. This money was allocated for transplant-related programs, and none for patient care. The program would provide training to educate physicians and the public of the need for cadaver kidneys, would support development of a cadaver retrieval program, including the actual collection and transplantation of cadaver kidneys, and would support immunology to provide tissue typing and matching. The Center would be most closely involved in the retrieval and transplantation portion of the program and would be working with kidney preservation methods and with a kidney perfusion machine that would arrive shortly. A request for funds from the Seattle Foundation had been made to convert space in Eklind Hall to a kidney perfusion laboratory. September was the anticipated date for the first human cadaver transplant using this equipment. A publicity drive to inform the public on organ donation would probably begin in October. Of the 80 patients anticipated to start at NKC in the next year, 40 or so would probably receive transplants, 25 related donor transplants and 20 cadaveric transplants

Northwest Kidney Center's Transplant Committee met on July 13, 1971. This committee was set up by the Executive Committee to become involved with the transplant and cadaver retrieval program and the cadaver retrieval laboratory that would be located at the Center. Dr. Maurice Ward of the Pacific Northwest Research Center had been retained by the Regional Medical Program and was currently involved in an attempt to preserve dog kidneys with the recently obtained kidney perfusion equipment. The first human transplant using this equipment would probably be in late September. The Committee agreed that the transplant program be expanded to include other Seattle hospitals in addition to University Hospital, and Dr. Gerald Kenny who has transplant surgery experience had expressed interest in being involved, perhaps at Swedish Hospital.

To obtain kidneys for preservation, it would be necessary to establish an organized systematic approach to hospitals and surgery, along with a public education program. The Transplant Committee recommended to the Executive Committee: 1) the Regional Medical Program, University Hospital, and the Northwest Kidney Center cooperate in development of an organization for organ retrieval and preservation; 2) contact be made with hospitals and surgeons concerning the program, and systematic follow-up procedures established; 3) Dr. Gerald Kenny be retained by the RMP, or, if necessary, Northwest Kidney Center, to work with Dr. Marchioro and the University of Washington transplant program, with a view to transferring a portion of renal transplantation to Swedish Hospital in the future. There was no action taken by the Executive Committee on these recommendations at that time. Dr. Blagg noted that the Transplant Committee had visualized transplantation as a joint program among hospitals with University Hospital and Swedish Hospital being the centers for actual transplantation and the Northwest Kidney Center handling the processing of transplant applications. However, the Executive Committee of Virginia Mason Hospital had decided to undertake a transplant program on its own. Dr. Blagg pointed out that there would be approximately 50 to 60 transplants per year originating in Western Washington and 50 additional transplant cases from Eastern Washington, Idaho and Montana, and that a transplant center should probably perform a transplant every other week in order to maintain proficiency. Thus, it would be possible with careful planning to have transplantation centers at the University Hospital, Swedish Hospital and Virginia Mason Hospital. Dr. Haviland suggested NKC delegates meet with Virginia Mason administration to discuss procedures involving Virginia Mason operating a transplant program in conjunction with Northwest Kidney Center and the RMP. There would be a meeting of the Transplant Committee and members of the Virginia Mason staff in early September.

In September, Dr. Blagg reported that he and Dr. Haviland had met with surgeons from Virginia Mason Hospital to discuss future transplantation programs. Some basic concepts about transplantation were discussed.

Virginia Mason surgeons would meet with Dr. Marchioro. They would start a transplantation program slowly, in an organized fashion. Virginia Mason was responsible for ten to twelve applications to NKC per year and statistics from the Regional Medical Program and other information had shown that a successful transplant program should do at least one transplant every two weeks. Dr. McCormack said the University Hospital's program was on an experimental basis and the time had come to make this service available to patients in private hospitals. Preparation for surgery and follow-up post-transplant should be done by nephrologists, with NKC in charge. Dr. Blagg said that the cadaver retrieval program was already underway. A request had been made to the Seattle Foundation for $4,600 to remodel space in Eklind Hall for a cadaver retrieval laboratory. The perfusion machine for this laboratory currently was being tested at the University Hospital dog laboratory.

A press conference in October had announced the beginning of the cadaver retrieval program and it was anticipated the organ retrieval laboratory would be fully functioning in Eklind Hall by January.

In December, Dr. Blagg reported that four cadaver kidneys had been retrieved, preserved using the perfusion equipment and transplanted. Construction of the Organ Retrieval Laboratory in Eklind Hall was progressing. There was considerable enthusiasm for this program. By becoming responsible for regional control of the RMP transplant program the NKC program became the second regional organ procurement in the United States, only the Boston program having been developed earlier. With the estimated cost of $1,500 per cadaver kidney, Northwest Kidney Center also had assumed the problems of billing for out-of-state patients. Unless a kidney recipient had gone through some sort of intake processing there might be difficulty billing proper insurance agencies, etc.; additionally, state funds could not be used for out-of-state patients, and there was general agreement that Washington state fund drive funds should not be used and there might be problems in billing patients direct. One solution might be to be sure all potential candidates in Western Washington and Alaska go through the patient intake processing at NKC, and Eastern Washington, Idaho and Montana patients go through the Spokane Kidney Center intake processing, with Spokane guaranteeing payment for these patients. The Executive Committee agreed that preliminary explorations with state agencies, insurance companies, etc., should be instituted regarding payment for cadaver retrieval costs and Spokane be approached about guaranteed payment for Eastern Washington, Idaho and Montana patients. Dr. Blagg would report to the Executive Committee at the next meeting.

## Patient Admissions Committee

At the January Executive Committee meeting, Dr. Eschbach reported the Patient Admissions Committee had three meetings in December 1970 at which 13 applications were presented and all were approved. Dr. Eschbach complimented the patient processing staff for its efficiency in expediting the heavy load of applications.

Dr. Eschbach reported that out-of-state patients until recently had been trained for home dialysis at the University of Washington, but this was being phased out. He proposed that the Center consider accepting out-of-state patients for home dialysis training, with the following provisions: 1) that patients be fully funded; 2) that accepting the patient did not interfere with the operation of the Center; 3) that no long-term commitment be made to the patient; and 4) that the patient's physician in his home state agree to follow the patient after training. Dr. Sawyer pointed out that now there was no facility to care for patients with end-stage renal disease who were referred to Seattle nephrologists in private practice from out of state, other than NKC. Therefore training out-of-state patients would be beneficial to these physicians, and also to the Center. If there were periods when the Center was not operating at capacity, training these patients would occupy the staff and facilities. He stressed, however, that there were questions which needed to be clarified before such patients were accepted, such as the drawing up of a contract to protect against on-going obligations (long-term care), the exact monetary requirement of the patient, utilization of Public Health monies, particularly in view of the recent Supreme Court decision regarding state money as applicable to out-of-state indigent patients, and so on. It was moved, seconded, and passed unanimously that NKC policy be altered so that, with proper safeguards, out-of-state patients be accepted at NKC for training.

During February, 12 applications were presented to the Patient Admissions Committee; 11 were approved and 1 was deferred; one NKC patient application for transplant was approved. Dr. McCormack asked if there was a definition of the concept of the Center's responsibility to approve applications of patients who were medically marginal, referring specifically to the recent approval of the application of a paraplegic who developed kidney failure. While in many cases paraplegia would be considered a contraindication to acceptance, in this particular case the Patient Admissions Committee felt the patient could handle himself satisfactorily on home peritoneal dialysis and was rehabilitable; his application was therefore approved. Acceptance criteria in general were discussed. Dr. Eschbach said that in the past various measurements had been used to determine social "values" but none had proved useful.

In March, Mr. Pollard reported the Patient Admissions Committee had considered five applications in the previous month; three were approved and two were rejected. Six transplant applications for previously accepted patients were approved, three for related donor transplant and three for cadaveric transplant. To improve the efficiency of processing applications, the Patient Admissions Committee would meet weekly, rather than bimonthly and routine applications would be processed by a quorum committee, consisting of Dr. Eschbach, Dr. Blagg and Mr. Pollard, who would meet every other Wednesday. The full committee would meet the alternate Wednesdays. Information on all applicants would be sent to all committee members, and any committee member might request that a particular application be held for a full committee meeting.

In April, the Patient Admissions Committee had held two meetings. Seven applications were presented; six were approved and one was approved for transplant only because of a social situation, which would preclude home dialysis. There were two NKC patient transplant applications: one was approved and one was deferred.

During May, there had been four Patient Admissions Committee meetings since the last Executive Committee meeting; 13 applications were considered and all were approved. Two NKC patients were approved for transplantation.

During June, there had been one meeting of the Patient Admissions Committee since the last Executive Committee meeting. Of five applications, four were approved and one was deferred. Three NKC patients were approved for transplant.

In August, the Patient Admissions Committee reported that over the previous two months there had been four meetings and two telephone polls. Sixteen applications were presented: 13 were approved, one was deferred and two were rejected. There were four NKC transplant applications and all were approved.

In September, Mr. Pollard gave the report of the Patient Admissions Committee. There had been two meetings since the last Executive Committee meeting. Nine applications were presented: eight were approved and one was deferred.

In October, Mr. Pollard reported there had been three meetings of the Patient Admissions Committee since the last Executive Committee meeting. Six applications were presented: five were approved and one was rejected.

In December, Dr. Eschbach reported there had been four Patient Admissions Committee meetings. Eight applications were approved; there were no deferrals and no rejections. Four NKC patient transplant applications were approved.


## FINANCES

Mr. Ginsey reported that the Finance Committee at its meeting on January 20, 1971, recommended that the Executive Committee adopt the following resolution: A special fund shall be established to be known as "Board Designated Fund," which shall consist of such funds as the Board designates as a reserve for future treatment of patients. The Board shall, from time to time, transfer funds to said Fund from the General Fund, or to the General

Fund from said Fund as, in its judgment, shall best serve the needs of the Center. It is further recommended that this fund be maintained at a level determined by multiplying the number of patients at the Center for which it is responsible as of the year-end times $2,000.

In March, Mr. Burns reported that the Finance Committee had met to review the financial statement for the fifteen-month period from July 1, 1969, through September 30, 1970, audited by Stokes & Company. Mr. Burns expressed appreciation to Stokes & Company on behalf of the Board of Trustees and Northwest Kidney Center's staff for their contribution in preparing the audit report at reduced cost and their donation of time and effort to help during the time the business office was without an accountant. The statements presented were in a different format from the traditional balance sheet and income statement. The restyling of financial statements was made to communicate better the financial position and operation of Northwest Kidney Center. Since these financial statements were prepared, there had been changes in the Business Office personnel. Mr. Kassa had a massive amount of work ahead of him, but within 30 days should have things in better shape. The Finance Committee recommended the Executive Committee approve the audited financial statement for July 1, 1969 through September 30, 1970. It was so moved, seconded, and passed unanimously.

Mr. Pollard reported that after prolonged negotiations between Northwest Kidney Center and Group Health Cooperative, its Board of Trustees had now approved Group Health coverage up to $10,000 per year, including equipment, for patients with kidney failure.

At the April meeting, Mr. Kassa presented financial statements for the period October through March 31, 1971, with comparison figures for the period ending September 30, 1970. Under Current Assets, cash was $17,541 less, but certificates of deposit had increased by $54,000; both were readily available and this represented a stronger cash position than in September 1970. Accounts receivable, even less $80,000 for doubtful accounts, had increased $190,000. Under Current Liabilities, there was a significant increase in University Hospital bills ($68,671). Total liabilities had increased

$67,001. Compared to total current assets, the position was favorable by $152,077. Approximately 40 percent of problem accounts were problems with Medicare, equipment charges, etc. However, cash receipts were up to $94,000 per month, as compared with the previous $50,000 per month. Under Statement of Operations and General Fund Balance, direct cost of patient services was $295,712, plus other costs of $298,074, for a total patient treatment cost of $593,786. With charges billed to DVR of $104,310, Department of Health $63,780, and patients and their insurance $354,568, a total had been billed of $522,658. The excess of costs over recoverable charges was $71,128, of which $65,024 was recovered from Designated Fund contributions, leaving $6,104 to be paid out of the general fund. The Northwest Kidney Center was now in a more favorable position by $136,568. The next goal of the business office would be to establish the actual cost of providing patient care. With this in mind, Mr. Burns offered the assistance of Price Waterhouse personnel to assist with these management studies.

In May, Mr. Pollard reported that following two meetings with Medicare representatives and NKC, Medicare had agreed to cover many charges previously not allowed, including 23 of 25 previously not covered catalog items, freight charges, carrying charges for equipment and other items. It had also agreed to check past accounts to see if some adjustments could be made. Mr. Kassa noted that recently the fiscal year-end was changed to September 30, although this was never officially approved. There were certain advantages in having June 30 as the fiscal year-end, particularly the fact that this was in line with those governmental agencies dealing most closely with NKC. It was moved, seconded, and passed unanimously that June 30 be the official fiscal year-end.

Mr. Burns reported that the Finance Committee had met on August 24, 1971. He presented the unaudited June 30, 1971 Financial Statements and outlined the Statement of Financial Position and noted the accounts receivable balance of $705,000 and the accounts payable balances, most important of which was with the University Hospital. The Statement of Operations and General Fund Balance were reviewed. Cost of patient treatment was $1,049,000. Charges for patient treatment and services were $987,000. This left an excess of cost of $62,000. Excess costs were received from designated contributions and interest income and provided for additional unrestricted monies of $39,000. Accounts receivable had increased $344,000 since September 1970 because of an increase in transplants and the policy of some insurance companies and Medicare to pay for equipment over two to four years. The Finance Committee recommended that accounts receivable be classified in a meaningful way on the financial statements. The investment policy for the Center was discussed and it was agreed that a subcommittee of the Finance Committee, consisting of Mr. Burns, Mr. Campbell, and Mr. Bangert, should manage the Center's investment portfolio. The investment policy would establish levels of investment for each type of security, thereby meeting the operational requirements of the Center. Mr. Kassa provided a listing of investments and their dates of maturity so proper action could be taken. Policy for disposal of gifts to the Northwest Kidney Center was restated. Stocks and similar securities would be disposed of immediately upon receipt and disposal would be handled by authorized officers of the board. Bonds, real property or other assets acquired would be analyzed to determine whether they should be sold immediately or retained as part of the Center's investment portfolio. Mr. Kassa presented the following corporate resolution necessary to implement this policy: Resolved, the president, Denver Ginsey, vice president, Richard C. Philbrick, DDS, the treasurer, Robert Burns, or any of them, be and they are hereby authorized to sell, assign and indorse for transfer certificates representing stocks, bonds or other securities now registered or hereafter registered in the name of this corporation. It was moved, seconded, and passed unanimously that the corporate resolution (above) be adopted.

In September, Mr. Derham informed the Executive Committee of the possibility of a suit against the estate of a deceased patient. The estate's assets were $250,000, but almost all assets were in land. The estate had offered to settle at 50 percent of the account balance; NKC counteroffered a discount of 5 percent with payment terms. Mr. Campbell expressed the opinion that it would be highly desirable to settle out of court. Mr. Burns suggested that if cash flow was the problem, that NKC take partial cash payment and one of the pieces of land. Mr. Ginsey requested a report at the next meeting.

Mr. Ginsey noted that the Long-Range Planning Committee, to which Executive Committee members belong, should consider the problems facing the Center and should discuss new developments such as the square meter hour hypothesis and cadaveric transplantation, and how these would affect future planning for the Center. The Long-Range Planning Committee should plan to meet after the first of the coming year.

In October, the Finance Committee had reviewed the financial statements for three periods – the audited period July 1, 1969 to September 30, 1970, the unaudited period October 1, 1970 to June 30, 1971, and the Statement of Financial Position for the period ending September 30, 1971. These financial statements provided a clear look at the Center operation and showed that if there were no deficit by Center-financed patients, present operation costs would still produce a deficit of about $40,000. Assets in the second period increased over the first period by $367,576 and liabilities increased by $340,000 ($218,000 in hospital services). Activities for the second period resulted in a net increase in the general fund balance of $12,000. The Finance Committee reported that a major portion of the difficulties revolved around payments to University Hospital – firstly, the large amounts involved, and secondly, the time lag between paying University Hospital and collecting from patients and insurance companies. In the future, the Statement of Operation would appear compared with the 1971/72 fiscal year budget for each quarter. Mr. Pollard said that in the last nine-month period, NKC had lost approximately $40,000, solely because the present fee structure did not allow billing for all costs. Charges to the patient have not increased, but costs had gone up and services to the patient had increased. The Center dialysis charge was now $133; the last increase in dialysis charge was in February 1968.

The proposed fee increase was not yet final and eventually there might need to be a separate fee per type of treatment – peritoneal dialysis and hemodialysis – and Mr. Pollard was continuing to do cost breakdowns to see if there was a significant difference in the costs of different treatments. Mr.

Burns was checking to see if fees could be increased under Phase II regulations. The proposed increase in fees was based on the proposed 1971/72 budget; with this fee increase and anticipated allocation from the state, even then NKC would need $298,120 in public funds. It was moved, seconded, and passed unanimously that Mr. Pollard proceed with implementing adjustments in the fee schedule after consulting Phase II regulations. The Executive Committee agreed that patients and third parties should be notified well in advance of fee adjustments. The proposed NKC 1971/72 budget was approved unanimously.

STATE FINANCING

At the beginning of the year, Clint Howard reported that the governor's budget included $935,000 for Washington State kidney centers, a $600,000 cut from the funds that had been requested and $100,000 less than was appropriated in the last biennium. A letter had been written to all legislators explaining NKC's request and patients had written urging the appropriation be increased. It was probable that the appropriation would be increased by the legislature. As a result, approaches to the legislature concerned getting the appropriation for kidney care treatment in Washington as it currently appeared in the governor's budget raised. By March, it appeared the legislature would either give Washington State kidney centers the full budget request or declare legislative intent to provide additional funds at the 1972 special session, if need were to be established, and in April it was reported that the final amount appropriated by the legislature for kidney care in Washington State was $1,067,000, which was $34,000 more than the last biennium's appropriation and $500,000 less than the amount requested. A request for this amount would be made at the special session of the legislature in 1972.

In June, Mr. Pollard reported that NKC would spend all money allocated for the current biennium by the Department of Health, and could spend $56,000 more than allocated. About $25,000 would be recovered from unspent Spokane funds. Division of Vocational Rehabilitation funds were also spent completely and $37,000 more could have been spent had it been available.

FUND DRIVE AND NORTHWEST KIDNEY FOUNDATION

At the January 22, 1971 meeting of the Executive Committee, Clint Howard announced that Billy Corbett, middle-weight boxer and karate expert, initiated a "brick breaking marathon" as a fundraising effort. Planning to break 2,000 bricks for a dollar a brick, he was unsuccessful in that 2,000 broken bricks resulted in only $278 in donations. He almost broke his hand and broke his heart when he realized how little had been raised. Then, following his emotional appeal on national TV, the Center received over $7,000 in contributions directly attributable to Corbett. This money came from virtually every part of the country and overseas. Corbett's response to this success was, "I want to do it again – you people need the money."

In February, Mr. Howard reported that the fund drive total to date was $165,231.84, including designated funds. Mr. Howard was excused so the Executive Committee could discuss extending his part-time position as he had been hired for the four-month duration of the fund drive, with the provision that at the end of the drive consideration would be given to extending the position to full time. Mr. Pollard recommended Mr. Howard be retained for the following reasons: he had become involved with the county chapters, helping them with their fund drives and establishing new county chapters, and he had been actively involved in legislative activities as they affected Northwest Kidney Center. Promotional activities were necessary year-round and Mr. Howard had supervised all activities of the fund office. He would be the logical person to head the endowment fund activities established at the last Executive Committee meeting and would be involved in the promotional program for the cadaver retrieval program. It was moved, seconded and passed unanimously that Mr. Howard be retained on a full-time bases.

By March, The total of fund drive to date was $200,083.22.

Mr. Schoenfeld suggested a new approach to fundraising for NKC, an endowment fund. The fund would represent a long-range plan for income for the Center and would be established as a separate organization. The committee agreed with the concept, and the initial organization and establishment of the fund would be investigated and started when feasible.

Dr. Blagg noted that on April 7, 1971, the Boeing Employee Good Neighbor Fund board would site visit Northwest Kidney Center, relative to NKC's proposal submitted to them.

Mr. Howard reported on a symposium he attended in San Francisco concerned with the new tax laws related to donations and endowment funds. The trend in fundraising was toward deferred giving, as each year it was harder to raise necessary funds. A deferred giving program takes ten to twelve years to establish, and then the yearly income from the fund should be the equivalent of a yearly fund drive. The fate of the request for funds from the state legislature was uncertain at present, but there was a fair chance the request would be met in full. More than two million Betty Crocker coupons had been received as a result of drives conducted by NKC auxiliaries. General Mills would authorize payment for two artificial kidney machines for 1,600,000 coupons, and a service van for 800,000 coupons. Dr. Philbrick and his committee would conduct a telephone marathon fund drive wrap-up. A fund drive chairman for the 1972 fund drive would be selected soon; suggested names were Kirby Torrance and Walt Daggett.

In September, Mr. Ginsey appointed himself, Elmer Nordstrom, Willis Campbell, Robert Burns and John McCormack as the Board of Trustees of the Northwest Kidney Center Foundation, to serve until the formal election in February.

The 1970-71 fund drive had exceeded the previous year's total by more than $10,000 and another $41,000 was expected during the next few months, exclusive of further public contributions. General Mills had received the 1,600,000 Betty Crocker coupons collected by public solicitation by NKC auxiliaries, and would be sending a check for $8,100 soon. There were an additional 2 million coupons being prepared for shipment for two more artificial kidneys and possibly a technician's van. The county fund drives were doing well; $15,000 was expected from Yakima and $10,000 from Clark County.

Mr. Howard reported there had been no progress in establishing a separate Board of Trustees for the endowment fund. Mr. Derham said this would be a public fund, so there would be no difficulties with the Internal

Revenue Service. The easiest way to start an endowment fund was with bequests, with the second phase being annuities. The Executive Committee recommended Mr. Derham prepare alternative sets of agreements of association and by-laws for presentation to the committee, and get an IRS tax ruling. At the next meeting, he would present a list of preliminary decisions to be made. The entire question may be presented to the board at its semi-annual meeting.

Mr. Howard reported on the 1971 fund drive. The total to date was $47,876.18, which included $13,000 from the Yakima County fund drive. The fund drive was well organized and would be formally opened on November 15. Business solicitation was to be concentrated in a one-month period. Alice Mickelwait had agreed to serve as chairman of the Foundation Solicitation Committee. Solicitation for the foundation would begin after the first of the year following a tax ruling. KING-TV would donate promotional spots this year and the Stewardess Emeritus Association was sponsoring the December 2 performance of Ice Capades as a fundraising benefit for NKC. It would be possible to receive a $10,000 donation from this event if the night was a sellout.

In December, Mr. Howard reported the fund drive total was $105,000 compared to $73,000 the previous year at this time. Mr. Pritchard especially complimented Alice Mickelwait and the Foundation Solicitation Committee for their work in this year's fund drive. The Betty Crocker coupons collection had resulted in another $4,000. The Ice Capades benefit, sponsored by the Stewardess Emeritus Association, did not do as well as was hoped, and probably would net only about $1,500.


## Personnel

At the Executive Committee meeting in February, Mr. Ginsey introduced Councilman Liem Tuai, a newly elected Board of Trustees member. Mr. Ginsey also made various committee appointments: Mr. Burns was appointed chairman of the Finance Committee. Dr. McCormack was appointed a permanent member of the Patient Admissions Committee, which was chaired by Dr. Eschbach. To fill the fifth vacancy on the Patient Admissions Committee, Mr. Ginsey asked each Executive Committee member to serve for two months. Mr. Bangert would attend March and April, Mr. Burns May and June, Mr. Phillips July and August, Mr. Baggott November and December, and Mr. Nordstrom January and February.

At the April Executive Committee meeting Mr. Ginsey introduced the new chief accountant, Thomas H. Kassa. Mr. Kassa formerly was employed by Mullin Corporation as manager, Project Accounts, had a strong accounting and economics background, and would be implementing improvements in the business office. Mr. Kirby Torrance had agreed to serve as 1972 fund drive chairman. Mr. Torrance had worked on the Kidney Center fund drive for the previous two years and had been one of the more effective solicitors.

At the June meeting, Mr. Ginsey introduced Richard A. Derham, attorney with Davis, Wright, Todd, Riese and Jones, the new legal counsel for Northwest Kidney Center.

At the August Executive Committee meeting, Mr. Ginsey announced the resignations of Jess B. Spielholz, MD and Mr. R. D. Ruble from the Board of Trustees. The resignations were accepted. Mr. Pollard recommended that Dr. Robert Leahy, Office of State Medical Consultant, Division of Vocational Rehabilitation, be considered to fill Dr. Spielholz's unexpired term. It was moved and seconded that Dr. Leahy be asked to consider this appointment. No immediate action was taken on filling Mr. Ruble's vacancy. However, Dr. Leahy felt he would be unable to accept the board position because of a possible conflict of interest with his position in the Washington State Department of Social and Health Services. As a result, there were still two vacancies on the Board of Trustees.

## PROPOSED BY-LAW CHANGES

By-law changes were presented to the Executive Committee at its January meeting for approval to present to the Board of Trustees meeting, February 23, 1971, for action:

Amend By Laws, Article II, Section 4, by deleting therefrom the sentence, "No trustee shall serve more than two (2) consecutive three (3) year terms in the same position."

Replace Article II, Section 8, with the following new Section 8: "Whenever any notice is required to be given to any member or trustee of the corporation by the Articles of Incorporation, by Laws, or by the laws of the State of Washington, a waiver thereof in writing, signed by the person or persons entitled to such notice, whether before or after the time set therein, shall be equal to the giving of such notice."

Amend Article II, Section 10, to read: "Such officers shall be elected for a term of one year, except the President, who will serve a term of two years, and if present at the meeting at which they are elected upon taking their seats, may participate thereafter in the meeting."

Add the following as Article II, Section 18: "Any corporate action required or permitted by the Articles of Incorporation or By Laws, or by the State of Washington, to be taken at a meeting of the members or trustees of the Corporation may be taken without a meeting if a consent in writing setting forth the actions so taken shall be signed by all of the members or trustees entitled to vote with respect to the subject of the meeting thereof. Each item shall have the same form and effect as a unanimous vote and may be designated as such."

Add the following Article VIII: "Each trustee and officer now or hereafter serving the Corporation and each person who at the request of or on behalf of the corporation is now serving or hereafter serves as a trustee or officer of any other corporation, whether for profit or not for profit, and his respective heirs, executors, and personal representatives, shall be indemnified by the Corporation against expenses actually and necessarily incurred by him in connection with the defense of any actions, suite, or proceeding in which he is a party by reason of being or having been such a trustee or officer, except in relation to matters as to which he shall be adjudged in such actions, suit, or proceedings to be liable for negligence or misconduct in the performance of duties; but such indemnification shall not be deemed exclusive of any other rights to which such person may be entitled under any By Laws, Agreement, vote of the members or otherwise." It was moved, seconded, and passed unanimously to present the proposed By Law changes to the Board of Trustees at the annual meeting where they were approved.

Mr. Pollard presented for approval the proposed By-Laws and Articles of Incorporation for the Northwest Kidney Center Foundation, establishment of which was approved by the Executive Committee on January 22, 1971. The Executive Committee agreed with the concepts and presentation of the By-Laws and Articles of Incorporation and recommended that they be presented to the Board of Trustees of the Center for approval at its meeting of September 15, 1971.

## OTHER ISSUES

In October, Dr. Blagg reported that the American Society for Artificial Internal Organs (ASAIO), the national organization covering most developments related to dialysis, would meet in Seattle in April 1972. This would be the first time this organization has meet west of Chicago. It was expected there would be great interest among attendees at this convention in seeing the institutions where long-term maintenance dialysis began--the University Hospital, the Coach House and Northwest Kidney Center; however, the logistics in transporting the expected attendees (1,500 anticipated) were formidable and so he proposed that an exhibit displaying the essential features of the Seattle developments be developed for the Olympic Hotel. This would have the added advantage of freeing the staff of the Seattle institutions to attend the meetings. The cost of these exhibits might be offset by donations from equipment manufacturers and the Olympic Hotel might donate space.

## THE 1971 ANNUAL MEETING OF THE ASAIO

The 17th Annual Meeting of the American Society for Artificial Internal Organs was held April 19 and 20 in Chicago. There were three papers presented from the University of Washington.

Drs. Babb, Popovich, Christopher and Scribner presented a paper on the genesis of the square meter-hour hypothesis. This was the culmination of several years of speculation at the University of Washington that so-called "middle molecules" play an important role in the toxicity of uremia. Middle molecules are of such a size that they are slowly dialyzable when compared to urea. This very low dialyzability is due almost entirely to a very high membrane diffusion resistance, since diffusion resistance through blood and dialysate films are not proportionately increased as molecular size increase. Two clinical observations favored this speculation about middle molecules. First, comparison of the results of hemodialysis and peritoneal dialysis suggest that since patients on peritoneal dialysis remain well and free of uremic neuropathy despite significantly higher average urea and creatinine levels, the peritoneum must be passing some toxic molecules better than cellophane does. The most logical explanation for this difference is that there are toxic middle molecules that more readily pass through the peritoneal membrane than through cellophane. The second line of reasoning is based on the observation that prevention of peripheral neuropathy is dependent upon an adequate number of hours of dialysis per week rather than maintaining certain predialysis levels of serum urea and creatinine. When neuropathy occurs in a patient on dialysis it can be arrested and reversed by increasing the length of time for each dialysis.

The plasma concentration of small molecules like urea falls rapidly during hemodialysis and the removal rate at the end of dialysis is very slow. Therefore extending the length of dialysis causes little net increase in total removal of such molecules. In contrast, net removal rate of middle molecules is so slow that the diffusion gradient remains high throughout dialysis and net weekly removal is proportional to the number of hours per week on dialysis. Therefore, since increasing the length of each dialysis has been repeatedly shown to arrest neuropathy, it is reasonable to speculate that middle molecules may be the cause.

Efforts to identify accumulation of middle molecules in dialysis patients had been unsuccessful and so the approach to the problem was made indirectly by carrying out hemodialysis at lower urea clearances to allow an increase in predialysis urea and creatinine levels approaching chronic pre-peritoneal dialysis levels. This was achieved using standard Kiil dialyzers by reducing the dialysate flow rate from 500 to 100 ml per minute. This would give a predialysis urea level about 20% to 25% higher than normal. Engineering analysis showed that when the dialysate flow rate was reduced over the proposed change range without channeling in the dialyzer the removal rates in middle molecules would essentially be unaffected. Complicated and detailed mathematical analysis was performed and clinical strategies were proposed. If these provided data supporting the square meter-hour hypothesis this would support the importance of middle molecules and a comprehensive program to try and identify them would be indicated. The trend occurring at that time toward design and optimization of dialyzers with respect to using high efficiency, low surface area hemodialyzers utilizing current membranes might actually cause the patient to develop neuropathy. The membrane permeability to middle molecules becomes the limiting factor to further improvements in hemodialysis performance. Membrane research should be directed toward increasing permeability to middle molecules. Improved membranes coupled with larger surface area might make feasible hemodialysis schedules of an hour a day six or seven days a week with dialyzers properly designed to avoid channeling despite low blood flow and/or low dialysate flow.

The next paper by Drs. Christopher, Cambi, Harker, Hurst, Popovich, Babb and Scribner was a clinical study of hemodialysis with lowered dialysate flow from 500 to 100 ml per minute for three months in four patients. Patient well-being was unchanged or improved despite a higher blood level of urea, there was no deterioration in nerve conduction or in some cases slight improvement, and platelet function was also improved. These preliminary results appeared to support the engineering hypothesis.

Doctors Quadracci, Cambi, Christopher, Harker and Striker studied serum abnormalities in uremic dialysis patients looking for evidence of depletion of vital substances with hemodialysis using a cell culture assay system. The preliminary results suggested a need for further studies.

## THE CLINICAL DIALYSIS AND TRANSPLANT FORUM

Because of the increasing developments in both dialysis and kidney transplantation, the American Society for Artificial Internal Organs and Dr. George Schreiner decided to start a new annual program, the Clinical Dialysis and Transplant Forum, as an annual event. In this regard they were assisted by the National Kidney Foundation and the American Society of Nephrology. The first meeting was held on November 21, 1971 at the Shoreham Hotel in Washington, D.C.

Twenty-five papers were presented at this initial meeting, four of which were from Seattle. Drs. Tremann, Chrzanowski, Tenckhoff, Moe, Quadracci, Rosenzweig, Striker and Marchioro discussed the effect of dialysis on kidney transplantation. Since the University of Washington program opened in January 1968, 66 patients had been transplanted: 54 were related donor transplants and 12 were cadaveric transplants. Eleven patients were never dialyzed prior to surgery, 27 were dialyzed for less than a year and 28 for more than a year. Eight cases were treated by peritoneal dialysis. Only seven of 50 patients tested had preformed lymphocytotoxic antibodies and six of these had been dialyzed more than one year. Patient survival in patients followed from 3 to 45 months was 94% and graft survival was 92% in those receiving related donor kidneys and 73% in the 12 recipients of cadaveric kidneys. Eighty-five of the surviving recipients had good-to-excellent kidney function. The length of time on dialysis had no adverse effect on the outcome of transplantation with respect to mortality, kidney loss or clinical grade.

Drs. Milutinovic, Halar, Harker, Babb and Scribner reported further experience with hemodialysis using a dialysate flow rate of 100 ml/min. Now a total of 10 patients had been treated by Kiil dialysis using the low dialysate flow rate for a total of 30 month. The resulting rise in predialysis levels of urea-like molecules and the absence of deterioration in nerve conduction velocity supported the hypothesis that middle molecules were responsible for uremic neuropathy. All patients showed improved platelet function and bleeding time showing that a low dialysate flow dialysis corrected a deficiency syndrome present with standard Kiil dialysis using a dialysate flow rate of 500 ml/min.

Drs. Rosenzweig and Babb, Mr. Vizzo and Drs. Scribner and Ginn compared the results of dialysis using a 1 m² Dow hollow fiber kidney for 6 to 8 hours three times a week with the results using three of the hollow fiber kidneys in a series for a third of the weekly hours. This resulted in clearance of middle molecules remaining constant because the square meter-hours/week of dialysis remained unchanged. However, removal of small molecules decreased and their predialysis levels rose. Preliminary results appeared to support the square meter hour hypothesis.

Drs. Blagg, Eschbach, Sawyer and Casaretto reported on a series of 12 patients with diabetic kidney failure treated at Northwest Kidney Center and the University of Washington. Ten patients were trained and treated by home hemodialysis and two were treated by home peritoneal dialysis. No particular problems were found with either form of treatment. The study accumulated 181 patient months of experience in ten male and two female patients with ages ranging from 33 to 58 years and an average duration of diabetes of 24 years.

Duration of dialysis ranged from 4 to 28 months and 8 of the 12 patients died 4 to 28 months after starting treatment for an overall mortality of 67%. Cumulative patient survival was poor in comparison with that for 216 non-diabetic patients treated at the same time. Seven of the eight deaths resulted from complications related to vascular disease or cardiac failure: four patients died from myocardial infarction; two from cardiac failure associated with hypertension and arterial disease; and one patient died from a cerebral hemorrhage. One patient died from pneumonia. Control of diabetes was relatively easy but nevertheless episodes of hyperglycemia and hypoglycemia were not infrequent in patients who were less than meticulous in the care of their diabetes. The patients appeared to have the metabolic defects of chronic uremia superimposed upon those of diabetes mellitus and consequently appeared to undergo vascular degeneration extremely rapidly. Peripheral neuropathy was found in all patients at the start of dialysis treatment but improved in some, presumably because of an effect on uremic peripheral neuropathy. However, three of the patients developed severe neuropathy with autonomic manifestation. Infection was common and seven of the ten patients on hemodialysis had episodes of cannula infection. Visual deterioration was also a serious problem. Rehabilitation, as judged by return to previous occupation or household duties, was considered good in 42% of patients and partial in 25% as compared with 73% and 24% respectively in non-diabetic patients on home hemodialysis. In those patients who deteriorated, both medically and from the point of view of rehabilitation, the most distressing features were the occurrence of progressively increased dialysis disability and physical and mental deterioration.

From the limited experience of this study there was little to encourage acceptance of diabetic patients routinely into a dialysis program. Nevertheless several patients did very well, at least for a period of time. This might have related to extremely careful control of the diabetes, uremia and hypertension – the patients who did best included two physicians and a college professor, all of whom cared for their diabetes meticulously.

The alternative treatment for diabetics with end-stage kidney disease would be kidney transplantation, although, in general, surgeons so far have been reluctant transplant diabetic patients because of other organ involvement and the necessity for use of steroids for immunosuppression. Nevertheless, a recent report on 20 diabetic patients transplanted reported that of 11 patients who received living related donor transplants nine were alive and well after 18 months. Of the nine who received cadaveric transplants only two remained alive and well after six months.

The experience suggested that extreme caution be taken in selection of diabetic patients for maintenance dialysis. The suggested minimum criteria would be minimal clinical involvement of other organ systems, good vision unless the family situation is exceptional, very stable family support, and both family and patient fully conversant with the fact that the patient's life may be prolonged for only a relatively short period of time and ultimately treatment might entail considerable suffering.

Since the first days of dialysis, a major ethical dilemma had been how to stop treatment once it had been started. In some of the diabetic patients in this series it would have been kinder to patient and family to withhold further treatment at an early stage in the course of the patient's deterioration. Consequently, if diabetic patients are accepted for dialysis, the family and patient must be aware of this problem, and the physician must be prepared to face and handle this situation should it develop.

Thus, at this time it would appear the most suitable form of treatment for the diabetic patient with terminal kidney disease who does not have other widespread complications would be a related donor kidney transplant. In the event this was not available, long-term hemodialysis might be attempted in a selected small number of patients, provided the multiple hazards of this treatment are understood by patient, family and physician.

This report was the largest series of diabetic patients reported to that time. A report published the previous year on regular dialysis treatment in Europe mentioned ten diabetic patients treated by maintenance dialysis with equally discouraging results. Four of the ten died within a year and at the time of the report only two patients had survived longer than 15 months. Rehabilitation was described as poor.

## THE 4TH ANNUAL CONTRACTORS CONFERENCE

This meeting was held in Washington DC, January 20-22, 1971. The meeting started with an overview of developments in the field of dialysis over the previous four years by Dr. Benjamin Burton from the NIH. This was followed by reports on the 66 ongoing contracts, six of which were from the University of Washington. There were 154 attendees, nine from the University of Washington, and 17 staff members from the NIH.

The section on hardware and mass transfer included reports from Dr. Tenckhoff on development of a home peritoneal dialysis system and a report from Drs. Babb, Scribner, Christopher and Popovich on fluid mechanics and mass transfer optimization studies on hemodialysis. The session on cannulas, membranes and nonthrombogenic surfaces included a report on cannula research at the University of Washington from Drs. Scribner, Thomas and Slichter and Mr. Cole. The session on clinical and metabolic studies included a report from Drs. Eschbach and Adamson on their studies of the anemia of kidney failure, a report from Dr. Tenckhoff on his studies of uremic neuropathy and one from Drs. Rich, Sherrard and Baylink on their studies of bone disease in uremia.

Doctors Krueger and Bryan reported on the National Dialysis Registry which now contained demographic data on approximately 4,600 patients of which about 3,500 were alive and being dialyzed in some 250 center and home programs throughout the country. The national patient load was 16.6 cases per million population. The average center size was 14 patients and there were many small centers with less than 10 patients, a lesser number of middle-size centers and a few large centers. Male patients outnumbered female patients by almost 2 to 1 but the age distribution was about the same, being 40.4 years for men and 39.2 years for women. Home dialysis accounted for 41.25% of all patients, almost all on hemodialysis.

The relative growth of home dialysis patients to in-center patients was significant. The annual growth rate in in-center patients over the previous year had been approximately 39% whereas the growth in home patients had been 90%, and 640 patients had been put on home dialysis compared with 550 who began in in-center dialysis programs.

CHAPTER 32

# The Year of HR-1 1972

---

THE YEAR 1972 WAS THE one that saw the most important financial development affecting treatment of kidney failure by dialysis and kidney transplantation when the Congress passed legislation making almost all such patients of all ages eligible for treatment under the Medicare program. The number of NKC patients continued to increase, more patients were receiving kidney transplants and the Center developed a regional organ procurement program.

## THE NINTH ANNUAL MEETING OF THE BOARD OF TRUSTEES

Since January 1972 was the tenth anniversary of the first dialysis at the Center, it had been suggested this be commemorated at the time of the annual meeting. The business meeting would be first, followed by refreshments and possibly a program on the history of the Center. Attendance of 300 was anticipated. This would have good fund raising and publicity potential, national publicity was planned, and there was a possibility that Life Magazine would write another story. Dr. Haviland had suggested a cost ceiling beyond which Executive Committee approval would be necessary and in January it was moved, seconded, and passed unanimously that the forthcoming annual Board of Trustees meeting be combined with the Tenth Anniversary, with expenses not to exceed $600.

The Annual Meeting of Northwest Kidney Center's Board of Trustees was called to order by the president, Denver Ginsey, on February 23, 1972. There were 75 attendees.

It was moved, seconded and approved unanimously that the following amendments to the Northwest Kidney Center By-Laws be adopted:

Article II, Section 2 was amended to read as follows: (a) The Board of Trustees shall consist of 45 trustees who shall be elected by a majority vote of the trustees in office whose terms have not expired; (b) The members of the Board of Trustees shall be divided into classes as follows: (i) Thirty-nine trustees shall be elected to serve for terms running for a period of three years from the date of the annual meeting for which said trustee was elected, unless said trustee was elected to fill an unexpired term, at which time such trustees term shall expire at the termination of said unexpired term. The 39 trustees comprising this class shall be divided into three groups such that 13 terms shall expire at each annual election. (ii) Six trustees shall be elected to serve for a period of one year from the date of the annual meeting at which said trustee was elected.

Article III was amended to read as follows: Fiscal Year. The fiscal year of the corporation shall be set by resolution of the Board of Trustees or its Executive Committee.

Dr. Haviland gave the nominating Committee report. It was moved and seconded that the following individuals be elected to three-year terms as members of the Board of Trustees, terms to expire in 1975: Robert Beaupre, Robert Burns, Denver Ginsey, John McCormack, MD, Alice Mickelwait, James Phillips, Rabbi Earl Starr, Joseph Eschbach, MD, Harry Machenheimer, Thomas Seifert, and Loretta Chin. Mr. Ginsey called for nominations from the floor; there were none. The motion passed unanimously. It was moved and seconded that the following individuals be elected as members of the Board of Trustees to fill unexpired terms, to expire in 1974: Belding Scribner, MD and Jerry Pendras, M D. Mr. Ginsey called for nominations from the floor; there were none. The motion passed unanimously. It was moved and seconded that the following individuals be elected to one-year terms as members of the Board of Trustees, terms to expire in 1973: The Reverend Webster Barnett, William McKee MD,

Charles Savage, Collings Miller, and Joan Russell. Mr. Ginsey called for nominations from the floor: there were none. The motion passed unanimously. It was moved and seconded that he following be elected as officers of the Board of Trustees: vice president, Richard Philbrick; secretary, James Phillips; treasurer, Robert Burns. Mr. Ginsey called for nominations from the floor; there were none. The motion passed unanimously. It was moved and seconded that the following be elected to the Executive Committee, terms to expire in 1975: Robert Burns, James Phillips, and Dr. Richard Philbrick. Mr. Ginsey called for nominations from the floor; there were none. The motion passed unanimously.

Mr. Ginsey gave the President's Report. The attendees had all received a copy of the Center's annual report covering all the activities for the past year that was prepared by Dr. Chris Blagg, medical director; Terry Pollard, administrator; Clint Howard, director of fund raising, and himself as president. The report summarized where the Center was ten years after the commencement of its activities. This being the tenth anniversary also was an excellent time to prognosticate and share some of the thoughts and hopes for the next ten years.

NORTHWEST KIDNEY CENTER AT TEN YEARS

The Center was not at all satisfied or content with the state of the art of dialysis as it existed now. It was hoped that with increased efforts on the part of the Board and the entire staff in conjunction with Dr. Scribner and his associates at the University of Washington Medical School that in ten years' time the current treatment methods would resemble flying to New York in a DC-3 versus the 747 – and this was within the realm of possibility.

The overall treatment of patients had changed with development of an active cadaveric kidney retrieval program during the last year. Initial funding for this was provided by the Regional Medical Program, and the Center had become the agency for coordinating this activity. As a result all patients could be offered either transplantation or dialysis, whichever was considered medically most appropriate for the individual patient.

As for dialysis, there continued to be new and exciting developments in equipment, which would have their effects in the future. The hollow fiber artificial kidney had been extensively tested at the University of Washington, was now about to be assessed at the Center and would probably come into widespread use during the coming year. New dialysate fluid supply systems were also under development and within the next few years these and successors to the hollow fiber artificial kidney might reduce dialysis to a push-button affair, requiring minimum patient effort and minimum time. Perhaps dialysis might become a one-hour-a-day process.

One year earlier it took an average of six weeks to train a patient for home hemodialysis. Thanks to a grant from the Boeing Employees Good Neighbor Fund, this had been reduced to approximately three weeks. With development of better equipment it could be possible to envisage the time when patients could be trained in as little as a week or so. Then, as the state the art advanced, it might be possible to visualize a patient coming home from work, sitting down in his easy chair, turning on his dialyzing unit while he leisurely sipped a martini and read his evening newspaper, waiting for dinner to be served an hour later, at which time his treatment was completed. There would be no need to spend additional time cleaning the equipment as this would be handled automatically. Considerable time and research also was being devoted to better access to the blood stream and he was confident these efforts would be successful.

Aside from the hemodialysis treatment, substantial strides were being made and knowledge gained regarding both related donor and cadaveric donor kidney transplants. For those patients who do not like martini sipping, newspaper reading and treatment every evening, a transplant would offer a very acceptable alternative and he believed the cost of treatment to the patient could be reduced.

The cost and quality of care offered to patients of Northwest Kidney Center must be continued. In the coming years the Center, in concert with other interested parties, would be constantly reviewing how best the public could be served; that is, with one major center or a number of major centers with smaller satellite centers. He hoped that with advanced planning it would be possible to assure residents of the area who might need the Center's services that the care they would receive would be the best in the world and, because of advance planning, at the lowest possible financial outlay. But the Center presently walked a financial tightrope with no reserve and what he called the 61-22-17 approach in financing: 61% of the Center's money came from patients' own resources, primarily insurance; 22% was derived from state and federal assistance; and 17% came from public contributions. To maintain these percentages would require increasing the dollar amount in each category by 15% annually.

The Center now had ten years of statistics which were probably the best in the world and the Center knows what it can do, what it wants to do, and how to do it. Because of this, the next ten years would be the most dramatic and exciting in the history of Northwest Kidney Center.

In the past, the Center had had outstanding individuals but he believed there had never been a more outstanding group of individuals and a smoother functioning team than in the persons of Drs. Chris Blagg and Tom Sawyer, Terry Pollard, Clint Howard and Marcia Clark. The esprit de corps of the entire Center was excellent.

He acknowledged the outstanding and exceptional efforts of all who had served on the Admissions Committee which, at a minimum, had met twice a month from 7:30 in the morning for at least two hours each session as well as having a number of hours of reading material that had to be digested before each meeting. He also pointed out for special recognition the efforts of the Finance Committee and the chairman, Bob Burns, in particular. Due to the growth and the additional services rendered, Bob had done a unique job in assisting staff in establishing accurate and efficient accounting and financial systems.

CERTIFICATES OF APPRECIATION AND FUNDRAISING

Mr. Ginsey then turned the meeting over to Mr. Phillips for presentation of certificates of appreciation to volunteer groups who had assisted Northwest Kidney Center during the past year. Mr. Phillips presented certificates to an outstanding group of individuals who had served on the Board of Trustees and whose terms were up this year. The Center had grown tremendously under their guidance and gratitude to each and every one was acknowledged. Walter E. Schoenfeld, member, Board of Trustees 1966–1972; Jess B. Spielholz M.D., member, Board of Trustees 1964–1971; David Simpson MD, member, Board of Trustees 1966–1972; E. D. (Del) Ruble, member, Board of Trustees 1970–1971; Charles M. Anderson, member, Board of Trustees 1969–1972; J. Nicholas Bez Jr., member, Board of Trustees 1970–1972; Frankie Frydenlund, member, Board of Trustees 1970–1972; Dale Smith, Snohomish County Chapter, Northwest Kidney Fund, 1971; Dave Kenny, Clark County Chapter, Northwest Kidney Fund, 1971; and Walt Hubbard, Yakima County Chapter Northwest Kidney Fund, 1971.

The Center was still working on its 1971-72 fund drive, but was running 35% ahead of the previous year and well on its way to meeting its goal of $270,000. Credit for this belonged to many volunteer solicitors who had been spearheaded by Kirby Torrance, Jr. – general fund drive chairman, Joel Pritchard – major gifts chairman, and Alice Mickelwait – foundation gifts chairman, who had produced a 20% increase over the previous year. They were all presented certificates of appreciation.

The Kidney Center was extremely fortunate in receiving support from many fine organizations that dedicated their time and efforts toward raising money for the Center. These included the Stewardess Emeritus Association, Somerset Auxiliary, Queen City Auxiliary, East Side Auxiliary, J. Garth Mooney Auxiliary, Brent Collette Auxiliary, Green Acres Auxiliary and Beta Sigma Phi. They had sponsored ice shows, fashion shows, dances, published telephone directories and cook books, sponsored bazaars and spaghetti dinners. Representatives of each organization were presented with certificates of appreciation for their help during the past year. Mrs. Kay Mahaffey, wife of energetic patient Virgil Mahaffey, was presented a certificate of appreciation for donating her time and artistic talents in decorating the Center's patient area. Boeing Employees Good Neighbor Fund helped found the Center and had contributed every year since 1965 for a total of $147,960. Mr. Clint Randolph, president of the fund, accepted the certificate of appreciation on behalf of the fund. Anne Jerome, Washington State Fraternal Order of Eagles and Auxiliary and member of the Kidney Endowment Fund Board had served as a valuable liaison between the Center and the Eagles. Her enthusiasm and dedication were appreciated and in particular her obtaining portable television sets for patients in the Center. She was presented a certificate of appreciation for her accomplishments. Ron Hansen, chairman of the Seattle Jaycees speakers bureau,-was presented a certificate of appreciation on behalf of the Jaycee Volunteers Committee. This committee had made speeches on behalf of Northwest Kidney Center to hundreds of service organizations. A special award was presented to Mrs. Jacquie McCall, chairman of Clippers Auxiliary, for two years of outstanding service to the Kidney Center. She, with the help of thousands of people throughout the state, had been responsible for clipping and counting four million Betty Crocker coupons and so obtaining $20,000 worth of equipment for the Center, namely four kidney machines and an emergency service van. She lost the use of her family room for a year and broke a pair of scissors in the process. The plaque with the scissors indicated Northwest Kidney Center's gratitude and appreciation.

The meeting was turned back to Mr. Ginsey for question and answers. There were none. Mr. Brent Collette, an NKC patient who had received a transplant, spoke on behalf of the patients in expressing appreciation for the activities and efforts of Northwest Kidney Center.

Finally, there was a display showing the evolution of equipment and a program produced by Clint Howard going over some of the achievements of the past ten years. Mr. John Myers, the longest surviving Kidney Center patient, was present. He received his first dialysis treatment in January 1962 and was treated in the Center for some five years and since then had dialyzed at home.

The meeting adjourned at 8:15 p.m. and was followed by a program in recognition of ten years' operation of Northwest Kidney Center.

## SEMI-ANNUAL MEETING OF THE BOARD

The second semiannual meeting of the Board of Trustees was held on September 13, 1972. Eighteen Board members attended and there were 49 other people in attendance including spouses and staff. The president, Denver Ginsey, opened the meeting, noting that the previous year's semi-annual meeting had been successful and he felt it important as the board expanded to meet more frequently than once a year.

Dr. Blagg reported that so far in 1972, 68 patients had been approved and 54 of these had started treatment. Forty-one patients had been trained for home dialysis and 26 patients had been transplanted. The current patient population was 265, of whom 66 were alive following transplantation, 135 were at home on hemodialysis, 16 on peritoneal dialysis and the rest were dialyzing in the center waiting training or transplantation, or had not yet started treatment. About 100 new patients were expected in 1972, about 10 or 15 more than last year. He believed there were potential candidates in the community that were not being referred and the possible annual patient load was likely 140.

On the medical side, the biggest event of the last year had been development of the new training program with the help of Mr. Gerald Stinson who reorganized it, and at the same time the Boeing Employees Good Neighbor Fund gave money to buy audio-visual television equipment. As a result, average training- time was reduced from about six to three weeks. This had economic advantages for patients by reducing the cost of training but more importantly they got home three weeks earlier and, if from out of town, did not have the expense of staying in Seattle an extra three weeks. As a result of this training program and its reorganization generally, the Center was acquiring a role as an educational institution. NKC had trained physicians, nurses and technicians from local hospitals about dialysis for acute kidney failure and from other parts of the country to learn about dialysis for chronic kidney failure. In April the meeting of the American Society for Artificial Internal Organs was held in Seattle hosted by Dr. Scribner's nephrology group at the University of Washington and the Kidney Center. It was a most successful meeting and several hundred attendees came through the NKC on conducted tours and were favorably impressed by the training program. As a result, parts of the training program were being translated into German and there had been enquiries from several European countries, as well as from many U.S. units.

The other big change during the year was that more NKC patients had received cadaveric kidney transplants from individuals who had just died. Much of this program was funded by the federal Regional Medical Program, and NKC was appointed the coordinating center for this in the Northwest. As a result, the newspapers had reported NKC retrieving kidneys from various hospitals around the city, around the state and as far away as Alaska, putting some of these into Center patients and, when there was no suitable local patient sending the kidneys out to other parts of the United States. This had been very successful and in return NKC was beginning to receive kidneys from elsewhere including a kidney from Salt Lake that was transplanted into an NKC patient. The program was getting much more active although there was still a need for more kidneys to supply the Center's needs.

There were other interesting developments as the number of patients increased. The Center was examining its responsibility for the rest of the region and the time was going to come when there would be a need for affiliated units in the other larger cities in the state. The other exciting area was the result of research at the university. During the previous year the Seattle Times had reported on the square meter-hour hypothesis and the university's research on improving dialysis. Perhaps in the future patients might dialyze for as little as an hour or two, three or four times a week. NKC was cooperating with the university and the patients were being extremely cooperative in volunteering to take part in this research.

Terry Pollard reported that progress made in management of the business affairs of the Center was just as dramatic and just as crucial to the future of NKC as the medical changes. NKC still had problems, especially in the area of accounts payable and accounts receivable. The Center owed the University of Washington more than $300,000 for transplants and related services and patients owed the Center more than $700,000 in accounts receivable. Nearly one-third of the accounts were over six months old. To resolve this, responsibilities were split between the chief accountant to deal with the accounts payable and John Morrow, manager of patient financing who was responsible for collection. This had made evident the need for a good overall plan for business control. The accounting system was archaic, purchasing and inventory control was ineffective, the billing system provided almost no collection follow-up of patient receivables and budgeting was almost nonexistent. With the approval of the Executive Committee, additional personnel were hired including Ernie Dantini, a young man fresh out of the University of Washington with an accounting degree. He had created a new chart of accounts which was conducive to cost accounting measurements, budget comparison and cost center techniques and would provide the Center with more timely, relevant, and reliable information as it was compatible with all the accounting and billing systems.

The fees charged patients again were not adequate to cover the costs of providing services. A rate increase proposal under Phase II Guidelines was developed and the rates were increased for the first time in four years so that revenue from operations matched expenses. A budget was developed that was comparable to the new chart of accounts and allowed comparison with actual results in cost centers on a quarterly basis so that positive and immediate action could be taken to resolve difficulties before they caused problems. Throughout all this drastic revamping, through the efforts of John Morrow, the accounts receivable balance was reduced from the previous year's $700,000 to less than $500,000 as of July 31, 1972, and instead of 30% of accounts payable having a balance over six months old only 13% now were in this category. The liability to the University of Washington for transplants was reduced $ 175,000 in one year. For the first time it was possible to reconstruct financial figures back to 1965 and compare costs with patients treated.

Mr. Ginsey closed the meeting by noting that it had been an exciting year and the Center had made great advances in both patient care and administration.

## Patient Numbers and Activities

Of the original seven patients who had started treatment at the SAKC in 1962, four were still alive and three of them were working fulltime. Of the three who died, the average survival after starting dialysis was 3.5 years. Figures from the United States and Europe were beginning to show that patients survived longest on home hemodialysis and the next best treatment was with a well-matched related donor transplant (although survival figures were less good, quality of life was better) Poorest was with a cadaveric kidney donor transplant. NKC figures indicated that for hemodialysis patients under 50 years of age, 93 to 94 percent of patients were alive at the end of the first year and more than 50 percent of patients would be alive at the end of ten years. The monthly census of patients on home hemodialysis had stabilized at 130 to 135 for the year because of deaths, the rate of transplantation of home patients, and transfers out. About one in six patients at home returned for a backup dialysis per month, mostly for medical reasons, with few being for technical or social reasons.

By December the Center was responsible for 274 patients: 23 patients were approved but had not yet started on dialysis; eight patients were dialyzing in center; three patients were being training for home hemodialysis; 138 patients were dialyzing at home on hemodialysis; 21 patients were on peritoneal dialysis at home; and 71 patients were living with a kidney transplant.

In March, a related donor kidney transplant was done at Virginia Mason Hospital, its first transplant, and in April Swedish Hospital performed its first kidney transplant, also from a related donor. Dr. Sawyer was asked whether transplanted patients coming back to dialysis presented any particular problems. He explained there were various medical problems to contend with, for example, they were in bad shape from the immunosuppressive drugs and from the surgery itself, and perhaps from complications following the surgery. They were usually uremic, and in addition, they were in poor psychological condition and depressed because the transplant had failed.

At this same time some new patients from the VA hospital were started on dialysis at the Center as there had been an outbreak of serum hepatitis at the VA hospital and it was undesirable to place new patients there until it was certain that the outbreak was under control.

Also in in March, the results of an evaluation of the Center's new shortened home training program were presented. Though the old program consisted of 18 patient contact days with 18 training dialyses, and the new had only 15 patient contact days and nine training dialyses, patients were learning and performing as well under the new program as the old. An interesting aspect of the evaluation was that, while it had been known for some time that the greatest number of technical visits was required by patients immediately post-training, it would appear that those trained under the new program ceased to need technical support earlier. The frequency of calls after training in both the old or new programs was identical, but under the new program, after the 15th week at home, the frequency curve plateaued, whereas in the old program this did not occur until about the 35th week. There were several potential reasons for this and, although it was unclear which ones were of prime importance, the finding was a good one. It was planned to present these results at the ASAIO meeting in Seattle in April.

Dr. Blagg noted that NKC was developing a large training responsibility and during the past year 320 days of one nurse's time was spent in training medical personnel. As a result a nurse's salary would be paid by the Regional Medical Program and then outside medical personnel would be trained free of charge.

Dr. Scribner and Dr. Blagg were invited to speak at a conference in Sydney, Australia in late November and visited dialysis centers in New Zealand and Australia then and in December.

In December, Dr. Sawyer reported that the Center was not meeting its obligations to patients because with the present staff and the current rate of incoming patients there was not suitable space in the center for home patients requiring backup dialysis and patients were being held in the Center who were medically able to be transferred to home dialysis training. The situation was frustrating to physicians working with the Center and a hardship for staff in addition to the problems it created for patients. There had been instances of patients having to be dialyzed in hospital because there was no space for a dialysis at the Center. The reasons for the present situation were the large increase in patients and a longer stabilization required for some patients because of medical problems. The nursing staff had been increased somewhat and would probably be increased by another two because of the need to increase the rate of output of patients trained for home dialysis. Construction had not begun on the proposed two new home training rooms that were approved by the Executive Committee at its last meeting. Dr. Eschbach said it was to be expected that the longer patients lived on dialysis more complications were to be expected. He did not feel the selection criteria could be criticized and was more concerned about the time that it took to get a patient "through the system." When home patients needed backup dialysis there were problems getting them scheduled and NKC should come to grips with the fact that it was presently working at maximum capacity. A selected few individuals could be taken care of in a limited care facility, something that had been brought up in the past by Dr. Blagg and was being considered. Mr. Pollard said the present problem could be resolved temporarily with two new training rooms, but there was no way of knowing if they would satisfy long-term needs because the effects of HR-1 on the input of new patients were not yet known. The consensus of the committee was that two new training rooms should be constructed immediately to solve the pressing need.

## Patient Admissions

At the January Executive Committee meeting Dr. Blagg reported there had been four meetings of the Patient Admissions Committee (PAC) since early December, 1971, and several telephone polls. Seventeen patients were presented; 15 were approved and two were rejected. One of the rejected applicants had diagnosed paranoid schizophrenia and the other was unemployed, could not speak English, had limited education, and had no helper. Two months later there had been six further Patient Admissions Committee meetings. Twenty-three patients were presented, one of whom was deferred pending further treatment, and two were rejected. One patient who was rejected did not have a helper here in Seattle but did have a sister in Ohio, and the patient's physician was referring this patient to the VA in Dayton, Ohio. The other patient was rejected due to her age, difficulty in trainability, little hope for rehabilitation and no finances or insurance.

In March, Dr. Blagg gave a brief history of the Patient Admissions Committee's structure since its beginning and then proposed the following change in admission policy: All routine referrals of patients to NKC would be approved by Dr. Blagg and any patients who might be rejected would be presented to the PAC, which met once a month. At the monthly PAC meeting a report also would be given on the financial position regarding funding patients. Mr. Ginsey suggested that a rotating Board member should continue to attend the PAC's monthly meeting and Dr. Blagg suggested that the physician representative from the Medical Advisory Committee also attend. Mr. Burns felt there would be no problem with the fully funded patient but would be with those that could represent a lien on future assets of the NKC. He suggested a guideline be established to resolve decisions as to financial obligations. Referring problem cases to the monthly meeting would reduce the possibility of embarrassment and liability to the Center for those patients who were rejected. It was recommended to try this form of admissions for a six months period. A motion was made: The Patient Admissions Committee meetings were to be held monthly, with prior patient acceptance to be at the discretion of Dr. Blagg, and that the power of rejection be given to the Patient Admissions Committee only. This new mode of admission was to have a trial period of six months. The motion was seconded and approved unanimously.

A letter of resignation had been received from Dr. Eschbach as chairman of the Patient Admissions Committee and he suggested Dr. Tenckhoff should take his place as representative of the Medical Advisory Committee on the Patient Admissions Committee and Dr. Blagg suggested this be tried for six months and that this post might then rotate to other physicians. Dr. Blagg proposed that Dr. McCormack assume the next rotation as chairman of the Patient Admissions Committee in place of Dr. Eschbach.

At the end of April, Dr. Blagg gave the PAC report. At the previous meeting it was agreed that he would be empowered to accept routine patients, would report to the PAC monthly and also present to them any problem cases. During the last month there was one regular meeting at which seven applicants were considered; six were approved and one was rejected. Dr. Blagg had accepted five patients, and in addition four current NKC patients were approved for transplantation. Dr. Eschbach said that the Medical Advisory Committee had agreed to the organizational change because many of the patient applications were straightforward and did not need extensive committee discussion and approval. In order to take care of the occasional problem patient, a once-a- month meeting would be sufficient. All the nephrologists in the community had been queried as to whether they would be willing to serve on this committee. Mr. Ginsey appointed Dr. McCormack as Chairman for one year.

Dr. Blagg reported there would be more than 100 new patients in the year if applications continued at the current rate. This could raise a problem with regard to space for home hemodialysis training classes and might mean the need to open a fifth training room. The question was raised as to whether this would require additional personnel and Dr. Blagg responded "yes" but with more patients coming in there would also be more revenue.

During June, the PAC had met and approved two patients and rejected one. The rejected patient was a transient who was an alcoholic, had cancer of the throat, a history of heart disease, and no relatives. In addition to the two patients approved at the meeting, Dr. Blagg approved six patients during the month; all had no particular medical, social, or financial problems and therefore were not referred to the committee. Three NKC patients were approved for transplantation.

The Patient Admissions Committee met once in July and considered an applicant who was subsequently rejected because of multiple medical problems, no helper, and marginal social problems. Dr. Blagg approved four other patients during the month.

In September, Dr. Blagg reported that since the last meeting he had approved 11 patients and one was approved unanimously by the PAC. In

March, the Executive Committee had agreed upon a six-month trial period during which Dr. Blagg would approve routine applications and the PAC would be convened only for problem applications, it was also agreed Dr. McCormack would serve as PAC chairman during this time. This approach appeared to have been very successful.

Dr. Sawyer also gave the Patient Admissions Committee report in December. Twenty referrals were received and 14 of these were approved by Dr. Blagg or Dr. Sawyer in Dr. Blagg's absence. Six were presented to the Patient Admissions Committee and of these, one was rejected and five approved. Thirteen of the 19 patients approved started treatment soon after their acceptance. Four of the patients presented were over 60 years old, four were between 40 and 60, and the rest were under 40 years of age.

## FEDERAL LEGISLATION

Dr. Sawyer had attended a National Kidney Foundation meeting in New Orleans where a presentation was made by a representative of the Kidney Advisory Group of the Social Security Administration to discuss the possible effects of HR-1 and the amendments to the Social Security Act. The Social Security Amendment provided Medicare coverage for almost all patients requiring dialysis and transplantation. A precedent had been established in that, for the first time, a specific disease had been singled out for government subsidization. Medicare would provide benefits at the beginning of the third month after a person started on dialysis. It was currently unknown how equipment would be covered and many provisions of the bill were currently not known. Mr. Phil Jos of the Social Security Administration had been directed by Senator Magnuson to visit Northwest Kidney Center so that NKC would have an opportunity to provide input into the formation of regulations and standards for kidney centers to be covered by the Social Security Amendment.

## STATE FUNDING

In 1971, the request for funds for NKC and the Spokane dialysis unit from the Division of Vocational Rehabilitation was appropriated by the legislature almost as requested but Department of Health funds were cut by about 50%. The Centers were told to come back to the legislature in January with cost figures for the first six months of the 1971-73 biennium appropriation. They did so and requested a total of $375,512 supplemental funds for the biennium: $208,938 in Department of Health funds and $166,574 in Division of Vocational Rehabilitation funds. This request represented $55,979 supplemental funds from the Department of Health for the present fiscal year, and $152,959 from the Department of Health, and $166,574 from the Division of Vocational Rehabilitation for the 1972-73 fiscal year. In March it was reported that the legislature had approved an additional $209,000 from the Department of Health for this biennium and as a result a total of $303,000 would be available between Seattle and Spokane for the 1972-73 fiscal year.

Northwest Kidney Center did not intend to take a position endorsing any proposed national health care plan.

In July the request made to the state for support of the two kidney centers for the next (1973-75) biennium was $1,954,000; in the 1971-73 biennium $1,508,000 was received (including both Seattle and Spokane DVR and DHS funds). The new request was for $1,080,000 in state funds, with $954,000 in federal matching funds, an increase of 51% over the last biennium. The state had expressed concern there might be a lessening of fund drive efforts because of state funding and that state involvement was increasing as a greater proportion of total funding support than the fund drive was. The request was sent to the state budget office, the Division of Social and Health Services, the Legislative Budget Committee and the governor. For the current year Spokane and NKC would try to get included in the governor's budget rather than try to get allocations from a supplemental budget. It was necessary to get DVR and DHS endorsement of the proposal.

In December Mr. Pollard reported that the Center faced the serious problem of running out of DVR funds within the next month or two. Because of the influx of new patients, there was only $50,000 of DVR funds left unencumbered out of $300,000 appropriated for Seattle for the fiscal year 1972-1973. Spokane was allocated $70,000 for the same time period. The main reason for the shortage of funds was the fact that the statewide kidney program did not receive full federal matching of state funds appropriated by the legislature. Full federal matching would have produced $495,000 this fiscal year, yet only $370,000 was available. Enquiries were being made as to the cause of this cutback but if these efforts did not prove fruitful, the alternatives left were to ask the legislature for a supplemental appropriation or to seek funds from the governor's Emergency Fund. It might also be possible to get Public Assistance to change its exclusion on kidney disease and thereby fund eligible patients through this program. Mr. Pollard, Dr. Sawyer and Mr. Howard intended to testify before a Legislative Budget Committee meeting in Olympia immediately after the Executive Committee meeting.

A second problem had arisen concerning the budget request for the 1973-75 biennium. Seattle and Spokane had submitted two combined requests to be included in the governor's budget for the next biennium. The first was submitted prior to the Congress signing HR-1 in November 1972, and totaled approximately $1,900,000 in DVR and health department funds. NKC was first informed that its request for health funds would not be included in the health department's budget and that NKC should seek funds through the legislative process. DVR funds for kidney disease were included, but at a lesser amount than requested. When HR-1 was signed by President Nixon on October 30, it was realized that it would probably have a profound effect on patient funding and a similar effect on the need for state assistance. However, estimating the extent of the effects of HR-1 involved much guesswork since the final form of HR-1 regulations was not totally known. Because of the uncertainties of HR-1, NKC felt the best approach would be to leave the original request to the state unchanged and if it turned out that HR-1 actually produced the funds anticipated, NKC would simply not use all the state funds available. However, NKC was told by the state to reduce the request showing the effect of HR-1, or it would be reduced by the two state agencies. NKC subsequently submitted a revised request for $1,100,000, based on what was known about HR-1. At the end of the year it was not known whether the revised request was included in the governor's budget.

## FINANCES

An analysis of individual charges in January showed a significant difference in the cost of peritoneal dialysis and hemodialysis and so proposed fee adjustments reflected this difference. If the Center did not increase fees, predicted difference in operating cost ($709,459) and revenue from current fees ($598,189) would be $111,270. The proposed fee averaged an 18.6% increase. Home training fees would go up 42%, mostly because of decreased time needed to train patients (the total cost to the patient for home training with the fee increase was still less with the shorter program than with the current fees and the previous six-week training program). Fees for doctors office calls would remain the same, but charges for other medical services would increase: for example technicians' hourly charge for home service calls would increase from $6 an hour to $9 an hour and supplies, which were originally being marked up 10%, were proposed to be marked up 12.5%. The Executive Committee agreed that these fee increases be submitted to the Price Control Board for approval.

The Compensation Review Committee had reviewed individual salaries and salary scales and approved them.

The Center now would claim the balance owing on a deceased patient's account against the estate. Several problems were the statute of limitations and lack of written agreements during the time a patient was being treated at the Center. NKC had also filed creditor's claims against two other estates where most of the estate's funds were tied up in real estate. Another estate problem needing discussion by the Executive Committee was that of an individual who died leaving an estate of $9,500. During the financial investigation prior to his becoming a patient, it was determined that he should pay a certain amount per month and it was agreed the Center would finance the rest. The patient faithfully fulfilled the terms of his agreement. The estate had been left to his grandson who also had kidney disease. The child's mother, the patient's daughter, donated one of her kidneys for his transplant. It was Mr. Derham's suggestion that for compassionate reasons and because it was not agreed that the patient was a full-pay patient, the Center not file a claim against the estate. Discussion followed, and there was general agreement that if the Center definitely decided that a patient was to be subsidized, fully or in part, by the fund drive or other Center funds, the amount agreed to be subsidized should be considered non-recoverable upon the patient's death. It was moved, seconded, and passed unanimously that the suit be dropped against the estate of this patient.

By March, the Center's request for fee increases had been filed with the appropriate agencies and the requested increases would produce an expected $144,000 of revenue annually. This would represent a 15.3% rate increase over the base period. The effective date would be April 1. NKC might be required to appear and produce additional information.

Mr. Burns reviewed the financial statement and explained how NKC was now doing all of the billing of Swedish Hospital and University Hospital for all Center patients and in the last year had replaced the chief accountant and had gone through a number of changes, thereby increasing accounts receivable. Stokes & Company suggested that on a regular basis a subcommittee of the Finance Committee meet and review aged accounts receivable and determine ways to collect overdue accounts. Two meetings had been held and favorable results were being accomplished. Dr. Haviland asked if there had been problems with University Hospital. Mr. Pollard answered that for six to eight months, bills from the hospitals were not in a form to send out for collection, but since then the outstanding amount had been reduced from $300,000 to $136,000. Mr. Burns also reviewed the unaudited financial statement as of December 31, 1971. A decrease in inventories was largely the result of stopping buying of new equipment and using the equipment from inventory. The cash balance of $138,000 was mainly savings accounts.

Terms of the patient agreement signed upon approval by the Patient Admissions Committee were discussed. Mr. Derham would check this agreement to see if there needed to be added a clause about the Center's position regarding estates left after a patient's death. Mr. Derham and Mr. Pollard would prepare a proposed policy statement regarding estate claims and present this for Executive Committee approval at the next meeting so that each individual case would no longer need to be considered by the Executive Committee.

As a result of Washington State's suit against Maynard Hospital for selling the hospital at a profit, the Center had received $25,000. The funds recovered by the state had been divided among other non-profit profit institutions in the state, including Children's Orthopedic Hospital.

Maynard Hospital, named after Seattle's first doctor, was founded in 1933 as a nonprofit organization by several doctors. It was sold to the Stewards Foundation, a nonprofit Chicago-based organization in 1960 and more than $300,000 of the proceeds from the sale was received by the hospitals trustees, three doctors and the estates of two others. However, the Internal Revenue Service said that the hospital's original articles of incorporation directed that any profits should go to charitable causes and no part of the net earnings "shall ever enure to the benefit of stockholders." Consequently, in 1969, the state Superior Court ruled this money should go to non-profit hospitals, particularly Children's Orthopedic Hospital, and to other charities. The Center received $25,000. The court ruled in 1969 but for whatever reason the Center did not get its share until 1972.

The auditors had recommended NKC increase employee financial dishonesty insurance and insurance coverage be in the amount of $300,000 could be purchased with a yearly premium of $494.00. A motion was made to purchase this and seconded and passed unanimously.


Policy on financial aid to patients

Mr. Pollard described two alternative plans for a policy on Center financial aid to patients:

ALTERNATIVE #1:

It is the policy of Northwest Kidney Center to grant financial assistance to patients who the Center determines, in its sole discretion, are unable to pay the full amount of their charges at any given time. Considering that the Center is able to provide this service only because of the generosity of public donors, the Center considers itself under an obligation to recover financial assistance whenever a change in patient circumstances permits recovery from the patient or his estate.

ALTERNATIVE #2:

It is the policy of Northwest Kidney Center to grant financial assistance to patients who the Center determines, in its sole discretion, are unable to pay the full amount of their charges at any given time. Considering that the Center is able to provide this service only because of the generosity of public donors, the Center considers itself under an obligation to terminate or reduce such assistance whenever a change in patient circumstances permits the patient to pay an increased amount or whenever other circumstances might dictate. In addition, the Center may choose to make "advances" to patients who shall be deemed conditional and which the patient or his estate shall be expected to repay. It shall be the policy of the Center to waive any claim for financial assistance denominated as grants (except such as are based on misleading or inaccurate financial information supplied by patients), and to reserve the right to reimbursement for any assistance denominated as advances.

Mr. Derham felt that perhaps a guideline should be worked up to determine the amount of recovery and in what circumstances the right would be exercised. Mr. Ginsey felt that if the Center had agreed to help fund a patient, with the patient making partial payment, that in the event of death, the Center would not deplete a small estate, especially if there was a family surviving the deceased. It was moved and seconded that Alternative I be adopted. The motion passed unanimously.

NKC had been providing supplies to the home patients and this had become a burden. The storeroom, which occupied a good part of the basement of Eklind Hall, was running out of space and so two companies had been asked to bid to provide supplies to home patients. It would cost a little more, but the subcommittee of the Finance Committee would review this possibility.

Two weeks earlier, 37 representatives from insurance companies met at the Center to discuss the costs of organ retrieval. Dr. Blagg spoke about the organ retrieval program, and Maurice Ward demonstrated the perfusion machine to the guests and explained how it worked. An hour and a half of questions and answers followed. Some good ideas came out of this open discussion period. It was found that the representatives were somewhat limited in what they could do regarding payment of the bills in this situation because of their underwriters and because of the way the policies are written. It was suggested that there be discussion with the purchasers of insurance to clarify this problem.

In April, Mr. Pollard reported that the price increase request for Northwest Kidney Center was submitted to the state Advisory Board and approved. It was originally thought this would be a fairly routine procedure that would not take too much time but after the Board had approved the original request, it might take three or four months to be approved by the Internal Revenue Service. The subcommittee of the Finance Committee had suggested that fees be raised so that the Center's total revenue did not increase by 6%. Some price changes would go into effect on May 1. The Center would still file for the original price increase request, but the price increases that would be implemented May 1 were inpatient center dialysis from $98 to $120, inpatient home hemodialysis training dialysis from $154 to $224, room and board for center hemodialysis from $35 to $40, room and board for a semi-private room for training dialysis from $35 to $55, and technician fee hourly charge from $6 to $9. These fee increases would produce $90,000 in annual revenue, a 5.58% increase of 1971 total operating revenue.

Mr. Derham reported on the estate of a patient who did not pay her bill for a number of years before she died. Claims were filed with the estate and were rejected and so NKC filed suit. The estate was encumbered with no cash assets. The balance of an apple orchard contract was $27,000, with $5,000 committed for a beneficiary. They had offered the equity of $22,000 as payment in full of her claim. The apple orchard contract would bring in a minimum of $2,500 or 30% of gross revenue, whichever was greater, until the contract, plus 6% interest, was paid in full. This would pay the claim. It was moved and seconded to accept the offer of the apple orchard and to attempt to get a guarantee from the patient's relative to manage the apple orchard and to see that these funds accrued to the Northwest Kidney Center. The motion passed unanimously. Mr. Derham was complimented for his efforts in working with this estate.

The current year's budget included an item for remodeling to consolidate all office space on one floor and the intent was to move as soon as possible. Twenty-five thousand dollars was the estimated cost for reconstruction on the second floor. An application to the Seattle Foundation for that amount was being prepared. Mr. Campbell suggested, since he did not feel that the Seattle Foundation would grant $25,000, it might be helpful to find out exactly what they would be able to help with by speaking personally with Mr. Ben Bowling of the foundation before the grant was submitted.

In May, Dr. Blagg requested funds be set aside in the next year's budget for research and development. NKC was offered new equipment to test, but did not have the staffing required to assess its clinical applicability. If funds were available for a technician to work with new equipment assessment and for necessary laboratory tests, the Center would be able to continue to provide its patients with the best up-to-date treatment. This was not meant to be pure research such as that performed at the University of Washington, but rather applied research, including assessment of equipment for use by the Center's own patients. It was moved and seconded that an amount not to exceed $20,000 of the 1972-73 budget be used for equipment research and development. The motion passed unanimously.

Mr. Pollard reported on the subcommittee of the Finance Committee that was established to review accounts receivable on a monthly basis as recommended by Stokes and Company. As of December 31, 1971, receivables were \$564,828 for 265 accounts. The total receivables currently were \$541,781, with the number of accounts having increased to 303. The average per account had decreased from \$2,100 at December 21, 1971, to \$1,800 at April 30, 1972. Another significant measure was the decrease in the amount receivable over six months. The total over six months at December 31, 1971 was \$139,164 and the number of accounts having balances over six months was 100; by April 30, 1972, the total over six months had been decreased to \$96,111 and the number of accounts decreased to 83. The average per account over six months had decreased from almost \$1,400 down to about \$1,150. In addition to the increase in patient population during this period, about \$200,000 of University bills had been added to the accounts receivable, demonstrating that the collection efforts had been fruitful. Another significant measure was that in reviewing these accounts monthly, certain accounts were placed at a higher priority than others, resulting in a top ten priority account list, which amounted to the majority of the money that was more than six months delinquent. Seven of these ten accounts had been solved, two of the remaining three were nearly solved, and only one of the original top ten still presented a problem.

INSURANCE PROTECTION AND OTHER EXPENSES

At a previous meeting the Executive Committee had authorized increasing NKC employee's financial dishonesty insurance policy from the previous \$10,000 coverage to \$300,000 coverage. This was implemented and put into effect as of April 1, 1972. In reviewing the total insurance protection portfolio, John Soderberg and Company made the following recommendations for additional coverage: 1) coverage for replacement or recovery of records for accounts receivable lost or damaged due to insured peril. Since receivables had run as high as \$700,000, protection for that amount would cost \$327 per year; 2) there were other valuable papers, such as medical records and personnel files that would be very costly to re-create. A policy in the amount of \$100,000 was recommended to cover the cost to re-create these valuable papers and would cost \$195 per year; 3) one hundred thousand-dollar coverage for the cost of temporarily relocating the Center in the event the building was destroyed. A one-year premium would be $108; and 4) that the umbrella excess liability coverage of $1,000,000 that cost $1,200 a year and covered everything beyond the basic liability coverage of $300,000 be increased to a total of $2,000,000 coverage with an additional annual premium of $450 year. It was recommended that Mr. Pollard communicate with Swedish Hospital to see if the Center could receive insurance benefits as being "attached" to the hospital, although NKC was not a member of the Hospital Association.

NKC now owned the contract to an apple orchard as settlement against the claim against an estate and Mr. Bangert had investigated the quality of land and crops and determined them to be satisfactory. He suggested in his appraisal the possibility of discontinuing the contract rather than carrying it to a five-year receivable. An attractive discount would be 10%. It was recommended Mr. Pollard explore this possibility.

The Center's additional space on the second floor would have to be reduced as Swedish had given the Pacific Northwest Research Center additional space. NKC did not have a lease with Swedish Hospital and Dr. Lobb had commented that he would give NKC a letter of intent, and Mr. Pollard was asked to follow this up.

The Finance Committee met again on June 27, 1972, and Mr. Burns reported that Mr. Tom Kassa, the accountant, had resigned and Mr. Pollard was looking for a replacement. Mr. Dantini, who had been hired two months earlier to help set up a more effective cash-budgeting system, was willing to stay on until the end of August when he would move to Price Waterhouse. He and Mr. Pollard were working to set up a budgeting and forecasting system with cost controls and Mr. Dantini was working closely with Stokes and Company. This system would record costs and compare them quarterly to the projected budget. The projected budget had been approved by the Finance Committee for presentation to the Executive Committee.

Mr. Pollard presented the Expense and Capital Budget for Fiscal Year 72/73, with a Pro Forma Statement of Operations & General Fund Balance. The budget and the chart of accounts were each broken down into six categories: Center, Training, Organ Retrieval, Tissue Typing, General Administration and Fund Office. Using the chart of accounts to match costs to the budget would provide a means for controlling costs in the various cost centers. The total anticipated expense for the fiscal year for the six cost centers was $967,181 and with costs of equipment and supplies for home patients totaling $544,000, the total expense budget was $1,511,181. Projected patient-incurred expense was broken down by areas where expenses were anticipated and whether they related to transplantation or dialysis. The total expense budget was $2,214,541, a ten percent increase over the previous year. Total anticipated revenue and deductions from revenue was $2,246,400, leaving $207,141 to be financed out of the General Fund. Capital budget items were listed by priority and included opening a fifth training room to take care of the projected input of patients over the coming year. It was moved, seconded, and passed unanimously that the budget be approved as presented and that the identifiable 1972-73 capital budget items be approved as presented.

Mr. Burns gave the September Finance Committee report. The report of the unaudited Statement of Financial Position was not yet finalized, due to changes in rules regarding reporting of hospital financial statements. Now all general fund drives must be reported as revenue in the current operations. Stokes and Company were researching the problem as they could not certify the statements as they are now prepared. There had been a slight increase in accounts receivable but the overall position was better due to improved management and control. The increase partly represented increased patient load. University Hospital bills had decreased by $173,000.

Mr. Pollard reported on creditors' claims since the Executive Committee approved action to file claims. Four claims had been filed totaling $45,000; $32,000 was collected. Only about 10 percent of patients who died had estates subject to probate. NKC presently did not have mechanisms to follow through on estate claims, and present policy was not to jeopardize the financial situation of a surviving family by pursuing collections.

Mr. Ginsey reported that the Long-Range Planning Committee met on August 22, and discussed current and future space needs and problems, development of a multiphase long-range plan, and formalizing an agreement with Swedish Hospital. A draft of a letter to the Swedish Hospital Board of Trustees was presented to the Executive Committee and after discussion the Executive Committee felt it might be appropriate to delay sending this letter until after informal discussion had been initiated. In the meantime Dr. Blagg and Mr. Pollard would attend the Swedish Board of Trustees meeting in October. After they had done this Mr. Nordstrom, Dr. Blagg and Mr. Pollard had met with Dr. Lobb to discuss space problems and future concerns. Dr. Lobb had said that he would be willing to sign a letter of intent. Mr. Derham said that a letter of intent would be legally binding for a short period of time, but probably not long term. He felt the letter was sufficient for the present needs of the Center in that it memorialized a moral agreement between the two institutions. If further documentation were required, it would be necessary to have a lease. The question before the Committee was whether the letter of intent was acceptable. It was moved; seconded and passed unanimously that the proposed letter of intent by Dr. Lobb be approved by the Executive Committee.

Mr. Baggott reported there had been two meetings of the Compensation Review Committee and they had agreed on salary increases within the 5.5% limitations of Phase II regulations and new salary ranges.

Mr. Derham asked for Executive Committee approval for starting suit against the insurance company of a deceased patient who had assigned life insurance policies to Northwest Kidney Center. Upon his death, he owed approximately $30,000, $12,000 of which was for services and material provided by Northwest Kidney Center, $11,000 owed to the University of Washington by Northwest Kidney Center for the patient, and $7,000 in university physicians bills. The Center was obligated to pay the University of Washington, whether or not it received payment from the patient's insurance company. The attorney for the patient's wife had offered to pay the $12,000 for NKC services and contended that the life insurance policies were signed to pay debts only for NKC and no others. The policies totaled $24,000. It was moved and seconded that Northwest Kidney Center sue the insurance company and the wife for the full amount. In discussion it was pointed out that the Executive Committee should be aware that bad publicity might be forthcoming from a suit against a widow of a kidney patient. It was also uncertain whether her estate would leave her adequately provided for after a suit. The motion then was amended that only the insurance company be sued, with the option to sue the widow for the balance if undue delays were experienced with the insurance company settlement. The motion was passed unanimously.

## Fund Drive

At the start of 1972 every category in the fund drive was running ahead of the previous year with the exception of public solicitation. It was believed that Neighbors in Need had received at least part of the funds normally sent to NKC. With committed amounts, $248,000 was anticipated, and there was every reason to expect the fund drive would reach the goal of $270,000 by the end of the year.

In the previous year, the Boeing Employees Good Neighbor Fund had funded video equipment in order to start the new home hemodialysis training program. The request for this year was for a sum to purchase more equipment to complete the program and to establish an intercommunication system. Subsequently NKC received $11,300 to complete the equipping of the training area and that should substantially take care of video equipment and an intercommunication system and other necessary equipment purchases. By April the fund drive was on schedule and was anticipated to teach its target of $325,000 by June 30th, with much of the credit going to Kirby Torrance, Fund Drive chairman. Between $40,000 and $50,000 would be given to the Center by the Washington State Eagles and its use would not be restricted to just Eagles patients. Kirby Torrance had agreed to be General Fund Drive chairman again for coming year and Joel Pritchard would be asked to be Major Gifts chairman.

Mr. Evans reported that the Public Relations Committee had met in June and determined that volunteer support should consist of capable people who understood the program. With this in mind, they had added several new members to the committee who were active in public relations and communications fields. The first meeting was devoted to orientation and explanation of the donor program. TV announcements for KOMO were to be produced.

The fund drive through June 29, 1972, essentially the results for fiscal year 1971-1972, had a goal of $325,000 and $328,335 was received - $3,592.53 over the goal and the most donated money ever collected in a NKC fund drive. The goal for 1972 was to be $370,000. The fund office would pursue computerization in compiling data and recording of names. Presently there were more than 4,000 names of people who donated $25 or less who were not solicited because of the effort of recording and re-soliciting them. With computerization, it was intended that one-half person could be cut from the fund office.

By December, $105,000 had been raised in the next fund drive and there had been a 20% response from the mass mailing. The public was not aware of HR-1 and since NKC did not know yet what the impact of HR-1 on funding for the Center would be, the fund raisers were stressing that NKC was raising money today for today's patients because HR-1 would not come into effect until July 1, 1973. People working on the drive were being kept informed of HR-1 developments.

## NORTHWEST KIDNEY FOUNDATION

Mr. Pollard reported that a nominating committee had been appointed to suggest the names of members to serve on the NKC Foundation Committee. The Nominating Committee, consisting of Dr. Haviland, Mr. Burns, and Mr. Pollard had nominated Mr. Schoenfeld, Dr. Philbrick, Mr. Guernsey, Mr. Bangert and Mr. Bayley for one-year terms as members of the Board of Trustees of Northwest Kidney Center Foundation. It was moved, seconded and passed unanimously that these nominations be approved. It would be the duty of these members of the Board to appoint the president, treasurer and secretary. The primary purpose of the foundation was to operate exclusively for the benefit of Northwest Kidney Center and its patients, and distribute its income and/or principal to the Center as needed.

Funds for the foundation would primarily be raised through the following forms of deferred giving:

1. BEQUESTS: The simplest of all forms of deferred giving in which an individual specifies an amount or a percentage in his or her will which should go to the Kidney Center;

2. INSURANCE CONSIGNMENT: A person takes out an insurance policy and names the NKC beneficiary. He also turns the policy over to the Center while he makes the premium payments, which are tax deductible;

3. GIFT ANNUITY: Probably the easiest and most common contracted agreement. The individual makes a donation and the foundation guarantees through all of its assets fixed annuity payments based on standard actuarial rates reflecting the age of the person and the value of the gift. The individual is also entitled to a tax deduction based on age and amount of the contribution;

4. POOLED INCOME FUND: A donor's contribution is pooled with other similar contributions and the donor receives income for life based on six per cent times fair market value. Upon death, the Center receives the remaining value of the donor's share. According to IRS regulations, the foundation cannot operate a pooled income fund; it would have to be operated by the Kidney Center;

5. ANNUITY TRUST: Under this trust, the foundation guarantees a fixed payment for life and the payment shall not be less than five per cent of the fair market value of the contribution at the time the trust was created. There is no evaluation of the trust on an annual basis;

6. UNIT TRUST: Similar to the Annuity Trust except that the donor receives a fixed percentage return (not less than five per-cent) based on the net fair market value of assets evaluated annually. There are three variations to this plan, including an ability to provide tax-free income to the donor.

Donors in the last four categories would be people of sizeable means who wanted to make a charitable contribution, enjoy the tax benefits now, and receive a guaranteed income for the rest of their lives. An example of a potential donor would be a woman, age 65, who purchased one of the following trust agreements with six percent return in income (gift annuity 5.6%).

|  | Tax Deduction | Annual Taxable Income | Income |
| --- | --- | --- | --- |
| Gift Annuity | $11,718.50 | $2,800.00 | $ 690.00 |
| Pooled Income | $22,100.00 | $3,000.00[*] | $3,000.00 |
| Annuity Trust | $22,200.00 | $3,000.00 | varies |
| Unit Trust | $21,150.00 | $3,000.00 | varies |

[*]Income would vary since it is six percent times the
fair market value of the investment.

Trevor Bayley accepted presidency of Northwest Kidney Center Foundation and the next move would be to expand the foundation Board of Trustees with people who were not currently on NKC's Board of Trustees. When the foundation gets enough funds, the Board would have to consider investment responsibility and this would be considered when appointing new board members. The Board intended to pursue sheltered tax annuity in the near future.

## THE NORTHWEST KIDNEY PATIENT ASSOCIATION

Northwest Kidney Center patients had formed the Northwest Kidney Center Patient Association, an organization for dialysis and transplant patients and any interested persons in the Northwest. Its goals were consistent with those of the Center, and they did not intend to be involved in fundraising. Primarily, they intended to be a group to help new patients and to provide assistance to each other. While the National Association of Kidney Patients was actively involved in political lobbying for insurance coverage and federal funding, the Northwest group did not intend to be active in these areas and would follow guidelines proposed by the Center. They had asked for representation on the Board of Trustees but after discussion it was decided that it would not be appropriate for a patient to attend Executive Committee meetings as this could inhibit free exchange of information and discussion. However, the Executive Committee agreed that a representative from the Northwest Kidney Patient Association be appointed to the Board of Trustees to fill a currently vacant term. They also agreed that at the annual meeting a representative from the patient group would be elected to a one-year term on the Board of Trustees. It was so moved, seconded, and passed unanimously.


## The Regional Medical Program and Organ Retrieval

As noted previously, legislation in October 1970 had extended the Regional Medical Program (RMP) to include kidney disease and as a result a committee was appointed to consider the best approach to dialysis and transplantation in Washington State, with eventual recommendations to the Washington State Medical Association. This tied in with the problems of having potential multiple transplant centers.

Early in the year, information became available about planning for the Regional Medical Program and transplantation in the Northwest. As part of the Kidney Disease Control Program it was desired to get donor organ retrieval and tissue typing onto self-sustaining bases. For each of these two activities there had to be an agency which could pay for all expenses and collect fees, and the transplant recipient or his sponsor was ultimately to be responsible for paying the charges. The RMP would assist in covering initial expenses for these activities but could not fund direct patient care. Consequently, Northwest Kidney Center was designated by RMP as the agency to reimburse various care providers for organ retrieval and tissue typing, and to collect the established fees.

In March, Dr. Blagg reported that two weeks earlier 37 representatives from insurance companies met at the Center to discuss the costs of organ retrieval. Dr. Blagg spoke about the organ retrieval program, and Maurice

Ward demonstrated the perfusion machine to the guests and explained how it worked. An hour and a half of questions and answers followed. Some good ideas came out of this open discussion period. It was found that the representatives were somewhat limited in what they could do regarding payment of the bills in this situation because of their underwriters and because of the way the policies were written. It was suggested that there be discussion with the purchasers of insurance to clarify this problem.

The proposed charge schedule was as follows:

<u>Cadaveric donor organ:</u> $1,500. This included a professional service fee for nephrectomy; donor operating room charges; all transportation from place of donor death to the place of recipient surgery; communications; all perfusion and preservation costs including supplies, services, equipment maintenance, facilities rental and standby personnel; and overhead and collection costs.

<u>Tissue typing, per recipient:</u> $250 (one-time charge). This typing fee included typing of recipient and all proposed donors for ABO and HL-A compatibility, cross-matching of recipient's serum with cells of proposed donors and routine testing.

<u>Operating plan for organ retrieval</u>: Northwest Kidney Center as the base for all organ retrieval operations in the region.

<u>Staff for retrieval and perfusion</u>: Dr. Blagg, project director; Maurice J. Ward, organ retrieval coordinator; John Bleifuss, perfusion technician and engineer and William Perlis, biochemistry technician.

<u>Equipment</u>: Kidney perfusion consoles, two - one at University Hospital and one at Northwest Kidney Center; transport modules, five - one each in Seattle (Northwest Kidney Center), Spokane, Great Falls, Skagit Valley (Mt. Vernon) and Anchorage; instrument packs (two at Northwest Kidney Center).

<u>Supplies</u>: Perfusion supplies to be provided by Northwest Kidney Center except that plasma for perfusion was to be provided by local blood banks and processed at the Northwest Kidney Center; stock to be maintained by perfusion team; surgical supplies to be provided where the nephrectomy is performed.

Communication and transportation: Initial contact usually to be between the physician attending the potential donor and the organ retrieval coordinator at Northwest Kidney Center; upon receipt of acceptable data and after verifying that the organs were likely to become available and the probable time, the organ retrieval coordinator would alert the perfusion team and the attending physician would alert the surgeon who will perform the nephrectomy if it is other than a transplant surgeon; the perfusion team would arrange for the necessary transportation.

Transplant surgery support: Perfusion team from Northwest Kidney Center would obtain the kidneys at the operating room where nephrectomy was performed, if within 150 miles; they would pick them up at the Seattle airport (SeaTac or Boeing) or at the helicopter pad if they were shipped by air; the perfusion team would deliver the kidneys to University Hospital or to Northwest Kidney Center and would maintain them until the surgeon desired to receive them for implanting in the recipient.

Maintenance: The perfusion team would be responsible for insuring that all perfusion equipment was in operating condition, including any transport modules that are stored at remote centers; they maintain reasonable amounts of spare parts; they schedule periodic inspections of all units; they train appropriate persons in the operation and maintenance of each unit.

Records: Northwest Kidney Center would keep records of all organ retrieval actions, including time required for various phases, expenses incurred, communications and transportation used, results, and after-action recommendations; keeps cost accounting records to substantiate established charge schedules.

Tissue typing operating plan: Northwest Kidney Center coordinates tissue-typing and cross-matching done in Seattle for kidney donors and recipients in Alaska, Idaho, Montana and Washington.

Definitions: tissue typing: A sample of blood is processed to remove red blood cells, platelets and granulocytes. The remaining suspension of pure lymphocytes is reacted with various defined antisera to determine which antigens the lymphocytes possess (assumed to be shared by other body tissues). On this basis the specific antigens, called HL-A antigens that a subject has are identified. Approximately 30 antigens are now recognized; except in rare instances, each subject has no more than four; Cross-matching: Lymphocytes from the potential donor are similarly reacted with serum from the prospective recipient. The reaction observed determines whether a donor and recipient will be compatible, that is, if the recipient has no specific antibody in his blood directed against the donor's tissues; Facility: Tissue-typing and cross-matching are done in the laboratory of E. Donal Thomas, MD, Division of Oncology, Room 1021, USPHS Hospital. Typing and cross-matching, or either procedure alone, requires approximately four hours for a single donor-recipient pair; Staff: One full-time Research Technologist I employed by Northwest Kidney Center. Other technologists of Dr. Thomas's share the on-call schedule when typing or matching is needed other than during normal working hours. On-call technologist carries a "bellboy" provided by Northwest Kidney Center; Equipment: Provided by Dr. Thomas; Supplies: To be ordered through Northwest Kidney Center or in coordination therewith; Specimens: For typing or cross-matching, a 5 ml sample of heparinized blood plus 2 ml of clotted blood (or serum) is required from each recipient, and 5 ml of heparinized blood is needed from each donor. Patients and donors may either report to the typing laboratory to have samples drawn, or the samples may be delivered from nearby institutions. When samples are to be sent by mail, subjects will receive instructions from and will send samples directly to Dr. Thomas' laboratory; For the routine screening of recipient's serum for antibody, mailing envelopes and instructions would be available at the Northwest Kidney Center and at Spokane and Inland Empire Artificial Kidney Center for furnishing to physicians and recipients; Requests: Typing and matching requirements are initiated by the physician who is evaluating the prospective transplant recipient or by the surgeon who will perform the transplant; <u>Results</u>: Furnished in writing to the referring physician, the transplant surgeon, and Northwest Kidney Center. Pre-transplant cross-matches and emergency typing results are telephoned directly to the transplant surgeon and other physicians concerned; <u>Cost Accounting</u>: Northwest Kidney Center keeps complete records of expenses in detail, issues invoices to patient or sponsor, keeps record of revenue and determines fair unit price.

In April Dr. Blagg reported on the Regional Medical Program Advisory Subcommittee that had been appointed to look at guidelines for the data regarding dialysis and transplantation and to report back to the Regional Medical Program. This was in an effort to unify management of patients with renal disease in the Regional Medical Program area and an effort to adopt policy regarding acceptance and standardized treatment of all patients in the area. The subcommittee consisted of Drs. Blagg, McCormack, Marr, Curtis, Hegstrom and Tenckhoff. Dr. Blagg said there would be more to report at the next Executive Committee meeting.

In May Dr. Blagg reported that the RMP Kidney Advisory Committee had met to review proposals for a grant for the years 1973-76. The following proposals considered directly involved NKC:

1.  Collection of statistics with regard to kidney patients.
2.  Funding for one or two nurses for follow-up care in the home.
3.  A program to study the problem of hepatitis in patients with renal disease.

Dr. Blagg was also a member of an RMP subcommittee which had the task of making recommendations on the facilities required for dialysis and transplant in the region. This subcommittee had met twice so far, and had made the following recommendations with regard to dialysis:

1.  That NKC and Spokane remain the two major centers in this state.
2.  That these centers should continue to be responsible for the training of patients and for the more specialized surgery including cannula and fistula surgery.
3.  That satellite centers might be established in the state. (St. Joseph's Hospital in Tacoma was in process of developing such a center in conjunction with Northwest Kidney Center.)
4.  That a satellite center would be developed only in an area with interested nephrologists with sufficient patients to require such a center, and only if both centers agree to the necessity for such a center at that site.

The object of these regulations was to keep dialysis in the state a high quality economical treatment.

There was discussion of the transplant problem at the subcommittee and also at the RMP Kidney Advisory Committee meetings, but no concrete resolutions developed because of the many different viewpoints. There seemed little doubt that University Hospital was approaching or might already have reached its capacity for transplants and the NKC must develop a policy to support appropriate people who were doing work elsewhere. Mr. Ginsey commented that Virginia Mason and Swedish Hospital were both doing kidney transplants without NKC's blessing, and that if we continued to be quiet, others might also begin doing transplants on their own. As a result NKC should support them or take a position. Dr. Blagg agreed that NKC should develop a position with regard to support of other hospitals doing transplants. Dr. Haviland commented that if NKC established its own criteria for transplantation it would be ahead, and this would put NKC in a very strong or key position since the Center handled the funding. Mr. Ginsey asked Dr. Blagg how soon NKC would have to have its position established. Dr. Blagg answered, "within the next two or three months, otherwise we will be too late". Dr. McCormack suggested the Executive Committee support Dr. Blagg to arbitrarily estimate what he considered to be the best patient care. Dr. Blagg noted that the only real sanction the

Kidney Center had was financial and that it would not be as economical to do transplants outside of University Hospital because of physician's fees. Dr. Haviland recommended establishing a strong policy regarding control of transplantation with NKC as focal point and that efforts be made to get the others involved to cooperate. It was moved and seconded that the Executive Committee support the concept be established regarding the approach to the transplant program with Northwest Kidney Center as the central focal point to be recommended by Dr. Blagg. The motion passed unanimously.

In June, Dr. Blagg reported that Northwest Kidney Center currently was the coordinating center for transplants in the Northwest Region and that there was a potential for a federal program to establish regional centers. The University of Washington had reached its maximum capacity for doing transplants. Dr. Blagg suggested the Executive Committee approve hiring a transplant surgeon, Dr. Gerald Kenny, to work with the Center on a part-time consultant basis and do perhaps 10 to 12 transplants per year at Swedish Hospital. Dr. Haviland pointed out that NKC could take a firm stand on regional transplantation; if the federal program went through, it would be controlled by NKC, and transplantation would still be handled equitably throughout the area. The Executive Committee agreed to the concept in principle and asked that Dr. Blagg, Dr. Haviland, Dr. McCormack, and Mr. Ginsey meet to discuss specific details, such as salary, etc., and report back to the Executive Committee.

In July, Dr. Blagg reported on the meeting of the subcommittee appointed to investigate the feasibility of appointing a transplant surgeon to the staff of the Center. They agreed it would be best to appoint Dr. Gerald Kenny as a part-time consultant to the Center from August 1, for a six-month period which might be extended at that time. He would receive $250 a month plus professional fees for transplants performed. It was moved, seconded and passed unanimously that Dr. Gerald Kenny be retained as a consultant at $250 per month for six months.

Mr. Ginsey inquired about the present status of kidney retrieval with the perfusion machine and Dr. Blagg replied that NKC had harvested kidneys in the previous month that had been sent to other areas of the country where there were patents with good matches. NKC would continue to send out kidneys of blood type AB or B since the Center had very few patients with these blood types who were potential recipients. In return it was hoped for some blood type O kidneys to be sent to NKC or to harvest some locally.

There appeared now to be funds in the national budget for setting up regional transplant centers as the legislation had passed both Houses. Dr. Kountz from San Francisco and Dr. Scribner were involved in drafting the plan. Dr. Blagg had submitted a proposal that would integrate the whole Northwest into a functioning transplant region with the NKC very much involved.

In December, Dr. Sawyer reported on the Regional Organ Retrieval Symposium. This was a meeting attended by representatives of dialysis centers in the area of Eastern Washington (Spokane), Montana, Idaho and Seattle to discuss patient referral to Washington State transplant centers. It was agreed that every such patient coming into the state for treatment should be sponsored by either the Seattle or the Spokane center, and that insofar as possible, Spokane would handle patients from Eastern Washington and Seattle would handle patients from the Western part of the state; that patients referred for transplantation should be sponsored by either of these two centers, but if they were not able to provide support the University of Washington might proceed with transplant if it so wished.

## Limited Care Dialysis

Limited care dialysis for indigent patients and those whose home circumstances were such that home dialysis would be very difficult was discussed by Dr. Blagg. A study in Hawaii was to explore this style of treatment. The cost for this form of treatment was two to three times the cost of home dialysis in Washington State, but was decreasing. NKC should look at this sooner or later, although there was no need take immediate action on this now. He would report further at a later date. Dr. Haviland asked what number of patients NKC turned down because of a home environment that would make home dialysis impossible. This was only two to three a year, but there was always worry about 10 to 15 percent of the patients accepted for home dialysis because of possible poor home conditions and other reasons. NKC has not rejected any patients strictly because of a poor home environment, but in some cases where the home environment was poor the cost of dialysis had been higher because of the need for more backup hospital dialysis.

## THE AMERICAN KIDNEY FUND (AKF)

It was reported in April that the American Kidney Fund had sent out flyers requesting financial support to individuals in Washington State. This organization appeared to be a dubious one-man organization in Washington D.C., which did have a charitable solicitation permit; however, it was "not qualified" by the National Information Bureau standards as there was no Board of Trustees, no information available and no books to audit. This, however, did not mean this operation was in question according to Washington D.C. laws. The problem was that it was now competing in Washington State with the NKC's fund drive efforts. The National Kidney Foundation (NKF) was also concerned about the AKF. No one knew whether the individual actually had given any money to patients, although the brochures suggested that this was what he was soliciting for. As a result, NKC had published a news release pointing out donations to either the American Kidney Fund or to the National Kidney Foundation left the state and therefore were not used for Washington state residents with kidney disease, and that donations to the National Kidney Foundation were used for research and not for patient care. Mr. Derham would continue to investigate the situation.

Three months later when some on the board were solicited to donate to the American Kidney Fund it was noted information was still lacking about this organization and about how the funds were to be dispersed and that the literature from the American Kidney Fund implied that Northwest Kidney Center was involved. Mr. Derham subsequently contacted the Postal Inspector in Washington D.C. to investigate whether fraud through the mails was involved. Several alternatives were discussed by the Executive

Committee such as having a Board Member write a letter posing as a patient and requesting financial assistance; however, it was decided to wait until after the Post Office investigation before initiating further action. In the future an injunction might be considered to prevent the American Kidney Fund from sending promotional mail to the state of Washington.

## The 1972 Annual Meeting of the ASAIO

Dr. Blagg reported that between April 15 and 18 there were visitors from all over the country and from various parts of the world attending the eighteenth annual meeting of the American Society for Artificial Internal Organs, the first ever to be held in Seattle. It was estimated that on each day at least 400 to 450 people visited Northwest Kidney Center. The meetings themselves were very successful and everyone agreed that it was one of the better meetings that had been held by the ASAIO. Papers from staff were presented at both the nurses and technicians meetings and the new home training program at NKC was reported at the physicians meeting. All were received enthusiastically by everyone present. There had been many subsequent requests for more information regarding the new home training program.

Six of the 87 ASAIO papers emanated from Seattle.

Mr. Stinson, Ms. Clark, and Drs. Sawyer and Blagg from Northwest Kidney Center described their home hemodialysis training program that reduced training time from about six weeks to about three weeks. Since 1967, as far as possible home dialysis had been the treatment for almost all the Center's dialysis patients other than kidney transplantation in order to be able to afford to offer treatment to more patients and experience had shown that home dialysis had many advantages over in-center dialysis Thus it was important to have a training program that would enable as many patients as possible to do safe home dialysis. Consequently they looked at program instruction and semi-automated teaching aids and decided to use half-inch black-and-white videotape because of its cheapness and versatility. Thanks to a grant from the Boeing Employees Good Neighbor Fund the equipment was acquired and a television studio was developed in a conference room. The training program was based on a core curriculum of materials and skills and provided some 20 hours of videotapes about identification of the equipment and its subsystems, the procedural format for doing dialysis, information about diet and the medical aspects of dialysis treatment. Humor, music and other techniques were used to relieve some of the tedium of instruction and a workbook was provided in which the patient was required to fill in missing words. Patients were expected to spend at least at least two weeks in the Center dialyzing before entering the training program. More than 80 percent of patients finished training in three weeks or less. The new training program had been extremely successful. However the media was not the message. The program success was attributed to the use of an empirically determined program format and nurses and technicians who had become teaching specialists and who appeared on the video tapes.

Doctors Babb, Farrell, Uvelli and Scribner from the University of Washington discussed hemodialyzer evaluation and solute molecular spectra. It was known that small molecule clearance was significantly dependent upon dialyzer flow rates as well as overall mass transfer coefficient and effective membrane area of the dialyzer, whereas middle molecules (greater than 1,000 MW) clearances are, within reasonable limits, independent of flow rate and dependent only on effective membrane area and overall mass transfer coefficient. Since middle molecules are area-dependent it should be possible to achieve equally adequate dialysis by keeping the area–time product constant for a given dialyzer–membrane system – the Square Meter-Hour Hypothesis. Data from dialyses in patients and in vitro showed that a low dialysate flow ($Q_D$ 100) on a standard Kiil dialyzer resulted in the predialysis concentration of small solutes rising by up to 30 percent but was not detrimental, patient well-being was significantly improved and dialysate costs were reduced by up to 80 percent. Long-term data using this protocol indicated that low molecular weight metabolites (less than 300 MW) were not toxic at the predialysis levels observed. The in-vitro predialysis concentration curves for the DOW HFAK, the Twin-coil UF–100 and the Mini-Dialyzer and accompanying clinical data discount the importance of greater than 2,000 MW molecules in causing uremic abnormalities. Data from three patients using large area dialysis and reduced time (3 $M^2$ at 1/3 of the normal weekly dialysis schedule using a 1 $M^2$ dialyzer) confirmed the technique was safe. The data suggested that molecules in the 300 to 2,000 MW range (and more probably the 300 to 1500 MW range) were the most likely solutes to produce uremic abnormalities at relatively low predialysis levels. As molecules in the 300 to 1500 MW range now seen more important for uremic toxicity it was suggested the term Square Meter–Hour Hypothesis be replaced by the Middle Molecule Hypothesis.

Dr. Farrell, Mr. Grib, Mr. Fry, and Drs. Popovich, Broviac and Babb from the Departments of Chemical, and Nuclear Engineering and Medicine at the University of Washington described a comparison of in vitro and in vivo solute-protein binding levels of selected waste metabolites, drugs, and essential amino acids in both normal and uremic subjects. Binding was determined by conventional ultrafiltration techniques and by in vitro and in vivo dialysis procedures. When binding occurred the levels in uremic patients were on average universally reduced and in some cases to significant levels. Reductions in binding were noted in uremic patients for several drugs, and proteins other than albumin appeared to be implicated in the drug binding interactions. It was confirmed that in vitro binding techniques reflected actual in vivo binding levels. Reduced binding in uremia could be important with respect to both drug administration and loss of vital endogenous compounds during dialysis.

Dr. Eschbach, Adamson, Anderson and Dennis from the University of Washington described studies of bone marrow regulation in uremic sheep. The anemia of chronic renal failure was still incompletely understood and seemingly adequate dialysis did not correct this. Because of the difficulty of maintaining a bilaterally nephrectomized sheep by dialysis a subtotal nephrectomy model was developed. This report described the animal model and the results of the initial studies that confirmed the anemia of chronic renal failure in sheep is physiologically similar to that seen in uremic man.

Dr. Schmer from the Department of Laboratory Medicine at the University of Washington had studied means to render foreign surfaces antithrombogenic by binding heparin to a polymer. A study showed that interposing substance between the polymer surface and heparin increased the amount bound as well as its biological activity. He studied various substances that assisted such binding and the extent of the binding was measured by use of $S^{35}$ labeled heparin.

Drs. Sherrard, Baylink and Wergedal from the Seattle VA Hospital and University of Washington described bone disease in uremia and discussed the importance of bone biopsy as a tool to improve understanding of renal bone disease. They presented data to document the progression with time from mild to advanced osteomalacia or osteitis fibrosa and showed that static and dynamic features distinguished the various pathologic disturbances. Biopsies had been of prime importance in the management of symptomatic bone disease and were beginning to be used to provide evidence for the efficacy of various prophylactic measures.

Dr. Tenckhoff and Mr. Meston and Mr. Shilipetar described a simplified automatic peritoneal dialysis system they had developed. The prototype was undergoing initial clinical testing in seven dialysis patients at the University of Washington and there had been no technical failures. Cultures before and after each dialysis remained sterile over six weeks even though the system was not resterilized between uses during the last four weeks of this period. All patients much preferred the new machine to any other system they had used. Undesirable side effects were limited to one patient who got slight shoulder pain at the end of dialysis due to a small amount of subdiaphragmatic air and which subsided within an hour. The new system used water purification by reverse osmosis (R.O.), was low cost, and provided virtually unlimited quantities of sterile, pyrogen-free dialysate from tap water and sterile concentrate. They believed this development would have a major impact on the cost and practical application of dialysis and in particular the role of peritoneal dialysis in the treatment of chronic kidney failure.

Mr. Cole, Drs. Dennis and Hickman, Mr. Coglon, Mr. Jensen and Dr. Scribner from the University of Washington described preliminary studies with the fistula catheter, a new vascular access prosthesis based on their experience working with dogs for various experimental purposes. They reasoned that placement of a catheter of appropriate design in the high flow environment in the vein just proximal to an AV fistula might result in creation of a thrombus-free, nonreactive semi-permanent blood access for hemodialysis. They described their experience with this, initially with a single implant of a Silastic tube with an attached Dacron cuff and an external fitting and most recently using a double lumen implant consisting of two Silastic tubes bonded together and introduced into the fistula at a single entry point. They suggested that the fistula catheter might provide new possibilities for long-term access to the vascular system for hemodialysis and might also be used for other forms of therapy such as long-term parenteral alimentation.

In addition papers from NKC staff were presented at both the nurses and technicians meetings.

A Workshop on Dialysis and Transplantation was held on the Sunday before the main meeting and speakers from Seattle and Spokane included Drs. Sawyer, Hickman, Donnell Thomas, Marchioro, Giblett, Blagg and Marr. In the section entitled How Much Should Dialysis Cost the keynote speaker was Dr. Blagg discussing the reduced cost of dialysis in the home and the clinical benefits (this was before the HR-1 legislation) and that self-dialysis in the home or center would be possible throughout the country if physicians could be convinced that this policy was the only financially tenable course to follow. Dr. Constantine Hampers from Boston gave the counter arguments and strongly disagreed with Dr. Blagg. A spirited discussion followed, moderated by Dr. Willem Kolff. Discussants included Drs. Ira Greifer, John de Palma, James Nicotero, Eli Friedman, Richard Balinsky, Jorn Hess-Thaysen, Fred Shapiro, Earl Newhart, Angus Rae and Arnold Siemsen, Miss Barbara Belino (a nurse) and Mr. William Litchfield (a patient).

The following morning was devoted to a symposium on Middle Molecules in Uremia. Speakers included Drs. Earl Ginn, Lee Henderson, Scribner, Mike Baccay, E. M. Halar, Peter Farrell, Babb, and Jean-Louis Funck-Brentano.

## THE CLINICAL DIALYSIS AND TRANSPLANT FORUM, 1972

This, the second Forum, was held at the Roosevelt Hotel in New Orleans on November 19, 1972. Thirty-four papers were presented, two of which were from the University of Washington.

Drs. George, Tremann, Quadracci, Striker and Marchioro presented a paper on the spleen in chronic renal failure and renal transplantation. Certain systemic diseases such as amyloidosis, tuberculosis, and systemic lupus erythematosus may affect both the spleen and kidneys. Excessive splenic sequestration of red blood cells had recently been described in patients on chronic dialysis and splenectomy had been suggested to improve their anemia, leukopenia and thrombocytopenia. Also, the merits of prior splenectomy in renal transplant recipients was an unanswered question.

The study was undertaken to examine the relationships between the spleen, chronic kidney failure and kidney transplantation. The records of 125 patients who had received 128 kidney transplants over the last five years, 34 of them of cadaveric, were analyzed. Forty-two spleens were available, (the others had been used in the production of antilymphocyte globulin). Mean splenic weights were compared with the weights of normal spleens and although there was considerable variation in both groups, on average spleens of chronic renal failure patients were more than one and a half times heavier than those of normal subjects. Splenectomy was associated with better ultimate kidney function and a higher mean peripheral white blood count and patients who had undergone splenectomy were able to take larger doses of an immunosuppressive drug and smaller doses of prednisone.

The other paper by Drs. Babb, Farrell, Strand, Uvelli, Milutinovic and Scribner looked at residual renal function in patients on hemodialysis. Of the first three Seattle dialysis patients in 1960, one had very severe neuropathy from the start of dialysis and the second suffered a gradual decrease in creatinine clearance from March until August at which point he began to develop clinical evidence of peripheral neuropathy while on once-weekly dialysis. The third patient continued to have residual renal function until he was eventually transplanted a number of years later and never developed any clinical evidence of neuropathy. All three received the same amount of dialysis in 1960. These findings were consistent with the idea that small amounts of residual renal function, by augmenting the weekly amounts of middle molecules removed, would indeed permit the use of shortened dialysis schedules for some patients. They believed it was particularly hazardous to shorten dialysis time when a patient first began treatment, since residual renal function often deteriorated rapidly at that point. Only after renal function had remained stable for several months should the possibility of shortening dialysis time be considered.

## CHAPTER 33

# January to June – Before the Medicare End-Stage Renal Disease (ESRD) Program 1973

———

THE YEAR 1973 WAS THE most far-reaching one since 1960 for patients with chronic kidney failure needing dialysis and kidney transplantation. This was because on July 1 the Medicare End-Stage Renal Disease (ESRD) Program began. The detailed history of the legislation leading to this is described in the next chapter. Because July 1, 1973 was a watershed date in the management of these patients, this chapter will be devoted to the first six months of the year and chapter 35 will discuss the second six months of 1973 following implementation of the program.

## THE TENTH ANNUAL MEETING OF THE BOARD OF TRUSTEES

The board met on the evening of February 21, 1973, called to order by the president, Mr. Denver Ginsey. Mr. Elmer Nordstrom gave the Nominating Committee report. The committee, consisting of Mr. Nordstrom, Mr. Baggott, Drs. McCormack and Haviland, submitted the following recommendations to the Board of Trustees: that the officers be president: Denver Ginsey; vice president: Richard C Philbrick, DDS; secretary: James W Phillips; and treasurer: Robert Burns. Members of the Executive Committee would be: Renaldo Baggott, Willis Campbell and Elmer Nordstrom. Trustees re-elected to three-year terms expiring in 1976 were: Renaldo Baggott, Bruce Baker, Emery Bayley, Willis Campbell, John Dare, Trevor Evans, John Kennedy, MD, Elmer Nordstrom, Richard C. Philbrick, DDS,

Jack D. Schwartz and T. Evans Wyckoff. New trustees with three-year terms expiring in 1976 were: Kirby Torrance and George Fleming. One trustee with a three-year term expiring in 1974 was: Thomas Marr, MD. Trustees with three-year terms expiring in 1975 were: Allan Lobb, MD; Roy Correa, MD; and Mrs. Holt Webster. Trustees with one-year terms were: William McKee, MD, Wenatchee; Representative Charles Savage, Mason County; Virgil Mahaffey, president, Northwest Kidney Center Patients Association; Mrs. Marilyn Dean, Stewardess Emeritus Association; Merle West, chairman, Snohomish County Kidney Fund; and Jack Larson, chairman, Yakima County Kidney Fund.

Mr. Ginsey noted that the theme of the Center during 1972 had been change. It had continued to accept and treat an increasing number of new patients and, during 1972, 95 new patients started treatment, an increase of more than 20% over the previous year. Also during 1972, 44 kidney transplants were performed, 61 patients were trained for home dialysis, and 26 kidneys were retrieved through the Center's organ retrieval program. Mr. Ginsey noted that during 1972 the Center treated more new patients per capita population than any other major center in the world. The videotape home hemodialysis training program had been improved and continued to attract attention in the U.S. and abroad and had attracted other centers to send staff to Seattle for training.

The tissue typing and organ retrieval programs funded by the Regional Medical Program were set in motion. Tissue typing was undertaken in the laboratory of Dr. E. Donnell Thomas at the Public Health Hospital in Seattle and results of the typing of potential transplant candidates were maintained on a computerized list at the Center. This list included not only the Center's patients but patients from Eastern Washington, Alaska and some from Idaho and Montana, and was used to select the best candidates for cadaveric kidneys which might become available for transplantation. The organ retrieval program also had proved a resounding success and was only the second such regional program in the United States. There was need for more publicity and public awareness of the need for cadaveric kidneys.

The previous year had seen the use of smaller, disposable dialyzers and new equipment to make dialysis easier for the patient, and the Center continued to work in conjunction with Dr. Scribner's group at the University looking at developing simpler and better equipment. The Center itself had been remodeled and the offices were now on one floor at Eklind Hall. Two new training rooms for home dialysis and a new clinic for outpatients had been developed.

Improvements had been made in accounting, purchasing and patient collections, resulting in stabilization of the financial position and securing a better financial outlook for the future. Fundraising under the direction of Kirby Torrance, Jr., had been extremely successful, having produced more than $500,000 during the previous year and a half. He had assembled an active group of volunteer solicitors and had started using computerized letters with amazing results, producing a more than 30% response at a cost of approximately 3 cents for each dollar raised.

The Center would continue to lead in directing treatment of renal disease in the state of Washington together with the Spokane and Inland Empire Artificial Kidney Center that served Eastern Washington. The Center, with the University of Washington Division of Nephrology, could provide the nucleus around which a statewide or regional program was built. Mr. Ginsey reminded the Board that donations of money and time would continue to be necessary but that now with the developing kidney transplant program he also urged the attendees to encourage their relatives and friends to sign donor cards as well as sign one themselves.

He recognized and thanked Bob Burns, the board treasurer and chairman of the Finance Committee for development of the new system of accounting and praised the staff for the excellent management of the Center and his predecessors as president, Drs. Haviland and McCormack.


THE MEDICARE ESRD PROGRAM
Dr. Scribner and Dr. Blagg described the coming Medicare ESRD program. (Note that this was based on current speculation and grossly underestimated

what actually happened. Further discussion of this topic is included later in this chapter.) The current reasonable estimate of the number of patients who would be involved at any one time was about 60,000, a number that should be reached in 5 to 10 years' time by which time the rate of intake of new patients would equal the death rate of patients in the program. The cost of kidney transplantation would average about $15,000 in the first year and only $1,500 per year thereafter, in contrast to the cost of dialysis which would continue for as long as the patient continued on dialysis. It cost four times as much to maintain artificial kidney patients in a hospital or center as it did for the patient to treat themselves at home or in a self-care center. If there were 30,000 patients using artificial kidneys and all the dialysis patients cared for themselves, the cost for dialysis would be $120 million a year, but if dialysis was done in institutions, the cost would be more than $480 million per year. Thus, a saving of $360 million per year for the taxpayer could be effected if the artificial kidney program was properly administered. It would be important to discuss the pros and cons of self-care dialysis versus hospital- or kidney-center dialysis and experience in the United States and Europe had shown patients on home dialysis were medically and psychologically better and better rehabilitated than those on long-term in-center treatment. Experience in the state of Washington over the previous five years had clearly shown that a dialysis program could be designed to favor self-care, ultimately saving millions of dollars a year and thousands of man-hours from medical and paramedical personnel. Currently there was no long-term institutional dialysis in Washington.

Even so, many doctors felt home dialysis placed undue stress on the family. Also, for new patients, the choice of institutional versus self-care dialysis was greatly influenced by the attitude of their physicians, and most new patients would choose institutional dialysis unless their physician encouraged them to do self-care dialysis. Some physicians felt that self-care dialysis discriminated against the poor who had inadequate housing and were ill-equipped to cope with self-dialysis. The solution to this would be to integrate dialysis treatment of such patients with social services such as re-housing, vocational retraining, other social service support, and even provision of a dialysis helper. The cost of such service would still be much less than the cost of maintaining such a patient in a center.

A new type of artificial kidney treatment facility, a limited care facility, had come into being in the last few years. (More information on this topic is included later in this chapter.) This was freestanding like the NKC and often entirely separate from a hospital, and was where patients received artificial kidney treatments three times a week. Recently there had been a proliferation of privately owned limited care facilities designed to make as much money as possible from the business of providing these life-saving treatments. The effort was quite proper as long as the proprietary centers continued to provide quality care at a competitive cost to the patient, but the problem was that most of these profit-making units were owned by physicians who were also treating the patients in the unit.

Dr. Scribner believed strongly that to answer these problems, regulation should provide that a physician with a proprietary interest in a profit-making dialysis unit should forfeit rights to collect professional fees for dialysis patients treated in the unit as well as the right to make professional decisions with respect to management of such patients. Administrative policy should be set up so that all patients were funded sufficiently to cover the cost of self-care dialysis, including the cost of training, equipment, backup dialysis and provision of a dialysis helper in the home, and also sufficient for the maintenance of low-cost self-care dialysis units. In the case of patients with poor housing conditions, funds from other relevant federal and state agencies should be made available for relocation of the family and vocational retraining. Finally, for those patients local authorities believed must remain on expensive institutional dialysis, Medicare should pay only an amount equal to the average cost of self-care dialysis and the additional funds necessary should come from sources other than Medicare. It was becoming increasingly important for physicians to pay attention to cost considerations in the use of this and other developing technologic areas of medicine and that legislators and the public become informed about the cost of this and similar programs. The final decision as to the approach to be taken with such an expensive program should be decided only after informed debate by all concerned.

FUND-DRIVE RESULTS

Kirby Torrance noted that his role as chairman of the Kidney Center Fund Drive had been much easier as a result of the group of organizations that had raised a lot of money while doing all the work. He presented certificates of appreciation to the Stewardess Emeritus Association, the Omicron Chapter of Epsilon Sigma Alpha Sorority, the Boeing Employees Good Neighbor Fund, the Xi Alpha Psi Chapter, Beta Sigma Phi Sorority, the Seattle Jaycees, the Queen City Auxiliary, the J. Garth Mooney Auxiliary, the Eastside Auxiliary, the West Seattle Eagles Auxiliary and Clippers Auxiliary, the Greenacres Auxiliary and the Somerset Auxiliary. He also gave special thanks to Gary Meisner who had been the major gifts chairman for the drive.

A building permit had been obtained for construction of two additional home dialysis training rooms in the patient area at Eklind Hall and this would be completed and put into use in May. The Boeing Employee Good Neighbor Fund had contributed $21,453 to finance the final cost of construction of the new training rooms.

VISITORS FROM THE SPOKANE CENTER

The January meeting of the Executive Committee was attended by Dr. Thomas Marr, medical director of the Spokane and Inland Empire Artificial Kidney Center; Florence Hansen, administrator, Spokane and Inland Empire Artificial Kidney Center; and Mr. Gerald Leahy, co-administrator, Sacred Heart Hospital, Spokane.

Dr. Marr said that he was interested in initiating a continuing dialogue between the two Washington State dialysis centers. These centers had the same purpose and goals and this was the first time communication at a Board level had occurred. Although the goals were the same, there was some dissimilarity between the two programs. The Spokane Center was the first center connected with a private nephrology practice in the United States and probably in the world. It was viewed as a unit of Sacred Heart Hospital and included facilities for treating both acute renal failure and chronic renal failure. Patients were trained for home hemodialysis, and there were currently 29 patients at home (54 having been trained altogether) and 42 transplanted. Patients came from Eastern Washington, Idaho and Montana. There were three criteria for acceptance into the program: 1) that the candidate be suitable for home dialysis; 2) that there was a family physician in the community to follow the patient after training; and 3) that there was reasonable funding support. Although there was no formal fund-drive campaign, about 20 percent of the budget came from funds raised in the local communities, usually for a particular patient. The large geographic area involved prohibited an effective fund drive. The medical director, Dr. Marr, spent about one hour per day in the facility and was involved in private practice at other times. Mrs. Hansen, administrator, was also the social worker for the center.

## Patient Numbers and Activities

In 1972, 106 patients had been accepted; 95 started treatment; 61 were trained for home dialysis, seven were on peritoneal dialysis and 54 on hemodialysis; 44 were transplanted, 28 received related-donor transplants and 16 cadaveric transplants; and 38 patients had died.

By January 1973 the number of patients treated in the center was down considerably as a result of doubling the number of patients in the home training program over the previous year and was a necessary solution to the increased in-center population. In addition, a dialysis helper had been trained for a patient who had no helper so that he might dialyze at home. The Center had 12 beds and normally operated five and one-half days per week. On this basis, in October, 1972 there was 85% occupancy, an average of 10.2 beds utilization per day; in November, 102% occupancy or an average bed utilization of 12.2 beds per day; and in December, 111% occupancy or an average bed utilization of 13.5 per day. The home training area had four beds and operated five days a week with dialysis three times a week and didactic training two days a week. In October, one bed was vacant for two dialyses because of patient complications, in

November one bed was vacant for one dialysis and there was 100 per cent occupancy in December. The patient census as of January 1973, was: outpatients, 26; in-center hemodialysis, 10; in-center peritoneal dialysis, 4; home training hemodialysis, 6; home-training peritoneal dialysis, 3; home hemodialysis, 144; home peritoneal dialysis, 15; and transplanted, 81, for a total of 289 patients. By the end of June there were 325 patients, 40 outpatients, 18 on in-center hemodialysis, six in home hemodialysis training, 157 patients at home on hemodialysis, 16 patients at home on peritoneal dialysis, two in home peritoneal dialysis training, and 8 to 6 patients transplanted.

TRAINING ROOMS
Because of the steadily increasing number of patients being trained for home hemodialysis further home dialysis training rooms had become essential. The Boeing Employee Good Neighbor Fund contributed $21,453 to finance construction and equipment of two more rooms that opened in May 1973.

HEPATITIS SCARE
There had been a serum hepatitis scare at the Center. Two nurses had developed hepatitis, probably from a patient from Alaska who was known to have had hepatitis. Special precautions were put into effect and alternate emergency plans including patient isolation would have been implemented should an epidemic have occurred. However, there were no new cases of hepatitis among staff or patients and so an epidemic appeared unlikely. The two nurses who had contracted hepatitis improved and were soon back at work part-time. This was the first report of hepatitis in a dialysis facility and was followed by a number of reports from facilities in the United States and Europe on hepatitis and deaths among staff and patients. Shortly thereafter, with availability of testing for hepatitis, this no longer continued to be a serious problem.

OTHER NEW MEDICAL DEVELOPMENTS

A survey of NKC patients and Veterans Administration patients was conducted by the Regional Medical Program on out-of-pocket medical expenses and rehabilitation.

On a trial basis, hollow fiber artificial kidneys were being used in the Center to shorten dialysis time by as much as 50%, without increasing the staff. The results would be evaluated in about three weeks to see if this approach should be continued.

## PATIENT ACCEPTANCE

During the first six months of 1973, 70 patients were approved for treatment, the great majority approved by Dr. Blagg. The age range was from 11 to 72 with the average age being 48 years. This compared with the national average of 45 years. The average number of patients approved per month was 11 and this increase might represent more referrals were occurring as entitlement under the Medicare ESRD program was approaching. Dr. Blagg had suggested that even if there were no problem patients to be considered, the Patient Acceptance Committee (PAC) probably should meet once a month to approve the patients approved by Dr. Blagg. In June it was decided not to change the role of the PAC at that time, as it was believed that a medical advisory panel might be required under the new Social Security regulations, but the exact requirements were not yet known.

## LIMITED CARE FACILITIES

Dr. Blagg had discussed so-called limited care facilities previously. For patients who were well but who experienced unforeseen problems, such as death of a spouse, it was inordinately expensive to dialyze them in-center. In addition to causing crowded center conditions, it would cause financial hardship for the patient and/or would use up his or her insurance rapidly. It would be beneficial if such patients could dialyze in a low-cost facility where assistance would be available but where specialized nursing and technician staffing would be unnecessary. This sort of facility would probably be part of the HR-1 legislative package, as the Department of Health Education and Welfare (HEW) had been led to believe that under optimum conditions nationwide, 80% of patients could be cared for on home dialysis, 10% would require a limited care facility, and 10% would require institutional dialysis in a hospital-like setting with specialized nursing and physician care. Dr. Lobb had indicated that NKC might be able to acquire the lobby area in Eklind Hall for a limited care facility, although ultimately such a period facility should be in a lower-cost building.

Mr. Ginsey said initiation of such a facility would require a philosophical decision by the Executive Committee and suggested a special meeting be devoted entirely to this issue. Background information would be provided to the committee members before the meeting or perhaps the Long-Range Planning Committee members should meet and make recommendations to the Executive Committee. Dr. Eschbach said that in practice, few persons were rejected for treatment because of initial lack of facilities for home dialysis, but that these problems occur later during the course of the patient's treatment. HR-1 would make it economically feasible for these patients to be kept alive – this was the intention of the law. These patients then would fill up the Center treatment area and the situation would be similar to that of five or six years earlier unless NKC came up with an innovative plan to take care of such patients.

Dr. Blagg requested that the Executive Committee convene soon, as the decision had to be made in the immediate future. Mr. Ginsey would arrange a special session of an ad hoc group to be devoted to the discussion of limited care facilities and report back to the Executive Committee.

Dr. Blagg also discussed the need for a policy position on affiliate centers in the state. There were nephrologists in other parts of the state who were going to want to do dialysis, which might or might not be appropriate; however funds would become available for this under HR-1. NKC could cooperate where feasible and appropriate. The Executive Committee should include the subject of affiliate centers in its discussion on limited care facilities.

## LIMITED CARE DIALYSIS AND HR-1

On the evening of February 27, a meeting was held at the Rainier Club in downtown Seattle to discuss the general philosophy of the NKC with regard to what was known of the federal legislation, limited care dialysis, and dialysis at centers other than the NKC in Washington State. Present at the meeting were Denver Ginsey, Drs. Blagg, Burnell, Haviland and Sawyer, Bob Burns, Terry Pollard and Tom Siefert.

An important new point involved clarifying the nomenclature. The Social Security Administration called dialysis in a non-hospital center, supervised by nurses or technicians, limited care dialysis. In previous discussions, NKC had used the term limited care dialysis to mean self-care dialysis. In the future it was important to distinguish between limited care dialysis that was in-center dialysis supervised by nurses or technicians as provided by the NKC prior to 1967, and self-care dialysis which was dialysis in a facility where the patients did most of the work for themselves.

Briefly, the provisions of HR-1, at least the little known about them at that date, suggested that NKC, in association with University Hospital, would qualify as the major regional center providing all services. Neither institution alone could qualify as this at the present time. There was discussion as to whether NKC wanted to provide all these services or should merely become a dialysis center. The general view was that NKC and the University of Washington, with a suitable agreement, should become the major dialysis and transplant center for the region. More details would become available for discussion when the final regulations were published. This approach would fit with the plan that Dr. Blagg had suggested before the meeting. For example, the regulations almost certainly would state that a transplant unit must do at least 25 transplants a year. The only way that the three or more hospitals in Seattle that wanted to do kidney transplants could continue to do so would be if they all combined to work with NKC – basically a "Seattle project."

With regard to dialysis, HR-1 would probably recognize four separate levels of dialysis. These would be: 1) hospital dialysis – only for the sick patient and it would be regarded as too expensive for long continued treatment; 2) limited care dialysis – dialysis in a kidney center outside a hospital provided by nurses, technicians or other trained personnel. This too would be expensive, and based on NKC experience should not account for more than 5-10% of dialysis patients. (The proprietary units already established elsewhere in the country were limited care centers.); 3) self-care dialysis – dialysis performed in a low-cost facility, the patient doing most of the treatment for himself with minimal technical supervision. This would be an alternative to home dialysis for the patient who could perform self-dialysis but whose home or other circumstances made home dialysis impractical; 4) Home dialysis.

There had been a philosophic discussion as to whether NKC should change its posture from its present one of "transplantation or home dialysis only." All nephrologists whose patients NKC was currently treating had had occasional patients doing badly on home dialysis and who would have been better supported either by limited care or self-care dialysis. There was general agreement that limited- care dialysis was a service that would be required under HR-1. If NKC was to have the role of a regional center it must supply this service.

With regard to self-care dialysis – this required more thought and experience in order to develop techniques to be used if the service was to be inexpensive and yet simple and efficient for the patient to perform. It was felt NKC should explore this further using either space on the ground floor of Eklind Hall or a low-cost facility elsewhere in the city. (Dr. Blagg's personal feeling was that the first effort should be in Eklind Hall where there was ready access to the Center.) This problem would be discussed further.

With regard to centers elsewhere in the state, the feeling was that NKC should be active in its approach. NKC already had a prototype agreement with St. Joseph Hospital in Tacoma and felt it appropriate to encourage signing of such affiliation agreements with other centers that might develop so that NKC would remain the focal point of a regional service. This too was going to fit with one of the likely provisions of HR-1 that would demand that all small dialysis centers be affiliated with a major regional unit. The feeling at the meeting was that when a nephrologist wished to do chronic dialysis in a hospital situation and NKC approved, the physician should be prepared to sign an affiliation agreement so that NKC could work with him or her.

After long and careful debate, the decision was made to report to the Executive Committee on these various subjects. In the case of limited care dialysis, the general feeling was that this was very similar to the in-center the Center already provided. Self-care dialysis should be approached with thought, and a decision made whether to attempt this in Eklind Hall. It was stressed that both limited care and self-care dialysis would be controlled by careful regulation and NKC should continue to maintain most of NKC's patients on home dialysis and avoid excessive use of expensive facilities. In the case of centers elsewhere in the state, the feeling was that active moves towards affiliation should be made where thought appropriate.

At the March Executive Committee meeting Dr. Blagg reported on the Ad Hoc committee meeting. He described the terminology that was expected to be used in the regulations for HR-1 and pointed out that in the past the NKC generally had accepted for treatment only those patients who would be able to perform home dialysis. However, even these patients might develop problems preventing their being able to do dialysis in the home; for example, death, divorce of spouse, transient illness, etc. In July, the new regulations under HR-1 (Social Security) undoubtedly would require all types of dialysis to be potentially available for all patients. The Executive Committee accepted the report of the Ad Hoc Committee and approved implementation of a limited care dialysis facility.

Also at the March meeting, Dr. Blagg reported on the current status of the HR-1 legislation. NKC had sent documents to persons involved with the development of this legislation, stating its position regarding the advantages of home dialysis over center dialysis and the economics of both. He had also attended a National Kidney Foundation sub-committee meeting in Houston to discuss the economics of dialysis. NKC's recommendations would be presented to the National Kidney Foundation, which would be giving its final recommendation to the Social Security Administration in the middle of April.

During March, the Center had been visited by Mr. Phil Jos who would be in charge of the ESRD program at the Medicare headquarters in Baltimore. He was not pleased when he arrived in Seattle and when Dr. Blagg asked him why he had come he replied that when Sen. Magnuson asked one to do something one did it. However, he soon realized how much he could learn from the Seattle program and he became a great friend of Dr. Blagg and was most helpful over the next few years.

At the April meeting Dr. Blagg reported there was no new information on HR-1 and the regulations, and that the Social Security Administration was re-writing a portion of the regulations and was currently behind schedule. Dr. Scribner was in Washington, D.C. to speak with representatives of Health, Education and Welfare and to various persons in the Social Security Administration. The National Kidney Foundation had developed a document of suggested regulations but NKC differed widely from some of the statements. Comments on these differences had been sent to the Social Security Administration.

Mr. Ginsey said that Dr. Blagg and Dr. Scribner should be complimented on the work they had done to inform the government of potential economic problems.

In May, Dr. Blagg reported that he had spoken with a representative from the Department of Health, Education and Welfare on May 24 and was told that regulations for HR-1 should be published by the end of June. During the last month, Dr. Blagg also had written to HEW explaining the operation of Northwest Kidney Center's program. It was hoped that the Center's program would remain essentially the same and that no major changes in overall function would result from HR-1 other than those related to the change in funding.

Dr. Blagg had discussed his concerns about the difficulties the Center might face with the new regulations with Dr. Haviland. Jim had introduced him to Mr. Joe Anderson who was the head of the Region 10 HEW serving the Pacific Northwest. Joe's response was to say that Dr. Blagg should not change anything as Baltimore was more than 2,000 miles away and it would be several months before headquarters knew what we were doing.

At the June 29 meeting, Dr. Blagg described and discussed the Interim Regulations for HR-1 (Medicare) received that week. These regulations would be in force for a few months to a year, after which final regulations would be developed and become effective. The Interim Regulations set limitations on reimbursement for limited care dialysis, training-fee dialysis limitations, limits for doctor's office visits for stable patients and other directions. The regulations as they were now written would not affect significantly the present operation of the Center. There would be meetings at NKC in the coming weeks with Social Security representatives, insurance carriers, Medicare intermediaries, hospital administrators and physicians to discuss these regulations.

## Kidney Transplantation

In May Dr. Blagg reported that Mr. Ward would be leaving the organ retrieval program in June to work with a cardiovascular surgery unit. Since May 1 NKC had become totally responsible for the regional organ retrieval program and Dr. Blagg planned to meet with the Seattle transplant surgeons in June to discuss organization of retrieval teams. NKC would continue to coordinate the program.

## NKC and NIH Research

The National Institutes of Health had contracted with NKC to develop a study for a comparison of peritoneal dialysis with hemodialysis. This study would commence shortly.

The NIH had also asked NKC to participate in a cost data study. Mr. Pollard reported that each patient's individual file for the fiscal year 1971-72 was analyzed. The average cost for a single patient, receiving dialysis in the Center, pro-rated over a 52-week period, was $31,000. This included drugs, medical care for treating complications, hospitalization, etc. The average cost for home hemodialysis training and equipment was $5,620. The cost for hemodialysis in the home, including backup dialysis and other costs, was $3,913 per year. Home peritoneal dialysis costs were divided based on equipment categories – new automatic cycler equipment was much more expensive and the average cost per year was $10,385 as compared to peritoneal dialysis with the equipment from the University of Washington which cost $7,840 per year. These data were based on the bills Northwest Kidney Center received and did not include bills for some outside charges which were not processed through the Center and were taken care of directly by the patient or his insurance. The accounting department would continue to study average costs through March 31, 1973, and would compare these costs with those from the last fiscal year. These combined costs then would be submitted for comparison nationally.

Two postgraduate students from the Department of Biostatistics at the University of Washington had been working with Northwest Kidney Center during the past year. One was primarily involved with creating a system for forecasting future events and situations based on past experiences at the Center using Markov chain analysis. This computer matrix had built-in allowances for changes, which could modify the future forecasting. The other student had been involved in developing data collection and creating a retrieval system to cover major medical activities at the Center including patient survival on dialysis and on transplantation, numbers and varieties of dialysis, blood access surgery and so on. This information had now reached the point where it was ready to be put into the computer and so Dr. Blagg requested $12,000 in funds from the Executive Committee for this project. This amount represented $5,000 for consulting with University of Washington staff and students, $400 for equipment, $1,000 for keypunching and $5,000 for computer time. A request for this funding would also be made to the Seattle Foundation. There were distinct advantages in communication in working with an academic biostatistician as opposed to a programmer or systems analyst from a commercial computer firm. This data retrieval program had become a necessary operational tool for the Center because data increased so rapidly that present personnel were unable to record it by hand in a fashion permitting easy retrieval. As a result of computerized data collection and retrieval, staff would be more able to choose alternate courses and would allow the Center to function more efficiently. It had been suggested the Center might wait and see what HR-1 would require in the way of data collection so that this could be included in the program, but Dr. Blagg felt the current program already included the materials which would be required by the government. It was moved, seconded, and passed unanimously that expenditure of funds be approved for one year for data collection.

## CENTER FINANCES

In January, the Finance Committee had met to review the quarterly financial statements for 1972. Accounts payable continued to decline during the year. Inpatient services were up by 45 percent in the second quarter compared with the first quarter and outside services continued at a higher rate than anticipated because more transplants were being performed than expected. Operating expenses had increased proportionately to increased activity.

At the March meeting, Mr. Burns reported that the Finance Committee had met on March 21, 1973 and there was now $365,000 tied up in receivables. The option of equipment leasing versus purchase of equipment and how this might be affected by the new regulations were discussed. (This issue is described in more detail later in this chapter.) The balance sheet showed there had been significant changes in the liquid position, and cash receipts for the last quarter had been heavy compared to previous quarters. This cash was in a savings account. Accounts receivable had declined since the beginning of the year, inventory was up slightly and plant and equipment depreciation was up because of the second floor remodeling and the experiment with renting equipment. Liabilities were down about $545,000 since December 31, 1972 and the Center was now current with payables. The Statement of Revenues, Expenses and Changes in Fund Balances showed the Center was doing more dialysis in-Center than budgeted and equipment and supplies sales were below budget, as NKC was selling or recycling more used equipment than budgeted, and also permitting some patients to rent equipment.

Comparison of statements showed the Center to be operating in a fairly similar fashion to the previous year. Review of Accounts Receivable and Age Analysis Summaries showed that total receivables had decreased from 1971 to 1973 even though the number of accounts increased by 130. There was now much better control over accounts receivable.

After negotiations, Swedish Hospital agreed on a reduced rent for NKC space in Eklind Hall of $2.94 per square foot. Dr. Lobb had signed the letter of intent regarding future relations between NKC and Swedish Hospital.

ESTATE CLAIMS AND DELINQUENT ACCOUNTS

Mr. Derham, the Center's attorney, had received approval to sue Jack Carnegie's insurance company for the amount owed to NKC prior to his death. As a result, $24,000 had been received from the insurance company. Also discussed was collection of specific older accounts and whether collection agencies should be utilized. The Committee agreed serious repercussion might result from the use of collection agencies, in that NKC might not be able to control pressures brought to bear on patients and the resultant publicity might be detrimental to community support. The Executive Committee concurred with this opinion.

A SECOND FULL-TIME STAFF PHYSICIAN

Dr. Blagg requested the appointment of an additional staff physician to assist Dr. Sawyer. With the steady increase in new patients and increasing number of medical problems, as well as the added responsibilities from assuming supervision of organ retrieval and tissue typing as NKC took these over from the Regional Medical Program, it had become necessary to acquire an additional full-time staff physician to provide adequate care and coverage. In order to get a conscientious, well-trained person, it would be necessary to pay a competitive salary. It was moved and seconded that the Executive Committee authorize Dr. Blagg to procure an additional full-time staff physician and to pay a reasonable salary. After discussion of various amounts constituting a "reasonable" salary, the motion was amended to read, "...authorize Dr. Blagg to procure an additional full-time staff physician and pay a salary not to exceed $30,000 per year." The motion passed unanimously.

LEASING VERSUS PURCHASING EQUIPMENT

The Finance Committee discussed whether NKC should be involved in leasing of equipment to rent to home dialysis patients. There was a remote possibility that Medicare would buy equipment outright; if it did not, the Center should be prepared to accept deferred payment on equipment, which would exclude recovery of financing costs. The philosophy involved was discussed, i.e., whether to use reserve funds to finance $250,000–$300,000 worth of equipment and wait two to three years for rental revenue to accrue, or whether to contract with a leasing firm or to borrow the capital and pass payments on to patients, thus preserving the Center's patient care reserve fund. With either agreement, the Kidney Center would be responsible for and hold title for the equipment at the end of the payment term. NKC currently had $50,000 in equipment that was being rented to patients on an experimental basis and the Finance Committee had asked for a policy statement from the Executive Committee. Mr. Ginsey proposed that alternate methods of providing equipment to patients be documented and be submitted to the Executive Committee. The financial impact of the following alternatives would be studied and a report made to the Executive Committee: 1) purchase equipment and sell to patients; 2) purchase equipment and lease to patients; 3) lease or purchase equipment in installments from Lease/Finance Company and lease to patients.

In the past, NKC had purchased equipment and resold it to patients but this would present problems to NKC when Medicare became the primary carrier for the patient, since its present policy did not allow reimbursement for purchase but would reimburse rental charges. Several alternative methods of coping with this situation, while at the same time maintaining the best financial position for the Center, had been considered. Mr. Rathman had investigated these alternatives and recommended cash purchase of patient equipment, with the purchase price passed to the patients as rental charges. The Finance Committee recommended the Executive Committee approve the investment of not more than $265,000 in equipment, with the stipulation that cash funds not be now reduced to less than $200,000. It was so moved, seconded, and passed unanimously.

At the May meeting there was continuing discussion of the problem created by possible deferred payments by Medicare for home patients' equipment. One thing to be considered was the current offer by the National Bank of Commerce for a $300,000 line of credit at 7¾% interest. The Finance Committee would consider the entire question of equipment financing when all information was prepared.

## ACCOUNTING SYSTEMS AND COMPUTERS

Mr. Pollard noted there had been several improvements in the accounting systems but further progress was impeded by having to use a 20 year-old accounting machine. There was presently a 6-to-8 week delay from the time a service was provided to the time the bill was sent. The present machine had very limited capabilities and required several additional manual operations and so a computerized system had been investigated. The accounting machines being considered would do as well at less cost. Burroughs and NCR were developing proposals for the preferred machines on a lease-versus-purchase basis and either machine would have the capability of linking to a computer, should that be desired. The machine also had the potential of reducing accounting personnel. Various other alternatives, such as the possibility of buying an accounting machine at a reduced price from a company that was going to a computer system, were being considered. After discussion by the Finance Committee, the Executive Committee approved the lease/purchase of a Burroughs L-7000 accounting machine.

## STATE FUNDING

In January Terry Pollard reported that funds from the state Division of Vocational Rehabilitation (DVR) were said to have been $100,000 short. After a meeting between NKC and legislative representatives it was discovered that an error had been made in disbursement of the funds and $88,000 was in fact available and another $29,000 probably would be freed up.

A request for funds for the 1973-75 biennium was currently in the governor's budget together with the revised request for DVR funding of $624,000. However, the revised request for $490,000 in Department of Health funds had been changed to $200,000. It was the Center's understanding that the intent was to get NKC through the first nine months of the biennium and then, after the effects of HR-1 were known and if more funding was required, the NKC could request a supplemental appropriation from the 1974 special session of the legislature. The Spokane Kidney Center was encouraged to request the entire amount of its original request and had done so. It was the unanimous opinion of the Executive Committee to request the full amount of the revised request, disregarding the possible effects of HR-1.

By April the legislature had approved funds for the Washington State kidney centers as contained in the original governor's request. The governor's budget office and the legislative budget office both recommended that the Center accept this amount and present a supplemental appropriation request in January 1974. It had been inserted into the senate records that the kidney centers would be returning in 1974 for a supplemental appropriation. A total of $824,000 was appropriated: $624,000 in DVR funds and $200,000 in Department of Health Funds.

## THE FUND DRIVE

After a slower start the fund drive had picked up and by March public solicitation contributions had increased by 42%, major gifts contributions had increased by 5%, and the general fund was 19% higher than the previous year, although the county fund drives were down 40%. By April the fund drive stood at $303,105.25, including $2,500 donated from Safeco. This represented a 5% increase over the previous year's fund drive and it was anticipated that the goal of $337,000 and would be reached.


## THE AMERICAN KIDNEY FUND

For some time, the Center had been aware of the questionable operations of the American Kidney Fund from an address in Falls Church, Virginia, and Mr. Pollard had written to the fund president, Mr. Swen Larsen:

> Dear Mr. Larsen:
>
> During the past two years, numerous contributors of ours have received letters from you asking for contributions. Many of these letters have been turned over to us asking for an explanation. In essence, your direct mail solicitation in the state of Washington has caused confusion on the part of contributors and drained vitally needed resources for Washington kidney patients.
>
> The Northwest Kidney Center is very dependent upon public contributions to meet the financial needs of the state of Washington kidney patients, and over the years we have been very successful--successful to the point that no patient in recent years has been denied kidney treatment for lack of financial resources. We accept every medically acceptable patient regardless of their ability to pay. This means that we now treat more patients per capita than any other treatment center in the world.
>
> While we seemingly are working towards the same goal, we are in conflict in raising funds for the same purpose. To this end, we respectfully ask that you no longer solicit contributions in the state of Washington. By doing this, you would greatly help in eliminating confusion and not drain the vitally needed resources to guarantee

kidney treatment for all state of Washington residents suffering from chronic renal failure.

I might add that the Washington State Legislature recently passed a Charitable Solicitation Act which requires all organizations raising funds within the state to make public disclosure of their financial statements. This may or may not influence your decision to continue to solicit funds in the state.

Thank you for the attention you have given this letter and we sincerely hope you will comply with our request.

Sincerely,

Terrance L. Pollard Administrator

This letter was not answered.

The Portland Better Business Bureau had prepared information on the American Kidney Fund, pointing out, in part, that the Kidney Association of Oregon was the only organization authorized by that state which utilizes contributions for direct care of kidney patients. They also said that the Council of Better Business Bureaus advised that the American Kidney Fund failed to cooperate in furnishing information relating to funding costs or planned distribution of funds received.

According to a news article in The Washington Post, $779,434 was raised in the first year of the American Kidney Fund's operation, and only $39,000 was spent on patient care. The AKF was being investigated by the U. S. Postal Service for possible violations of mail fraud laws. The organization also spent $132,000 to distribute 2,000 kidney donor cards at a cost of $66 per card. This compared with the National Kidney Foundation's Washington D. C. chapter, which distributed 400,000 cards at a cost of 22 cents per card.

## PERSONNEL

At the April executive meeting Mr. Ginsey announced that Terry Pollard, the executive director, had resigned after 11 years at the Center. Mr. Pollard had made a significant contribution to the Northwest Kidney Center and would stay on until pending problems were resolved. Dr. Haviland, on behalf of the Board of Trustees and the Executive Committee, presented Terry with a plaque of appreciation for his service to the Kidney Center.

In May, Mr. Ginsey reported that with Terry Pollard's resignation, the Executive Committee had given much thought to reorganization and had met with the Compensation Review Committee. It was agreed that Dr. Blagg be made medical and executive director of Northwest Kidney Center and that Harold Rathman be made business manager. Mr. Rathman would report to Dr. Blagg on operating matters and on fiscal matters would report to the Board of Trustees. Mr. Rathman introduced Richard (Huey) Powell, who would become the chief accountant, having spent the last year at Northwest Kidney Center as purchasing agent. In his capacity as chief accountant, he would be responsible for patient finances, accounting, billing and purchasing.

It was moved, seconded and passed unanimously that the following Corporate Resolution be adopted. Resolved: That National Bank of Commerce, First Hill Branch, be authorized to honor and pay checks or other orders for the payment of money drawn in the name of Northwest Kidney Center when signed by any two of the following: Christopher R. Blagg, MD, medical and executive director; Harold Rathman, business manager; Richard C. Powell, chief accountant; Denver Ginsey, president; James W. Phillips, secretary; and Robert Burns, treasurer.

## Northwest Kidney Foundation

With regard to Northwest Kidney Foundation, it was the responsibility of the Executive Committee to elect trustees to the foundation. At the April meeting it was moved, seconded, and passed unanimously that the present board be continued for another year. The present Board consisted of Richard Bangert, Walter Schoenfeld, Richard Philbrick, Lisle Guernsey and Emery Bailey.

# The 1973 ASAIO Annual Meeting

The 1973 meeting of the ASAIO was held in Boston, Massachusetts and two papers from Seattle were included in the program.

Drs. Casarreto, Marchioro and Bagdade presented a paper reporting on the frequency of hyperlipidemia and associated abnormalities in lipid transport in patients who had a successful kidney transplant. Patients were subdivided into ages 10 to 19, 20 to 29 and 30 to 39 because plasma lipids correlate with age. Mean serum triglyceride levels in all three age groups were significantly increased above values for normal subjects matched by age. Serum cholesterol values and mean serum cholesterol levels also were significantly increased in each group. Lipoprotein lipase activity is reduced in dialysis patients but their measurements suggested lipoprotein lipase-related triglyceride removal was normal in the transplant patients. This suggested that the hypertriglyceridemia following kidney transplantation may be a consequence of increased triglyceride production alone, since the process of removal appears normal. Consequently the hyperlipidemia in transplant patients would appear to relate to tissue insulin resistance resulting from the corticosteroids used in treatment causing a compensatory hypersecretion of insulin by pancreatic beta cells and exposure of the liver to increased insulin levels, as insulin is known to be a sensitive regulator of hepatic lipid synthesis. The changes in insulin availability probably resulted in increased synthesis of both triglyceride-rich and cholesterol-rich lipoproteins which were then released into plasma. Similar changes are seen in steroid treated animals. The hyperlipidemia and the basal hyperinsulinism in uremic patients results from both the production and removal of triglyceride-rich lipoprotein and are closely related to the clinical severity of the uremic state. These changes appear to persist after successful renal transplantation but probably results from increased production of both cholesterol-rich and triglyceride-rich lipoprotein and may be a consequence of steroid immunosuppressive therapy. These cardiovascular risk factors continue to contribute to premature morbidity and mortality after kidney transplantation.

Drs. Counts, Hickman, Garbaccio and Tenckhoff presented a paper on home peritoneal dialysis in children. They had treated 12 children in this way between 1968 and 1972 and who were maintained in good health for prolonged periods of time. Indwelling Tenckhoff catheters were used for access, and dialysis fluid was either obtained in bulk from the University of Washington Dialysis Laboratory or prepared at home using an automated dialysate supply system. Overnight dialysis three times a week or on alternate nights was accomplished using a closed automated system programmed to allow variable times for inflow, diffusion, and outflow. Patient and parents slept in separate rooms. Each dialysis lasted an average of 12 hours and in all but the youngest patients 30 to 35 L of dialysate was used per dialysis. No significant electrolyte or fluid volume disturbances occur during home dialysis. All patients were instructed in a high protein, low sodium and limited potassium diet tailored for individual needs and degree of residual renal function.

Home peritoneal dialysis was well accepted by all families and scheduled into the family routine. Children and parents preferred to be at home in familiar and comfortable surroundings for routine treatment. Complete rehabilitation with routine school attendance was the goal for all patients and only one, an adolescent with many years of chronic illness, was not successfully returned to normal functioning. Nine of the 12 patients were pre-pubertal and three had arrested puberty. The age range of patients was from two years ten months to 15 years ten months. The 12 children were on peritoneal dialysis from three to 38 months, and 11 were alive at the end of the study. One patient died following aspiration unrelated to dialysis and one was placed on hemodialysis because of poor peritoneal clearances after recurrent infections. Three patients eventually received a kidney transplant but at the end of the study eight patients remained on home dialysis by choice of their parents and themselves. Peritoneal dialysis is easily performed in children and well accepted by child and parents. Hemodialysis is more complicated to perform and peritoneal dialysis is relatively free from complications, making it safe for use in the home even with small children. Nearly normal activities and some growth and development make peritoneal dialysis a reasonable alternative to transplantation when growth-suppressive doses of immunosuppressive agents or urologic problems complicate transplantation in children.

## THE 6TH ANNUAL CONTRACTORS CONFERENCE

The meeting was held in Bethesda, Maryland, on February 12-14, 1973 with 166 participants, including 16 from the University of Washington, and 23 staff members from the NIH. There were reports on 67 contracts of which seven were from Seattle.

The first session was on biochemistry and pathophysiology. This included a section on divalent ions and bone metabolism and included a report on acid-base chemistry and human bone by Dr. Burnell and Ms. Elizabeth Teubner from the University of Washington. The next section was on neurological and psychological measures and on diet in uremia, and these were followed by a section on metabolic studies in uremia. This included a report on pharmacological studies both in the laboratory and in patients examining the dialysis of furosemide and gentamicin by Drs. Cutler, Christopher, Forrey and Blair from Harborview Hospital. The next section on the anemia of uremia included a report from Drs. Adamson and Eschbach on continuing studies using their animal model together with other in vitro studies.

The next session was on therapy and its evaluation, and the first section on dialysis included two reports from the University of Washington. Drs. Scribner, Babb, Strand and Milutinovic reported on the current status of their studies on the middle molecule hypothesis and Dr. Tenckhoff, Mr. Meston and Mr. Pete reported on further development of their home peritoneal dialysis system. The next section was on dialyzer evaluation and reuse and included a report by Dr. Eschbach and Mr. Vizzo on evaluation of the Dow hollow fiber artificial kidney. This was followed by sections on gastrointestinal absorption, and hemoperfusion and dialysate delivery. The next session was on non-thrombogenic surfaces and this was followed by a session on cannulae. The latter included a report on cannula developments at of the

University of Washington from Drs. Scribner, Thomas, Hickman, Dennis and Mr. Cole. The final session was on membranes and other materials.

As in other years, Dr. Krueger and Dr. Brian reported on the National Dialysis Registry. After 3 ½ years, the registry had collected data from about 11,000 patients being treated in the more than 370 dialysis programs across the United States. The largest centers were in the Northwest, which also had the highest percentage of home patients, and the smallest centers were in the Southeast. On average, there were 37.4 patients per million population and 371 centers. The average center size was 20 patients and on average 36% of all patients were being treated at home. Over the past year the mean age of the dialysis patient population had increased by almost two years, being slightly over 44 years for men and 43 years for women. Recently there had been a significant increase in the male and female populations in the higher age groups and the age groups 60 to 65 and 65 to 70-plus years had increased by more than 100% over the previous year. The predominant age group overall was the group aged 40 to 59 years. Men comprised 64% of the dialysis population and were being treated 40% in centers and 24% at home; women comprised 36% of the population and were being treated 24% in centers and 12% at home. Slightly more than 98% of the population was treated by hemodialysis, the remainder being on peritoneal dialysis.

The program finished with reports from the chairmen of the working sessions, and chairman of the cannulae session was surgeon Dr. George Thomas from Seattle.

CHAPTER 34

# History of the Legislation HR-1 and the Medicare End-Stage Renal Disease Program The Beginnings: 1962-1966

---

As discussed in Chapter 13, it was on May 6, 1962 that the New York Times published an article by Harold Schmeck on the Seattle selection process for dialysis titled "Panel Holds Life-or-Death Vote in Allotting of Artificial Kidney." Perhaps as a result of this, in the summer of 1962, Life magazine sent a young reporter, Shana Alexander, to write an article about the Seattle Artificial Kidney Center and Scribner's University of Washington program and the Seattle chronic dialysis program. It was also in mid-1962 that John Merrill from the Peter Bent Brigham Hospital in Boston visited Seattle to look at the results of Scribner's program. Whether his visit was related to the New York Times article or the forthcoming Life magazine article is uncertain, but Merrill became convinced that Scribner's program was able to prolong worthwhile life in patients with terminal chronic renal failure for periods of a year or more. Consequently, in October 1962, he wrote to Dr. James Shannon, director of the National Institutes of Health, describing Scrib's success and noting that this had already been reported on the front page of the New York Times and was soon to be described in detail in Life magazine. His letter also alerted the Department of Health, Education and Welfare (HEW) and the White House that questions might be asked following publication of the Life article in November – but these did not occur.

The following year the Veterans Administration announced the intention to establish 30 artificial kidney treatment centers in VA hospitals across the country over the next three years, the first one to be at the Seattle VA Hospital. In 1964, the National Institutes of Health established a program in transplant immunology in the National Institute of Allergy and Infectious Diseases and in 1965 started the Artificial Kidney/Chronic Uremia program in the National Institute of Arthritis and Metabolic Diseases. Also in 1965, the U.S. Public Health Service started the Kidney Disease Control Program that awarded 12 grants to establish dialysis centers around the country, and a year later awarded 14 home dialysis contracts. The program also began development of regionalization of kidney retrieval for transplantation and establishment of tissue typing laboratories.

In October 1965, President Lyndon Johnson signed Public Law 89-239, the Heart Disease, Cancer and Stroke Amendments, establishing "regional medical programs" and by the end of the year the Advisory Council on Regional Medical Programs (RMP) met for the first time. Originally established in the National Institutes of Health, in 1968 the RMP was moved to the newly created Health Services and Mental Health Administration. In 1970, Public Law 90-115 extended the life of the RMP and expanded its activities to include kidney disease, leading to support for kidney retrieval and tissue typing programs. As a result, the Northwest Kidney Center (NKC – previously the Seattle Artificial Kidney Center), was awarded a grant from the RMP to establish what became the regional center for kidney and other organ retrieval and the regional tissue typing center for kidney transplantation for the Northwest and to support the related tissue typing program in the laboratory of Dr. E. Donnal Thomas who later got the Nobel Prize for having done the first successful bone marrow transplant. The RMP functions were phased out during 1976 by which time the Medicare End-Stage Renal Disease Program had been functioning for three years but the NKC continued its regional role for the local transplant centers.

In March 1965, Scribner testified before Congress about dialysis and in November NBC aired a television documentary featuring Dr. Scribner's work and the Seattle kidney program. The program also included comments by Rep. John Fogarty, Democratic chairman of the House Appropriations Subcommittee and an expert on health care policy, and Rep. Melvin Laird, ranking Republican on the committee, both of whom expressed their support for development of a national dialysis program. However, although Fogarty controlled Department of Health and Human Welfare appropriations in the House, he was not a member of the Ways and Means Committee that was responsible for health legislation. Because of his interest, he visited Seattle in December to see the program for himself.

On October 20, 1965, Senators Henry Jackson and Warren Magnuson from the state of Washington introduced the Kidney Act of 1966 (S. 2675) to amend the Public Health Service Act to assist in meeting the costs of establishment and operation of programs for the care of patients with kidney diseases and to train professional personnel needed to conduct such programs and for other purposes. They introduced similar bills each year thereafter. Senator Jackson was always a strong supporter of Dr. Scribner and the Seattle program because one of his schoolgirl friends was now on dialysis at the Seattle Artificial Kidney Center. Unfortunately, Senator Lister Hill, chairman of the Senate Committee on Labor and Human Welfare, was not interested and the bill went nowhere.

On the House side, in 1966, Congressman Fogarty was prepared to sponsor a counterpart bill to the Senate bill but before he could do so Scrib, with his characteristic enthusiasm, had already pushed Washington freshman Representative Brock Adams to introduce the corresponding bill in the House. Unfortunately, House rules at that time restricted sponsorship of a bill to only one member. The legislation did not pass in 1966 but it was expected that Representative Fogarty would reintroduce the bill himself in 1967. Unfortunately, he died suddenly on the opening day of the 90th Congress in 1967.

Even so, the number of dialysis patients and transplanted patients and the number of dialysis units and transplant programs were gradually increasing, funded by several resources including the U.S. Public Health Service, the National Institutes of Health, a number of state kidney disease programs, community support and the patients themselves. By 1966 there were about 1,000 dialysis patients in the United States.

## THE BUREAU OF THE BUDGET AND THE GOTTSCHALK COMMITTEE: 1966-1967

In 1966, as plans for a possible dialysis program in the Public Health Service were being discussed, the White House Office of Science and Technology Policy prompted the Bureau of the Budget to form a committee to review dialysis and kidney transplantation in the United States and to consider what the role of the government should be. The committee was headed by Carl Gottschalk, a nephrologist from the University of North Carolina, and included an immunologist, three other nephrologists, a professor of medicine and psychiatry, and a transplant surgeon. The committee also included two economists. Scribner, Kolff, and Merrill were not members of the committee because of their potential bias. The committee, which came to be known as the Gottschalk Committee, collected information from all the federal agencies concerned with dialysis and kidney transplantation. They also held four meetings with nephrologists experienced with dialysis and with transplant surgeons. One of these meetings was a three-day visit to Seattle by the committee in October 1966 to meet with staff and patients from the University of Washington and the Seattle Artificial Kidney Center.

The confidential Report of the Committee on Chronic Kidney Disease was written in the summer of 1967 and submitted to the Bureau of the Budget in September of that year. The report noted that the committee agreed that hemodialysis and kidney transplantation were now no longer experimental and already were being used clinically by a number of physicians in the United States and elsewhere. In addition, it recommended that a national treatment program should be developed for "all the American population for whom it is medically indicated" and that financing of patient care should be through title XVIII of the Social Security Act (Medicare), and that necessary manpower and physical resources should also be developed. The report had no obvious effect at the time as it was not widely distributed and the Bureau of the Budget, the Bureau of Health Insurance (BHI) of the Social Security Administration and the House Ways and Means and Senate Finance Committees were preoccupied with problems resulting from the introduction of the Medicare Program in 1965, and the war in Vietnam.

## THE NATIONAL KIDNEY FOUNDATION: 1967-1973

The National Kidney Foundation (NKF) had evolved from the National Kidney Disease Foundation as dialysis and transplantation came to be recognized as effective treatments in the middle 1960s. It was the organization most responsible for the development of the legislation that led to the Medicare ESRD program. In 1967, an important event was admission of the NKF to the federal government's Combined Federal Campaign (CFC), as this allowed federal employees to commit funds to certain charities by payroll deduction. Until then the CFC had been dominated by the American Heart Association and the American Cancer Society. Membership in the CFC allowed the NKF a further source of funds that could be used to pay for travel to Washington, DC to testify, to fund research on public policy, to support advocacy and to cover costs associated with having an office in Washington, DC.

In 1968, only a small number of dollars were available, as resources related to kidney care and federal funds could not be used to directly support patient care. Consequently the NKF organized a planning session held in Washington, DC, attended by Drs. Neil Bricker, Don Seldin, Lou Welt, Belding Scribner, George Schreiner and Paul Teschan. They developed a five-year plan to expand federal support for kidney disease. This included: 1) amending the Vocational Rehabilitation Act to include kidney patients; 2) adding kidney care to the Regional Medical Program (RMP); 3) increasing support for pediatric patients with kidney disease through the Crippled Children's Act; 4) expanding the authority of the Chronic Disease Control program; 5) tripling appropriations for the NIH; 6) renaming the NIH Institute of Diabetes and Digestive Disease to include kidney disease or 7) obtaining congressional language to create a separate Kidney Institute;

8) opening the Veterans Administration to non-veteran patients in need of dialysis; and 9) working toward a new program to assist in payment of patient care. All of the proposed programs were amended by Congress or changed administratively but they served to increase congressional awareness of the problems for patients with kidney disease. As a result, many legislators began to look for alternative solutions, and because of the "life and death" issues with kidney disease a large number of bills were introduced. In addition, the congressmen and senators who sponsored and cosponsored these bills came from every state and more than 50% of the congressional districts

One major factor helping to lead to passage of the ESRD legislation was the publicity for the National Campaign for a Uniform Anatomical Gift Act that was passed in 1968. This required all the states to pass their own version of the Anatomical Act. The publicity associated with this increased public awareness of kidney failure and of kidney transplantation. Each potential donor had to sign a donor card and have this witnessed by two persons who were not family members, and this eventually involved millions of individuals. Behind these efforts were the NKF and its affiliates, the NIH, the American Bar Association and the Public Health Service. This was followed by increasing national and local press coverage.

George Schreiner, professor of medicine and chief of nephrology at Georgetown University, was probably the single most important individual in spurring Congress to legislative action when he became involved with the National Kidney Foundation (NKF). He served as its president from 1968 to 1970 and he hired Charlie Plante, his next door neighbor and who had previously been a Senate aide, to be the Washington representative of the NKF.

## THE CONGRESS: 1971-1972
During this time, the NKF made the decision to concentrate its strategic policy efforts on the House of Representatives Ways and Means Committee and the U.S. Senate Finance Committee as these were the key congressional

committees dealing with Medicare entitlement. This became important at the start of the 92$^{nd}$ Congress in 1971, when the Nixon administration proposed a number of new amendments to the Social Security Act. The House Ways and Means Committee, under its powerful chairman, Democrat Representative Wilbur Mills from Arkansas, was responsible, among other things, for the Social Security Act that included Medicare and Medicaid. During the summer of 1971, the Committee was working on a large omnibus bill, H.R. 1, a bill concerned with Social Security, welfare reform and Medicare, including the extension of Medicare benefits to the disabled and many other issues. The bill required considerable debate as it contained, among many other provisions, the first set of major amendments to Medicare and Medicaid since these programs were originally legislated in 1964. Both houses of Congress were anxious to have the resulting legislation on President Nixon's desk before the November 1972 election.

During the extended debates throughout most of 1971, the issue of kidney disease was not considered in either the House or Senate apart from a brief appearance by dialysis patients at a hearing on national health insurance before the Ways and Means Committee in November (see below). By this time, information on the rapidly rising cost of the first five years of the Medicare and Medicaid programs was available and so much of the early discussions focused on cost-containment by limitations on physician and hospital payments, the establishment of peer review organizations, and efforts to encourage health maintenance organizations.

At the same time, a consensus was growing that some form of national health insurance was coming. The costly Medicare program was very popular with the public and pressures for its expansion were growing. Senator Edward Kennedy wanted to see universal health insurance and a health security bill in particular was a major legislative goal. At the same time, President Nixon was starting to put together a modest yet sweeping piece of legislation calling for an employee mandate to provide health insurance coverage. Also in 1972, the American Hospital Association, the Health Insurance Association of America and even the American Medical Association were preparing and introducing national health insurance bills.

At the time both the House and Senate and both political parties thought there were only two questions concerning national health insurance. The first was timing, and a consensus began to develop that the committees should first work on H.R. 1 with all its cost control provisions before starting on broader health insurance bills in the next Congress. The other question was unsettled but had to do with the scope of any eventual legislation. Senator Kennedy and labor wanted a very broad universal, comprehensive, payroll-tax financed program. President Nixon and most of the major health organizations were in the middle and backed broad universal comprehensive measures, but measures that depended more on employer contributions or tax credits than on payroll taxes. The conservatives, led by Republican Senator Russell Long of Louisiana, chairman of the Senate Finance Committee, were concerned about the ballooning costs of Medicare and Medicaid and were looking toward a more incremental expansion of coverage rather than universal coverage.

Senator Long and Democratic Senator Ribicoff of Connecticut agreed that a universal comprehensive health insurance bill was too much at that time and put forward a more targeted measure aimed at the two problems most often cited by proponents of national health insurance – catastrophic illnesses and medical bills, and the problems of the poor. The bill they introduced was to provide coverage against the cost of catastrophic illness and to federalize and improve the Medicaid program for the poor, and it aimed to complement and support, rather than replace, private health insurance for the middle-class employed population. This Long/Ribicoff bill was strongly supported by the Senate Finance Committee and was expected to be introduced in the next congress.

## THE NATIONAL ASSOCIATION OF PATIENTS ON HEMODIALYSIS (NAPH), SHEP GLAZER, THE HOUSE WAYS AND MEANS COMMITTEE AND THE COMMITTEE HEARING, NOVEMBER 4, 1971

In October and November 1971, the House Ways and Means Committee held hearings on H.R. 1 and it was at the November 4 hearing that a patient was dialyzed very briefly on the meeting- room floor. Six patients from the National Association of Patients on Hemodialysis (NAPH) attended the hearing, including 43-year-old Shep Glazer, vice president of NAPH, and Peter Lundin, a medical student who had been trained to do home hemodialysis at the University of Washington while an undergraduate at Stanford. (He had not been accepted to the University of Washington School of Medicine despite the strong recommendations of Drs. Scribner, Blagg and Marchioro, but was accepted by Dr. Eli Friedman at Downstate Medical Center in Brooklyn). He continued on home hemodialysis, having married a dialysis nurse, and eventually became a nephrologist and an associate professor of medicine in Dr. Friedman's Division of Nephrology.

Glazer made the official statement from NAPH and afterwards was the patient who dialyzed briefly on the floor of the committee room. Previously he had consulted with Ways and Means staff who were far from enthusiastic about this, concerned that he might die in front of the committee. One of the senior committee aides who had not been consulted beforehand is said to have asked "What the fuck is going on here?" when he saw Glazer dialyzing. Glazer had also conferred with staff at the National Kidney Foundation and its president, George Schreiner, who were all strongly against the dialysis, concerned that any accident would immediately negate the progress the NKF had been making with the legislators over the last few years.

Despite this, on the day before the hearing, Glazer held a press conference in New York to announce what he would be doing the next day. That evening he called Schreiner at home asking for a dialysis machine from Georgetown University to be sent to the Longworth House Office Building. Schreiner was astonished and angry but made arrangements that a machine be made available and that Dr. James Carey, one of his nephrology fellows, would attend the hearing rather than Schreiner himself. Carey was instructed that in the event of any problem he should clamp off the blood lines, turn off the artificial kidney and declare that the dialysis was over. In fact, Glazer developed ventricular tachycardia shortly after the dialysis was started and so Carey clamped the blood lines and switched the machine off. The whole treatment lasted at most five minutes but was described by committee members as "excellent testimony," even though at that time they were concerned primarily with Medicare generally and not with patients with kidney failure. As a result of this episode and the ensuing publicity, the NAPH and later the American Association of Kidney Patients (AAKP) came to believe the myth that this was the important event that set on course Section 299I, the kidney section of H.R. 1. However, a week later on November 11, George Schreiner, Charlie Plante and Pat Flannigan, the chief of nephrology at the University of Arkansas in Little Rock, Arkansas, the home town of Wilbur Mills, the committee chairman, testified before the same committee on behalf of the National Kidney Foundation. There was no mention or question at this hearing about the dialysis before the committee the previous week.

One month later on December 6, 1971, Mills himself introduced a bill to amend the Social Security Act and provide financing for persons with chronic kidney disease "to make available ....the necessary life-saving care and treatment for such disease and will not be denied such treatment because of his inability to pay for it." (H.R. 12043.) This was not an entitlement program but was a budgeted program to provide financial assistance only to the extent that payment "does not exceed the cost of the least expensive form of dialysis which is or would be medically sufficient." There was also a project grant program to assist in development of new treatments with emphasis on "less costly methods" and training of staff and education on the prevention of chronic kidney disease. Most significantly, it supported establishment of hemodialysis centers but including "only those centers that make home dialysis equipment available to those who require it."

## THE SENATE FINANCE COMMITTEE: 1971-1972

Meanwhile, the Senate Finance Committee also had held hearings on H.R. 1 in the summer of 1971 and January and February of 1972. In addition to many cost control provisions, the Omnibus bill included the first major expansion of Medicare to expand coverage to the disabled and this was potentially a very costly expansion as the disabled had such high health care costs. In order to reduce the cost of covering the disabled, the committee structured the provision that limited coverage only to those people who had been receiving disability benefits for at least two years. This drastically reduced the cost of coverage because the most expensive medical costs were often incurred during the first year of treatment of a disability and also about half of the disabled died during the first two years of disability.

This postponement of coverage of the disabled until after two years of disability became important in the arguments which eventually led to the legislation for what became called the Medicare End-Stage Renal Disease (ESRD) Program. In early 1972, Schreiner, Plante, Lowell Becker, president of the National Kidney Foundation, and others had contacts with Senator Russell Long, chairman of the committee and Democratic Senator Herman Talmadge of Georgia, chairman of the Senate Finance Subcommittee on Health. During debates and discussions with the senators and their staffs, a special argument for coverage of those with irreversible kidney failure began to emerge because a two-year waiting period like that for disability benefits would be impossible for most kidney patients. They were a definable group with an available treatment who would die while awaiting coverage unless they were lucky enough to have the funding or private insurance to cover the cost of the first two years of treatment. Some members of the committee believed that a catastrophic coverage bill would be passed during the course of the next Congress. They understood the unique needs of kidney patients and came to believe that coverage of them by Medicare might be a pilot or demonstration program for the inevitable broader catastrophic bill to come in the next Congress. As a result, they supported amending the bill in a way that would "deem" those suffering from irreversible kidney failure to be eligible for coverage under Medicare. This argument was not completed until after the committee had completed action on H.R. 1 and so the actual amendment was added to the bill during debate before the full Senate later in the year.

In February, Senators Vance Hartke of Florida and Alan Cranston of California introduced a bill (S. 3210) to amend the Public Health Service Act to provide aid to various non-federal programs to establish community programs for patients with kidney disease. Meanwhile Schreiner and Plante maintained contacts with the Senate Finance Committee and staff and it was at one of these staff meetings that Dr. Jim Mongan pushed for including a kidney provision in the bill, pointing out that money was all that was needed to save the lives of many more patients with kidney failure and that such an amendment could be considered as a pilot study or demonstration program for catastrophic health insurance.

The Senate Finance Committee report was published on September 26, 1972, and was almost 1,300 pages long, included 49 additions to the House bill, but did not include a provision for kidney disease. However, on Saturday morning September 30, Indiana Senator Vance Hartke introduced a kidney entitlement amendment during a debate before the full Senate that was co-sponsored by Senator Long and Senator Burdick of North Dakota. Within a few minutes they were joined by Senator Chiles of Florida and Senator Dole of Kansas. Senator Hartke noted that cost estimates suggested the amendment would cost about $75 million in the first year and then $90 to $100 million each year. Senator Dole noted that the one possible reservation was that the amendment approached support for catastrophic illnesses in a piecemeal way but at least was a step in the right direction. Both Senators Jackson and Magnuson from Washington State spoke in support of the amendment, commenting on the Seattle experience, and Magnuson said that years before he had been asked "to be on the committee that would dip into the fishbowl to pick out the names" in Seattle but had said "No, thank you." He also commented on a current HEW bill that included support for kidney transplantation, rehabilitation services and staff training. Senator Wallace Bennett of Utah spoke against the amendment, pointing that on the previous day the Senate had voted "$2.5 billion for eye glasses, hearing aids, and foot massages" and a more than $5 billion addition to Social Security funding. He was reminded of a television ad in which a very happy housewife opens her cupboard up and says, "Christmas in September; isn't it a wonderful idea? I can sit at home and have all these good things brought to me." He realized the amendment would pass but would vote against it as he was concerned that no one was worrying about other serious medical problems such as hemophilia. He was also concerned that H.R. 1 might die of its own weight in the Senate. Senator Long, who had long had an interest in providing insurance to cover the costs of catastrophic health problems, responded that the next Congress would deal with health insurance generally and hopefully with catastrophic health insurance. The Hartke-Long-Burdick-Chiles-Dole amendment was debated for only about 35 minutes before being passed by 52 votes to three, so adding Section 299I to H.R.1.

## THE JOINT HOUSE-SENATE CONFERENCE COMMITTEE: OCTOBER 12-OCTOBER 14, 1972 AND PRESIDENT NIXON'S SIGNING: OCTOBER 30, 1972

The Joint House-Senate Conference Committee met from Thursday morning, October 12, until Saturday evening, October 14 and discussed the kidney amendment on Saturday evening. Conference committees are the most political and arbitrary part of the legislative process and often occur near the end of legislative sessions when time is running out and are often dominated by a few leaders from both Houses, even more so then than now. This was where the last piece of the kidney legislation fell into place.

The House bill did not include the kidney amendment because of cost concerns, and House members in the conference were disinclined to accept the Senate amendment. However, the Senate Finance Committee had included another amendment in their bill that was far broader and more costly – a provision to cover prescription drugs under Medicare. Senator Long personally strongly supported drug coverage and fought for the conference committee to approve this but ultimately did not prevail. An hour or so later the smaller Senate amendment to cover kidney disease came up in conference and Senator Long argued that the Senate had to come away with something from the conference and so the House yielded. So the kidney legislation ultimately survived in exchange for the more expensive prescription drug coverage. The only other change was that the Hartke amendment had required a six-month waiting period after the first treatment for chronic kidney failure before eligibility would be established and the House proposed shortening this to three months. This was accepted.

Thus was legislated Section 299I in the Social Security Amendments of 1972 and after adoption of the bill in both House and Senate it was sent to President Nixon who signed it into law on October 30, 1972.

The HR 1 legislation was a huge package that included controversial welfare reform provisions and Medicare and Medicaid changes and as a result little attention was paid to the kidney legislation at first. Kidney patients were understandably very pleased but the reaction in the provider community was relatively muted except for concern by physicians regarding the method of payment for dialysis. This led to the founding of what became the Renal Physicians Association.

## THE REACTION: 1972-1973

The main public reaction came on January 14, 1973, about three months after passage of the legislation when the New York Times attacked the kidney legislation as irresponsibly broad in an editorial titled "Medicarelessness." It noted that the Congress now was learning that the program might require annual expenditures of $1 billion in 10 years' time and that Representative Paul Rogers of Florida, an acknowledged congressional specialist on health issues, had admitted publicly that "We in Congress had no idea that the costs would be anywhere near that large." The editorial noted that the belated discovery of the financial problem was reminiscent of what happened after enactment of Medicare and Medicaid in the mid-1960s by legislators who had little understanding of the huge fiscal and other consequences that would flow from their actions. It was not that kidney disease patients were unworthy of help, but government resources had to be allocated to meet many other needs as well. One billion dollars to prolong the lives of thousands of kidney disease victims was $1 billion that could not be used to eradicate slums, improve education or find a cure for cancer. Society had a right to expect legislators would understand the magnitude of the commitment they were making when they passed special interest legislation, whether for kidney disease or anything else. There was mild criticism from conservatives, some of whom described the legislation as getting the camel's nose (or kidney as a humorist suggested) under the tent on behalf of national health insurance. They were completely wrong. Ironically, rather than seeing it as demonstration or pilot project, the kidney legislation proved to be the last piece of legislation affecting the Medicare program for many years. In fact, when the subject of catastrophic health insurance was raised several years later it proved to be wildly unpopular.

## CHAPTER 35

# July-December, 1973

———

THE NEXT MEETING OF THE EXECUTIVE COMMITTEE OF
NORTHWEST KIDNEY CENTER'S BOARD OF TRUSTEES WAS HELD
ON JULY 27, 1973 IN THE B-FLOOR CONFERENCE ROOM OF
SWEDISH HOSPITAL.

THE MEDICARE ESRD PROGRAM

DR. BLAGG REPORTED THAT THE Medicare End-Stage Renal Disease interim regulations went into effect on July 1. These regulations allowed current programs to continue to run almost as before, although with some
limitations. The limitation causing discussion was the charge for stable in-
center dialysis; this charge was set at $150 and did not include a physician
fee unless a specific service had been provided. Physicians caring for sick
patients and patients being treated for other problems could be reimbursed
on a fee-for-service basis after the physician provided documentation for the
service. The cost of any supervision by the physician during dialysis was to
be included in the overhead Medicare paid to the facility. This latter point
was specified because Dr. Scribner and others had told Medicare that only
some 5 percent of routine dialysis treatments actually required physician's
personal services during dialysis.

Because the proposed physician reimbursement was seen as the government specifying how doctors should practice medicine, many nephrologists
were incensed. An angry meeting was held at O'Hare Airport in Chicago

on "Black Friday," July 13, attended by some 40 nephrologists from both private practice and academia. This led to the formation of a new society, the Physicians for Renal Replacement Therapy (PRRT), later to become the Renal Physicians Association (RPA), to protest the regulations related to nephrologists and to work with the Medicare program to improve the regulations generally. Dr. John Sadler from the University of Maryland was elected president of the PRRT and Dr. Stuart Kleit from the University of Indiana and Blagg were elected vice-presidents.

Medicare would not be in a position to start reimbursing dialysis centers for at least three or four months. Northwest Kidney Center currently had not been assigned a fiscal intermediary. Intermediaries would be supplying questionnaires to all dialysis facilities and these would be used as the basis for establishing dialysis charges. It was anticipated that the final regulations would become available for review by nephrologists and dialysis centers by the end of the year.

MEDICAL ACTIVITIES THROUGH JULY 1973

Dr. Sawyer reported the total patient census was 336 on July 27, 1973. This included 22 patients on in-center hemodialysis, 1 on in-center peritoneal dialysis, 6 in home hemodialysis training, 1 in peritoneal dialysis training, 161 on hemodialysis at home, 17 on peritoneal dialysis at home, 86 transplanted and 42 outpatients. Sixteen patients were accepted during the month, 12 patients started treatment and 8 patients finished home training, including 2 on peritoneal dialysis.

There were two cadaveric transplants during the month: a 40-year-old woman who had been on peritoneal dialysis for ten months and a 31-year-old woman who had been on dialysis for six months. There was one related donor transplant, a 26-year-old man who had been on dialysis 3½ years. All were doing well. There were three deaths during the month: a 48-year-old man on dialysis seven months who died of a heart attack; a 67-year-old man on peritoneal dialysis for one year whose kidney disease had improved and had been taken off of dialysis since May of 1972 and who died in University

Hospital of currently unknown causes; and a 53-year-old woman who had been on dialysis for seven years and who was found to have extensive cancer at surgery and treatment was stopped.

## Patient acceptance through July 1973

Blagg reported that 15 patients were approved during the last month, their average age was 48 and two were aged 70. Six of the applications were emergency applications. The average processing time of each of these was three days.

## The Next Meeting of the Executive Committee of Northwest Kidney Center's Board of Trustees was Held on October 26, 1973 in the Auditorium of Eklind Hall.

### Additional concerns regarding the Medicare program

Blagg reported that NKC had requested an exception to the present Medicare dialysis charge screen of $150 for in-center dialysis in light of the fact that the Center's costs were higher than this. The exception process was not yet developed by Social Security but there was a possibility it would be expedited in the near future. This situation had caused a serious billing problem in that bills with dialysis charges for Medicare-eligible patients were being held until some word was heard on the exception request. Currently those Medicare-eligible patients with other charges were being billed; however, no action had been taken by the intermediary for reimbursement so far. The following week a decision would be made whether to bill Medicare for dialysis charges at the lower approved rate of $150 and then to rebill if an exception was granted, or whether to continue pending the bills.

The next regulations for the Medicare program, which might be out in January 1974, would emphasize home dialysis and self-dialysis more than the present Interim Regulations. They would also include provisions for peer review.

The Social Security Administration had assigned Northwest Kidney Center the status of a non-provider limited care facility, which did not really describe the activities performed by NKC. Presently the Center's charge for an in-center stabilization hemodialysis that would be ordinarily performed in a hospital setting in many other parts of the country was $160; the screen prescribed by the present regulations was $145. This same screen, $145, also was applicable to in-center peritoneal dialysis. This did not take into account the higher charge for the equipment necessary for peritoneal dialysis, bringing the cost to NKC to $185. Additionally, because the home hemodialysis training program had been intensified and shortened, the Center was charging $312 per dialysis, as opposed to the $185 screen set forth in the regulations. However, most training programs existing in the country at that time took six to eight weeks. Thus, the total cost of the Center's three-week training program was still lower than in other centers, even with NKC's higher per dialysis charge.

NORTHWEST KIDNEY CENTER FINANCES AND THE FIRST THREE MONTHS OF THE MEDICARE ESRD PROGRAM

The Finance Committee had met in early October and Mr. Powell had presented statements for the quarter July 1 to September 30, 1973. Assets were relatively stable and current cash, although down $37,000 from June 30, was not as low as had been anticipated in light of the delay in Medicare payments. It was thought that the next quarterly statements would reflect more accurately the problems caused by Medicare. Liabilities were greater, mostly attributable to purchase of many new kidney machines since July 1. The Statement of Revenue, Expenses, and Changes in Fund Balances, showed revenue increasing proportionately to the increase in the total number of dialyses performed, which was 83 percent over the same quarter last year. Equipment and supplies sales were up 46 percent over the previous year, due primarily to disposable dialyzers being used in the Center. In addition, 13 home patients had been retrained on disposable dialyzers. Another factor was that patients had been asked to defer major supply purchases until after July 1, which many of them did.

There had been no significant purchases of kidney machines since NKC began renting all machines, but until about three years had passed, rental revenue would not equal the figure of past major equipment sales. In future internal statements, the category Equipment and Supply Sales would be broken into a rental figure and the rest of supplies and sales categories so as to be able to follow this rental figure for a number of months.

Outside hospital service revenue had declined sharply due to the Medicare program, which required hospitals to do their own billing. Other outside services were higher, largely as a result of payments to dialysis helpers who assisted home hemodialysis patients.

At Northwest Kidney Center, internal expense was up about 46 percent and revenue was up about 83 percent. Increased expense in the Center was due largely to additional staff members and the use of disposable dialyzers. NKC had not expected the great increase in activity that had occurred since the Medicare program began, and was providing more billable services without corresponding increases in reimbursement. Even without additional revenues from hospitals, NKC was maintaining a strong gross revenue position.

Despite Medicare delays, accounts receivable was up only $50,000 and was now $552,000 as compared with the June 30 figure of $496,000, and 80 percent of all June 30 balances had been collected. An active pursuit of problem accounts had begun. Account analyses were being performed, and where money might be collected every effort was being made to do so. Twenty thousand dollars had been collected from problem accounts in the last quarter. Billing would be sending separate statements for the June 30 balance and new statements for monthly charges starting July 1. In addition, the Patient Financing Department had interviewed more than 200 patients to try and update their financial background and to inform them of Medicare procedures.

Because of the current situations in Medicare, billing had been forced to pend some billing. Of $552,000 to be billed, $133,000 had been billed. Half of the unbilled Medicare charges could not be billed because patients were not yet considered enrolled in the Social Security System (that is, they had not been determined as eligible Social Security beneficiaries).

NKC dialysis charges were in excess of charges allowed in the facility category in which Social Security had placed NKC and a request for an exception to this charge had been made. Denver Ginsey, Blagg and Mr. Rathman had gone to Baltimore the previous week to meet with Medicare staff to press the Center's case for an exception and learned that a ruling likely would be made by the end of November. It had been difficult to date to accumulate master files, but getting people enrolled should be going faster now. If within a short time NKC had not heard further information on the request for exception for dialysis charges, the billing department would bill the intermediary for all charges and then rebill if an exception was granted. This would obviously affect the cash position in the second quarter statement. The cash position dropped $37,000 during the last quarter but NKC was still collecting on June 30 balances. Emergency payments were available for providers or provider-based facilities only and Medicare had placed NKC in the non-provider category.

Blagg said that some problems currently existed between Social Security and Health, Education and Welfare (HEW). In spite of this, things seem to be going faster in Baltimore than in the past. A committee, which would pass on exceptions, had not yet been formed but would be shortly. At that point a questionnaire would be made available to those centers seeking exceptions and upon receipt of the questionnaires in Baltimore, decisions would be made. The ceiling was a screening ceiling only and exceptions should not be difficult to get.

The ESRD Program was regarded by some as being a forerunner of national catastrophic health insurance and so policy people in HEW and Social Security were concerned about making the program work.

The "stumbling start" of the Medicare ESRD Program

Victor Cohn, a Washington Post staff writer, wrote an article published on October 7, 1973 under the headline "Delays Slow U.S. Aid for Kidney Care." He noted that the Medicare ESRD Program was intended to pay for dialysis and kidney transplantation but in the first three months little or nothing had been paid out to patients, doctors or facilities in several parts of the country. The Social Security Administration estimated that about $550,000 had been dispersed, mostly in the preceding 10 days, meaning that only about one-fortieth of the estimated first-year monthly treatment cost of $20 million had been reimbursed so far. Phil Jos, chief of the dialysis staff of the Social Security Health Insurance Bureau, noted that so far nothing at all had been paid out to the West Coast.

Dr. George Schreiner of Georgetown University described the problem as "a big bureaucratic snafu" in HEW and its Social Security Administration. Charlie Plante, the National Kidney Foundation lobbyist, described the lag as "appalling" and blamed the problem on policy conflicts within HEW, HEW's desire to keep down the costs of this expensive program and poor performance by payment intermediaries like Blue Cross. Dr. Ron Klar in HEW said that the government had not started receiving bills from facilities until August 1 and starting such a large program obviously took time. He noted that the intermediaries had been unclear on the payment policies and that this also contributed to the delay. There were also arguments from the Physicians for Renal Replacement Therapy (see above) and other nephrologists about the inclusion of physician fees in the reimbursement to facilities for dialysis. At the time of the article, Phil Jos estimated that some 14,000 patients might be eligible for about $240 million in benefits during the first year.

One of the other problems was for home dialysis patients because suppliers of dialysis equipment and supplies were asking patients to prepay for six months of supplies but no information had been given to the patients about how they would be eventually be reimbursed from Medicare. In fact, the Interim Regulations said that patients would themselves have to bill Medicare after paying the suppliers.

MEDICAL ACTIVITIES THROUGH OCTOBER 1973

Sawyer reported there were 45 patients in the outpatient category; 191 patients were on hemodialysis – 22 in the Center, 6 in home training and 163 at home; 18 patients were on peritoneal dialysis – 3 in the Center, 1 in training and 14 at home; 6 were on limited care dialysis, 1 at the Center and 5 at the University of Washington's Coach House dialysis facility; and 96 had been transplanted, for a total patient census of 356.

It had been three months since the last Executive Committee meeting and during that time 32 patients were accepted, 27 started treatment, 22 finished home hemodialysis training and two finished peritoneal dialysis training. Twelve patients were transplanted: six related donor transplants and six cadaveric transplants. Of the six related donor transplants, all were successful although one patient subsequently died from other causes. Of the six cadaveric transplants, one had rejected, one was in borderline rejection and one subsequently died of a stroke. Three other transplanted patients had returned to dialysis.

There had been 11 deaths. The age range of these patients was 31 years to 77 years and five of them died of strokes, three of heart attacks, one from a high blood potassium level, one of a ruptured aortic aneurysm, and one patient voluntarily stopped treatment for social and medical reasons. During this three-month period, there were 355 in-center dialyses per month and the average number of home training dialyses per month was 98. This was a 70 percent increase over the same time period the previous year.

The Center was still working on details of establishing a limited care center on the first floor of Eklind Hall.

A new social worker had started at NKC in August and NKC was still looking for a case worker. The Center was also acutely in need of a nurse educator. This person ideally would have a master's degree and experience in teaching. The previous year, staff at NKC had provided 250-260 training days.

## Patient acceptance through October 1973

Blagg reported that 28 patients were approved during the three-month interval, the age range being from 14 to 71 years. The average age of these patients was 35 years, lower than the average age prior to the introduction of the Medicare program. Since July 1, 1973, 60 patients per million population were being referred to NKC.

## Leasing equipment

With regard to the Center's leasing equipment, it was moved, seconded and passed unanimously that the following corporate resolution be adopted: Resolved, that this corporation lease personal property from time to time from People's Leasing Company, Inc., in such amount and upon such terms as may be agreed upon.

## Finance Committee

Mr. Burns reported that the Finance Committee had met twice during the past three-month interval. It had reviewed the audited yearly financial statement and the first quarter financial statement. Accounts receivable was looked at in two ways: prior to June 30 and those accumulating since the Medicare Program began. The Center had done well toward liquidating old problem balances and on June 30, 1973, $120,000 was uncollected, of which $100,000 had been previously reserved for uncollectible accounts. Since then the balance of uncollected accounts was largely unprocessed because of Medicare. Cash reserves were up very slightly compared with a year ago.

STATE LEGISLATURE

As described in chapter 33, after the NKC's budget request to the legislature for the biennium was submitted, the requested amount from the Division of Vocational Rehabilitation was allocated, but the requested money from the Department of Health, $490,000, was reduced to $200,000 because of the uncertainty of the effect of the Medicare Program on dialysis and transplant facilities. The Center was told to come back to the interim legislative session with a supplemental budget proposal for the current year. NKC now had asked the legislature to reinstate the total amount requested in the original budget. Blagg and Rathman went to Olympia to substantiate this request with figures and to answer questions, and it was possible that this request might be included in the governor's budget.

FUND DRIVE

Fund drive results through the first part of 1973 were up $7,000 more than the comparable period the previous year, owing to the amount collected in Wenatchee, WA, which was to be used to set up a one-machine acute and backup dialysis operation there. Fundraising during the current fiscal year should be carefully monitored to try to detect any trends as they might relate to Medicare.

Later, Mr. Howard reported additional information to date about the fund drive. A comparison between the 1973 fund drive and the previous year's fund drive at the same time period showed that NKC was $18,000 ahead of the previous year. Fifteen thousand boxes of Halloween candy were being sold as a Beta Sigma Phi project and the profit to the Center expected from this sale was $8,000. The Seattle Foundation gave $4,000 to the Center to purchase two peritoneal dialysis machines. During Christmas, Shakey's Pizza Parlor would do a promotion for the NKC and would guarantee $6,000 from this. November 14 was to be the kickoff to the 1974 fund drive and the goal would be $350,000. The total raised during the 1973 fund drive was $338,000, the most ever raised in the NKC fund drive.

Gary Meisner would be chairman of the fund drive and there would be both direct mail solicitation and personal solicitation.

## The Final Meeting of the Executive Committee of Northwest Kidney Center's Board of Trustees for the Year was Held on November 30, 1973, in the B-Floor Conference Room of Swedish Hospital.

### Medical activities through November 1973

Sawyer reported that there were 42 outpatients and 198 patients were on hemodialysis (22 of them dialyzing in-center, 6 were in home training, and 170 were dialyzing at home). Sixteen patients were on peritoneal dialysis (1 in-center, 1 in home training and 14 at home). Currently, there were still 6 patients in limited care (1 at NKC and 5 dialyzing at the Coach House). Ninety-seven patients had functioning transplants.

Since the last Executive Committee Meeting on October 26, seven patients had been accepted, nine had started treatment, nine had completed home hemodialysis training and five had been transplanted. Three of these transplants were cadaveric: one performed at University Hospital and the other two at Swedish Hospital. The remaining two transplants were from related donors, one of which was performed at Virginia Mason Hospital and the other at University Hospital. There were three transplant rejections: the transplants lasted one month, three months and four months, respectively. There were no deaths during this time period and two patients transferred out to the Spokane Center. The total number of dialyses per month seemed to be stabilizing at about 460.

### Patient acceptance through November 1973

Blagg reported that 12 patients had been approved since the last Executive Committee Meeting, their ages ranging from 8 to 62, with an average age of 40. There were no major medical problems with this group of patients. The admission rate presently was 44 to 45 new patients per million population per year.

PERSONNEL ISSUES

Rathman announced that Miss Kay Olheiser would be leaving NKC's position of executive secretary to undertake classes at the University of Washington winter quarter. Arlene Thomas would be assuming Ms. Olheiser's responsibilities.

Mr. Baggott reported that the Compensation Review Committee had met to discuss salary ranges and salary increases. A subcommittee was appointed to study the proposed salary ranges in consideration of NKC's incoming monies from public sources. Mr. John Dare was appointed chairman of this sub-committee with Mr. Evans Wyckoff and Dr. Allan Lobb acting as committeemen. The Compensation Review Committee approved the proposed, modest salary increases, the change in Blagg's title to director and the change in Clint Howard's title to development director.

Currently the Center needed a person in a supervisory position to initiate and handle a more formal orientation and continuing education program for NKC's nurses, technicians and aides. This program would also be open to outside medical personnel desiring training for dialysis situations. There was also a need for someone to supervise changes in the curriculum of NKC's home hemodialysis training program and to develop an in-service education program on non-renal diseases (cardiac disease, lung disease, diabetes, etc.) for NKC's staff in order to serve as a refresher course. This would enable nursing personnel to better assist physicians with treatment of non-renal diseases in their dialysis patients. Burns moved that such a position be created and be filled, be termed training supervisor, and that the compensation level should be in accordance with Compensation Review Committee salary ranges. The fee schedules for training outside individuals should be set at levels sufficient to recover NKC's investment. There was no discussion and the motion was seconded and passed unanimously.

BILLING MATTER RELATING TO MEDICARE

Blagg reported that the Center had received a draft of a questionnaire with reference to the financial information NKC had submitted to Social Security to implement the request for an exception to the dialysis fee ceiling. This particular questionnaire would be submitted to all dialysis centers and the data collected and used as a basis for providing the information used by Social Security in granting exceptions. Thus, there would continue to be delays in resolving whether the Center's previous dialysis charges could be approved for an exception. Because of this delay, NKC had started billing Medicare for dialysis charges at the standard rate and Medicare had begun remitting monies for the previous one-month period.

PHYSICIANS FOR RENAL REPLACEMENT THERAPY

As noted earlier in this chapter, the Physicians for Renal Replacement Therapy organization was formed in July to represent physicians on a nationwide basis. Its objective was to gather information from Medicare on issues related to provision of dialysis care by physicians and to achieve consensus on comments to be submitted to Social Security from an organization rather than from individual physicians and small groups. The Social Security Amendments of 1973 had come to the floor of the Senate a few days earlier and, at the invitation of Blagg, Senator Jackson spoke at the request of the PRRT to encourage rapid implementation of all aspects of the Medicare ESRD Program.

FUND DRIVE RESULTS THROUGH NOVEMBER 1973

Howard reported that the total amount received as a result of the Fund Drive as of November 29, was $96,233.95. This was 21 percent ahead of last year at the comparable time. The Fund Office was completing and in the process of sending out solicitation letters to 7,445 organizations, foundations, corporations and clubs. A good response was expected, and reaching the $350,000 goal looked favorable. Shakey's Pizza Parlor was now guaranteeing a $13,500 contribution near Christmas time and was currently putting 50 cents in a jar for every family-size pizza sold, to go toward its total contribution.

## The 1973 ASAIO Annual Meeting

The 1973 meeting of the ASAIO was held in Boston, Massachusetts and two papers from Seattle were included in the program.

Drs. Casarreto, Marchioro and Bagdade presented a paper reporting on the frequency of hyperlipidemia and associated abnormalities in lipid transport in patients who had a successful kidney transplant. Patients were subdivided into ages 10 to 19, 20 to 29 and 30 to 39 because plasma lipids correlate with age. Mean serum triglyceride levels in all three age groups were significantly increased above values for normal subjects matched by age. Serum cholesterol values and mean serum cholesterol levels also were significantly increased in each group. Lipoprotein lipase activity is reduced in dialysis patients but their measurements suggested lipoprotein lipase-related triglyceride removal was normal in the transplant patients. This suggested that the hypertriglyceridemia following kidney transplantation may be a consequence of increased triglyceride production alone, since the process of removal appears normal. Consequently, the hyperlipidemia in transplant patients would appear to relate to tissue insulin resistance resulting from the corticosteroids used in treatment causing a compensatory hypersecretion of insulin by pancreatic beta cells and exposure of the liver to increased insulin levels, as insulin is known to be a sensitive regulator of hepatic lipid synthesis. The changes in insulin availability probably resulted in increased synthesis of both triglyceride-rich and cholesterol-rich lipoproteins which were then released into plasma. Similar changes are seen in steroid treated animals. The hyperlipidemia and the basal hyperinsulinism in uremic patients results from both the production and removal of triglyceride-rich lipoprotein and are closely related to the clinical severity of the uremic state. These changes appear to persist after successful renal transplantation but probably results from increased production of both cholesterol-rich and triglyceride-rich lipoprotein and may be a consequence of steroid immuno-suppressive therapy. These cardiovascular risk factors continue to contribute to premature morbidity and mortality after kidney transplantation.

Drs. Counts, Hickman, Garbaccio and Tenckhoff presented a paper on home peritoneal dialysis in children. They had treated 12 children in this way between 1968 and 1972 and who were maintained in good health for prolonged periods of time. Indwelling Tenckhoff catheters were used for access, and dialysis fluid was either obtained in bulk from the University of Washington dialysis laboratory or prepared at home using an automated dialysate supply system. Overnight dialysis three times a week or on alternate nights was accomplished using a closed automated system programmed to allow variable times for inflow, diffusion and outflow. Patient and parents slept in separate rooms. Each dialysis lasted an average of 12 hours and in all but the youngest patients 30 to 35 L of dialysate were used per dialysis. No significant electrolyte or fluid volume disturbances occurred during home dialysis. All patients were instructed in a high-protein, low-sodium and limited potassium diet tailored for individual needs and degree of residual renal function.

Home peritoneal dialysis was well accepted by all families and scheduled into the family routine. Children and parents preferred to be at home in familiar and comfortable surroundings for routine treatment. Complete rehabilitation with routine school attendance was the goal for all patients and only one, an adolescent with many years of chronic illness, was not successfully returned to normal functioning. Nine of the 12 patients were pre-pubertal and three had arrested puberty. The age range of patients was from two years ten months to 15 years ten months. The 12 children were on peritoneal dialysis from 3 to 38 months, and 11 were alive at the end of the study. One patient died following aspiration unrelated to dialysis and one was placed on hemodialysis because of poor peritoneal clearances after recurrent infections. Three patients eventually received a kidney transplant but at the end of the study eight patients remained on home dialysis by choice of their parents and themselves. Peritoneal dialysis is easily performed in children and well accepted by child and parents. Hemodialysis is more complicated to perform and peritoneal dialysis is relatively free from complications, making it safe for use in the home even with small children. Nearly normal activities and some growth and development make peritoneal dialysis a reasonable alternative to transplantation when growth-suppressive doses of immunosuppressive agents or urologic problems complicate transplantation in children.

## THE 6TH ANNUAL CONTRACTORS CONFERENCE

The meeting was held in Bethesda, Maryland, on February 12-14, 1973 with 166 participants, including 16 from the University of Washington, and 23 staff members from the NIH. There were reports on 67 contracts of which seven were from Seattle.

The first session was on biochemistry and pathophysiology. This included a section on divalent ions and bone metabolism and included a report on acid-base chemistry and human bone by Dr. Burnell and Ms. Elizabeth Teubner from the University of Washington. The next section was on neurological and psychological measures and on diet in uremia, and these were followed by a section on metabolic studies in uremia. This included a report on pharmacological studies both in the laboratory and in patients examining the dialysis of furosemide and gentamicin by Drs. Cutler, Christopher, Forrey and Blair from Harborview Hospital. The next section on the anemia of uremia included a report from Drs. Adamson and Eschbach on continuing studies using their animal model together with other in vitro studies.

The next session was on therapy and its evaluation, and the first section on dialysis included two reports from the University of Washington. Drs. Scribner, Babb, Strand and Milutinovic reported on the current status of their studies on the middle molecule hypothesis, and Tenckhoff, Mr. Meston and Mr. Pete reported on further development of their home peritoneal dialysis system. The next section was on dialyzer evaluation and reuse and included a report by Dr. Eschbach and Mr. Vizzo on evaluation of the Dow hollow fiber artificial kidney. This was followed by sections on gastrointestinal absorption, and hemoperfusion and dialysate delivery. The next session was on non-thrombogenic surfaces and this was followed by a session on cannulas. The latter included a report on cannula developments at of the University of Washington from Drs. Scribner, Thomas, Hickman, Dennis and Mr. Cole. The final session was on membranes and other materials.

As in other years, Dr. Krueger and Dr. Brian reported on the National Dialysis Registry. After 3 ½ years, the registry had collected data from about 11,000 patients being treated in the more than 370 dialysis programs across the United States. The largest centers were in the Northwest, which also had the highest percentage of home patients, and the smallest centers were in the Southeast. On average, there were 37.4 patients per million population and 371 centers. The average center size was 20 patients, and on average 36 percent of all patients were being treated at home. Over the past year the mean age of the dialysis patient population had increased by almost two years, being slightly over 44 years for men and 43 years for women. Recently there had been a significant increase in the male and female populations in the higher age groups and the age groups 60 to 65 and 65 to 70-plus years had increased by more than 100 percent over the previous year. The predominant age group overall was the group aged 40 to 59 years. Men comprised 64 percent of the dialysis population and were being treated 40 percent in centers and 24 percent at home; women comprised 36 percent of the population and were being treated 24 percent in centers and 12 percent at home. Slightly more than 98 percent of the population was treated by hemodialysis, the remainder being on peritoneal dialysis.

The program finished with reports from the chairmen of the working sessions. The chairman of the cannula session was Surgeon George Thomas from Seattle.

CHAPTER 36

# The First Full Year of the Medicare End-Stage Renal Disease Program 1974

———

DURING THE YEAR, THE NUMBER of dialysis patients increased steadily while the issues with Medicare reimbursement continued. Medicare was planning to develop a program of networks throughout the country to follow and promote effective coordination of its end-stage renal disease (ESRD) program, believing that integration of hospitals and other health facilities into organized networks was the most effective way to assure delivery of needed ESRD care.

THE 11TH ANNUAL MEETING OF NORTHWEST KIDNEY CENTER'S BOARD OF TRUSTEES WAS HELD IN THE AUDITORIUM OF THE WASHINGTON ATHLETIC CLUB ON FEBRUARY 21, 1974, CALLED TO ORDER AT 7:40 P.M. AND PRESIDED OVER BY PRESIDENT DENVER GINSEY.
Proxy votes of Trevor Bailey, Monte L. Bean, Willis Campbell, Mrs. Loretta Chin, John Dare, Joseph Eschbach, MD, Trevor Evans, Gerald Grinstein, Lisle R. Guernsey, John Kennedy, MD, Jack Larson, Allan Lobb, MD, Tom Marr, MD, Jerry P. Pendras, MD, Richard Philbrick, DDS, Belding H. Scribner, MD, Thomas Seifert and T. Evans Wyckoff were recorded and a quorum was established.

James W. Haviland, MD, read the report of the Nominating Committee and it was moved and seconded that the following individuals be re-elected to three-year terms as members of the Board of Trustees, terms to expire in 1977: Richard E. Bangert; M. L. Bean; James Burnell, MD; Ross Cunningham; Gerald Grinstein; Lisle R. Guernsey; James W. Haviland, MD; Tom Marr, MD; William McKee, MD; Jerry P. Pendras, MD; Representative Charles Savage; Belding H. Scribner, MD; James Sullivan; H. Sedge Thomson; and Liem Tuai. There were no nominations from the floor and the motion passed unanimously.

It was moved and seconded that the following individuals be elected to one-year terms as members of the Board of Trustees, terms to expire in 1975: Father R. J. Queen, Yakima County Fund; George Wallace, Snohomish County Fund; Virgil Mahaffey, Northwest Kidney Center Patient Association; and Marilyn Dean, Stewardess Emeritus Association. There were no nominations from the floor and the motion passed unanimously.

It was moved and seconded that the following individuals be elected as officers of the Board of Trustees: vice president, James W. Phillips; secretary, Liem Tuai; and treasurer, Robert P. Burns. There were no nominations from the floor and the motion passed unanimously

It was moved and seconded that the following individuals be reelected to the Executive Committee, terms to expire in 1977: Richard E. Bangert and James W. Haviland, MD.

It was moved and seconded the following individual be elected to the Executive Committee, term to expire in 1977: Liem Tuai.

Ginsey called for nominations from the floor for these latter appointments and there were none. The motions passed unanimously.

There was no old business and there was no new business.


PRESIDENT'S REPORT, DENVER GINSEY

Ginsey reported that the previous year had probably been the most eventful year for the Northwest Kidney Center since its inception. The reason for this was the implementation of Public Law 92-603, which provided Medicare coverage for most patients requiring dialysis or kidney transplantation. As a result, the whole operation of the Center was in the process of changing and there were a number of problems that had not yet been resolved. The first of these was merely getting the program going and receiving payment from the government. At the time of this meeting, the Center was owed more than a quarter of a million dollars, much of it from Medicare. But the problem went much deeper than the mere money coming from Medicare, because until this was received the Center was also unable to bill the co-insurers, the health insurance companies with which the Center had had such a good relationship in the past, and the state of Washington, which had been so helpful to the Center. NKC had also been struggling with the Social Security Administration, to have it accept some of the aspects of the Center's program, which differed from those of most other programs in the United States and yet were responsible for our excellent results. Unfortunately, for one reason or another, we just could not get decisions out of Baltimore, this despite the close relationship between the Center and the senior staff of HEW Region X (our region here), and also with some of the senior staff in Baltimore. Hopefully these problems would be resolved in the very near future.

Also, during the last year there had been many changes in the staff of the Center. Mr. Terry Pollard, who had been associated with the Center for some 10 years in many different capacities, resigned from his post as administrator to take up a senior position with the Drake-Willock Company in Portland, Oregon. Christopher Blagg, MD, became medical and executive director and Mr. Harold Rathman, previously the chief accountant, became business manager. Mr. Huey Powell became chief accountant and Ms. Cynthia Shadle became head of the patient financing department when Mr. John Morrow left. On the medical side, a third physician, Daniel Franklin, MD, was added to the staff and a number of new nurses and technicians also joined.

The number of patients continued to increase, and the increase in the current year was more than 10% over that of the previous year. This resulted in more dialysis treatments and some general expansion of the program. In order to handle the increasing number of patients, the television training program, which had attracted so much attention in the past, had been revised and shortened even further. This would help improve the efficiency of the Center.

The transplant program had continued to be successful, with transplantation now being performed in University, Swedish and Virginia Mason hospitals. Patient results from all three hospitals were good so far, being considerably better than the national average. Nevertheless, with the increasing number of patients, there was a continuing need to obtain cadaveric kidneys for transplantation for those patients who did not have a living related donor. During the coming year the plan was to devote more effort to encouraging the public and the medical profession to think of transplantation and to refer kidneys to the Center.

The Center had maintained its close association with the research of Dr. Scribner and the Division of Nephrology at the University of Washington. A number of the Center's patients were cooperating by being subjects for research, which was aimed at providing more efficient and possibly shorter dialysis. These results would benefit all patients.

The Center continued its strong emphasis on home dialysis with more than 85 percent of current dialysis patients being treated at home. The results of this program spoke for itself. The Center's patients were the most enthusiastic advocates of home dialysis in the United States.

During the past year the Center had been cooperating with the Department of Biostatistics at the University of Washington to develop a data collection system. As a result of this, a new system was in the process of being tried out and should permit more accurate data retrieval and forecasting of future trends. A system devised for the Center by Dr. Kirby Cooper of the Department of Biostatistics had already attracted national interest by forecasting that by 1984, 10 years hence, there might be 55,000 patients in the United States living on dialysis and transplantation.

Last year the Center received funds from the National Institutes of Health and the Regional Medical Program for a study of the use of peritoneal dialysis, for developing a program for training staff from the region, and for developing the data collection system. In addition, the Boeing

Employees Good Neighbors Fund continued its generous support to maintain the patient training program.

Turning to individuals, several of the staff had been involved in national activities during the last year. Marcia Clark, RN, had been working with the American Association of Nephrology Nurses and Technicians (AANNT), Sawyer had been active on the committee that organized the annual Chronic Dialysis and Transplant Forum, and Blagg was vice president of the Renal Physicians Association. However, the success of the Center really depended on the efforts of the nurses and technicians, the staff in the business office and the fund office, and the other administrative staff.

It is difficult to say why the dialysis and transplant program in Washington State had worked so well for so many years. Probably because the NKC, by coordinating so many aspects of the treatment of these patients, had been helpful and responsive to the needs of the patients, the community physicians and the specialists involved in these treatments. Only those who had seen similar programs elsewhere in the country could realize the chaos that can occur without some central organization. It was this organizational role of the Center, together with the dedication of all the staff, that was the keystone of the success of Northwest Kidney Center.

What of the future? Simply put – it could be more of the same. However, the Center needs more office space, more space for dialysis, more kidneys for transplantation, more money, and so on. But even prior to Medicare, we were not turning down patients who were medically suitable for treatment. We were anticipating expansion.

However, there were two things needed, which the board could help us with. One of these was a continuing source of money. The Medicare program would probably provide some 60 percent of the total budget for the Center and so there would be continuing need for state monies, monies from patients' insurance and an effective fund drive. We had been successful in all these areas this past year, and we hope to be so again in the future. In addition, the Center also needed the public's generosity in terms of the provision of more kidneys for transplantation. This too was something the board would be hearing more about in the future.

PRESENTATION OF AWARDS, R. CLINTON HOWARD

Howard presented certificates of appreciation to the following groups and individuals: Mrs. Connie Anderson, State Project Board, Beta Sigma Phi Sorority; Mrs. Hazel Slater, State Project Board, Beta Sigma Phi Sorority; the Stewardess Emeritus Association (accepted by Mrs. Pat Berger); Mr. Ed Jerome, West Seattle Eagles and Auxiliary; Mrs. Ann Jerome, Kidney Board, Washington State Eagles and Auxiliary; Mrs. Lois Matlock, Grand Royal Matron, Washington State Amaranth; Miss Letie Batchelder, Grand Worthy Advisor, Washington-Idaho Rainbow Girls; Mrs. Joella Morrison, King County Police Wives Auxiliary; Mrs. Jo Anne Danielson, president, West Seattle Auxiliary of NKC; Mrs. Kathryn Kennedy, president, Queen City Auxiliary of NKC; and Mrs. Connie Anderson in the place of Mrs. Jo Burrell, Antique Show, Beta Sigma Phi Sorority.

A plaque of appreciation was presented to the Boeing Employees Good Neighbor Fund and accepted by Mrs. Grace D. Pierce, vice president.

Those presented certificates but unable to attend were: Shakey's Pizza Parlors; Somerset and Greenacres Auxiliaries of NKC; and Jack Larson, retiring board member from Yakima.

The meeting adjourned at 8:18 p.m. following a brief question and answer period.

THE FIRST MEETING OF THE EXECUTIVE COMMITTEE WAS HELD JANUARY 25, 1974, PRESIDED OVER BY PRESIDENT DENVER GINSEY AND ATTENDED BY LONGTIME PATIENT VIRGIL MAHAFFEY.

MEDICARE ISSUES

The Center's exception request and the related questionnaire had been completed and returned to Baltimore. Word had been received that approval or disapproval would be decided in February, although it might not be made effective until April 1974. A patient who was a personal friend of Senator

Henry Jackson had talked with him about applying pressure on NKC's behalf if needed to get a timely decision.

Major problems continued with the billing of Medicare and it was becoming most unlikely that Medicare would pay anything toward support of the dialysis helper program at the Center. However, the Secretary of HEW had agreed to look at the use of home dialysis helpers during the course of the year and the Center had proposed itself as a test location for establishing policies for such a program.

In accordance with the expected Medicare regulations, the Patient Admissions Committee would have to be revised. It seemed likely the committee would have to consist of three physicians, one of whom would be a transplant surgeon. At the present time Blagg was acting for the Patient Admissions Committee unless a serious problem applicant required the decision of the whole committee. Plans for the future organization of the committee would be developed.

Another serious problem for NKC since the beginning of the Medicare ESRD program was that with universal entitlement the number of patients was steadily increasing, resulting in the need for more staff and more space for dialysis. A four- or five-bed space on the first floor of Eklind Hall had been suggested but had not yet been developed.

Patient activities through January 1974

Sawyer reported that the Center's total patient population was 370 as of January 24, 1974. Eighteen patients had been accepted since the beginning of December 1973; 8 had completed home dialysis training; 21 home dialysis patients had been retrained on new dialyzers; 4 patients had received kidney transplants, 3 being cadaveric transplants and 1 being a transplant from a related donor; and 7 deaths had occurred, 2 of them Alaska patients. Sawyer noted that the death rate might be higher as a result of the Center now accepting patients into the treatment program with less rigid medical selection criteria than prior to the Medicare program.

Even though there would be fewer training dialyses in January because of the closure of the training unit for a week in order to revise the patient training program, by the end of the month there would be an increase in the total number of dialyses at the Center.

With the availability of new smaller disposable dialyzers, the Center was changing from using the large flat plate Kiil dialyzers in the Center and at home to using these new dialyzers. Instructions were being developed for their use and reuse and techniques were being simplified, as was the vocabulary used in training patients for home hemodialysis to help them better understand pertinent information. It was anticipated that this revised training program might be shorter for patients of average and above average intelligence and yet at the same time would assist the patient of below average intelligence in acquiring basic information.

In terms of nurses, the University of Washington nurse who had been offered the position of training supervisor had turned this down. No other outside person was being considered for this position because the Regional Medical Program would provide salary for the supervisor only through June 1974. Because of the increasing number of dialyses being performed, the Center would be hiring two new nurses to handle dialysis during the evening shift.


PATIENT ADMISSIONS THROUGH JANUARY 1974

Blagg reported that since the Executive Committee meeting at the end of November 1973, 19 patients had been approved: eight females and 11 males. Ages ranged from 23 to 72 with the average age being 45 years.


THE REGIONAL MEDICAL PROGRAM (RMP)

Blagg reported that the Regional Medical Program that had supported development of kidney retrieval programs and tissue typing for transplantation at NKC and elsewhere and provided financial support for training staff, would continue until at least July 1, 1974 as a result of the release of some impounded funds for fiscal year 1974. From these funds, NKC had been promised about $9,000 to support training staff and $4,000 for computerization of statistics. However, late in 1974, Congress passed the National Health Planning and Resources Development Act of 1975 (Public Law 93 – 641), which combined into one local organization the functions formerly carried out by the RMP and various other programs. In consequence, over the next year, the RMP was phased out of existence.

### LIMITED CARE DIALYSIS

The Medicare program had introduced the term "limited care dialysis" to cover routine dialysis in a dialysis unit, either in-hospital or as a freestanding unit. The Center differed from most programs in that it had a much larger proportion of patients on home dialysis, and Seattle experience to date had shown that only a small number of patients were unable to dialyze at home because of social or other reasons. However, this was changing with the changing patient population and so a request had been made to Lobb to use part of the first floor of Eklind Hall as a limited care facility and this was being considered.

The dialysis unit in the basement of Eklind Hall would also be regarded by many as a limited care unit. Remodeling was going to be necessary there in order to link up with the tunnel providing access to Swedish hospital under the street nearby (Broadway) and also to make better use of the space in the basement. Plans for this were being developed. It was noted that if major space requirements were needed in the future, the possibility of building out on the roof of the Center might also have to be considered.

### LONG-RANGE PLANNING

Blagg reported he had contacted Dr. Robert Leahy and Haviland on the subject of future requirements for dialysis and transplantation facilities in the state of Washington. State and Social Security Administration officials would be helping determine the appropriate locations for dialysis and transplantation and NKC was providing them with this information.

## FINANCES

The Finance Committee had met earlier in the month and Rathman had reported that the contract with Cascade Medical Leasing Company had been approved. He had then contacted eight of the 10 members of the Executive Committee, all of whom also approved the lease plan. The two nonvoting members were out of town at the time. The cost to the patient remained identical with the previous NKC rental system, and NKC still earned the 10 percent markup to cover billing and administration costs. This new leasing plan allowed better cash flow since it was not tied up in the outright purchase of dialysis equipment.

Rathman also reported that the billing backlog resulting from waiting for Medicare to approve or disapprove the Center's exception request had resulted in slow movement of funds. There was $450,000 worth of bills either in the process of being prepared or sitting at NKC's intermediary, Blue Cross. To date, $50,000 had been received from Medicare, but NKC was doing well in this regard when compared with many other facilities.

Powell presented the financial statements ending December 31, 1973. There were three points of interest: 1) the total cash and short-term investments for the period ending December 31, 1973 were less than for the period ending December 31, 1972, due to the difficulties with Medicare that had been discussed previously; 2) the accounts receivable net allowance for doubtful accounts was $100,000 and the accounts receivable total for December 31, 1973 was greater than the total for the previous year, again due to the backlog of billing and the slow movement of funds with reference to the Medicare process; 3) the Statement of Revenue, Expenses, and Changes in Fund Balances for the six months ending December 31, 1973 showed that net revenues for the six months ended December 31, 1973 was down almost 25 percent from the previous year's total. The reasons for this decrease in net income were the added cost of disposable dialyzers now being used by the Center and the increase in Center activities and staff resulting from the increasing patient numbers.

## STATE FINANCES

At this time it appeared likely that the 1974-75 budget request to the state of Washington was likely to be granted.

## FUND DRIVE REPORT

Howard reported that the fund drive was approximately 20 percent ahead of last year at this time and that Medicare did not appear to have affected contributions to the fund drive. The cost per $1.00 raised was $0.11. Three large donations received before the end of 1973 totaled $35,000 and two of these were unsolicited. The goal of $350,000 for the year appeared possible.

Howard also reported that Mr. Gary Meisner, the current year's fund drive chairman, had resigned effective January 1, 1974 to take a position at the Everett Trust and Savings.

## THE NEXT MEETING OF THE EXECUTIVE COMMITTEE WAS HELD ON MARCH 29, 1974 IN THE B-FLOOR CONFERENCE ROOM OF SWEDISH HOSPITAL. IN THE ABSENCE OF BOTH PRESIDENT GINSEY AND VICE PRESIDENT PHILLIPS, TREASURER ROBERT BURNS PRESIDED OVER THE MEETING.

## THE LATEST ON THE MEDICARE ESRD PROGRAM

Blagg reported that NKC's exception request had been granted by Medicare and the dialysis reimbursement rates that had been requested by the Center were cut by something less than 2 percent.

New regulations on the "network" concept were being developed and would shortly be circulated.

MEDICAL-RELATED ACTIVITIES THROUGH MARCH 28

Sawyer reported that the total patient census as of March 28 was 380. There were 37 outpatients; 210 on hemodialysis; 22 on peritoneal dialysis; 5 limited care patients, 4 of whom were dialyzing at the Coach House; and 106 patients with a functioning kidney transplant.

Since the January Executive Committee meeting, 19 persons had been accepted into NKC's program; 25 patients had completed home dialysis training, 22 on home hemodialysis and three on home peritoneal dialysis; 25 patients had been retrained on the new disposable dialyzers and, in addition, 4 patients had received an accumulated total of eight weeks of retraining with the Kiil dialyzers; 7 patients had received kidney transplants, 6 cadaveric transplants and 1 related donor transplant (one of the former was suffering a severe rejection and another was expected to go back on hemodialysis); and 9 deaths had occurred.

The total number of dialyses performed in the Center in the month of January was 512, consisting of 418 in-center dialyses, 71 training dialyses and 23 limited care dialyses. The corresponding numbers of dialyses performed during the month of February was 481, consisting of 368 in-center dialyses, 95 training dialyses and 18 limited care dialyses. The total number of dialyses for the period March 1 through March 28 was 506, consisting of 393 in-center dialyses, 101 training dialyses and 12 limited care dialyses. The increased Center activity was due to the increased number of older patients since the beginning of the Medicare program as these patients generally required longer stabilization periods and also tended to require more backup care for both medical and surgical reasons. Also, on occasion, there was need for prolonged backup dialysis following rejection of a kidney transplant.

Because of the increased patient load, NKC would be increasing patient care staff by 1 to 2 persons per shift and another shift would probably be opened on Sunday mornings. It had also been deemed necessary to maintain a highly professional patient care staff due to the less rigid medical selection of patients, even though, technically, dialysis was becoming simpler. Unfortunately, several members of the patient care staff were considering resigning and would take with them years of experience and valuable knowledge.

As a result of the increased population and the increasing number of social problems, the Center had hired a caseworker to assist the social worker in his duties. In addition, several persons were being interviewed for the position of nurse educator but a suitably qualified person had yet to be found.

## PATIENT ADMISSIONS THROUGH MARCH 28

Blagg reported that since the last Executive Committee meeting 23 persons had been approved: nine males and 14 females. Ages ranged from a four-year-old male to a 72-year-old male; the average age was 43. Recently the average age of persons approved for treatment had risen from 35 to 46 years of age due to the fact that older patients and those with a number of complicating conditions were being approved for treatment (as was stated previously).

## LIMITED CARE

Blagg reported that Scribner had offered the facilities at the Coach House to be used by NKC as its limited care unit. A committee consisting of Ginsey, Eschbach, Blagg, Haviland, John McCormack, MD, and Richard Paton, MD, had been formed to discuss this possibility.

Meanwhile, an application for $70,000 to construct a seven-bed limited care unit in the Eklind Hall lobby had been submitted to the Boeing Employees Good Neighbor Fund for approval. NKC had been given permission to build a limited care unit in the lobby of Eklind Hall and the architect had drawn up the plans but, as yet, construction had not started.

## RENAL PHYSICIANS ASSOCIATION

The organization formed by nephrologists in July 1973 as the Physicians for Renal Replacement Therapy (see previous chapter) had been renamed the Renal Physicians Association. The objective of the organization was to help renal physicians work with problems concerning health care for persons with renal disease on a nationwide basis.

Blagg had attended several meetings of the RPA as vice president and a member of the Board of Trustees. His attendance at two of these meetings had been charged to the Center since the RPA did not have an overabundance of funds at the time. As a result, Bangert made a motion to allow the Center to cover Blagg's expenses for the past and future meetings of the RPA. Tuai seconded the motion and it was passed unanimously.

FINANCIAL ACTIVITIES

The state Division of Vocational Rehabilitation (DVR) and the Department of Social and Health Services (DSHS) had approved a plan allowing NKC to pre-bill for DVR and DSHS funds before completing billings to Medicare. This plan was instigated because of the lengthy turn-around time caused by Medicare and it would allow NKC to use DVR and DSHS funds while waiting for Medicare to pay.

A letter had been received from John Beare, MD, director of the Department of Social and Health Services, Health Services Division, to assure the Center that an additional $245,000 had been allotted by the Division of Vocational Rehabilitation for kidney treatment. In addition, DSHS was now covering kidney treatment for up to $45,000 using Title XIX funds. (Today, title XIX of the Social Security Act is administered by the Center for Medicare and Medicaid Services and provides federal grants to the states for Medicaid and some other medical assistance programs). The state expected that at this time no change would be necessary in the Center's billing procedures or its patient acceptance criteria.

FUND DRIVE

Howard reported that the fund drive was 10 percent ahead of the same time the previous year and it was expected that the current fund drive would reach a total of at least $327,000 by the end of the year, based on what was known to be coming in. The cost of fundraising was between $0.13 and $0.14 per $1.00 raised, one of the lowest fundraising costs in the Seattle area for a major fundraising charity.

## THE NEXT MEETING OF THE EXECUTIVE COMMITTEE WAS HELD IN THE B-FLOOR CONFERENCE ROOM OF SWEDISH HOSPITAL ON APRIL 26, 1974 AND PRESIDED OVER BY PRESIDENT DENVER GINSEY.

Among the guests attending were Albert Babb, PhD, engineering professor from the University of Washington, George Irvine, MD, from the Division of Nephrology at the university and Virgil Mahaffey, a patient.

### LIMITED CARE

The first item of business was a discussion led by Scribner and Sawyer regarding the proposed sites for the Center's construction of a limited care facility: 1) the lobby of Eklind Hall; and 2) an apartment adjacent to the now existing Coach House dialysis facility of the University of Washington. Summaries of the proposals for the two facilities and the advantages of each had been distributed prior to the Executive Committee meeting.

Scribner presented the three main reasons for establishing a limited care facility at the Coach House. These were:

a) Establishing the limited care facility at the University of Washington Coach House would create a unique opportunity to innovate. The University of Washington had in the past set the precedent for advancement in the dialysis field and wished to continue to do so;

b) The limited care facility could be used as a field testing unit for improving dialysis equipment and/or inventing new ideas for equipment and would enhance the University of Washington's already established reputation. Since it would be situated next to the now existing Coach House, which was a research unit, safety proven innovations could be further tested in the limited care facility;

c) The University of Washington Hospital could not run a teaching dialysis center because there were no longer chronic dialysis patients there. At the present time, the acute dialysis service was virtually non-existent, and establishing a limited care facility at the Coach House would provide dialysis patients needed for teaching and research.

Babb, professor of chemical and nuclear engineering at the University of Washington and a colleague of Scribner's, elaborated upon the research aspects of the three points Scribner had presented. However, Babb also stated that he would gladly work at either site to develop new and/or better techniques and equipment for improving patient care.

Sawyer presented several reasons for establishing a limited care facility on the premises now housing the Northwest Kidney Center:

a) The architect had been contacted and had been requested to draw up plans for the necessary remodeling before NKC personnel even knew the University of Washington was interested in establishing a limited care facility;

b) A proposal for establishing a limited care facility and a request of $70,000 to build the facility had been submitted to the Boeing Employees Good Neighbor Fund before NKC personnel knew the University of Washington was interested in it establishing a limited care facility;

c) Northwest Kidney Center had hired a nurse for the limited care facility and had begun her training before NKC personnel knew of the University of Washington's interest;

d) Northwest Kidney Center had an efficient location as it was within walking distance of Swedish Hospital, and when the Cancer Center tunnel was completed and in use, accessibility to both buildings would be even easier;

e) Northwest Kidney Center had already obtained the necessary space to construct a seven-bed limited care unit, and the availability of services from NKC personnel, Swedish Hospital personnel and private practitioners was extremely advantageous.

During the lengthy discussion that followed, Campbell suggested a geographic breakdown of the patients eligible for treatment in a limited care facility might someday show the need for construction of two limited care facilities: one at the University of Washington and one at the Center. However, at the present time there was no need for two units as only 5 to 10 percent of the total local patient population required this type of care.

After prolonged discussion, Campbell made a motion to establish the limited care facility on the premises of Northwest Kidney Center, with the stipulation that Center personnel go out of their way to cooperate fully with the University of Washington and Scribner in an effort to solve his problems. The motion was seconded by Elmer Nordstrom and passed unanimously. After passage of the motion, Sawyer announced that Blagg, who was out of town that day, had requested that the Long-range Planning Committee meet in the very near future in order to assist Scribner in solving his problem.

CENTER ACTIVITIES

Sawyer reported that the total patient census on April 25 was 383. There were 220 patients on hemodialysis of whom 191 were at home, 3 were in training, 21 were dialyzing at the Center and 5 were on limited care dialysis, 4 of whom were being treated at the Coach House. Twenty-two patients were being treated by peritoneal dialysis, of whom 19 were at home, 2 were in training and 1 was dialyzing at the Center. And there were 100 transplanted patients and 41 outpatients who had not yet started on treatment.

Since the last Executive Committee meeting six patients had been accepted into the Center's program. Only one new patient started treatment, five patients had completed home hemodialysis training and one patient had completed training for home peritoneal dialysis. Nine patients had been retrained on new dialyzers. There were now 12 patients on limited care dialysis, excluding the 4 patients being dialyzed at the Coach House. During the month, no patients were transplanted even though there were several potential kidney retrievals, all of which eventually fell through. There were four transplant rejections. There were three deaths.

### PATIENT ADMISSIONS COMMITTEE REPORT
Sawyer reported that since the last Executive Committee meeting 11 patients had been approved for treatment: six males and five females. Ages ranged from 20 to 63 years with only one patient, the 20-year-old, being under the age of 40. The mean age was 47.5 years.

### FINANCE COMMITTEE MEETING REPORT
Rathman reported that more Medicare payments were now coming in. He also reported that at the recent Finance Committee meeting the main topic of discussion resulted in a motion being passed with reference to instigating a rotation of Northwest Kidney Center's banking business, especially to those banks that might have contributed time and/or funds to NKC's programs.

### FUND DRIVE
Howard reported that the fund drive was slowing down but was still approximately 15 percent ahead of the previous year's fund drive at the same time. The current total contributions stood at about $270,000, with another $214,000 in various stages of coming into the drive. One item in the $214,000 figure was a $90,000 bequest, which would be finalized in three-to-four months.

THE NEXT MEETING OF THE EXECUTIVE COMMITTEE OF THE BOARD OF TRUSTEES WAS HELD MAY 31, 1974 IN THE B-FLOOR CONFERENCE ROOM OF SWEDISH HOSPITAL, WITH VICE PRESIDENT JAMES PHILLIPS PRESIDING IN THE ABSENCE OF PRESIDENT DENVER GINSEY.

Guests included Irvine from the Division of Nephrology at the University of Washington, Lobb from Swedish Hospital and Mahaffey, a patient.

STATUS OF THE MEDICARE END-STAGE RENAL DISEASE PROGRAM

Blagg reported that at this time the Medicare program was involved in three principal areas of planning: 1) data collection on a national basis; 2) establishing guidelines for peer review in judging the quality of treatment in various programs; and 3) development of the proposed treatment networks.

Northwest Kidney Center already provided patient treatment but also served regionally in an organizational role as coordinator of the Northwest network of treatment facilities. Hopefully, these two roles could be continued in the future without interposing further bureaucracy.

LIMITED CARE

Blagg reported having met with Scribner following the Executive Committee's decision to place a limited care facility at the Northwest Kidney Center. Blagg planned that the Long-range Planning Committee would meet with Scribner in July to discuss ways in which NKC could assist his program.

Before the limited care facility could be established, applications to Comprehensive Health Planning at the state level and to the Bureau of Health Insurance had to be approved. The Boeing Employees Good Neighbor Fund had refrained from acting upon NKC's request for $70,000 to build a limited care unit until state Comprehensive Health Planning approval was obtained. Blagg estimated that it would be some three to six months before actual building could take place.

Sawyer had also met with Scribner from the University of Washington, Eschbach from Swedish Hospital and Burton Orme, MD, from Virginia Mason Hospital to discuss patient admission to the Center's future limited care facility. He had also met with Eschbach with reference to planning to provide an attractive and useful limited care unit.

## MEDICAL ACTIVITIES THROUGH MAY 1974

Sawyer reported that the total patient census as of May 30, 1974 was 388. There were 39 outpatients not yet started on treatment. Twenty-six hemodialysis patients and one peritoneal dialysis patient were dialyzing in-center and there were six limited care patients, of whom four were being treated at the Coach House. Eight patients were in home dialysis training: six for home hemodialysis and two in peritoneal dialysis training. Currently, there were 209 patients on home dialysis, consisting of 189 on home hemodialysis and 20 on home peritoneal dialysis. There were 99 patients living with a functioning kidney transplant.

Since the April 26 Executive Committee meeting, 14 new patients had been accepted into the Center's program; 16 patients had started treatment, 12 on hemodialysis and four on peritoneal dialysis; six patients had completed home hemodialysis training, two had completed home peritoneal dialysis training and three patients had been retrained; one patient had received a related donor transplant at University Hospital and two patients had rejected their transplanted kidneys, one at Madigan Hospital and one at Swedish Hospital. There had been nine deaths since last Executive Committee meeting: six from cardiac causes, two from strokes and one due to multiple factors.

The total number of dialyses per month during the last five months ranged between 481 in February and 579, the last in the month of May when there were many new patients and a large number of backup dialyses.

## PATIENT ADMISSIONS COMMITTEE REPORT

Blagg reported that since the last Executive Committee meeting, 14 individuals had been approved for the Center's program: eight males and six females. Ages ranged from 14 to 77, the average age being 46 years.

## PERSONNEL

Sawyer requested Phillips to request that Ginsey write a letter on behalf of the Board of Trustees to Ms. Charlene Sowles, RN, a head nurse who was leaving the Center and to thank her for contributions to Northwest Kidney Center.

He also reported that Dan Franklin, MD, NKC's first full-time staff physician, was planning to leave the Center.

## FUND DRIVE REPORT

Howard reported that for the first time in the current fiscal year the fund drive trailed the previous year's total at the same time. He pointed out that patient designated funds were down, due to the fact that emphasis on fundraising for specific patients had been redirected toward fundraising for counties. Also, the restricted funds were down because NKC was still waiting for the Boeing Employees Good Neighbors Fund's decision as to what portion of the requested $70,000, if any, would be allotted to NKC to build the limited care facility.

Howard anticipated additional monies totaling $137,000, and if all came in before June 30 the fund drive total would exceed $400,000. The goal had been $350,000.

Howard also indicated that since 1966, 633 contributors of $100 or more had donated in excess of $1 million to the kidney fund. He also stated that 90 percent of the donations came from 10 percent of the contributors.

Rathman requested adoption of the following resolution so that NKC could continue to transfer securities that might be donated to the Center:

Resolved, that the president, Denver Ginsey, vice president, James W. Phillips, the treasurer, Robert Burns, or any of them, be and they are hereby authorized to sell, assign and indorse for transfer, certificates representing stocks, bonds or other securities now registered or hereafter registered in the name of this corporation.

Tuai made a motion that the aforesaid resolution be adopted and it was seconded by Campbell. The motion passed unanimously.

## THE NEXT MEETING OF THE EXECUTIVE COMMITTEE WAS HELD ON JUNE 28, 1974 IN THE B-FLOOR CONFERENCE ROOM OF SWEDISH HOSPITAL AND WAS PRESIDED OVER BY VICE PRESIDENT JAMES PHILLIPS IN THE ABSENCE OF PRESIDENT GINSEY.

### THE 1974-75 BUDGET

Burns announced that the Finance Committee had met on the previous day to review the 1974-75 budget. The Finance Committee passed a motion to recommend to the Executive Committee approval of the budget with the stipulation that one item, capital contributions for the year, on the financial sheet entitled Pro Forma Statement of Revenues and Expenses for the Year Ended June 30, 1975 (unaudited), should be changed from $25,000 to $95,000 as the expected Boeing Employees Good Neighbor Fund contribution of $70,000 should appear on this fiscal year's statements.

Burns then asked Rathman to elaborate on specific points of interest throughout the 1974-75 budget. Rathman stated that overall revenues and expenses were expected to increase slightly over the year. However, the equipment and supply costs were expected to stay fairly stable as a direct result of the Center's ability to keep supplier costs to NKC at approximately the same level as the year just ended, with one exception: a 14.3 percent cost increase on one specific dialysis machine.

As stated previously, the impact of limited care was not expected to be felt until approximately the fourth quarter of the fiscal year. This expectation was derived from the fact that the Boeing Employees Good Neighbor Fund would not approve NKC's requested monies until the state Comprehensive Health Planning Commission and the federal Bureau of Quality Assurance had approved and accepted NKC's application to establish a limited care unit. Once final approval was received, the building might begin. The anticipated completion date of the limited care facility now stood at winter 1975.

Rathman stated that for the 1973-74 fiscal year, revenues and expenses exceeded the budget because the large increases in the number of patients had not been anticipated.

It was anticipated that additional personnel would be hired during the coming fiscal year, and the registered nurses were negotiating a new contract so labor costs would increase. However, with the continued public support, the 1974-75 budget would be in balance.

Campbell made a motion that the 1974-75 budget be approved as presented with the understanding that approval would include the $70,000 increase in capital contributions for the year. Burns seconded the motion and the motion passed unanimously.

MEDICAL ACTIVITIES THROUGH JUNE 1974

Sawyer reported that the total patient census for June 27, 1974, was 392 patients. There were 38 outpatients not yet started on dialysis; 229 hemodialysis patients, of whom 24 were dialyzing in-center, 4 were in home hemodialysis training, 6 were in limited care (4 at the Coach House) and 195 were on home hemodialysis. There were 22 peritoneal dialysis patients of whom 1 was in the Center, 1 was training and 20 were on home peritoneal dialysis. In addition, there were 103 patients with functioning kidney transplants.

In the last month, six patients had been accepted into the program. Six patients had started treatment (five on hemodialysis and one peritoneal dialysis) and ten patients had completed home dialysis training, nine on home hemodialysis and one on home peritoneal dialysis. There had been six kidney transplants: two related donor transplants and four cadaveric donor transplants. All transplants were doing well in the early stages but there were two other patients who had rejected their transplanted kidneys. There had been two deaths since the last Executive Committee meeting in patients aged 40 and 53. Monthly figures for the number of dialyses from January through June 27 was 512, 481, 506, 484, 578 (corrected total) and 515.

PERSONNEL

Sawyer reported that the community renal nurse position had now been filled. A registered nurse/medical social worker from Salt Lake City had accepted the position and it would be her responsibility to visit home dialysis patients with the intent to watch for technical service needs, further training requirements and social or medical problems that needed professional attention. She would act as NKC's liaison between the community and local physicians, and she would seek out community social support for dialysis patients.

Franklin, the staff physician, would be leaving in mid-July and a physician from the Mayo Clinic was coming for an interview for the open position.

PATIENT ADMISSIONS COMMITTEE REPORT

In Blagg's absence, Sawyer reported that since the last Executive Committee meeting eight patients had been approved: two males and six females. Ages ranged from 19 to 70, the average age being 50 years.

BOARD RESOLUTION

The Executive Committee resolved that the Pacific National Bank of Washington would be selected as a depository for the funds of Northwest Kidney Center. Designated individuals with access to the account were:

Rathman, business manager; Richard Powell, chief accountant; Blagg, director of Northwest Kidney Centers; Ginsey, president, Board of Trustees; and Burns, treasurer, Board of Trustees. The motion was made by Campbell, seconded by Phillips and passed unanimously.

## FUND DRIVE REPORT

Howard reported that the county funds were about 20 percent over the previous year at the same time due to the fact that county fund donations had been encouraged rather than patient designated funds. The restricted funds were way down because the Center was still waiting for action on the $70,000 Boeing Employees Good Neighbor Fund request.

He also reported that the Washington/Idaho Rainbow Girls Association had raised $28,000 for the Center's patients since February 1974 and the NKC paper drive had produced approximately $5,000.

## THE NEXT MEETING OF THE EXECUTIVE COMMITTEE WAS HELD ON AUGUST 23, 1974, IN THE B-FLOOR CONFERENCE ROOM OF SWEDISH HOSPITAL AND PRESIDED OVER BY PRESIDENT GINSEY.

## PERSONNEL

The first order of business was the formal introduction of Mr. Richard (Rick) Drottz and Mr. Ed Stein. Upon the resignation of Powell, Drottz had assumed NKC's chief accountant responsibilities. Stein had assumed Mr. Jim Anderson's role at University Hospital as Anderson had accepted a position with Methodist Hospital in Rochester, Minnesota.

## LIMITED CARE

Northwest Kidney Center's proposed limited care facility had been approved by all concerned agencies except the state Bureau of Health. Its response was not expected until mid-November. If approval was received, construction would probably not commence until the first of the year. NKC had now received the check in the amount of $70,000 from the Boeing Employees Good Neighbor Fund for the purpose of constructing the limited care facility.

## SOME OF WHAT YOU HAVE ALWAYS WANTED TO KNOW ABOUT MEDICARE BUT WERE AFRAID TO ASK

The planning to divide the country into a number of end-stage renal disease networks was going ahead. It was anticipated that NKC would be in the HEW Region X that consisted of Alaska, Idaho, Washington, Oregon and part of Montana. After the networks were established, among one of their activities would be to set up local medical review boards for the purpose of commenting on and overseeing the appropriateness of treatment recommended for specific patients.

## MEDICAL ACTIVITIES THROUGH AUGUST 1974

Sawyer reported that as of August 22, 1974, the total patient census was 400. This consisted of 38 outpatients awaiting dialysis; 236 hemodialysis patients of whom 209 were at home, 5 were in training for home hemodialysis, 5 were limited care patients (4 at the Coach House) and 17 were currently dialyzing in the Center; there were 21 peritoneal dialysis patients of whom 19 were dialyzing at home, 1 was in training, and 1 was dialyzing in-center; and there were now 105 patients with functioning transplants.

Since the previous Executive Committee meeting in June, 10 persons had been accepted into the NKC's program, 9 patients had started hemodialysis, 15 patients had completed home hemodialysis training and 2 had completed peritoneal dialysis training. There had been 7 kidney transplants since the previous meeting: 2 related donor transplants and 5 cadaveric donor transplants. Ages of the transplanted patients ranged from 9 years to 47 years. Five patients had rejected their transplanted kidneys.

There had been 4 patient deaths since the last Executive Committee meeting, with ages ranging from 27 to 57 years. In July there had been 546 total dialyses and since there had been a decreased input of new patients in the last two months, most of the dialyses consisted of backup dialyses for NKC patients and dialysis for out-of-state visitors.

Sawyer reported that the Center treatment area would be remodeled, painted and generally cleaned up. Mrs. Kay Mahaffey (patient Virgil Mahaffey's wife) would be responsible for the planning and proposed decorations.

PATIENT ADMISSIONS COMMITTEE REPORT

Blagg reported that since the last Executive Committee meeting, 13 individuals had been approved: six males and seven females. Ages ranged from 10 to 71, the average age being 45 years.

FINANCE

Rathman reported that the Finance Committee had met on August 7 for the purpose of reviewing the unaudited statements. Upon completion of the audit, the financial statements were to be presented for approval at the next Executive Committee meeting. Between March 31, 1974 and June 30, 1974, the accounts receivable balance dropped 25 percent. The Medicare payments had at last been coming in regularly and much of the last year had been spent straightening out old accounts receivable that might have been neglected for years, resulting in the 25 percent decrease.

At the last Executive Committee meeting, a board resolution had been adopted giving Rathman, Powell, Blagg, Ginsey and Burns authorization to sign on all NKC bank accounts, with two signatures required in accordance with the bank signature policies and procedures. As Powell had now resigned, the board resolution was reintroduced using authorized positions rather than individual authorized names. The positions were president, treasurer, director, business manager and chief accountant.

Campbell made a motion that the authorized positions be accepted and it was seconded by Nordstrom. The motion passed unanimously.

FUND DRIVE

Howard reported that for the fiscal year ending June 30, 1974, the general fund category totaled $242,810.51, the designated category totaled $64,413.92 and the restricted category totaled $74,000, bringing the total – all contributions – to $381,224.43. Of the restricted funds reported, $70,000 was actually received after the end of the fiscal year and would be reported in the 1975 audited financial statement. However, the funds were applicable to 1973-74 fund drive activity. The 1973-74 fund drive goal had been $350,000.

Howard also reported on the Center's newest promotional activity. KING radio had decided to sponsor a haunted castle during Halloween at the Seattle Center to benefit NKC's patients. It would be constructed on the northwest corner of the Seattle Center grounds and all the building materials and labor had been donated. The haunted castle would run from October 23 through October 31 and admission would be $1.00 per person. It was estimated that between 80,000 and 100,000 persons might "haunt" the haunted castle during the nine-day run. Until public interest was to drop off, this benefit would be a yearly fund.

THE SEMI-ANNUAL BOARD OF TRUSTEES MEETING OF THE NORTHWEST KIDNEY CENTER'S BOARD OF TRUSTEES WAS CALLED TO ORDER AT 6:14 P.M. ON SEPTEMBER 18, 1974, IN THE THIRD-FLOOR AUDITORIUM OF THE SEATTLE FIRST NATIONAL BANK BUILDING BY PRESIDENT DENVER GINSEY.

NORTHWEST KIDNEY CENTER: PAST, PRESENT, FUTURE.
CHRISTOPHER BLAGG, MD

Blagg reminded all that in 1960 Dr. Belding Scribner invented the shunt and that it took a quarter of a million dollars to keep three patients alive.

The success with these first patients established the need for a dialysis center, and Haviland, then president of the King County Medical Society, was approached. As a result, in January 1962, the first out-of-hospital kidney center in the world was established in the basement of Eklind Hall.

At first, funding for patients was a major concern as treatment was extremely costly and very few persons could afford the life-saving treatments. However, with NKC's annual public solicitation for funds and with state support during the most recent three to four years, patient acceptance into NKC's treatment program had not been hindered by funding problems. No medically acceptable applicants in that time had been turned away for lack of funds.

In late 1972, Senators Hartke and Long introduced to Congress an amendment to the Social Security Act, which covered dialysis and kidney transplantation under Medicare. On July 1, 1973, the Medicare End-Stage Renal Disease (ESRD) Program began. At the present time 95 percent of NKC patients were eligible for Medicare, although it did not cover all the costs of treatment, and ongoing state and fund-drive support were still needed.

Along with Medicare coverage came a number of problems affecting particularly the financial arrangements of the Center. However, many of these problems have since been resolved.

In accordance with Medicare regulations, regional networks will be established across the country. Northwest Kidney Center will be in HEW Region X consisting of Washington, Oregon, Alaska, Idaho and Montana.

The Center's future will involve continuing our treatment program much the same, with continuing involvement with the University of Washington and other hospitals and with more involvement in public education.

FUND DRIVE REPORT

Mr. Kirby Torrance, chairman of the Fund Drive Committee and a member of Northwest Kidney Center's Board of Trustees, gave a fund drive report for the year ending June 30, 1974. This was a record year with a total collection of $381,224. He noted that four factors contributed toward reaching this total: Meisner was a good fund drive chairman and had a very fine group of volunteers and solicitors; the public relations program pointed out how important NKC is to good community health care; Howard and his staff did a fantastic job in coordinating and promoting the fund drive; and $70,000 was received from the Boeing Employees Good Neighbor Fund, $28,000 was contributed by the Rainbow Girls and $13,500 was donated by Shakey's Pizza Parlors. These gifts amounted to 30 percent of the total funds raised. Torrance went on to say that this year's fund drive may expect approximately $50,000 from the KING Radio Haunted Castle, $11,000 from sales of Halloween candy by Beta Sigma Phi and bequests totaling about $100,000.

Torrance then introduced Mr. John Gilleland of Safeco as NKC's new fund drive chairman. Gilleland said he was flattered and a little bit worried at being named the new fund drive chairman, but that he had had experience in three different fundraising programs and, since the Kidney Center is a sellable item, he expected a good campaign for the coming year.

Ginsey thanked all the speakers and with no further business to be discussed the meeting was adjourned to the Seattle-First Executive Dining Room on the 45th floor for cocktails and dinner.

## THE NEXT MEETING OF THE EXECUTIVE COMMITTEE WAS HELD ON OCTOBER 25, 1974 IN THE B-FLOOR CONFERENCE ROOM OF SWEDISH HOSPITAL, PRESIDED OVER BY PRESIDENT DENVER GINSEY.

PERSONNEL

The first order of business was an announcement by Ginsey of Rathman's resignation from his position as business manager of Northwest Kidney Center. Rathman had taken a position with VMC Corporation as treasurer. Ginsey thanked Rathman for having done a tremendous job for the Center.

There still had not been a replacement for Franklin, the staff physician. However, there were two possible candidates and one from Tennessee was coming for an interview in mid-November. Meanwhile Dr. Vernon Rice, an Everett nephrologist, was working at NKC two half-days a week to carry some of the load and to gain knowledge and experience of the Center's operation. Rice would be Snohomish County's first nephrologist.

MEDICAL ACTIVITIES THROUGH OCTOBER 1974

Sawyer reported that the total patient census as of the day of the meeting was 445. There were 35 outpatients not yet on treatment; 230 hemodialysis patients of whom 209 were home, 4 were in training, 5 were on limited care dialysis (4 at the Coach House) and 12 patients were dialyzing in-center; there were also 20 peritoneal dialysis patients, 17 of whom were dialyzing at home, 2 were in training and 1 was dialyzing in-center; and there were 160 patients with a functioning kidney transplant.

During the previous four months the monthly number of dialyses were 546, 498, 488 and for October (through October 24) 383. The total number for October was anticipated to be 492.

Since the last Executive Committee meeting in August, 14 persons had been accepted into the program: 2 for training only and 12 patients started treatment, 9 on hemodialysis and 3 on peritoneal dialysis. Fourteen patients completed home hemodialysis training. There had been 12 kidney transplants: 1 related donor and 11 cadaveric donors, with ages ranging from 11 to 51 years with an average age of 34 ½ years. Three of the 12 persons transplanted had received their second transplant and 2 of the 12 had since rejected their transplanted kidneys and 1 was marginal. There had been 10 deaths since the last Executive Committee meeting, including one that had occurred six months earlier and had not been previously known. Ages at death ranged from 25 to 73, with an average of 52 ½ years. Length of time on dialysis ranged from two weeks to seven years-eight months, with an average of 20 months on dialysis before death. Causes of death included one suicide, one auto accident and various medical problems.

NKC was now using the new PhysioControl peritoneal dialysis equipment and had been experiencing some minor problems with this, which were in the process of being resolved. The new equipment was simpler to operate, cheaper to run and required less preparation time, resulting in less chance of an error by the patient. At the present time NKC personnel was developing a new home peritoneal dialysis training program using videotapes.

## Patient Admissions Committee report

Blagg reported that since the last Executive Committee meeting, 15 persons had been approved: 5 males and 10 females. Ages ranged from 6 to 77, the average age being 42 years.

## The University of Washington

Blagg reported that the Long-range Planning Committee had met recently. Present were Haviland, Ginsey, Thomson, Lobb, Eschbach, Scribner, Sawyer, Rathman and Blagg. The meeting discussed the difficulties Scribner was having with the University of Washington dialysis program. The Long-range Planning Committee approved a plan to offer support from the Center for a second renal fellow for at least two years.

Scribner had research funds through 1975-76, but funding beyond that time frame was doubtful, especially since the University of Washington dialysis program had received numerous previous grants. Several ways in which NKC could assist Scribner's dialysis program in the future included: 1) NKC could make a cash contribution to research; 2) NKC and the Coach House dialysis unit could be housed under the same roof; and/or 3) the NKC public fund drive could be slanted more toward research, since government funds would now be paying for the majority of patient care. It was planned to have an ongoing dialogue with the university to see where NKC and the university program could have mutual benefits.

FINANCES

The Finance Committee had met on the previous day and one topic of discussion was investment guidelines. It was decided that security investment decisions should be made jointly by the NKC business manager and the treasurer of the Board of Trustees or his or her designee.

Thompson, Kittoe and King, a respected Seattle accounting firm, was the accountant for Northwest Kidney Center. Its management letter was reviewed and all recommendations were implemented except one, as it was felt to be unnecessary in the present-day situation to implement the recommendation requiring two persons to open the mail and to record cash receipts. Rathman pointed out that actual cash receipts were very minimal. The Finance Committee felt it was not necessary to implement this recommendation at this time.

Rathman had reported that Mr. Windy King had left Thompson, Kittoe and King after completing NKC's audit to take up the position of controller of Lang Manufacturing Company. Mr. Jim Thompson would probably become involved again within NKC's accounting details as he had been two and more years earlier. He proceeded to discuss the June 30, 1974 auditors report and stated that the results were good and fairly predictable.

Rathman referred to the Comparative Statement of Revenues, Expenses, and Changes in Fund Balances where net revenues for the year of $248,437 compared to last year's net revenue of $115,932. A lower net revenue was predicted for the current year as a result of staffing and other activities having caught up to the demand for services.

He also referred to the Comparative Statement of Revenues, Expenses, and Changes in Fund Balances in order to introduce a recommendation the Finance Committee had made to the Executive Committee for approval. The recommendation was to transfer $200,000 from the General Fund to the Patient Care Fund for the purpose of meeting the long-term responsibilities NKC would have to patients for their care. Rathman asked for a resolution to authorize the transfer of funds and Burns so moved, Phillips seconded and the motion passed unanimously.

Rathman pointed out that accounts receivable had gone up approximately 67 percent since June 30, 1973. Contributing factors included a 20 to 25 percent increase in the number of patient accounts now being processed as compared to the previous year, and the implementation of the Medicare program, which had included a built-in time lag in turnaround time. This latter issue was caused by monthly Medicare billing and having to wait to bill the secondary insurance sources until the Medicare payment had been received.

The present incoming monies provided for patient care were approximately as follows: 55 percent from Medicare; 25 percent from commercial insurance carriers; 10 percent from the state of Washington; and 10 percent from the public fund drive. The 1974-75 budget was now close to $3 million.

Drottz then presented the unaudited September 30, 1974 quarterly financial statements. He referred to Statement of Revenue, Expenses, and Changes in Fund Balances for the three months ended September 30, 1974 (unaudited), pointing out that under the column "Total All Funds," September 30, 1974, net revenue for three months was $21,057. There had been an increase in revenues and an accompanying increase in expenses over the same quarter in 1973. Short-term investments had also increased. Receivables were down $15,000 from June 30, 1974, and the goal was to have $700,000 as a workable balance. Liabilities had not changed significantly from September 30, 1973 or June 30, 1974. The quarter's results generally showed the Center was operating favorably in relation to the 1974-75 budget.

FUND DRIVE

Howard reported the fund drive was running 20 percent ahead of the previous year in undesignated monies. He had knowledge of an additional $165,000 coming in within the next few months. A total of 25,000 Tootsie Roll banks sold at $1.00 per bank would net NKC $0.45 on each bank sold, or approximately $11,000. He also reported that the haunted castle being promoted by KING Radio had experienced an initially low attendance but it was anticipated that this would increase appreciably in the weekend before Halloween.

## THE 1974 ANNUAL MEETING OF THE ASAIO

This year only two papers from Seattle were presented.

The first paper was a preliminary report on the clinical impact of residual kidney function on dialysis time by Drs. Milutinovic, Strand, Casaretto, Follette, Babb and Scribner from the University of Washington. It was only recently that the effect of residual kidney function had been considered in planning dialysis schedules. However, the residual nephrons work continuously for 160 hours/week and may pass middle molecular weight substances much more efficiently than the dialyzer, and so the potential importance of residual renal function needs to be considered. In order to test this, they reduced weekly dialysis time in 15 stable chronic dialysis patients, the time being reduced in proportion to the amount of residual kidney function. The object was to show a correlation between the minimum amount of dialysis and amount of residual renal function. To do this it was necessary to reduce time to a point where some evidence of underdialysis became evident but this only happened in three of the 15 subjects.

Predialysis concentrations of urea and creatinine serve as indices for removal of small molecular weight toxins, and the investigators developed a ratio called the dialysis index ($D_1$) representing the weekly amount of substances with a molecular weight of 1500 removed during dialysis and residual kidney function divided by the minimum weekly amount of these substances necessary to be removed to maintain the patient free of symptoms of underdialysis. $D_1 = 1.0$ and represents the minimum value for each patient. In a particular patient, if the combined residual glomerular filtration rate (GFR) and the dialysis schedule gives a $D_1$ less than 1.0, symptoms of underdialysis should occur sooner or later.

Preliminary results showed support for the conclusion that even small amounts of residual renal function would permit significant shortening of dialysis time from what was previously considered optimal. Secondly, it appeared that $D_1 = 1.0$ represented a good estimate of the minimum amount of dialysis needed to prevent symptoms of underdialysis with respect to middle molecules in patients stabilized on chronic dialysis. Nevertheless the investigators did not advocate drastic reductions in dialysis time except under strictly monitored protocols that are clearly experimental.

The reasons for this were that significant reduction in dialysis time might take as much as several years before any long-term ill-effects became apparent, including effects on the pathogenesis of coronary artery disease. Also, patients on reduced dialysis time have no reserve to protect them in times of stress such as infection, trauma or a high-protein diet. Thirdly, severe serious complications of shortening dialysis time continue to plague the technique. Potassium and phosphate retention cause only moderate difficulty, but the need for rapid ultrafiltration, especially with patients who have difficulty controlling sodium intake, presented the greatest problem, especially in older patients in some of whom sudden severe episodes of hypotension had occurred. Thus until the possible long-term effects of drastic reductions in dialysis time are better delineated and until some of the complications are eliminated, the technique must be considered strictly experimental.

Nevertheless, the results to date were consistent with the middle molecule hypothesis, which states that one factor causing uremic neuropathy is accumulation of middle molecules.

The second paper reported 12 years' experience with the treatment of chronic renal failure since the opening of the Seattle Artificial Kidney Center in 1962 and was presented by Drs. Samuels and Charra, Ms. Olheiser and Blagg. The study population was 533 patients, 307 males and 226 females who had started hemodialysis or peritoneal dialysis at the Center or had received a kidney transplant prior to December 31, 1973. The only excluded patients were transients or visiting patients.

As of December 31, 1973, 156 of the patients had died. Dialysis was the initial treatment in 512 patients, 380 patients were treated only by dialysis, and 153 patients had been transplanted one or more times. The patient population changed with time as more funds became available and patient acceptance criteria became more liberal. The acceptance rate of new patients was more than 50 new patients per million population per year by 1973, and the average age of new patients increased from 35 in 1962 to 46 in 1973. Chronic glomerulonephritis and polycystic kidney disease accounted for about half of both male and female patients but there was a higher percentage of females with malformations of the kidney and urinary tract.

Previous data from this Center have suggested that age at the start of dialysis had little effect on patient survival for patients between the ages of 15 and 54. The current data suggested that in patients older than 35 there was a direct relationship between age and survival, perhaps related to more kidney transplants in the younger age group. There was no significant difference between survival in male and female patients on dialysis.

Survival was also related to diagnosis and showed that males with a diagnosis of chronic glomerulonephritis had about the same five-year survival as all the other male and female patients combined. In the case of polycystic kidney disease, both male and female patients had survival that was much better at five years than that of the remaining patients. This was probably related to residual renal function and a higher hematocrit in such patients. The patients studied included 17 with a primary diagnosis of diabetes as cause of their kidney disease and, as previously reported, there was a 25% estimated mortality in the first year of treatment in these patients.

Causes of death showed that two thirds of the patients treated only by dialysis died from cardiovascular disease and there was no difference in causes of death between male and female patients. The frequent deaths from cardiovascular disease confirmed the findings of Lindner et al. studying some of the same group of patients.

In the transplanted patients, graft survival results were slightly better than those reported by the US Transplant Registry and the European Dialysis and Transplant Association. Graft survival was 78% at two years for living related donor transplants and 50% for cadaveric grafts. With regard to patient survival following transplantation, there was an 86% two-year survival for living related donor patients and recipients of cadaveric grafts but most of the deaths of recipients of cadaveric kidneys occurred in males. There was no significant difference between graft and patient survival in those patients who had been dialyzed for less than or longer than one year prior to transplantation. Of the 22 deaths in transplanted patients, 45% resulted from infection and 32% from cardiovascular disease.

Following transplant rejection, patients returning to dialysis had been reported to have considerable morbidity and mortality, presumably related to the immunosuppressive treatment given during rejection. Thirty-six patients were returned to dialysis after rejection of the transplant and six died within 90 days. The estimated one-year survival was 77%, compared with 55% reported elsewhere.

The results of this study at one center suggest there may be an effect of age, sex, and disease on the survival of patients treated by dialysis and transplantation. Further study in larger populations is required. Many other risk factors influence survival, including some not considered in this study. These include race, medical history, associated diseases, exact mode of treatment, immunological data, and so on. The presence of various risk factors means patient populations will be heterogeneous with respect to survival, and survival varies with age and disease, but age is often correlated with disease so that separating the effects of the two is difficult. Consequently, summary survival studies may be very misleading because of the heterogeneous history of the population.

A new national data retrieval program for chronic renal failure patients was being developed in conjunction with Medicare and although this will have access to a larger number of patients for analysis, adjustments must be made for the simultaneous presence of more than one risk factor. Similar comparisons between different patient populations or different centers also will be misleading if no adjustment is made for variation in populations and policies. The large national investment for the care of patients with end-stage renal disease will also require an appropriately large investment in research on the exact epidemiology of this disease.

## THE SEVENTH ANNUAL CONTRACTORS' CONFERENCE OF THE ARTIFICIAL KIDNEY PROGRAM OF THE NATIONAL INSTITUTE OF ARTHRITIS, METABOLISM AND DIGESTIVE DISEASES WAS HELD IN BETHESDA, MARYLAND, JANUARY 28-30, 1974.

The first session was devoted to biochemistry and pathophysiology. Drs. Ralph Cutler, Graham Christopher, Arden Forrey and Andrew Blair from Harborview Medical Center and the University of Washington presented an update on their pharmacokinetic studies in chronic renal disease and hemodialysis. They discussed in vitro and in vivo studies on gentamicin, ethambutol, procainamide, and furosemide.

Dr. John Bagdade from the University of Washington described a study of hyperlipidemia in chronically uremic rats. Current efforts were underway to study increased triglyceride production rates in association with decreases in triglyceride levels.

Dr. James Burnell, Dr. Donald Sherrard and Elizabeth Teubner had been studying acid-base chemistry and human bone at the University of Washington. They had performed 78 bone biopsies on patients and compared these to 35 normal biopsies. The data suggested that the most effective dialysate concentration of calcium was 3.5 – 4.0 mEq/L and that calcium carbonate supplement was necessary to lower bone magnesium toward normal. Of six patients with osteofibrosis treated with 1,25-dihydroxycholecalciferol only one showed marked histologic improvement.

The second session was devoted to membranes, cannulas and non-thrombogenic surfaces. Scribner, Jack Cole, Mel Dennis and Dr. Robert Hickman discussed cannula research at the University of Washington. They were examining the feasibility of long-term vascular access with an indwelling Silastic catheter placed in the high flow environment of the proximal vein draining an arteriovenous fistula. They studied catheters of various lengths and in each case the catheter was reinforced by increasing the wall thickness with additional Silastic laminate. In vivo flow studies were done in sheep. All catheters had problems with vessel wall erosion and thrombosis. Longer catheters (six – 20 cm) were much better than shorter catheters of up to 3 cm in length. Movement of the catheter tip appeared to be the cause of the problem. They had also started work on the Sparks mandril graft concept, and preliminary studies in two sheep had shown the grafts remained functional at 14 and 21 days without anticoagulation.

Dr. Gottfried Schmer, Cole, Joe Vizzo and Jenny Krys reported on binding heparin to artificial kidney membranes to produce a local anticoagulant or antithrombogenic effect and so avoiding the need for repeated systemic anticoagulation. They had done studies in normal sheep using two groups of hollow fiber artificial kidneys, one with heparin grafted to the membrane and the other ungrafted to serve as control. Grafted units ran for seven hours with a stable blood flow and controls averaged five hours with a continuous drop off in blood flow. Thrombin time, the most sensitive indicator of heparin activity in plasma, showed no measurable heparin release from the grafted surface. They were continuing these studies with alterations in the grafting technique.

The third session was devoted to device development, therapy and its evaluation. Dr. Henry Tenckhoff, Bruce Meston and Michael Pete described the development of a new home peritoneal dialysis system. The system used reverse osmosis (RO) for both water purification and water sterilization. The major concern was the possibility of a membrane leak and they had developed techniques for leak detection and protection of the patient in case of a bacterial contaminated leak. As a result of their studies with five prototypes, they decided to incorporate an ultraviolet light source into the fluid pathway as a backup device and this was being investigated. In June 1973, the first commercially produced prototype was placed in a patient's home and by the time of the presentation five prototype units were operating in homes. There had been one infection as a result of a bacterial leak from the reverse osmosis unit and so they were reevaluating both the RO monitor and the backup devices. Simultaneously they were evaluating a new proportioning pump to further simplify operation of the system, which also would reduce the cost of the equipment itself as well as recurring dialysis expenses.

Blagg from Northwest Kidney Center reported on a comparison of home hemodialysis and home peritoneal dialysis in patients under the care of a community dialysis center. A study was anticipated to commence early in 1974 when issues related to payment for peritoneal dialysis by the Social Security Administration had been resolved. Meanwhile Northwest Kidney Center had been providing home peritoneal dialysis as an alternative to home hemodialysis for the last two years. At any one time there had been between 12 and 20 patients on home peritoneal dialysis, this being 10 to 15% of all patients on home dialysis. Patients had been selected for peritoneal dialysis on the basis of unsuitability for hemodialysis for various reasons.

For the forthcoming study, patients treated by hemodialysis and peritoneal dialysis would be comparable and patients with specific indications for home peritoneal dialysis would be excluded. All patients used the Tenckhoff catheter for peritoneal access and for most patients peritoneal dialysate was provided by the COBE peritoneal dialysate fluid supply equipment, although several patients used 40 L bottles of pre-sterilized dialysate supplied by the University of Washington. Between November 1972 and November 1973 there was an average of 17 patients on home peritoneal dialysis at any one time, 22 patients were started on peritoneal dialysis for the first time, and 12 of these were trained for home peritoneal dialysis, three of these with helpers because of lack of family support. Average training time for home peritoneal dialysis was nine dialyses per patient or three weeks. During the year five patients were transferred to home hemodialysis and five patients died. Backup dialyses for patients on home peritoneal dialysis during the year totaled 191, or 11.2 backup dialyses/patient/year compared with an average of 6.5 backup dialyses/patient/year for patients on home hemodialysis. One hundred and fifty-nine of the backup peritoneal dialyses were for medical reasons, of which 106 (67%) were in-hospital peritoneal dialyses. Sixty-five of the latter were in three patients with continuing problems. The need for in-center backup peritoneal dialysis because of technical problems with the peritoneal equipment at home was 0.9 backup dialyses/patient/year as compared with 0.32 backup dialyses/patient/year for patients in the home hemodialysis program. The cost of home peritoneal dialysis based on the 1972 experience in ten patients using the COBE equipment averaged $6,104/patient/year exclusive of physician fees. This was appreciably higher than the cost of home hemodialysis. Detailed comparison of the results to date were presented and discussed in relation to the forthcoming study.

Drs. Scribner, Babb and Jovan Milutinovic, Michael Strand and William Follette described the clinical engineering research in hemodialysis at the University of Washington. During the preceding year two basic facts were emerging from their research: 1) residual renal function has an enormous impact on the amount of dialysis required; and 2) 24 to 30 hours of standard Kiil dialysis might represent significant overdialysis for most anephric patients. They had studied criteria for objective evaluation of patient wellbeing and found the Activity Index particularly promising in showing or predicting clinical deterioration. They also now had considerable experience with the Continuous Performance Test (CPT). Deterioration in CPT scores reflected deterioration as evidenced by the fact that daily scores in one patient dropped for more than a week prior to the point where deterioration became clinically evident. Measurement of motor nerve conduction velocity (MNCV) had been greatly improved since setting up the technique in the dialysis unit under the care of the nurses. Reproducible results were now being consistently obtained and use of the regression line method of plotting serial measurements had further increased the usefulness of this parameter. In terms of reduced dialysis time, eight patients had been studied using standard Kiil dialysis for four to five hours, three times weekly for periods of up to 22 months. Surprisingly, contrary to expectations, all had done as well or better than expected. None had developed clinical evidence of neuropathy and only one had shown significant slowing of MNCV without any clinical detectable change. No other adverse clinical effects had been noted despite predialysis creatinine values as high as 15 mg/dl. They had also started using a protocol of reducing dialysis time to six to nine hours per week expecting that the patients would quickly manifest obvious symptoms of underdialysis. To date none of the seven patients who had been in the study for as long as nine months had yet manifested any clear-cut evidence of inadequate dialysis, although the patient who had been studied longest had recently demonstrated a highly significant decreasing MNCV. However, so far there was no clinical evidence of neuropathy and the experiment was being continued.

They had also studied residual renal function in 20 patients with levels of residual renal function from 0.1 ml/min to 2.0 ml/min. Simultaneous measurements of inulin, creatinine, iothalamate and urea clearances indicated that in this low range creatinine clearance agrees sufficiently well with inulin measurements that it can be relied upon for clinical use. Based on these results, they had devised a simple practical technique for serial measurement of residual GFR in dialysis patients.

In another experiment to look at possible middle molecule intoxication, they had returned a patient to using small surface area Kiil dialyzers, intending to confirm earlier data showing that slowing of MNCV occurred on a 21-hour per week (3×7) dialysis schedule. The intent was to continue this regimen until clinical evidence of neuropathy appeared. After 7.5 months of dialysis on the small surface area Kiil dialyzers, and with time shortened to 15 hours per week during the final two months, they had not found any evidence of clinical neuropathy or changes in MNCV. On the other hand, toward the end of this protocol they suddenly and belatedly discovered the patient had lost nearly 10 kg in real weight and had become more anemic. The weight loss had been masked by a simultaneous increase in extracellular fluid volume that had led to hypertension with severe headaches and finally mild heart failure. However, it was impossible to say that this deterioration was due to middle molecule intoxication. They felt they must repeat this protocol several more times using much more reliable objective data that now had become available to them.

# The 4th Clinical Dialysis and Transplant Forum, November 16-17, San Francisco

Two papers were presented from Seattle: one from Northwest Kidney Center and the other from the University of Washington.

A paper on patient financing in the first year of the ESRD program was presented by Ms. Shadle, Ms. Hallam and Blagg from Northwest Kidney Center. The Center, in addition to coordinating the medical aspects of dialysis and transplant treatment, also plays a central role in the financing of care for ESRD patients from Western Washington State. It administers state appropriations from the Division of Vocational Rehabilitation and the Department of Health Services, has an annual fundraising campaign which provides as much as $350,000 a year for patient care, and a long history of successful dialogue with private insurance companies regarding coverage for these patients. In addition, the Center has a patient financing department to advise and assist patients with the multiple financial concerns and to coordinate the best use of available funding sources for treatment. This financial role of the Center provides a unique environment in which to study the impact of the ESRD Medicare Program on the funding of dialysis treatment and how this may alter the need for funds from other sources.

Data were collected during the year prior to ESRD Medicare, (July 1, 1972 to June 30, 1973) and the first year of the Medicare program (July 1, 1973 to June 30, 1974). The first group consisted of 89 patients and the second of 97 patients, and in both cases the increase over the previous year was 13%. Fifty-four percent of patients were male in the first year and 56% in the second year. The average age was 45 years and 43 years and the average number of months of treatment was 5.7 months and 5.8 months. The average annual cost of treatment in the first year was $10,800 and in the second $9,300. The apparent reduction of cost resulted from a number of changes following institution of the Medicare ESRD Program. These included the change to equipment rental rather than outright purchase and the exclusion of most of the physician costs for hospitalization, which were no longer routed through the Center. These apparent reductions were offset in part by a change to disposable dialyzers from Kiil dialyzers for all patients both in the Center and at home. Thus, if the costs of physician charges for hospitalized patients were included, the actual cost per patient post-Medicare is greater than the year before.

In the year after July 1, 1973, Medicare provided only 39% of the total funding for the first 5.8 months of dialysis treatment because patients not already Medicare-entitled due to age or disability had a 60 to 90 day waiting period before coverage was effective. In addition, there had been obstacles to collecting even this 39% from Medicare, and 12% of the Medicare payments were in the form of anticipated payments now more than four months outstanding. Slow payment, delays in establishing patient entitlement, slowness in obtaining policy decisions at the national level, and delays in interpretation of regulations locally by intermediaries and carriers created problems and frustrations for a previously effective and efficient patient financing system.

In the year after Medicare, 97 new patients started treatment, four of whom were ineligible for Medicare coverage. Of the remaining 93 patients, 22 were already Medicare eligible when treatment was begun, either due to age or having been under Social Security disability for more than two years. For this group, Medicare paid 73.5% of total dialysis-related charges during the 5.8 months, much higher than the average of 39% for all new patients. This higher level was due to the fact that these patients were not subject to a waiting period prior to coverage. However, even for these patients, Medicare did not pay 80% of all dialysis-related charges, mainly because the Medicare program did not cover all aspects of home dialysis care. This difference (6.5% of total costs) appears small but may represent several hundred dollars for the individual. In addition, 50% of patients in this group had no insurance coverage other than Medicare. For the remaining 71 patients whose Medicare coverage was not established until 60 to 90 days after starting dialysis, Medicare paid only 30% of total dialysis-related costs in the first 5.8 months of treatment. This was because these patients have the costliest period of treatment prior to becoming Medicare-entitled, the first week of treatment alone often costing more than $1,000, including hospitalization, access surgery, etc. In addition, in this program many patients are trained for home dialysis as soon as they are medically stable and, therefore, an appreciable number of patients were not entitled to Medicare coverage until after expensive home dialysis training had begun. The costs in the year before the Medicare program included hospitalization, physician services, and equipment purchase. This changed with Medicare to include the use of disposable dialyzers and equipment rental and excluded hospitalization and physician services.

The 13% increase in the number of patients starting dialysis in both years had been a characteristic of this program for several years and had not altered significantly with introduction of ESRD Medicare. In the year before Medicare, 24% of patients starting treatment had no insurance other than Medicare itself for some aged patients, while after Medicare the number of patients without insurance was 39%, a gain relatively consistent with previous experience in which approximately one third of all patients had no private insurance.

This experience shows that on average Medicare coverage provides for less than 40% of dialysis-related costs during the first six months of treatment. Although the experience at this Center related mainly to patients trained and treated by home dialysis, the situation is not much different for those patients treated by in-center dialysis. Depending upon when the patient becomes entitled to Medicare coverage, as much as 50 to 60% of the first six months of dialysis-related costs are not covered by Medicare for most dialysis patients under the age of 65, whether treated by home dialysis or in-center dialysis, and have non-covered charges of $5,000-$8,000 during the first six months.

While the philosophy of the Medicare ESRD program was never to pay all costs for patient care, it is possible the benefits of the new program are somewhat less than may have been the intent of Congress. Also there is no doubt the benefits are less than anticipated by most facilities, private insurers, state agencies and patients. Because of a widespread belief that Medicare pays 80% of the cost of dialysis treatment, some insurance companies and state agencies have attempted to reduce support for patients and, further, such reductions are likely to develop. This analysis emphasizes the need for continuing support of dialysis patients by other sources such as private insurance programs, state agencies and public contributions. Although the Medicare program may reduce the dollars required per patient, the increasing number of patients needing treatment undoubtedly will increase the total expenditure required. Thus, despite the ESRD Medicare program, continued additional support remains essential if all patients at risk are to be treated without prohibitive personal financial burdens.

The other paper was by Drs. Riella, Hickman, Striker, Slichter, Harker and Quadracci from the University of Washington and described renal microangiography of the hemolytic-uremic syndrome in childhood. This occurs when acute renal failure is accompanied by fragmentation hemolysis and thrombocytopenia developing a few days after the onset of gastrointestinal symptoms such as vomiting, diarrhea and abdominal pain in a previously well child. The cause is unknown and treatment had been diverse including dialysis, anticoagulation, and exchange transfusion.

A retrospective study had been done on 18 children admitted to the Children's Orthopedic Hospital and Medical Center and the University Hospital in Seattle between 1967 and 1973. Clinical features, hemostatic mechanisms, and renal histology were assessed during the illness. While most of the determinations were in the normal range, thrombin time was prolonged in most patients. In four patients during the first week of illness, platelet count was reduced and platelet survival was shortened. Platelet turnover was increased nearly 3½ times over normal. Fibrinogen turnover was not different from normal. Twelve specimens were obtained by renal biopsy from nine of the patients and showed major structural abnormalities in the glomeruli and their blood vessels.

The first six patients were treated with heparin, corticosteroids, and supportive therapy and the following six children received only heparin and supportive therapy. The last six children treated in the most recent few years had received only supportive therapy consisting of correction of fluid and electrolyte abnormalities, administration of red cells and/or platelets, and dialysis if indicated. Most patients survived with normal renal function, and treatment with corticosteroids or heparin appeared to have no advantage over careful supportive therapy alone.

## CHAPTER 37

# 1975

THE YEAR 1975 WAS THE second full year following implementation of the Medicare ESRD Program and, as had become usual, there was an increase in the number of patients referred for treatment by both dialysis and kidney transplantation. The total number of patients continued to increase although the number of patients on home dialysis and who were transplanted was not increasing as rapidly as before. This was because of an increase in the number of new patients with multiple medical and social problems, including diabetes and old age that may prevent transplantation or treatment by home dialysis.

The Center's kidney retrieval unit continued to coordinate procurement of cadaveric kidneys for transplantation from the four-state area of Washington, Alaska, Idaho and Montana. This cooperative program included transplant surgeons from University, Swedish and Virginia Mason hospitals, as well as community surgeons and hospitals.

In conjunction with the Lions Eye Bank and similar programs, the Center continued efforts with public education about the importance of organ donation. During the year the Center was involved in passage of state legislation to provide a donor card with each driving license. The original intent had been that the donor card be on the reverse of the permanent driving license but because of technical problems the donor card appears only on the reverse side of the temporary driver's license. It is hoped to change this in the future. In addition, the Center, the Lions Eye Bank and other programs that use donated organs or tissues have developed the Organ

Donor Information Center to provide the public with information about donation of any and all organs and tissues. This is staffed by volunteers and NKC provides accommodation, management and advice.

Antilymphocyte globulin (ALG) is a substance important in reducing the risk of early rejection of transplanted kidneys. It is prepared from horse serum by the University of Minnesota and had been used at the University of Washington but not at the other transplant hospitals. The Center made arrangements for ALG to be available for all transplants performed in Seattle.

Financially NKC had adjusted to many of the changes since Medicare had become a major source of funds. Even so, Medicare only provided about two thirds of the total costs of the program because of deductibles and various items which were not covered. The Center continued to need support from the state of Washington and monies raised from public donations in order to support patients without other resources. As the federal government might become increasingly concerned about the cost of health care, the need for local support was likely to become more important rather than less.

A major problem with the Medicare program was that it discriminated against home dialysis because of items and services which were not covered. To a lesser degree this also applied to transplant patients. Dr. Blagg and others continued their efforts to encourage passage of legislation to right problems. The seriousness of the issue was shown by the fact that there were private insurance companies that would no longer pay coinsurance to maintain a patient on home dialysis and yet were prepared to pay much more to have the same patient dialyze in a center or a hospital. Continuing political and educational pressures were needed to make the necessary changes.

Pressure on space in Eklind Hall had increased as the number of patients and number of staff increased. Some relief from the serious overcrowding and congestion should occur in 1976 when the home dialysis training unit would be transferred to one of the floors of Swedish Hospital. As a result of the space that would become available, NKC would then be able to open the limited care unit that had been discussed previously.

During the year, two new full-time physicians came on staff, Dr. Millie Tung and Dr. Jay Honari, as did a number of new nursing and business staff to meet the needs of the increasing numbers of patients. Clint Howard, the director of development, left NKC and Lucy Ransdell, previously his deputy, took over his role. Marcia Clark, RN, the renal coordinator, became president-elect of the American Association of Nephrology Nurses and Technicians (AANNT), a national organization with a membership of more than 1,700 nurses and technicians involved in the care of dialysis and transplant patients in the U.S. and Canada. And Blagg became president of the Renal Physicians Association. The Northwest Kidney Patients Association continued to be successful under the presidency of Mr. John Noel.

THE 12ᵀᴴ ANNUAL MEETING OF NORTHWEST KIDNEY CENTER'S BOARD OF TRUSTEES WAS CALLED TO ORDER AT 7:35 P.M. IN THE AUDITORIUM OF THE WASHINGTON ATHLETIC CLUB ON FEBRUARY 20, 1975, BY THE PRESIDENT, DENVER GINSEY.

Mr. Robert Burns was appointed temporary secretary for the meeting.

The proxy votes of Bruce Baker, Richard E. Bangert, M. L. Bean, Sr., James Burnell, MD, Willis Campbell, Ross Cunningham, John Dare, Trevor Evans, Gerald Grinstein, Allan Lobb, MD, Harry Machenheimer, Thomas Marr, MD, Jerry Pendras, MD, Richard Philbrick, DDS, Jack D. Schwartz, Belding H. Scribner, MD, Rabbi Earl Starr, Mrs. Holt W. Webster and T. Evans Wyckoff were recorded and a quorum was established.

John McCormack read the report of the Nominating Committee. It was moved and seconded that the following individuals be elected as officers of the Board of Trustees for one-year terms: vice president, Richard E. Bangert; secretary, Liem E. Tuai; and treasurer, Robert P. Burns; and that Elmer Nordstrom be elected as president of the Board of Trustees for a two-year term. There were no nominations from the floor and the motion passed unanimously.

It was moved and seconded that the following individuals be elected to one-year terms as members of the Board of Trustees, terms to expire in 1976: Pat Berger, Stewardess Emeritus Association; James Takemoto, Northwest Kidney Center Patients Association; Father R. J. Queen, Yakima County Fund; and Shirley Keltner, Snohomish County Fund. There were no nominations from the floor and the motion passed unanimously.

It was moved and seconded that the following individual be elected as a member of the Board of Trustees to fill an unexpired term to expire in 1976: George Kinnear. There were no nominations from the floor and the motion passed unanimously.

It was moved and seconded that the following individuals be reelected to three-year terms as members of the Board of Trustees, terms to expire in 1978: Robert Beaupre; Robert P. Burns, Roy Correa, MD; Joseph Eschbach, MD; Denver Ginsey, Allan Lobb, MD; John L. McCormack, MD; James W. Phillips; Rabbi Earl S. Starr; and Mrs. Holt W. Webster; and that the following individuals be elected to three-year terms as members of the Board of Trustees, terms to expire in 1978: Dutton Hayward; James F. Henriot; Frank Pritchard; and Walter Schoenfeld. There were no nominations from the floor and the motion passed unanimously.

It was moved and seconded that the following individuals be re-elected to the Executive Committee, terms to expire in 1978: Denver Ginsey; John L. McCormack, MD; and James W. Phillips. There were no nominations from the floor and the motion passed unanimously.

There was no old business and no new business.

THE PRESIDENT'S REPORT

Ginsey gave the president's report. He began by thanking the retiring board members for their past support and encouraging them to think of and help the Center in the future even though they were joining emeritus status. The retiring board members were: Thomas Seifert; Loretta Chin; Harry Machenheimer; Marilyn Dean, Stewardess Emeritus Association; Virgil

Mahaffey, Northwest Kidney Center Patients Association; and George Wallace, Snohomish County Fund.

He welcomed the new board members and was sure they would find the coming years most interesting. The new board members were: Frank Prichard; Walter Schoenfeld; James F. Henriot; George Kinnear; Dutton Hayward; Pat Berger, Stewardess Emeritus Association; Jim Takemoto, Northwest Kidney Center Patients Association; and Shirley Keltner, Snohomish County Fund.

Ginsey thanked the members of the Executive Committee for their support during not only the past year, but the previous four years. Members of the Executive Committee were: James W. Phillips; Robert P. Burns; Liem E. Tuai; Elmer Nordstrom; Willis Campbell; John McCormack, MD; James W. Haviland, MD; Renaldo Baggott; and Richard E. Bangert.

He also acknowledged the untiring efforts of Burns, the treasurer and chairman of the Finance Committee.

Ginsey noted that everyone associated with the Center, particularly the patients, were indebted to the total dedication and untiring energy of the staff, in particular Blagg, Tom Sawyer, MD, Marcia Clark, RN, and Clint Howard. There were many others whose untiring efforts had made the Center the success it was today. On behalf of the board and the patients, he gave all of them sincere thanks.

The new man on the scene was the new business manager, John Pollock, and Ginsey mentioned how fortunate the Center was in having John aboard. It was always interesting how new people had new ideas, all of which seem to benefit the Center. As a matter of interest, the Center had had three executive directors or business managers whose names started with "P" – Jim Phillips, Terry Pollard and now John Pollock – and also two business managers whose names started with "R" – Harold Rathman and Earl Rice. If your name did not start with a "P" or an "R" there' was very little chance for you to have a position of authority in the kidney center. Actuarially speaking, this was impossible, but nevertheless, the impossible happens at Northwest Kidney Center rather routinely. He wanted to point out that the above was not totally actuarially sound because one "S" did slip in in the form of Tom Siefert, but only for a six-month period that did not really count.

Ginsey introduced and welcomed Tung, a new member of the Center medical staff.

He said that the past four years as president of Northwest Kidney Center had been most interesting. Talking about numerical probability, he thought it of great interest that in the first year of operation of the kidney center in 1962 seven patients were treated. Four years ago on December 31, 1970, the Center treated 193 patients, including 20 patients who had been transplanted, and on December 31, 1974 the Center treated 415 patients, 117 of whom had been transplanted.

The Center had experienced dynamic growth. Three years ago at the Annual Meeting, Ginsey had mentioned that the Center was not satisfied with state-of-the-art as it exists today and that ten years hence would compare treatment methods in a manner similar to flying to New York in a DC 3 versus a 747 today. He even had had the audacity to mention that a person could come home, sip on a martini, plug into the dialyzer, and one hour later enjoy a dinner and go about his business without any further problems or concern. Three years have passed and, although that is not yet the situation, the Center had almost totally eliminated the use of the old Kiil kidney. The new disposable artificial kidneys do not need to be torn down, washed, and put back together, a process that could consume an hour routinely and, if problems developed, substantially more time. Were we satisfied? Not at all. There are continuing studies of methods whereby the entire dialysis procedure can be mechanized, thus minimizing the time required for dialysis and less effort on the part of the patient.

It was interesting to know what happened to the old Kiil kidneys that were approximately 3 to 4 feet long and 18 inches wide. Scribner had a renal fellow from Chile who worked for a time at Northwest Kidney Center. On his return to Chile, he wrote asking if the Center had any spare Kiil kidneys. He was told that if he would pay for the transportation and pay NKC $25 for each dialyzer to clean it up and check it out, the Center would provide Chile with all they could use. Payment was arranged through the Rotary Clubs of Seattle and Santiago, Chile. Today, ex-Seattle kidneys were in use in Chile, Brazil, and other places where labor was not a consideration.

What were some of the other accomplishments in the last four years?

Through Blagg, the relationship between the University of Washington Medical School and Northwest Kidney Center had been strengthened.

The Center now had its own organ retrieval laboratory, so that NKC coordinated organ retrieval and tissue typing for patients from Washington, Alaska, Idaho and Montana. In the last three years, NKC had been responsible for harvesting 172 kidneys, which had been used not only in this area but throughout the United States.

With the aid of Gerald Stinson, the educational consultant, the Center had developed a videotape patient training program for home dialysis. This program was so successful that it was copied by several large centers in the United States as well as in centers in Europe and Australia.

With the signing of Public Law 92–603 by President Nixon, payment for dialysis and transplantation was included under the Medicare program. However, early experience with the Medicare program was very frustrating, and there were delays of many months in receiving reimbursement for equipment and services. In spite of this rather rocky beginning, the Center's relationships with the Medicare program were excellent and in fact Medicare looked more to the Center for guidance than the Center did to it. Illustrating this particular point was the fact that Virgil Mahaffey, who had been the patient representative on the board, recently moved to Philadelphia. Virg continued to maintain medical contact in Seattle, making about four trips a year to see his local physician. His home dialysis unit was recently sent to Seattle for repair and Virg called, saying "Please hurry up and fix my machine and return it as the in-center dialysis I am receiving in Philadelphia is interfering with my work." He had signed up with an in-center dialysis unit, which treated approximately 30 patients. Not one of the 30 had ever tried home dialysis or was working, and not one of the 30 could believe that Virgil worked full-time. They also thought he was really pulling their leg when he said he slept during dialysis. It seems that this particular center closed at 9 p.m. and Virg worked a full schedule and did not have time to dialyze between 6 and 9 p.m. in the evening. NKC could not have a better man than Virg on the East Coast to expound on the advantages of home dialysis.

Another new development, particularly in the last two years, had been the coordination of transplant activity by Northwest Kidney Center. In addition to University Hospital, transplants were now performed at Swedish and Virginia Mason hospitals. The cadaveric kidney retrieval program was becoming increasingly successful year by year and in the last three years, 172 kidneys had been retrieved of which 112 had been transplanted in Washington State and 26 sent to patients elsewhere. The Center still provided home dialysis for the great majority of patients, although facilities were being developed for limited care dialysis for those patients who had major problems in performing home dialysis.

Another innovation at Northwest Kidney Center during the last two years was the use of a new peritoneal dialysis machine developed by Henry Tenckhoff, MD at the University of Washington, manufactured locally by Physio-Control and which was being used for a number of patients on home peritoneal dialysis.

In the last two years, an average of 100 patients a year had been trained for home dialysis.

The success of Northwest Kidney Center depended on the staff at all levels. From a small "family" operation in 1962, it had grown to be a large enterprise working in cooperation with both patients and physicians, both in the community and at the university. It was nationally recognized as one of the major centers, and visitors came from all over the world. Members of its staff were involved in national organizations and committees related to dialysis and transplantation and have had some role in influencing the development of the national program.

What faces the next president? Continuing change. The Medicare program presently operates under Interim Regulations, and final regulations will be promulgated in the next year or so. So far, most government regulations have not been designed for a program like the Center's but rather for the in-hospital or in-center programs common on the East Coast and elsewhere. Continuing efforts were being made to modify the legislation to provide incentives for home dialysis, more efficient use of dialysis services and to minimize problems for patients.

The Center's most recent endeavor had been to have organ donor cards placed on the blank space on the back of the Washington State driver's license. This legislation was currently being considered.

It was unlikely that technical or other advances within the next few years would eliminate the need for either dialysis or transplantation, and the kidney center's role would continue to be that of coordinating resources for the individual patient, coordinating services with institutions throughout the region and cooperating with physicians caring for these patients.

Ginsey said that it had been a real pleasure to serve as the president of Northwest Kidney Center for the previous four years and that he found it hard to describe the personal satisfaction that he had derived from his association with the Center. The uniqueness of Northwest Kidney Center had left no doubt in his mind, nor should it in those of other members of the staff or of the board, as to their important contributions to the community. This experience had meant more to him than he could express. With this four-year term behind him, he believed he was safe in recommending it to everyone as an experience not to be missed.

## INTRODUCTION OF THE NEW PRESIDENT

Ginsey introduce Elmer Nordstrom as the new president of Northwest Kidney Center's Board of Trustees and commented that Nordstrom was definitely not a new face since he was one of the seven originators of the Center and had served on the Board of Trustees since the incorporation of NKC in early December 1963. Ginsey then turned the meeting over to Nordstrom, and Nordstrom commented that the kidney center started out small with no guarantee of success, but due to good management it blossomed and grew and was still growing. Nordstrom indicated that being president of the Board of Trustees should be an easy task because of the fine staff at the Center.

RECOGNITION OF VOLUNTEERS AND ORGANIZATIONS
During the 12th Annual Meeting of the Board of Trustees, the board recognized individuals and organizations that had worked tirelessly over the years on the Center's behalf. They included the following:

- *Xi Alpha Psi Chapter, Beta Sigma Phi.* One of the members of the sorority was a friend of Clyde Shields, who was the first artificial kidney machine patient in the world. As an antique buff, she decided to help the Center by sponsoring an antique show, which has been running now for six years. To date the group – comprised of 13 women – had raised $7,078.72 by sponsoring the show the first weekend in November.

- *Greater Seattle Area Sweet Adelines.* This group of 350 women chose the Northwest Kidney Center as the recipient of proceeds from its first benefit concert "Harmony Potpourri," at the Seattle Center Playhouse in September 1974. Their four-part harmony, barbershop style, and their beautiful costumes is popular. They raised $3,121.76.

- *Eastside Auxiliary.* For four years the auxiliary has helped raise funds for the Center. In the previous year it raised $1,000 by sponsoring a fireworks stand, a car smash and several dances.

- *King County Council, Epsilon Sigma Alpha.* This non-academic sorority supervised the construction of a haunted castle at the Seattle Center, haunting 15 rooms for 9 nights prior to Halloween. In 1974 it raised $11,000. Thirteen chapters of the sorority, including 75 women, took part.

- *Mr. Bill Forrester, Assistant Professor, University of Washington School of Drama.* Mr. Forrester designed the haunted castle, an elaborate labyrinth with special fright features built into it.

- *Mr. Leo Cooper, Seattle Occupational Income Maintenance Center.* Mr. Cooper's carpentry classes got on-the-job training by actually building the haunted castle.

- *West Seattle Auxiliary.* For the second year, the West Seattle Auxiliary donated proceeds from its pre-holiday bazaar to the kidney center. The auxiliary raised $2,000 from its one-day benefit.

- *Queen City Auxiliary.* The auxiliary sponsors a day at Longacres Racetrack to benefit the Center. The day sells out every year and features a luncheon, fashion show and a day at the races. The auxiliary has been helping the Center for six years and has given a total of $8,209.

- *Stewardess Emeritus Association.* This organization holds a special place at the Center because it was the Center's first auxiliary. The group has sponsored art shows and boutiques, luncheons and grand balls, all to raise money to benefit kidney dialysis patients. Organized in 1966, it has donated more than $25,000 to the kidney center.

- *Mrs. Edna Vinson of Exeter House.* Mrs. Vinson volunteered to help the Center by clipping coupons. In the past year, she and her crew at the Exeter House Retirement Residence clipped more than 1,161,400 coupons – the Betty Crocker variety – to raise more than $6,500 for the Center. Mrs. Vinson had 10 volunteers working with her, with the oldest being 94 years of age.

- *Beta Sigma Phi Sorority of Washington State.* For the second year, 2,500 women in 250 chapters throughout the state sold Halloween Candy to benefit the Center. This year it was Tootsie Roll banks. The Center was Beta Sigma Phi's statewide service project for the year and as such the group raised $11,000.

- *The Boeing Employees Good Neighbor Fund* and the *Somerset Auxiliary* were also recognized for their many years of financial support and received certificates of appreciation.


PRESENTATION OF A GIFT TO MR. DENVER GINSEY
Haviland presented Ginsey with a desk-model pen set bearing the following inscription: *The Northwest Kidney Center Gratefully Acknowledges the Outstanding Contribution and Public Service of Denver Ginsey as President, Board of Trustees 1971-75, Presented February 20, 1975.*

Following a brief question and answer period, the meeting was adjourned at 8:20 p.m.

# CENTER ACTIVITIES REPORT, JANUARY 24-MARCH 27, 1975

## DIALYSES DURING THE FIRST QUARTER

During the first quarter of 1975, there was a monthly average of 538 dialyses performed at the Northwest Kidney Center with 505, 520 and 589 in the first three months respectively. The March number of 589 dialyses set a new record, the previous one being 578 dialyses performed in May of 1974. In comparison, the average for the first three months of 1974 was 499.7 dialyses and the average for the year 1974 was 512.5 dialyses per month.

Since the Executive Committee meeting of January 24, 28 patients were accepted for treatment of which 3 were from out of state and for training only. Thirty-one patients started treatment: 28 on hemodialysis and 3 on peritoneal dialysis. Sixteen patents completed home dialysis training, all of them on hemodialysis. Others were retrained on hemodialysis because of a change in their mode of blood access or type of hemodialyzer used, or changed from peritoneal to hemodialysis. Those patients retrained in peritoneal dialysis were done so on the Physio-Control Model 200 machine. Previously, these patients had been treated using the Physio-Control prototype or the obsolete Cobe machine.

## ORGAN RETRIEVAL AND TRANSPLANTS

The organ retrieval unit retrieved 14 kidneys in the quarter. All were retrieved from the Puget Sound region. Three of those kidneys were transplanted locally and three shipped to other units for transplantation.

Since the Executive Committee meeting of January 24, there were 4 transplants: 1 from a related donor at the University of Washington and 3 cadaveric grafts, one each at Swedish Hospital, University Hospital and Virginia Mason Hospital. One patient received a second transplant after loss of his first graft. Of the 4, 3 were male and 1 female, ranging in age from 25 to 46 years, with an average age of 31 years. They had been on treatment for 6 to 38 months with an average of 17 ¾ months.

Three patients who had received cadaveric transplants prior to January 24 rejected their grafts and returned to hemodialysis 1 to 8 months, with an average of 4 1/3 months, post-transplantation.

## PATIENT DEATHS
Seven Northwest Kidney Center clients/patients plus 1 Alaska patient died since the January 24 meeting: 4 males and 4 females, with ages ranging from 32 to 67 years and with an average age of 49.9 years. They had been on treatment for periods ranging from 1 to 43 months, with an average treatment period of 17.1 months. Three died of heart attacks, arrhythmias or arrest. Two died of complications of transplantation, 2 of bacterial septicemia and 1 of influenza pneumonia.

## NKC's PERITONEAL DIALYSIS PROGRAM
Nancy Gallagher, RN, who came to NKC in December 1974 to supervise the peritoneal dialysis program after 8 years' experience as a dialysis nurse, including positions as head nurse in two dialysis centers, completed – with Dr. Tenckhoff's assistance – the rewriting of all of the peritoneal dialysis procedures. After testing the procedures they will be videotaped to make the peritoneal dialysis training program comparable to that of hemodialysis.

## THIRD NORTHWEST NEPHROLOGY WORKSHOP
Clark, NKC's renal coordinator, again chaired a committee comprised of nurses from University, Veterans and Children's Orthopedic hospitals to present the third Northwest Nephrology Workshop on April 25-26, 1975. Bruce VanDeusen, NKC social worker, Dr. Bill Hamlin, Swedish Hospital

pathologist, and Dick Derham, attorney and NKC legal consultant, all participated in the program. The workshop was held for health care personnel engaged in the care of patients with end-stage renal disease and was sponsored by the Division of Continuing Education, School of Nursing, University of Washington, and by the American Association of Nephrology Nurses and Technicians (AANNT).

Clark, president-elect of the AANNT, was also promoted to assistant chief nurse of the 40ᵗʰ Air Evacuation Squadron at McChord Air Force Base where she is a flight nurse instructor.

### LIMITED CARE CENTER

An agreement was reached with Swedish Hospital for NKC's limited care facility to be constructed in the eastern portion of the first floor of Eklind Hall. The limited care center will utilize two classroom areas and the university nurse educator area for the initial six-bed unit, with plans to remodel the majority of the present lounge and adjacent offices as space for fundraising and public relations. This area is ideally situated for such function adjacent to the main entrance of the building. Construction was to commence as soon as final approval was received from the Health Department.

## DIRECTOR OF DEVELOPMENT REPORT, OCTOBER 31, 1975

### FUND DRIVE REPORT

A report on the previous year's fund drive was given by Howard who stated that 1974 was the biggest fund raising year in the history of the kidney center. A total of $373,544 was contributed, topping the previous year's total by 6 percent. He noted that individuals contributed the most: $113,508.50, with an average contribution of $30.76 from 3,690 donors.

Clubs and organizations contributed the next highest amount –
$89,745.13 – with an average donation of $304.22 from 295 groups. The
third highest contribution came from employee groups, which donated
$72,160.48, with an average donation of $2,886 from 25 employee groups.

LEGISLATIVE REPORT

The 1975 state legislature unanimously passed a bill directing the
Department of Motor Vehicles to distribute donor cards to every license
holder in the State of Washington. While the kidney center's hope was
to have the donor card imprinted on the back of the driver's license, this
proved to be impractical at the present time. Precisely how the donor cards
will be distributed has not been determined, but should be resolved shortly.

The kidney center's budget request for $1,028,240 appears to be in good
shape. No opposition had yet been raised but hearings on the appropriation
have not been held. Since this request is for less than the last appropriation
(and less than the governor's budget request), there should be little difficulty
in obtaining the appropriation, which should be adopted within the next
20 days.

ORGAN DONOR INFORMATION CENTER

An Organ Donor Information Center at Northwest Kidney Center is to be
established in cooperation with the Lions Eye Bank, Harborview Hospital's
Skin Bank, the University of Washington Department of Biological
Structures for Whole Body Donations and the Human Growth Foundation
for Pituitary Glands.

The information center will be located at NKC's Retrieval Center on
the first floor of Eklind Hall, staffed mostly by volunteers from the various
agencies and financially supported by all the participating agencies.

The Washington State Insurance Council is providing the brochures
and on-site counter displays to be located in the Department of Motor
Vehicles' auto license centers.

# THE 1975 ASAIO ANNUAL MEETING

The 1975 ASAIO annual meeting was held in Washington DC, April 17-19. There were no presentations from Seattle.

## CHAPTER 38

# 1976

———

In this year, patient numbers continued to grow steadily, primarily because the availability of Medicare funding resulted in increasing numbers of older and sicker dialysis patients with increasing pressure on space at the Center. It was also the year of publication of the final regulations for the national end-stage renal disease networks.

## The 13th Annual Meeting of Northwest Kidney Center's Board of Trustees was Called to Order at 7:30 p.m. on February 17, 1976 by the President, Elmer Nordstrom.

Mr. Robert Burns was appointed temporary secretary for the meeting.

The proxy votes of Robert S Beaupre, Willis L Campbell, Ross Cunningham, Trevor Evans, George Kinnear, Allan Lobb, MD, Thomas Marr, MD, William McKee, MD, James W Phillips, Frank Pritchard, Rabbi Earl Starr, James Takemoto, Kirby Torrance, Liem Tuai and Kate Webster were recorded and a quorum was established.

John McCormack read the report of the Nominating Committee. It was moved and seconded that the following individuals be elected as officers of the Board of Trustees for one-year terms: Richard E. Bangert, vice president; Liem Tuai, secretary; Robert Burns, treasurer; and Elmer J. Nordstrom, president. There were no nominations from the floor and the motion passed unanimously.

It was moved and seconded that the following individuals be appointed to the Board of Trustees for a term of three years: Renaldo Baggott; Bruce Baker; Willis L. Campbell; John Dare; Trevor Evans; George Kinnear; Jack D. Schwartz; Kirby Torrance, Jr.; T. Evans Wyckoff; Betty Magnuson; and Walter T. Hubbard. (The last two would replace Richard C. Philbrick, DDS and Senator George Fleming, both of whom had asked to be relieved of further responsibilities). To replace a position that had been held by Representative Charles Savage, Representative Don Charnley was nominated for a one-year term.

In addition, the following were appointed for a one-year term to the Board of Trustees: Pat Berger, Stewardess Emeritus Organization; George Buxton, Snohomish County group; John Kennedy, MD, Pierce County group; Rick Webb, Yakima County group; and John Noel, NKC patient.

Baggott, Campbell and Evans were appointed to three-year terms of membership on the Executive Committee and Noel, representing the patient group, and Berger, representing the Stewardess Emeritus Organization, were proposed for one-year terms.

There were no nominations from the floor and the motions passed unanimously.

There was no old business and no new business.

THE PRESIDENT'S REPORT

Elmer Nordstrom gave the president's report. He noted that it was now more than 14 years since the kidney center first opened as a three-bed unit in the basement of Eklind Hall, which at that time was the Swedish Hospital nurses residence. This original unit was an experiment to get dialysis out of the expensive hospital setting and to develop a community dialysis program. It proved so successful that there was now a system of treatment for end-stage kidney disease in Western Washington, which not only was among the best, most efficient and least expensive in the United States, but also served as an example of how physicians in private practice and physicians from the academic world of the university could work together through a centralized facility to provide high-quality care for a large number of patients.

Nordstrom briefly mentioned the challenges that had faced the Center in the previous year, namely the increase in the number of patients referred for treatment by both dialysis and kidney transplantation. There also were continuing issues with the Medicare program as it provided only two-thirds of the cost of dialysis. The Center was thus reliant on state monies and on monies raised by public donation to support the many patients who did not have other resources. Additionally, Medicare legislation continued to discriminate against the home dialysis patient and somewhat against the transplant patient because of the items and services that were not covered.

Because of the increasing numbers of patients being treated at the Center, and the subsequent increase in the number of staff, the Center was outgrowing its space in Eklind Hall. Some relief had occurred with the transfer of the home dialysis training unit to one of the floors of Swedish hospital. This provided space in the Center for opening a limited care unit to provide in-center dialysis for those patients unable to do home dialysis. The long-term solution to the space problem was still being discussed and looked to be about a year away.

Last year, the Center welcomed two new full-time physicians, Dr. Millie Tung and Dr. Jay Honari, and various new nursing and administrative staff members. Center staff also presented our activities at local and national scientific meetings related to kidney disease, so that the Center continues to have a national reputation for excellence. Clark, the renal coordinator, was president-elect of the American Association of Nephrology Nurses and Technicians and Dr. Blagg was president of the Renal Physicians Association. Additionally, the Northwest Kidney Patients Association, a voluntary organization of patients run by the patients and assisted by the Center, publishes a newsletter that is read, it seems, by patients in many other parts of the country and abroad. The success of the organization reflects well on its organizers, and, in particular, Mr. John Noel, the retiring president of the patients' association.

What about the current year? The number of patients and activities will undoubtedly continue to increase and the Center will continue its cooperation with nephrologists in Seattle and elsewhere in Washington and the adjoining states to provide treatment for patients with end-stage kidney disease. Further administrative complications are to be expected with implementation of the final rules for the Medicare End-Stage Renal Disease Program expected. Among other things, it will link together several Northwest states as a network. How it will affect the operation of the Center as a regional resource remains to be seen. However, the Center's aim will be to continue to provide high-quality medical care in the form of both dialysis and kidney transplantation through Northwest Kidney Center, the university and affiliated hospitals and physicians for all patients in Western Washington state who have the misfortune to suffer from end-stage kidney disease.

## The First Meeting of the Executive Committee was Held January 16, 1976 at 12 Noon in Eklind Hall and Called to Order by Elmer Nordstrom.

It was reported that the patient census had increased by 18% over the previous year, and that 11 patients had started treatment on hemodialysis, 1 on peritoneal dialysis, and 11 patients had finished home dialysis training in the previous month. In terms of the kidney retrieval program, in 1974, 50 kidneys were retrieved and 14 were received from outside, 10 were discarded and 34 were transplanted locally. In 1975, 44 kidneys were retrieved and 5 were received from outside, 8 were discarded and 34 were transplanted locally. A new program was being instituted with federal support to generate more kidneys. There had also been several episodes of hepatitis among staff, but the patients had not been affected. The new home training unit would be located in Five South of Swedish Hospital.

Since the last meeting, 12 patients had been approved for treatment: 3 females and 9 males, ranging in age from 24 to 74, with an average age of 51.4 years.

Blagg noted that the Department of Social and Health Services (DSHS) money previously requested from the state would not be adequate due to sharp cost-per-patient increases, but the state had indicated additional funds might be available. The fund drive to date had received $319,515.09.

Solicitations from the American Kidney Fund had appeared again and the Executive Committee was discussing what to do about it.

## Restructuring of Northwest Kidney Foundation

A suggested restructuring of the organization of Northwest Kidney Foundation in relation to Northwest Kidney Center was discussed, detailing the proposed responsibilities of the Center and the foundation. In essence, the foundation would be responsible for fundraising, research and public education activities with its own employees, but directly managed by administration of the Center. The primary purpose of the Center would be to provide care and treatment for renal disease. This would eliminate fundraising and research overhead from the Center and would have a significant impact on the Center's cost and overhead. The issue would be studied further.

## NKC and federal agencies

Blagg reported that Northwest Kidney Center was negotiating a contract with the Centers for Disease Control (CDC) in Atlanta to stimulate availability of kidneys for transplantation and to provide education to hospital staffs to encourage organ donation.

Blagg reported that Congress did not pass anticipated legislation to help home hemodialysis and transplantation in 1975 but that there would be continued efforts in hopes to have such legislation in 1976.

The agreement between NKC and Dr. Scribner for research funding was discussed at length and would be discussed further.

## THE FEBRUARY EXECUTIVE COMMITTEE MEETING WAS HELD AT 12:30 P.M. ON FEBRUARY 20 IN SWEDISH HOSPITAL AND PRESIDED OVER BY ELMER NORDSTROM.

At the February meeting it was reported that there were currently 272 patients on hemodialysis: 41 in the Center; 5 in training; 10 in limited care; and 216 at home. There were 25 peritoneal dialysis patients: 20 at home; 4 in the Center; and 1 in training. The number of transplanted patients alive was 138. Six patients had started training in the last month and 7 had completed home dialysis training.

### ORGAN RETRIEVAL ACTIVITY

Organ retrieval activity included 8 referrals, 4 kidneys retrieved from two donors, no kidneys retrieved from outside or discarded, 2 local transplants and 2 kidneys sent out.

The home hemodialysis training unit was now located in Five North at Swedish hospital.

Since the last meeting, 8 new patients had been approved for treatment: 3 females and 5 males, ranging in age from 16 to 69 with an average age of 42.

### RESEARCH GRANT FOR SCRIBNER

There was discussion about the details associated with a proposed research grant for Scribner. The first phase of 18 months would be developmental, the second phase would be experimental, and the third phase would be marketing and sales. This was a study to develop new equipment, and so far a new blood pump, an air extractor and a sensor mechanism had been developed. The Division of Nephrology at the University of Washington felt it should retain all rights to these specific components, and there was discussion whether NKC wanted to be involved and participate in the future. There was discussion as to NKC's share of any income from phase 2 of the study. Scribner suggested this should be 10% and Nordstrom suggested 25%. A contract would be developed.

The restructuring of Northwest Kidney Foundation was discussed further and a motion was made to elect new trustees and to proceed further.

Fund drive receipts for the fiscal year were $375,000.

### Discussion with CDC terminated

Blagg reported that the discussion with the Centers for Disease Control on how to stimulate the availability of kidneys for transplantation and provide education to hospital staffs had been terminated because basic irreconcilable philosophical differences between the CDC and NKC became apparent.

### Seattle Veterans Administration and dialysis at NKC

The Seattle VA had asked NKC about a possibility of NKC dialyzing some of its patients. This could be accomplished, provided the patients could be handled in a manner that would not require changing or compromising NKC's established policies.

### The April Executive Committee Meeting was Held at 12:30 P.M. on April 30 in Swedish Hospital and Presided Over by Vice President Richard Bangert.

Lobb, executive director of Swedish Hospital, attended the meeting to discuss the situation with regard to Marycrest Villa, across the road from both Swedish Hospital and the kidney center. NKC had originally hoped Swedish Hospital would purchase this from Seattle University, a large portion of which could then be used for the purpose of housing the NKC facility. However, it now looked more likely that Marycrest would be demolished and a new hospital to house Seattle General and Seattle Doctor's hospitals would be developed there. The whole project was still under consideration. NKC staff would look at other possibilities for relocation of NKC.

PATIENT CENSUS AND KIDNEY RETRIEVAL ACTIVITY

There were now 287 patients on hemodialysis: 43 in the Center; and 2 in training, together with 3 retrains; 13 in limited care; and 226 on home hemodialysis. There were 23 patients on peritoneal dialysis: 3 in the Center and 20 at home. There were now 143 patients living with a kidney transplant. Since the previous meeting, there had been 32 new patients approved for treatment: 17 females and 15 males, ranging in age from 13 to 70 years, with an average age of 46 years. Twenty-one patients had started treatment and 11 had completed home training. There had been 7 kidneys retrieved in the last month from four donors, 3 kidneys received from elsewhere, 2 kidneys discarded, 8 local transplants (6 of which were functioning well) and no kidneys had been sent out.

Cumulative dialyses through April 30, 1976, showed a 39% increase over the same period in 1975: 3,039 compared to 2,190.


STAFF ATTENDING OUTSIDE MEETINGS

A number of staff had attended the American Society for Artificial Internal Organs (ASAIO) meeting and the American Association of Nephrology Nurses and Technicians (AANNT) meeting. Marcia Clark, RN, director of nursing at NKC, was the current president of the latter association. Papers were presented by several members of staff. Bangert, vice president of NKC, expressed congratulations to the staff for taking part in these meetings. Haviland mentioned that during a recent meeting of the American College of Physicians on the East Coast, the question was raised as to why patients in the Seattle area found it easier to receive treatment with home dialysis. It was felt that the staff of NKC was largely responsible for this and were to be congratulated.

Since NKC employees had been withdrawn from the Swedish Hospital retirement program it was now being considered how a practical and meaningful retirement program could be developed for NKC employees.

## FUND DRIVE

The contributions to the fund drive now totaled $421,606. Lucy Ransdell, who gave the fund drive report, noted that sometimes there are unusual circumstances under which donations are made: one donor, for example, made $10 donations upon the death of certain celebrities or other famous people.

## NORTHWEST KIDNEY CENTER FOUNDATION

The foundation officers elected under the new system were Ned Turner, president, Betty Lou Magnuson, vice president, Richard Bangert, secretary, and Dick Derham, treasurer. Funds in the foundation at the end of March were $63,000.

## AUTOMATED HOME HEMODIALYSIS MACHINE

A progress report on the automated home hemodialysis machine project was distributed by Dr. George Irvine from the Division of Nephrology at the University of Washington.

## THE MAY EXECUTIVE COMMITTEE MEETING WAS HELD AT 12:30 P.M. ON MAY 27 IN SWEDISH HOSPITAL AND PRESIDED OVER BY PRESIDENT ELMER NORDSTROM.

At the May meeting it was reported that there were now 283 hemodialysis patients: 39 in the Center; 5 in training; 11 in limited care; and 228 on home hemodialysis. There were 23 peritoneal dialysis patients: 19 at home; 3 in the Center; and 1 in training. There were 142 transplanted patients. Since the last meeting, 7 patients had started dialysis: 3 had been home trained and 4 patients had been retrained.

NKC was seeing 212 more patients per month than it had in 1975.

## Organ retrieval activity

Organ retrieval activity included 7 referrals, 4 kidneys retrieved from 2 donors, no kidneys received from elsewhere, 2 kidneys discarded and 2 local transplants.

Fourteen new patients had been approved for treatment: 7 females and 7 males, ranging in age from 17 to 69, with an average age of 40 years.

## Cost of home dialysis

The cost of home dialysis after equipment had been placed in the home was reported as being in the neighborhood of $7,000 a year. Noel, a patient, commended NKC on its excellent service and equipment for home hemodialysis.

## Final federal regulations for ESRD

Blagg reported that the final federal regulations for the end-stage renal disease networks had now been published, and Washington State was part of the five-state grouping that had been expected. Steps were being taken to arrange planning meetings, formulate bylaws, etc. The first organizational meeting would probably be held in August, and the Northwest Kidney Center would offer to provide office space for network administration.

## Future planning for NKC headquarters

There was discussion of future planning for NKC. Various locations were being considered for relocation but the site had to be reasonably contiguous to Swedish Hospital. The most favorable site was the Seattle Medical Surgical Clinic Building at 700 Broadway. This was a fairly new four-story building with 40,000 square feet, and it was estimated that NKC needed approximately 30,000 square feet to have adequate space. Staying at the present location and remodeling was also being considered. The Long-range Planning Committee was reviewing the issues.

### FUND DRIVE

The fund drive now totaled almost $580,000. Funding in the Northwest Kidney Foundation account was approximately $100,000.

It was noted that the two vans Northwest Kidney Center now owned had covered more than 160,000 miles in service calls, etc., and a new van had been purchased by the Center.

The organ donor card was being revised. This was the card on the reverse of the temporary driver's license. A flyer was also to go out with driving license renewal notices explaining the organ donor program. Northwest Kidney Foundation was developing a pamphlet entitled *Your Gift of Life* for public distribution.

A report from the University of Washington was submitted on the progress with automated home dialysis.

### THE JULY MEETING OF THE EXECUTIVE COMMITTEE WAS HELD AT 12:30 P.M. ON JULY 23, 1976 AT SWEDISH HOSPITAL AND CALLED TO ORDER BY PRESIDENT ELMER NORDSTROM.

There were now 287 patients on hemodialysis: 48 in the Center; 2 in training; 12 in limited care; and 225 at home. There were 28 patients on peritoneal dialysis: 22 at home; 4 in the Center; and 2 in training. The number of transplant patients was 148. Since the past meeting, 21 patients had started treatment, 9 had completed home training and 13 patients had been retrained.

### ORGAN RETRIEVAL ACTIVITY

Organ retrieval activity for June was 14 referrals, 4 kidneys retrieved from 3 donors, 1 kidney received from elsewhere, 2 kidneys discarded and 3 kidneys transplanted locally.

## INCREASE IN DIALYSIS TREATMENTS

Despite the shortage of space and the limited increase in personnel and costs, dialysis treatments had increased by 42% over the previous year. For example, NKC was treating an average of 809 patients per month (January through June) in the current year compared to 568 patients per month for the same period in 1975. Even so, patients were not being referred early enough to get a thorough understanding of their illness and their treatment. The importance of educating all physicians about kidney disease and its treatments was realized together with the need for their cooperation with NKC staff in providing social, psychological and financial support to patients.

Since the May meeting, there had been 31 new patients approved for treatment: 12 females and 19 males, ranging in age from 11 to 72, with an average age of 45 years.

## ESRD NETWORKS

Blagg reported that ESRD Network 2 would consist of Washington, Oregon, Idaho, Montana and Alaska. He and Dr. George Porter, of the University of Oregon in Portland, had set up an organizational meeting to develop a network council. Again, NKC offered space for a network office. The network would play a dual role in providing medical review and in advising on planning activities and related areas.

## NKC FINANCES

During the past year, there had been a $1 million increase in revenues. Income loss, before public support, dropped from $64,000 in 1975 to $52,000 in 1976. Public contributions were up, partly due to a number of sizable probates. In the three years since the Medicare ESRD program came into effect there had been no increase in dialysis rates in spite of inflation. Public contributions increased from $378,500 in 1974/75 to $580,300 in the present year.

## NATIONAL KIDNEY FOUNDATION

Blagg had received a letter from the president of the National Kidney Foundation requesting consideration of setting up a chapter in Washington State. As the National Kidney Foundation was similar to the Northwest Kidney Foundation, except on a national scale, NKC would gain nothing that it did not already have by joining the National Kidney Foundation and would have to send 25% of all donated moneys to the national organization.

## NURSES' STRIKE

It was reported that the current nurses' strike had not affected services at NKC, as NKC nurses did not belong to the union. NKC nurses were, however, paid per the contract schedule, so Center costs would be affected by the negotiations.

## THE ROSELLINI BUILDING

The Long-range Planning Committee had held two meetings and considered both the possibility of purchasing Dr. Rosellini's building at 700 Broadway and the possibility of remodeling Eklind Hall as the future home of NKC. This was to be discussed further with more cost analysis.

## AUTOMATED DIALYSIS RESEARCH CONTRACT

Irvine from the University of Washington reported that the prototype blood pumps had been fabricated for the automated dialysis research device and that preliminary trials of various components of the blood circuit had been concluded satisfactorily. The next step would be to assemble these components as an integrated unit.

**MINUTES FOR THE AUGUST 27 MEETING OF THE EXECUTIVE COMMITTEE ARE MISSING EXCEPT FOR A REPORT FROM IRVINE AT THE UNIVERSITY OF WASHINGTON.**

Irvine reported that all elements of the automated dialysis research device had been integrated into a single unit and mounted on the chassis of a Drake supply unit. A gauge isolator had been developed and was being tested for reliability. Additionally, a heparin delivery system was ready to try.

**THE SEPTEMBER MEETING OF THE EXECUTIVE COMMITTEE WAS HELD ON SEPTEMBER 24, 1976 AT 12:30 P.M. IN SWEDISH HOSPITAL AND CALLED TO ORDER BY PRESIDENT ELMER NORDSTROM.**

It was reported that 25 patients had started treatment since the last meeting and 16 patients had been trained for home hemodialysis and 11 patients were retrained. The total number of patients was 491. Currently 150 patients had a functioning transplant.

## ORGAN RETRIEVAL ACTIVITY

Organ retrieval activity for August included 20 referrals, 8 kidneys retrieved from 5 donors, 1 kidney received from elsewhere, 3 kidneys discarded and 6 kidneys transplanted locally.

It was reported that 19 beds, excluding training beds, were now in use compared to 15 beds the previous year, with an increase of 42% in the number of dialyses over the last year.

Since the previous meeting, 30 new patients had been approved for treatment: 18 females and 12 males, ranging in age from 16 to 72, with an average age of 46 years.

## REQUEST TO STATE FOR ADDITIONAL FUNDING

A request had been made to the secretary of the Washington State Department of Social and Health Services in an effort to acquire further funding for both

Northwest Kidney Center and the Spokane and Inland Empire Artificial Kidney Centers for the dialysis and transplantation program in the state. Presently, appropriated funds were insufficient to support the program because of the increasing and aging population since the Medicare program began and the problems with funding from the Division of Vocational Rehabilitation. Estimates for 1977-1979 were provided to state government.

ORGANIZATIONAL MEETING FOR ESRD NETWORK 2

The initial organizational meeting for establishment of ESRD Network 2 had been accomplished and bylaws were being established. Additionally, the membership and nominating committees had been appointed. It was hoped that NKC could become the nucleus of the council because of its past experience. Federal regulations required facilities to be documented, and each facility would be surveyed in the same fashion hospitals were surveyed by the federal government.

FINANCIAL REPORT

It was reported that funding for NKC was still dependent upon public support, although to a lesser extent than before.

ROSELLINI BUILDING

A bid had been made to buy the building owned by Dr. Rosselini at 700 Broadway, and hopefully progress would occur within the next two weeks. Campbell, Bangert and Nordstrom had met with Rosselini regarding the initial bid. If that building were to be acquired, Rosselini could be permitted to retain one floor for two-five years. The basement at Eklind Hall would be retained for that period of time also.

NORTHWEST KIDNEY FOUNDATION FUND DRIVE

Northwest Kidney Foundation was revving up for its fall campaign to raise funds for 1976-1977. The fund drive would consist of a mail solicitation campaign to 10,000 former donors, and personal solicitation from local business executives directed by a volunteer chairman. Bruce Baker, a Northwest Kidney Center trustee, had been asked to direct the fund drive.

### Upgraded computer system

The program to design and implement an integrated computer system for NKC was scheduled to begin in January 1976, but because of the need to have the systems analyst become more familiar with NKC requirements most activity was postponed until July of 1976. The process was proceeding and an NKC programmer was to be appointed in October 1976. Swedish Hospital had offered some program support on a time-available basis. The program abilities of the various applicants for the post were being considered. The expenses to date had been $16,508, representing 21.4% of the budget.

## The October Meeting of the Executive Committee was Held at 12:30 P.M. on October 22, 1976 in Swedish Hospital and Called to Order by President Elmer Nordstrom.

Dr. Tom Sawyer reported that there were now 297 hemodialysis patients, which included 233 on home hemodialysis. A total of 38 patients were on peritoneal dialysis, which included 28 on home peritoneal dialysis. Additionally, 148 patients were living with a kidney transplant.

Blagg reported that since the last Executive Committee meeting, 15 patients had been approved for treatment: 5 females and 10 males, ranging in age from 14 to 68, with an average age of 44.4.

### Organ retrieval activity

Organ retrieval activity during the month of October included 8 referrals, 3 retrievals for a total of 6 kidneys, all of which were retrieved in this region.

Three kidneys were discarded, no local transplants were performed and 3 kidneys were sent out.

## ESRD NETWORKS

With regard to the ESRD networks and national developments, Blagg reported that there had been two organizational meetings held with 28 council representatives from the states of Oregon, Washington, Idaho, Montana and Alaska. This would be designated as Network 2, but no further meetings would be held until it had been officially designated by the Department of HEW. The Northwest Kidney Center had been temporarily chosen as the Network Support Facility and would provide two or three individuals to handle paperwork for the network.

## WESTERN DIALYSIS AND TRANSPLANT SOCIETY MEETING

Blagg reported on the Western Dialysis and Transplant Society meeting that had been held in Seattle in October and attracted more than 600 registrants, including the heads of the Bureau of Health Insurance and the Bureau of Quality Assurance for the ESRD programs. One highlight of the program was a symposium on peritoneal dialysis, which involved Blagg as program chairman, Dr. Henry Tenckhoff from the University of Washington, and Nancy Gallagher, RN, Carla Bush, social worker, and Marcia Clark, RN, from Northwest Kidney Center.

## THE ROSELLINI BUILDING

A bid had been made to Rosellini for purchase of his building, and a counter bid had been received. It was anticipated that further negotiation would ensue, but if negotiations did not progress in the near future, and because of the need to relocate or renovate Northwest Kidney Center, other decisions would have to be made.

## Northwest Kidney Foundation and the NKC fund drive

The foundation printed 10,000 booklets on how to donate money to the kidney center. The fund drive for 1976-1977 was beginning on October 21 with the haunted castle at Seattle Center. The event is sponsored by KING Radio and Epsilon Sigma Alpha Sorority. Jim Owens was to be chairman for the coming year.

## Automated dialysis unit

Irvine reported on the status of the automated dialysis unit being developed at the University of Washington. The university was re-fabricating the blood circuit using polyurethane tubing. The dialysis circuits were finished and would be tested on sheep soon.

## The December Meeting of the Executive Committee was Held at 12:30 P.M. on December 10, 1976 in Swedish Hospital and Called to Order by President Elmer Nordstrom.

Sawyer reported that there were 39 patients on hemodialysis pre-training or pre-transplant, 2 patients from the VA in extended care, and 14 patients, including 1 VA patient, on limited care. Additionally, there were 7 patients in home hemodialysis training, and 236 patients were on hemodialysis at home.

There were now 33 patients on home peritoneal dialysis, 11 in pre-training, and 3 in training. The total number of patients transplanted was 149. Since the last Executive Committee meeting, 30 patients had been approved for treatment and 20 had started treatment: 12 on hemodialysis and 8 on peritoneal dialysis. Twelve hemodialysis patients had finished primary training and 7 peritoneal dialysis patients had finished primary training.

Cumulative dialyses for the year stood at 9,982, a 45% increase over the 1975 figure of 6,860.

## Organ retrieval activity

Organ retrieval activity to December 10 included 20 referrals, 6 retrievals for a total of 10 kidneys within the region, 4 kidneys received from elsewhere, 1 kidney discarded, 8 kidneys transplanted locally and 1 kidney sent out.

Since the last Executive Committee meeting on October 22, 30 new patients were approved for treatment: 15 females and 15 males, ranging in age from 15 to 76, with an average age of 43. This rate of admission represents 90 new patients per million population per year.

## ESRD networks

There were no new developments with Network 2 since the last meeting. The activity of Network and Medical Renal Research will take considerable time as mandated, and it is still uncertain where the money to fund these activities will come from. The future of the networks is uncertain at the present time, and activities are more or less at a stand-still pending a new administration in government.

## Rosellini building and future home of NKC

Another meeting was held with Dr. Rosellini regarding negotiations for purchasing the Rosellini building. However, no agreement had been reached as yet.

## Construction at Swedish Hospital

Construction in 5 South should be completed in a few weeks to the extent that the temporary home training unit can be moved sometime around the end of December.

## Personnel changes

John Noel, a dialysis patient who represented patients on NKC's Board of Trustees, passed away. He was an inspiration to all and will be missed.

Pollie Crawford, the Center's dietitian for 8 ½ years, is retiring and will be replaced by Ann Grant.

Clay Jackson, a computer programmer, is a new NKC employee in charge of setting up the new computer system.

## NORTHWEST KIDNEY FOUNDATION AND NKC FUND DRIVE

Computerized mailings went out for the yearly donation request and will be followed by another mailing. The haunted castle at Seattle Center was visited by more than 18,000 people. The Stewardess Emeritus group brought in $6,000 in NKC donations. And coin banks, in the shape of plastic kidney shells, were distributed in Tacoma and Bellevue and are successful, averaging $3.00 per week.

A house, which was willed to NKC, sold for $36,800, an appreciable increase over the amount it would have sold for just a year ago.

## AUTOMATED HOME HEMODIALYSIS MACHINE

Irvine of the University of Washington submitted a progress report. The machine's system is approximately 15% completed. In total, about $4,000 of NKC research monies have been spent thus far on the project.

It was suggested that Scribner be invited to the next meeting to give a complete rundown on the progress of this project.

# ABOUT THE AUTHOR

---

"That lovely English gentleman." The soft words of Dr. Christopher Blagg have resounded loudly throughout the international nephrology community for over five decades. Dr. Blagg's contributions to the renal field are immense and broad. He led dialysis care delivery as executive director of the world's first program for 27 years. Throughout his career he's been a stalwart champion of home hemodialysis and rehabilitation. He is a dogged policy advocate for adequate federal and state government support of kidney patients. He is a supreme historian in our field, dedicated to accurate reflection of what actually happened. His contributions live on through this book.

Joyce F. Jackson, president and CEO, Northwest Kidney Centers

It was the experience of the Seattle program that encouraged a group of us in Tennessee to challenge the belief that hemodialysis had to be performed in a hospital setting. Indeed, without their example, I can only now wonder whether we would have been brave enough to proceed with the establishment of not-for-profit Dialysis Clinic, Inc. Of course, along with demonstrating the feasibility of freestanding dialysis, came the challenge of funding this experience. The process of engaging the federal government to provide this funding is a story in itself – one in which Dr. Chris Blagg and Northwest Kidney Centers played a crucial part.

H. Keith Johnson, MD, founder and chairman
of Dialysis Clinic, Inc., Nashville

Seattle is proud to be the home of Northwest Kidney Centers, the first out-of-hospital dialysis provider in the world. Under the leadership of pioneers such as Dr. Christopher Blagg, it has grown from a single dialysis unit to one of the preeminent nonprofit dialysis providers in the country. Throughout its storied history, Northwest Kidney Centers has supported innovations that improve kidney care and raise the quality of life of countless patients. To this day, it continues to provide high-quality care, and the people of the Puget Sound region are fortunate that it will do so for years to come.

14-term Congressman Jim McDermott, retired, former
co-chair of the Congressional Kidney Caucus

DR. CHRISTOPHER R. BLAGG HAS made significant contributions to dialysis therapy for more than fifty years. He trained as a physician in his native England and became interested in acute dialysis for patients whose kidneys were temporarily damaged. In 1963, he traveled to Seattle to learn about Dr. Belding Scribner's innovations in dialysis for people with permanent kidney failure. Blagg eventually spent 27 years as executive director of Northwest Kidney Centers, the dialysis organization Scribner had co-founded in Seattle. Blagg became known as an effective, tireless advocate for U.S. government policies in support of kidney patients as well as an international champion of home dialysis performed by patients themselves.